ARCHITECTURE AND THE SITES OF HISTORY

For Florence and Jack Birks

ARCHITECTURE AND THE SITES OF HISTORY

Interpretations of buildings and cities

Edited by

Iain Borden and David Dunster

Butterworth Architecture
An imprint of Butterworth-Heinemann Ltd
Linacre House, Jordan Hill, Oxford OX2 8DP

⧆ A member of the Reed Elsevier plc group

OXFORD   LONDON   BOSTON
MUNICH   NEW DELHI   SINGAPORE   SYDNEY
TOKYO   TORONTO   WELLINGTON

First published 1995

British Library Cataloguing in Publication Data
Architecture and the Sites of History:
Interpretations of Buildings and Cities
 I. Borden, Iain II. Dunster, David
 720.9

 ISBN 0 7506 0756 4

Library of Congress Cataloguing in Publication Data
Architecture and the sites of history: interpretations of buildings
 and cities/edited by Iain Borden and David Dunster.
 p. cm.
 Includes bibliographical references and index.
 ISBN 0 7506 0756 4
 1. Architecture. 2. City planning. I. Borden, Iain.
 II. Dunster, David.
 NA9040.A67 1995   95-20187
 720-dc20   CIP

Composition by Scribe Design, Gillingham, Kent, UK
**Printed and bound in Great Britain by
Hartnolls Limited, Bodmin, Cornwall**

CONTENTS

Preface · vii

Acknowledgements · ix

Contributors · xi

Sources of Illustrations · xv

1 Architecture and the sites of history · 1
Iain Borden and David Dunster

Part One Time and Place

2 Greece seen from Rome (and Paris) · 23
Martin Goalen

3 Urban classicism and modern ideology · 38
Graham Ive

4 Versailles – a political theme park? · 53
Adrian Forty

Part Two Interpretation

5 The rib, the arch and the buttress: the structure of gothic architecture · 67
Francis Woodman

6 The power and the glory: the meanings of medieval architecture · 78
Alexandrina Buchanan

7 The piazza, the artist and the Cyclops · 93
Iain Borden

8 The palazzo type · 106
David Dunster

9 Demand and supply in renaissance Florence · 119
Graham Ive

10 City of spectacle: renaissance and baroque Rome · 131
Jeremy Melvin

Part Three Theory and Practice

11 Three revolutionary architects: Boullée, Ledoux, Lequeu · 149
Richard Patterson

12 Building classicism: speculative development in eighteenth century Paris · 163
Maxine Copeland

13 Common sense and the picturesque · 176
Adrian Forty

Part Four Society

14 Architecture and philosophy: the case of G.W.F. Hegel   189
    Jeremy Melvin
15 Architecture and the industrial revolution: Pugin and Ruskin   200
    Mark Swenarton
16 The politics of the plan   214
    Iain Borden
17 Frank Lloyd Wright as educator: the Taliesin Fellowship Program, 1932–59   227
    Richard Cándida Smith
18 Modernism and the USSR   243
    Jonathan Charley
19 Patching the future: the evolution of a post-war housing estate   258
    Joe Kerr
20 Form and technology: the idea of a new architecture   271
    Andrew Higgott

Part Five Cities

21 The birth of a modern city: fin-de-siècle Vienna   291
    David Dunster
22 The city without qualities   304
    Adrian Forty
23 Gender and the city   317
    Iain Borden
24 Theorizing European cities: Aldo Rossi, O.M. Ungers and Rob Krier   331
    David Dunster
25 Industrialization and the city: work, speed-up, urbanization   344
    Jonathan Charley

Part Six Present Future

26 What is going on?   361
    Richard Patterson
27 Commercial architecture   372
    Graham Ive
28 Cities, cultural theory, architecture   387
    Iain Borden

Index   401

PREFACE

The history of architecture and cities has always been a disputatious field, constituted from a myriad of architectural concerns, historical events and authorial subject positions. The present situation is no different, indeed it has intensified. Relatively clear cut divisions between Anglo-American empiricism, Hegelian philosophy, social history and art historical iconography have ceded to a splintered and fractured kaleidoscope twisted out from camps drawn up along lines of politics and aesthetics, intellectual discipline and personal obsession. Voices clamour to be heard from all directions, favouring new objects of study and new approaches to the writing of history.

As a result, architectural history is becoming more explicitly concerned with the implications of its own practices, and so more able to set the boundaries and scope of its own visions. More interpretations and theories to expound, more things and processes to investigate – these are the developments of a newly invigorated discipline.

To us, as editors, it seems an appropriate time to present some of these ideas together, not so much as a finite rank of answers, but as potentialities – provisional and often oppositional propositions that could be thought of as active components in divulging the contradictory character of architecture. At the same time, we have set ourselves the task of alluding to some of the vast range of objects, spaces and activities that might conceivably be called architecture. Beside cathedrals, museums and villas sit shops, streets and construction sites; alongside designing, procuring and inhabiting are looking, walking and fearing. In these aims, we have been undeniably limited by the usual practical exigencies but also by our own implicated role as editors. In general, we have tended away from rampant pluralism, away from the apolitical stance of accepting that anything goes, toward a more purposeful set of histories that just might add up, in the reader's mind, to an explanation and understanding of architecture and cities. There are no ready-made answers here, still less any prescriptions as to what to do next, but simply an enquiry into what could have been, maybe is, and might be.

ACKNOWLEDGEMENTS

Architecture and the Sites of History has received no sponsorship, no institutional funding and is the product of no research grant. Instead, it is the creation of sixteen teachers and writers who believe the project to be worthwhile, and who have invested greatly in it. The text is in no way a manifesto, but it contains a number of inter-weaving arguments constructed by those who have done the writing. The editors therefore acknowledge first all these contributors who have made the book and its thematics possible. We thank them for their efforts and engagement, and for their diligence and patience in what has been, of course, a rather more drawn out period of gestation than was originally intended.

A book of this kind is a collaboration not only of its contributors but also of the many people we have all spoken to and with whom we have discussed our ideas. Too numerous to list, they deserve our thanks nonetheless. The idea for this book initially derived from a course taught at The Bartlett, University College, London, and we are grateful there to Michael Edwards, Joanna Saxon and Christopher Woodward who have all at times given freely of their time and ideas. We acknowledge the students at The Bartlett, for many of the essays were placed first before them for their attention and questions. We thank also the staff of the photographic service and libraries of University College London, particularly Anna Piet and Ruth Dar. The editors would especially like to recognize the support of Paul Finch, Rose Ive, Paul Monaghan and Alicia Pivaro, who have listened on many occasions and made invaluable suggestions as to what to do next. We have more often than not followed their advice. Iain Borden would also like to thank Jane Rendell for her many invaluable comments and advice. One way or another, all these people have together helped shape the project in ways too varied to list and often too profound to readily identify.

The illustrations used are numerous and extremely diverse, and we are grateful to all those who graciously granted us access to their photographic collections and permission to reproduce them here. Beside the contributors themselves, these include Tim Benton, Peter Cook, Thomas Deckker, Tadj Grajewski, Laurie Hallows, Felix Mara, John Lautner, Geoffrey Payne, Cedric Price, John Simpson, Jeremy Till, Philip Wells, Michael Webb and Sarah Wigglesworth. Others we would like to thank for their help are the Bibliothèque Nationale; the British Library; Naomi Clifton; Katy Harris, Lois Carleton and Foster Associates; Diane Hutchinson, Simon Templeton and Nicholas Grimshaw and Partners; Clare Endicott and Michael Hopkins and Partners; Nasjonalgalleriet, Oslo; National Gallery, London; Ed Amatore and the John and Mable Ringling Museum of Art,

Florida; Harriet Watson and the Richard Rogers Partnership; Norah Gillow and the William Morris Gallery, London; and Indira Berndtson and the Frank Lloyd Wright Archives. We are deeply indebted to Geoffrey Fisher, Philip Ward-Jackson and Lindy Grant at the Conway Library of the Courtauld Institute of Art whose fine collection and detailed knowledge of architectural photography proved invaluable. Without the help of all of these individuals and institutions, this book would simply not have been possible.

We would like to thank Caroline Mallinder for discussing with us our first ideas, and subsequently the publishers Butterworth Architecture throughout, and in particular Paddy Baker, Neil Warnock-Smith, and Diane Chandler for guiding us through the project.

Finally, we are obliged to the architectural practice of Allford Hall Monaghan Morris who kindly allowed us to reproduce their sensitive conservationist montage of London's Paternoster Square on the front cover.

Iain Borden
David Dunster

CONTRIBUTORS

Iain Borden

Iain Borden is Lecturer in Architectural History at The Bartlett, University College London, where he has taught since 1989. He has a degree from the University of Newcastle Upon Tyne and master's degrees in architectural history from the University of London and the University of California at Los Angeles. He has published in Europe and America, and with Jane Rendell is currently editing a book on architectural history and critical theory. With Joe Kerr and Alicia Pivaro, he is curator of 'Strangely Familiar' (1995), an exhibition of urban narratives at the Royal Institute of British Architects. The *Strangely Familiar* book will be published in 1996.

Alexandrina Buchanan

Alexandrina Buchanan completed her PhD at the University of London on the nineteenth century scholar Robert Willis and architectural historiography. She also holds a degree in history and history of art, and a master's degree in architectural history from the same institution. She is the 1995–6 Munby Fellow in Bibliography at the University of Cambridge, and is currently funded by the Royal Institute of British Architects to study the medievalist architectural historian John Bilson.

Jonathan Charley

Jonathan Charley is Lecturer in Architecture at Strathclyde University. He studied architecture at Portsmouth, worked for six years in a building and design co-operative, and has a master's degree from The Bartlett, University College London. He studied history for a year at the Moscow Institute of Construction and Engineering, and has recently completed a PhD concerned with a materialist theory of the production of the built environment, the labour process and the history of Russian and Soviet experience; a book on the subject is on its way. He has published widely in Europe.

Maxine Copeland

After taking a degree in the history of art at the University of Sussex, Maxine Copeland worked as a historic buildings officer. She later received a master's degree in the history of architecture from the University of London, and is completing a PhD at the University of Leicester on Parisian architecture 1871–86. Since 1992 she has taught art and architectural history to adult education groups for the WEA and the University of Cambridge, and currently teaches urban history at the University of Leicester. She has published in architectural periodicals and in the exhibition catalogue *Chaillot, Passy, Auteuil: Métamorphose des Trois Villages*, (1991), and is translating a history of Paris, to be published in 1995.

David Dunster

David Dunster is Professor of Architecture at South Bank University. He is the author of *Key Buildings of the 20th Century*, volumes 1 (1985) and 2 (1990). Educated at University College London, where he also taught, he has been visiting professor at various universities including Rice, Chicago and Melbourne. Apart from interests in architectural theory and history, he is currently engaged in writing a history of infrastructures in Chicago, and in the development of new approaches to urban planning and architectural education. He organizes the Events Programme at the Royal Institute of British Architects.

Adrian Forty

Adrian Forty is Senior Lecturer in the History of Architecture at The Bartlett, University College London, where he directs the master's course in the History of Modern Architecture. He was educated at the Universities of Oxford and London, in history and history of art. His book *Objects of Desire* was published in 1986, and he is now writing a book on the history of the relationship between architecture and language.

Martin Goalen

Martin Goalen practises and teaches architecture. His published design work includes new buildings, notably his own studio in Kentish Town, and work with important existing buildings, such as the Palace of Westminster and Pugin's St Mary's, Derby. He has also published on the response of architects in the modern world to the architecture of ancient Greece and Rome. Trained at the University of Cambridge, where he taught for a number of years, he is a Lecturer in Architecture at University College London. He was 1992–3 Sargant Fellow in Fine Art at the British School in Rome, and is presently working on a monograph on the Villa Adriana in Tivoli.

Andrew Higgott

Andrew Higgott is Senior Lecturer in History and Theory in the School of Architecture at the University of East London. He has taught both there and at the Architectural Association School of Architecture since 1984. His publications include studies of the architectural photographers F. R. Yerbury and Eric de Maré, and the book *Travels in Modern Architecture* (1989). His current work concerns the relationship of modern architecture to contemporary art theory.

Graham Ive

Graham Ive is Lecturer at The Bartlett, University College London, where he has taught since 1977. He studied economics at the University of Cambridge, and specializes in the economics of the construction industry. He directs the MSc in

Construction Economics and Management at The Bartlett, and has written exten-
sively on that subject. He is currently working on a book entitled *The Economics
of the Modern Construction Industry*.

Joe Kerr

Joe Kerr is Senior Lecturer at the University of North London, and at Middlesex
University where he has taught since 1986. He holds a degree in art history and a
master's degree in architectural history from University College London. He has
written articles, delivered papers and broadcast on the radio on the history of modern
architecture, particularly social housing and early British modernism. He is currently
writing, with Murray Fraser, a book entitled *The Special Relationship: the US Influence
on Post-war British Architecture*. With Iain Borden and Alicia Pivaro, he is curator
of 'Strangely Familiar' (1995), an exhibition of urban narratives at the Royal Institute
of British Architects. The *Strangely Familiar* book will be published in 1996.

Jeremy Melvin

Jeremy Melvin divides his time between journalism and academia. He edits
London Architect, launched under him in 1994, and is Senior Lecturer in History
of Architecture at South Bank University. A regular contributor to *Building Design*,
he has written for various architectural, property and general interest publications,
and has made several broadcast appearances. Graduating from University College
London with degrees in architecture and architectural history, his research projects
include British modernism of the 1930s and nineteenth century architectural
theory; both have formed research papers in Britain and America.

Richard Patterson

Richard Patterson is an architect and Lecturer in Architecture at De Montfort
University. He has worked in commercial practice in Britain and America, and has
taught in Britain, America and Germany. He has degrees and diplomas from the
Architectural Association and the Universities of Cambridge and Princeton. He has
published on architectural representation in the classical and late renaissance periods.

Richard Cándida Smith

Richard Cándida Smith is Assistant Professor of History at the University of
Michigan, Ann Arbor, where he teaches modern American and European intellectual history. He is the author of *Utopia and Dissent: Art, Poetry and Politics in
California* (1995), as well as articles on the politics of culture, oral history and
the history of subjectivity. He has been deeply involved in exploring the nature
of oral narratives, memory and identity. From 1988 to 1993, he was executive
secretary of the Oral History Association of the U.S. He is currently working on
a study of the relation of psychological theory and aesthetic practice in Europe
and America between 1880 and 1930.

Mark Swenarton

Mark Swenarton is a publishing editor of *Architecture Today*, which he co-
launched in 1989. He is author of *Homes Fit for Heroes* (1981) and *Artisans and*

Architects (1989) as well as numerous articles in architectural and historical periodicals. Formerly a lecturer at The Bartlett, University College London, he has also lectured and examined at many architecture schools in America and Europe. He holds degrees in history and history of art from the Universities of Oxford and Sussex, and a PhD in architectural history from the University of London. He is a Fellow of the Royal Historical Society and an Honorary Research Fellow at The Bartlett.

Francis Woodman

Francis Woodman is a Panel Tutor for Cambridge University School of Continuing Education. A medieval architectural historian, his publications range from *The Architectural History of Canterbury Cathedral* (1981) and *King's College Chapel* (1985) to *Blue Guide: South West France* (1994). A former lecturer at the University of East Anglia, where he gained his first degree, he has a PhD from the Courtauld Institute and is a Fellow of the Society of Antiquaries. Currently, he is preparing a book on medieval building in Europe for the new series of the *Oxford History of Art*.

SOURCES OF ILLUSTRATIONS

L.B. Alberti, *De Re Aedificatoria*, (Leoni edition, 1755): 7.5
L'architecture vivante: 23.8
Alexandrina Buchanan: 6.7
American Magazine (October 1932): 23.4
Arch. Phot. Paris/SPADEM (© DACS 1995): 4.3
Architecture Review, (1960): 19.6
Architecture Today, n.11 (September 1990): 13.1, 13.2
Arts and Architecture: 16.6
Catherine Bauer, *Modern Housing*, (Houghton Mifflin, Boston & NY, 1934): 16.4
Tim Benton: 8.2
Bibliothèque Nationale de France, Paris: 1.1, 11.2, 11.11
Iain Borden: 1.1, 1.2, 1.10, 1.11, 1.12, 1.13, 3.1, 3.2, 3.3, 3.4, 3.9, 8.3, 15.3, 17.10, 19.1, 19.3, 23.6, 23.7, 25.6, 25.7, 25.8, 25.9, 26.1, 27.9, 28.1, 28.2, 28.3, 28.4, 28.5, 28.6
By permission of the British Library, London: 4.2
Jonathan Charley: 18.5, 25.5
Auguste Choisy, *Histoire d'architecture*, (Gauthier-Villars, Paris, 1899): 2.2, 2.3, 2.4, 2.8
Maxime Collignon, *Le Parthénon. L'histoire, l'architecture et la sculpture*, (Librarie central d'art et d'architecture, Paris, 1914): 2.1, 2.7, 2.9, 2.10
Conway Library, Courtauld Institute of Art: 1.3, 1.5, 5.3, 5.5, 6.1, 6.2, 6.3, 6.4, 6.5, 7.1, 8.5, 8.6, 9.1, 10.2, 10.4, 10.5, 10.6, 10.7, 12.1, 12.2, 23.1
Peter Cook: 20.3
Maxine Copeland: 11.5, 11.6, 11.7, 11.8, 12.3, 12.4, 12.5, 12.6, 12.7
Das Neue Frankfurt, v.4 ns.2–3 (February–March 1930): 16.2
Thomas Deckker: 11.3, 18.4, 21.5
Gustav Doré, *London: a Pilgrimage*, (1871): 22.4
David Dunster: 8.1, 24.2, 24.6
Description de l'Égypte, (Paris: 1809): 14.1
David Dunster, *Key Buildings of the 20th Century, vol.1, Houses 1900–1944*, (Architectural Press, London, 1985): 16.5
Josef Durm, *Die Baukunst der Griechen*, (Kröner, Leipzig, 1910): 2.5
Sergei Eisenstein, 'Strike', (1925): 18.1
Adrian Forty: 15.8, 19.7, 20.11, 25.3
Foster Associates/Ian Lambot: 20.12, 20.13
Foster Associates/Tim Street-Porter: 20.8

Christine Frederick, *Scientific Management in the Home: Household Engineering*, (1920): 16.3

David Friedman, *Florentine New Towns: Urban Design in the Middle Ages*, (The Architectural History Foundation and Cambridge, Mass.: MIT Press, New York, 1988): 7.3

Martin Goalen: 2.6

Tadj Grajewski: 27.8

Nicholas Grimshaw and Partners: 20.6, 20.15

Laurie Hallows: 27.5

Ludwig Hilberseimer, *Grossstadt Architektur*, (Julius Hoffmann, Stuttgart, 1927): 22.7

Ludwig Hilberseimer, *Grosstadbauten*, (Apossverlag, Hanover, 1925): 22.6

Stephen Holl: 26.6

Michael Hopkins and Partners: 20.14

Joe Kerr: 1.6, 1.7, 1.9, 8.4, 15.10, 16.1, 17.3, 17.4, 17.5, 17.6, 19.2, 19.4, 19.5, 19.8, 21.10, 21.11, 25.10, 26.3, 26.4, 26.5, 26.7, 26.8, 26.9, 27.1, 27.2, 27.4, 27.6

Rob Krier: 24.7

Heinrich Kulka, *Adolf Loos*, (Vienna, 1931): 21.7, 21.9

Marc-Antoine Laugier, *Essai sur l'architecture*, (1753): 1.4

John Lautner: 17.9

Le Corbusier, *Oeuvre Complète*, (Zurich, 1935): 22.2

Paul Letrarouilly, *Édifices de Rome Moderne*, (Paris, 1860): 10.1, 10.3, 10.9

Charles-Nicholas Ledoux, *L'architecture considerée*, (1804): 11.4, 11.9, 11.10

El Lissitzky, *Russia: an Architecture for World Revolution*, (Germany, 1930): 18.2, 18.3, 18.6

Felix Mara: 21.3, 21.6, 21.8

Alfred Marie, *Jardins français classiques des XVII and XVIIIe siècles*, (Éditions Vincent, Paris, 1949): 4.4, 4.5

William Morris Gallery, Walthamstow, London: 15.6

Nasjonalgalleriet, Oslo: 22.5

Reproduced by courtesy of the Trustees, The National Gallery, London: 7.2

Allan Nevins, *Ford: the Times, the Man, the Company*, (Charles Scribner's Sons, New York, 1954): 25.1

Ourselves in Wartime, (London, n.d.): 23.2

Pierre Patek: 4.1

Geoffrey Payne: 25.4

Cedric Price Architects: 20.1, 20.2

A.W.N. Pugin, *Contrasts*, (1836): 15.1, 15.2

A.W.N. Pugin, *True Principles of Pointed or Christian Architecture*, (1841): 15.4

Humphrey Repton, *Sketches and Hints on Landscape Gardening*, (J. and J. Boydell and G. Nicoll, 1794): 13.4

John and Mable Ringling Museum of Art, Sarasota, Florida: 9.2

Richard Rogers Partnership: 20.7

Richard Rogers Partnership/Richard Bryant: 20.10

Richard Rogers Partnership/Martin Charles: 20.9

Matthias Roriczer, *Wimpergbüchlein*: 6.6

Aldo Rossi: 24.1

Saturday Evening Post, (21 September 1929): 23.5

K.F. Schinkel, *Collection of Architectural Designs*, (Butterworth Architecture, Guildford, 1989): 14.2

Scroope, n.3 (June 1991): 26.2

Gyula Sebestyén, *Large-Panel Buildings*, (Akadémai Kiadó, Budapest, 1965): 25.2

Robert Shoppell, *Modern Houses, Beautiful Homes*, (Co-operative Building Plan Association, New York, 1887): 23.3

John Simpson: 13.3

State Russian Museum, Leningrad: 18.7, 18.8

Mark Swenarton: 15.5, 15.7, 15.9, 21.1

Courtesy of Taliesin Architects: 17.7

Town Planning Review, v.17 n.1 (June 1936): 3.5, 3.6, 3.7

O.M. Ungers: 24.4, 24.5

Unidentified: 7.4, 18.9, 18.10, 20.5, 22.1

Raymond Unwin, *Town Planning in Practice*, (1909): 22.3

Viollet-le-Duc, *Dictionnaire raisonné de l'architecture française*, (1854–68), vol. IV: 13.5

Michael Webb: 20.4

Philip Wells: 19.9

Sarah Wigglesworth and Jeremy Till: 1.08, 1.14, 3.8, 10.8, 17.8, 21.2, 21.4, 24.3, 27.3, 27.7

Francis Woodman: 5.1, 5.2, 5.4

Courtesy of The Frank Lloyd Wright Archive: 17.2

Copyright © The Frank Lloyd Wright Foundation 1962: 17.1

1

ARCHITECTURE AND THE SITES OF HISTORY

Iain Borden and David Dunster

This book is grounded on a simple assertion: that the history of architecture and cities is capable of being explained and interpreted in many different ways, and that any understanding of these subjects should excavate below the surface of facts and objects to unearth and confront the multiplicity of possible meanings. In short, there is no single way, and still less any 'right' way, of knowing what architecture and cities are all about.

At first sight, the problem seems to be simply one of an overwhelming quantity of evidence, in that, with buildings and urban spaces all around us, it is hard to know what to look at or where to start. This is the problem which the large encyclopaedic survey of architectural history tries to address, seeking to document the most important projects and to guide the reader as to their relative significance. Such an approach is given its most exemplary demonstration in the magisterial *Sir Banister Fletcher's A History of Architecture*, first written in 1896 and still undergoing near continual revision.[1] Here, just about every famous building is given a short description, complete with essential factual details such as its location and time of construction. Other less ambitious, but equally valuable, publications seek to cover a more specific historical territory in a similar way, each dealing with, for example, renaissance France, nineteenth century Britain, or twentieth century modernism.

The reader of such books, however, is left with a certain unease, for while the information presented is undoubtedly useful in helping to delineate the objects of study – identifying exactly which buildings might constitute the subject of architectural history – ideas about how we might go about thinking about them are given far less attention. The concentration on factual documentation and the search for comprehensiveness tend to close off the discussion of the meanings of the urban realm. Yet just looking at and visiting buildings is not enough, for they are more often than not singularly resistant to exploration purely by the eye, or purely by empirical knowledge. Other forms of enquiry are also necessary if a larger range of meanings is to be unpicked from architecture. Nor is this the end of the story, for the closure of debate and argumentation itself casts doubt upon the basis on which material has been selected in the first place; if we do not know how buildings might be thought about, how do we know which ones to look at? On what basis do we choose to focus on one building over another? What, even, constitutes architecture at all?

There is then another way of looking at architecture, which is not just about recognition, identification and empirical observation, but which prefers explanation, interpretation and speculation. Of course many architectural historians have realized as much, and in doing so they have created an enormous array of interpretive themes, ranging from architectural style, constructional methods and artistic vision to modernity, philosophy and science, to patronage, social class and professionalism, and so on. While often considerably more thoughtful than the encyclopaedic survey, such books nonetheless raise their own problems. A first objection is intellectual, in that while architectural historians may explicate their own interpretations to the reader, they often present them as if they were the only way of looking at a particular subject. To expect all historians to lay out all possible interpretations would of course be wholly unreasonable, yet some contextualization, some setting of boundaries, some recognition of the possibility of other histories, is always welcome. A second objection is more practical, in that for someone to gain an insight into the plethora of ways of understanding architecture and cities, an enormous amount of material has to be read. Again, it would be wholly unreasonable to expect historians to condense their life's work into a series of readily digestible sound-bites, but it is nonetheless a turn-of-the-millennium truism that there have been more books published in the last decade than in the rest of the entire course of human history. As a result, it is not only simply impossible for one person to read everything, but it is equally difficult to get a grip on the range and diversity of what is on offer. Deciding what to read becomes as much of an issue as deciding what architecture to investigate.

We are left here with a conundrum. What kind of book is it that not only displays a wide range of architectural and urban examples, covering great geographical distances and temporal periods, but also throws into the ring a range of possible interpretations? To some extent, Spiro Kostof tried to provide exactly this in *A History of Architecture*, in which the kind of globalizing totality of the survey, starting with the Stone Age and ending with post-war twentieth century modernism, is set within a more relaxed interpretive framework, one which goes beyond physical form to address some of the gamut of issues suggested above.[2]

Architecture and the Sites of History, however, differs from Kostof's book in a number of ways. Firstly, we have tended much more toward the side of varied interpretations, and while we have certainly tried to give some of the flavour of changing architectural practices and meanings over the centuries, we have not in any way tried to repeat the comprehensive historical coverage yielded by survey works. More about less, rather than less about more, has been our key. This book is then in no way a substitution for comprehensive, historical knowledge; rather we feel that it is also equally important, in addition to such knowledge, to think about architecture in different ways.

Secondly, and perhaps more significantly, we have not tried to come to any definitive conclusions about things, in that rather than trying to explain everything, we have instead generally tried to explain just a few of the many different aspects of architecture and cities. Our idea here has been that while a particular essay might, for example, use the economic concepts of supply and demand to interpret renaissance Florence, as Graham Ive does in Chapter 9, so such ideas might equally apply, with some appropriate modification, to eighteenth century London, or to twentieth century Seoul. Similarly, the examination of picturesque theory undertaken by Adrian Forty in Chapter 13 unravels assumptions about the purely visual analysis of architecture that have been pervasive ever since. Essays are not intended to supply the definitive account of any particular subject, rather they demonstrate that such an interpretation of architecture is possible, and therefore are suggestive of different ways of interpreting architecture and cities in general. And in the light of our comments about the number of books now being published, each chapter has been made as short as possible; while this greatly limits the amount of historical detail and evidence put forward, it should have the advantage of making both the subject matter and the line of thinking more accessible.

There is also one other characteristic which should be noted, and that is a deliberate case of implicit argumentation between some, if not all, of the essays. This, we feel, is a more accurate representation of how architecture has actually operated historically. Buildings and cities are not only all around us, but we are all around them; architecture is more than a set of objects with which we come into occasional contact. It constitutes the very processes, practices and spaces that make up the physicality of life. It forms the spaces in which all aspects of our lives reside and flow. In short, we cannot live without buildings and cities, for they are an integral, not separate, part of how we go about things. And as we know, the history of our going-about-things is not a seamless, homogeneous path toward a commonly desired future; the myth of progress is exactly that – a constructed idea that purports to represent the common good but in fact serves to legitimize and facilitate the aspirations of a dominant social class. Architecture then is part of the conflicting and contradictory struggle of differing forces, interest groups and movements, and the essays in this volume try, in their own way, to mirror some of this turbulent dynamic. For this reason, we have not followed architectural history's more common preoc-cupations with things such as function, materials, exterior, site, styles, periods and artistic creators; although these are all concerns addressed at various points of the book, we prefer not to legitimate their supposed centrality by making them the immediate focus of our attention. Essays set architectural ideas against architectural practices, patrons against archi-tects, and architects against building users; they posit philosophy next to industry, popes next to craftsmen, and cultural theorists next to property developers; they raise design education alongside technology, construc-tion alongside aesthetics, class alongside gender. This variation yields the text's – and architecture's – sites of history.

In doing so, the aim is not to be deliberately confusing; we do not want to render architectural history opaque and perplexing. We would like, however, from the very beginning to raise the problematic of interpretation, so that at the same time as we are suggesting different ways of thinking about architecture we also make clear that such interpretations cannot always be in agreement with each other, and that we must think out their differing suggestions in the face of specific historical events. We do not propose, therefore, to justify pluralism in interpretations – that all interpretations are somehow equally valid. Rather we argue that no single interpretation is likely to hold all the clues for understanding architecture, and that if the contradictory nature of human history is to be grasped through architecture, more than one set of conditions must be brought into play. History must be constructed through the confrontation of different meanings.

Before explaining the overall structure of the book, it would be as well to point out that this is very much a discussion of western architecture and cities; however much we might hope that some of the interpretations might be of some use in the study of other cities and cultures, we have been inevitably constrained by our own knowledge and experience. The conventions adopted are then those commonly used in western history, including the Christian calendar.

Secondly, although many of the buildings and projects discussed here are indeed to be found in even the most empirical of textbooks, in this book they are appraised from architectural, economic and cultural viewpoints; and themes which recur in history are equally treated from differing perspectives. Thus while great monuments are given their due weight, the tissue of everyday life in town and country is also given some importance; essays concentrate more than usual attention on everyday buildings, on how cities and landscapes have grown and changed.

Thirdly, many of the architectural meanings elucidated here have been generated from two different directions. Firstly, from buildings and cities themselves, seeking to draw out from behind the obscuring veils of time and space their relevance and importance both then and now. Secondly, from our own contemporary history as writers, practitioners and teachers of architecture. This has involved inspecting our own concerns about aesthetics, economics, gender relations, politics and so forth, and it has also involved a continuous dialogue with ideas generated outside of architecture.

There are therefore theories embedded in these essays that owe a debt to those as diverse as the semioticians Roland Barthes and Umberto Eco, historians Fernand Braudel, Michel Foucault, Eric Hobsbawm and Hayden White, art historians T.J. Clark, Griselda Pollock and Janet Wolff, philosophers Jacques Derrida, Gilles Deleuze, Félix Guattari, G.W.F. Hegel, Martin Heidegger and Paul Ricoeur, political intellectuals Louis Althusser, Henri Lefebvre and Karl Marx, psychoanalysts Sigmund Freud and Julia Kristeva, economists Ernst Mandel and Thorstein Veblen, geographers David Harvey and Edward Soja, social theorists Jean Baudrillard, Anthony Giddens and Georg Simmel, literary critics Terry Eagleton and Raymond Williams, and cultural critics Theodor Adorno, Walter Benjamin, Marshall Berman, Fredric Jameson and Elizabeth Wilson. With a few notable exceptions, we have not used the ideas of these thinkers to explicitly drive the content of the essays, but their presence is often there nonetheless.

A word also on scholarship. In some cases, authors have relied on secondary sources for their factual material, particularly when looking at the development of a particular architectural theme over a long period of time. Such reliance on the work of others is an almost inevitable part of interpretive essays, and while some might see this as a drawback, we prefer to consider it a distinct advantage, allowing us to draw upon the many highly erudite studies of specific architectural works and periods. These publications are noted both in the references and the bibliography to each chapter. We would hope that any one wishing to learn more about a particular subject would turn first to these sources. They will, no doubt, come to conclusions different to our own.

There are many ways to skin a rabbit, and in this book, we consider six of them. Underlying Part One, Time and Place, is Heinrich Wölfflin's assertion that 'not everything is possible at all times',[3] to which we add another dimension – that of space – to note that not all things are possible in all places. When Martin Goalen raises the question of classical Greek architecture and its significance for the Roman theorist Vitruvius and for more modern architectural theorists such as Choisy and Le Corbusier, as he does in Chapter 2, the effect is to highlight the essential

Figure 1.1

Classical architecture: an
ancient form. The Roman
Temple of Zeus, Euromus,
Turkey, (2nd century AD), is
one of the six best preserved
examples in the old territory
of Asia Minor.

Figure 1.2

Classical architecture: a late
capitalist form. Sainsbury
Wing, National Gallery,
London, (1986–91), architects
Venturi, Scott Brown and
Associates.

malleability of architectural ideas, even within such an
apparently long-lasting tradition as classicism. Each
period, each country, makes of it what it will. Graham
Ive, in Chapter 3, also addresses the re-use of classicism over the centuries, but this time on a more urban
scale. London's Trafalgar Square, Chicago's and
Washington's City Beautiful plans and fascist Italy's
new towns are assessed for their political, ideological
character, showing how the classical tradition has been
used to legitimize ruling classes and to construct
hegemonic cultural values. Another version of this
politicized implementation of classicism is shown in
Chapter 4, where Adrian Forty, in considering the case
of Versailles, concludes that only the most general of
political themes is likely to survive through its attachment to architecture; the presence of people, either as

occupiers or interpreters of buildings, is required for the production of meanings.

In contrast to this traverse over the centuries, Part Two, Interpretation, focuses on the way particular architectural periods can be interpreted in different ways according to the analytical lens adopted. The first pair of essays therefore provide two alternative accounts of the medieval period. First Francis Woodman in Chapter 5 expounds an explanation of gothic architecture which focuses almost entirely on the development of constructional systems. Gravity, experimentation and accidental discoveries here provide the primary forces. In a different assessment, Alexandrina Buchanan in Chapter 6 delineates the significance of medieval architecture as it appeared to the three main social groups of the clergy, the patrons

Figure 1.3

A building, an urban space or a set of socio-economic conditions? Santa Maria del Fiore (the Duomo), Florence, (1296–1462), seen from a side street.

and the laity – disparate interests which combined to imbue gothic cathedrals with their rich meanings and symbolism. Both these essays make reference to a large number of churches, including Durham, St.-Denis, Notre-Dame, Salisbury, Tewkesbury Abbey and Westminster Abbey, rendering their individual explanations equally convincing.

The following quartet of essays move sideways through space and onward in time to consider, in a similar variety of interpretations, the Italian renaissance. In Chapter 7 Iain Borden considers the implications of the transformation of medieval Florence for renaissance perceptions and representations of urban space, particularly the perspectival experiments of Brunelleschi and Alberti. David Dunster, in Chapter 8, however, treats the same development of the renaissance as a set of typological objects (a concept to which he returns in relation to twentieth century urbanism in Chapter 24), with the specific example of the *palazzo* type used to bridge the chasm between the architectural and the sociological. The evolution of this palace type from the early medieval towers to the quattrocento humanist palaces of the Strozzi, Medici and Rucellai families mirrors both the evolution of theories of architecture and the changing social needs of palace owners, while ultimately reflecting the architectural humility of these patrons. Graham Ive, in Chapter 9, suggests a more economically-based version of these events and, in opposition to Dunster, interprets the palazzo type as evidence of ostentatious conspicuous consumption on the part of wealthy owners. Through a detailed exposition of Richard Goldthwaite's *The Building of Renaissance Florence*, Ive places architecture not only within the context of the patron class but also that of fluctuating trade patterns at the regional and international scale, and that of guild labour at the local scale. In the concluding Chapter 10 of this section, Jeremy Melvin turns toward Rome, and explores how the papacy consciously turned it into a city of spectacle, using the very appearance of edifices like St. Peter's, the Palazzo Farnese, San Carlo alle Quattro Fontane, San Andrea Quirinale and the Piazza del Popolo to impress residents, rivals and visitors alike. He suggests that, in doing so, Rome became a work of art not just for its state politics but also for its architectural and urban splendours.

A smaller Part Three, Theory and Practice, looks at a recurring problem in architectural history, that of the divergence between ideas about architecture and architectural practices. Rather than just noting that architects' intentions are not always translated unproblematically into built form – a conclusion which we feel the book as a whole should make clear – this part considers the disparity between theory-based and more practice-based approaches to architecture as a

Figure 1.4

Classical architecture as theory. The 'primitive hut', frontispiece to Marc-Antoine Laugier's *Essai sur l'architecture*, (1753), one of the fundamental principles of neo-classical architecture.

whole, and so questions the validity of any one conceptualization of what architecture should be. The first pair of essays here show how the same fundamental set of architectural ideas underlie some apparently diverse practices. In Chapter 11, Richard Patterson elucidates the various ways in which the highly academic architecture of Boullée, Ledoux and Lequeu draws upon the classical tradition, and in particular shows how these architects variously utilize metonymic, hieroglyphic and mystical signs according to their own intellectual programmes. In sharp contrast to this theorized neo-classicism, in her essay, Chapter 12, Maxine Copeland demonstrates how classical architecture was readily adapted to the needs of the speculative apartment market of eighteenth century Paris. Divested of cerebral justification, classicism nonetheless found its way into schemes like the Halle au Blé, the Théâtre de l'Odeon and the rue de Rivoli, making an important contribution to their formal design and commercial success.

Figure 1.5

Classical architecture as practice. Surrey Square, one small part of the speculative development of Georgian London's West End during the eighteenth and early nineteenth centuries.

In the last part of this part, Chapter 13, Adrian Forty considers a different strand within eighteenth century architectural theory, that of the picturesque. Here the privilege given to the eye in the experience of architecture is systematically debunked, showing how this theory of the 'common sense' deliberately bypasses reason and understanding to set up an illusion of innate good taste within 'properly' educated people. Rather than a shared, commonly-held ability available to all, the picturesque helped and continues to help secure the judgements and position of a social élite.

We have already asserted that architecture is far more than a set of isolated objects which we encounter as objects separate to ourselves, and in fact makes up an integral part of how we live. Part Four, Society, addresses this contention head on and, while it is obviously impossible to delve into them all, seeks to represent at least some of the possible mechanisms by which such an inter-dependent relation might take place. Jeremy Melvin in the first essay in this part, Chapter 14, investigates the connection between architecture and philosophy. Although such an erudite, abstract enterprise as philosophy might at first glance seem to be a somewhat perverse way of opening an exploration into the connection between architecture and society, Melvin's treatment of Hegel's *Aesthetics* shows not only how important architecture and art in general were to this profoundly influential nineteenth century philosopher, but also suggests how his thoughts were far from dissimilar to leading architectural theorists of the nineteenth century, such as

Figure 1.6

Architecture and society (1). Form and technology synthesized in the Brooklyn Bridge, New York, (1883), designed by John A. Roebling.

Ruskin, Semper and Viollet-le-Duc. Ruskin makes another, more substantive appearance in Chapter 15, where Mark Swenarton considers how Ruskin and Pugin each sought, in their different ways, to respond to the perceived threats of the industrial revolution. Through their theories, attitudes to urbanization, religion and contemporary labour arrangements duly found expression in architectural form, structure and production. As a result, gothic revival architecture was established not as one choice of architectural styles among many, but as the one true style.

In Chapter 16, Iain Borden turns to the architectural interior, and its representation by the architectural plan. The inter-war German *existenzminimum* and the contemporaneous Kings Road Studios designed by Schindler in Los Angeles in turn show how the plan is a necessary part of the design process, allowing the particular social relations of building users to be conceived, diagrammed and controlled. A different kind of social control is identified by Richard Cándida Smith in Chapter 17, this time concerning architects themselves. Through the experiences of those trained at Taliesin, Smith describes the influence of Frank Lloyd Wright over those he taught and employed, even after his death. He also highlights another feature common to many architects' practices: the blurry demarcation of labour and authorship of specific architectural projects.

Perhaps more than in any other period or for any other form of architecture, twentieth century modernism has been continuously and inextricably

Figure 1.7

Architecture and society (2). Philosophy at the second Goetheanum, Dornach, (1923–8), designed according to the spiritualistic principles of Anthroposophy by architect Rudolf Steiner.

Figure 1.8

Architecture and society (3). Housing provision was an over-riding concern of modernist architects in the 1920s and 1930s. Villa Savoye, Poissy, (1929–31), architect Le Corbusier.

linked with politics, and consequently the next pair of essays, Chapters 18 and 19, each provide a differing account of how modernism was harnessed to the purposes of the State. In the first, Jonathan Charley rejects simplistic accounts of the Russian revolution to separate the experimental avant-garde of the 1920s, the Constructivists and Rationalists, from the reactionary Socialist Realism of the 1930s. In both cases, nonetheless, architecture is linked to the needs and aspirations of the state, operating in a national if not international context. By contrast, in the second of this pair, Joe Kerr sets the modernist architecture of post-war Britain in the micro-context of municipal government, showing how the Regent's Park Estate was linked not only to the national government's housing policy but also to the peculiar nature of the politics of that part of London. This, too, is a revisionist history, rejecting conventional interpretations of modernist housing in the period of reconstruction as an activity entirely of the centralized state, throwing the spotlight instead onto the important human agency of particular architects and politicians active on the local stage. Kerr also raises the issue of conservation, something presently facing much modernist architecture: which buildings should be spared from the bulldozer, and by what right?

If intellectual philosophy, the rise of capitalism and industrialization, social relations and politics form some of the most important connections between architecture and society already addressed in this section, then that of technology is of equal importance

Figure 1.9

Architecture and society (4). The museum epitomizes the cultural aspirations of late capitalism. Neue Staatsgalerie, Stuttgart, (1977–83), architects Stirling Wilford & Associates.

and persistent, pervasive influence. In Chapter 20 Andrew Higgott focuses on the rise of a new technologically-driven architecture in the 1960s, and notes its sources in Prouvé and Fuller, its later transmogrification through Archigram and Price, and its development onward into the 'high-tech' designs of Foster and Rogers in the 1980s. While offering the promise of high performance in both social and economic terms, functional architecture, Higgott concludes, is impoverished as a totalizing conception of architecture.

Part Five, Cities, on the face of it, covers much the same historical ground as the previous one, in that it deals primarily with the twentieth century. Here, however, we turn outward from buildings to consider a different spatial context, that of the city. The city is far more than the simple physical confines of the

Figure 1.10

The modern metropolis requires agri-business to feed the urban population. Grain elevator, Illinois, 1994.

urban realm (as Georg Simmel pointed out long ago its influence 'overflows by waves into a far-flung international area'[4]), such that it is, above all, the city which has provided much of modern architecture's *raison d'être* — the need for public buildings, housing, the architecture of the welfare state, industrial buildings, transport and roads – and also has suggested many of its most important concerns: questions of social control, physical context, the role of technology and innovation, the whole burden of industrial and economic growth and so on. Beyond such material considerations, the city has also provided the focus of attention for many contemporary critics who have sought to identify what they see as the problematic of modern life. In other words the city has provided not only many of the problems which architecture has tried to address, it has also been the intellectual symbol by which people have sought to get a grip on reality. It is should then come of no surprise to find that it is at the spatial and conceptual level of the city that many of the most important and widespread issues in modern life are best seen to map onto architecture. In Chapter 21, David Dunster identifies one of the most pervasive of these, that of modernity itself. In fin-de-siècle Vienna, first the bourgeois promoters of the Ringstrasse and then architects like Wagner and Loos sought to give physical form to their own vision of modern life. Adrian Forty, in Chapter 22, picks up on this theme of modernity, but here explores the experience of the city as a place of fear and ambivalence. Without the qualities of direct social relations,

Figure 1.11

More than just a functional problem, the city is also an intellectual symbol by which people struggle to comprehend the world around them. Los Angeles, 1988.

the city was considered with both anxiety and exhila-
ration by contemporary commentators ranging from
Engels and Baudelaire to Simmel and Benjamin, and
was translated into architectural form by Hilberseimer.

In Chapter 23, Iain Borden considers the relevance
of gender relations to architecture and cities, and
shows how beyond the internal realm of the domestic environment issues of gender have informed the
suburbanization of cities, the creation of a consumer
ideology, the development of the architectural and
planning professions, and various genderized conceptions of urban space and spatiality. David Dunster, in
Chapter 24, returns to the concept of type he raised
in Chapter 8, but this time in the context of the urban
theories of Rossi, Ungers and Rob Krier. Applied to
the more historic cities of Europe, the notion of type
has allowed architects to address the problem of post-
war urban planning without ignoring either the cultural
sensitivity that such cities demand, or the continual
search for new ways of designing architectural and
urban forms. In the last essay of this section, Chapter
25, Jonathan Charley looks at some of the effects of
industrialization, categorizing them into transformations
of the labour process, space, and of everyday life. Such
fundamental processes seep into all our cities, into all
their corners and resting places. Charley concludes that
whatever the reality created by industrialization and
urbanization, we are now presented with an increasing commodification of the social world, in which
more and more people seem to know (and care) less
and less about the world in which they live.

Charley's closing remarks bring us in turn to the last
section of this book Part Six, Present Future. Three
chapters deal here with the problem of seeing through
the veil created by contemporary conditions, for the
present and the immediate future always seem less
intelligible than the past. In Chapter 26, Richard
Patterson begins by asking the question 'what is going
on?' His response, which delineates much of the confusion surrounding theories of science, architecture,
language and philosophy, is simply that, as the new
millennium approaches, we do not know and cannot
know. By contrast, in Chapter 27, Graham Ive provides
one part of a possible answer, outlining the current
and future state of the construction industry, and, in
particular, the artistic role left for architects within it.

Figure 1.12

Spying into the future. Offices of the advertising agency Chiat Day, Ocean Park, Los Angeles, (1989–91), architects Frank O. Gehry and Associates and sculptor Claes Oldenburg.

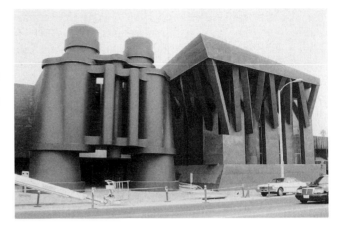

Figure 1.13

The spectacular side of the present/future. 900 North Michigan Avenue, Chicago, (1987–9), architects Kohn Pederson & Fox, and Perkins & Will, seen from the John Hancock Centre.

Figure 1.14

Surviving the present/future. The spectacular is suffered, resisted, and fought back against in a myriad of different ways. The Lower East Side, New York, 1991.

Architecture, he argues, is increasingly a matter of the marketing and sale of property developments. Underlying Ive's consideration of the construction sector of the economy is the conception that capitalism is far from over, and indeed that we have now entered an ever-intensifying form of capitalist development. The notion of 'late capitalism', developed by the economist Ernst Mandel,[5] provides the foundation for the analysis of many cultural forms of society, as, notably, undertaken by Fredric Jameson in his seminal text *Postmodernism, Or, the Cultural Logic of Late Capitalism*. In the closing Chapter 28, Iain Borden notes the increasing tendency of cultural theorists like Jameson and others who seek to understand the contemporary condition in general to incorporate architecture into their formulations. Through the particular example of Jameson's text, Borden considers the value of architecture to such theories, and, in turn, the value of such theories to architecture.

One last point. As is evident from the above, we should point out that although this book starts by referring to ancient Greece, and progresses more or less consistently through the centuries until ending with one eye upon the 21st century, this chronology is by no means adhered to throughout. Le Corbusier will be encountered before Brunelleschi, Washington before renaissance Florence, and high-tech before Loos' attack on ornament. We hope that this does not seem too incongruous, but in any case we expect readers – as is customary for a book of essays – to make their own selection and running order. For this reason, despite the inevitable redundancy it creates, we have tried to supply dates of individuals and buildings whenever mentioned for the first time in any single chapter. Finding the birth and death dates for Leon Battista Alberti (1404–72) in this book is not difficult, for having argued throughout for the cause of interpretation over facts, we have found that old habits die hard.

REFERENCES

1   John Musgrove (ed.), *Sir Banister Fletcher's A History of Architecture*, (Butterworths, London: nineteenth edition, 1987).
2   Spiro Kostof, *A History of Architecture: Settings and Rituals*, (Oxford University Press, Oxford: 1985).
3   Heinrich Wölfflin, *Principles of Art History: the Problem of the Development of Style in Later Art*, (Dover Editions, 1950), p. 11. First published in 1915 as *Kunstgeschichtliche Grundbegriffe.*
4   Georg Simmel, 'The Metropolis and Mental Life', (1903), reprinted in P.K. Hatt and A.J. Reiss (eds.), *Cities and Society: the Revised Reader in Urban Sociology*, (Free Press, New York: 1951), p. 642.
5   Ernst Mandel, *Late Capitalism*, (New Left Books, London: 1975).

Part One

TIME AND PLACE

2

GREECE SEEN FROM ROME (AND PARIS)

Martin Goalen

Why must I, like so many others, name the Parthenon the undeniable Master (the tyrant, the dictator), as it looms up from its stone base, and yield, even with anger, to its supremacy?

Le Corbusier, *Journey to the East*[1]

THE PARTHENON

The image of the Parthenon, the fifth century BC (447–32) temple to Athena set on the acropolis at Athens, has been a powerful one in the production of architecture and histories of architecture since the rediscovery of ancient Greece in the eighteenth century. A recent response is that of Nikolaus Pevsner in his *Outline of European Architecture*:

> The Greek temple is the most perfect example ever achieved of architecture finding its fulfilment in bodily beauty . . . It is the plastic shape of the temple that tells, placed before us with a physical presence more intense, more alive than of any later building . . . there is something consummately human in all this, life in the brightest lights of nature and mind: nothing harrowing, nothing problematic and obscure, nothing blurred.[2]

The idealizing note in Pevsner's description has its origin in antiquity; the historian Plutarch (c.46–120 AD) wrote of the buildings on the Athenian acropolis:

> Such is the bloom of perpetual newness . . . which makes them ever to look untouched by time, as though the unfaltering breath of an ageless spirit had been infused into them.[3]

Plutarch tells us, too, that it was a sculptor, Pheidias, who was in overall charge of all the work on the acropolis at Athens and that other great artists and architects were employed on the individual buildings. Of these, Iktinos, the architect

Figure 2.1

The Parthenon, Athens,
(447–32 BC), retains its power
in the present day.
Photograph by Frédéric
Boissonas, reproduced in Le
Corbusier, *Towards a New
Architecture*, (1923/1927).

(with Callicrates) of the great temple to Athena – the
Parthenon – and of temples at Bassae and Eleusis, was
the author of a now lost book describing the work.
We know from the single ancient book on architecture that has survived into the modern world, *De
Architectura* by the Roman architect Vitruvius, that it
was quite usual for architects in the ancient world to
write technical treatises explaining either general
principles or individual buildings. Vitruvius, who wrote
in the last quarter of the first century BC, gives a long
list of such treatises and tells us that it is from their,
mainly Greek, authors that he himself drew 'as it were
like water from springs' in the compilation of his own
treatise.[4]

Vitruvius' aim in *De Architectura* is, he tells us, to
disclose 'all the principles of the art.' He deals with
practical matters of building methods and materials,
but also seeks to place the practice of architecture
within the humane disciplines, the 'liberal arts', of the
ancient world:

So architects who have aimed at acquiring manual
skill without scholarship have never been able to

reach a position of authority to match their pains,
while those who only trust to theories and
scholarship obviously follow the shadow, not the
substance.[5]

Architecture was not the only art in the ancient
world to have such a tradition of commentary by
practitioners. Manuals of rhetoric had appeared from
the fifth century BC onward. The sculptor Polykleitos
wrote his famous *Canon* in the third quarter of the
fifth century BC and we know too there to have been
treatises on painting and perspective. All these
treatises, however, have been lost, apart from
Vitruvius' text. We have the tantalizing knowledge that
a good proportion of the architects of the major buildings of ancient Greece wrote detailed commentaries
about their work but that none has survived, except
at second hand reflected through the pages of
Vitruvius. It is the aim of this chapter to trace, through
a reading of Vitruvius' *De Architectura*, the themes and
explanations that ancient Greek architects thought
important, and to seek to discover what, if anything,
links these themes and explanations to our modern
critical responses.

VITRUVIUS

We know that Vitruvius drew from a great variety of
sources, and that he wished to present architecture as
a liberal art. He lists the branches of knowledge with
which architects need to be familiar – literature,
drawing, geometry, optics, arithmetic, history, philosophy, music, and medicine – 'for a liberal education
forms as it were, a single body made up of these
members.' Fundamental abstract aesthetic principles,
clearly borrowed from a Greek source, or sources, are
listed, but nevertheless, the structure of Vitruvius'
exposition is functional rather than abstract.[6] It is based
on the idea that the province of the architect encom-
passes all the tasks in the building of a city: the choice
of the site, its fortification, the division of land by the
laying out of streets, the distribution of sites for public
and for private buildings, the principles governing the
design of those public and private buildings, as well as
water supply, and machines for the attack and defence
of cities. This notion of the range and hierarchy of tasks

necessary for *political* life – the life of the city – gives Vitruvius the structure for his treatise.

Vitruvius' second guiding notion is that of typology. Rectangular temples, for instance, have seven types of plan, each differing from the other in the relationship of columns to walls; the classification follows a simple logical formal sequence. And types of elevation follow types of plan with the same formal progression between the types. In private houses, too, there are 'five different styles of atrium, termed according to their construction as ... Tuscan, Corinthian, tetrastyle, displuviate and testudinate,' and so on. Typological systematization runs throughout *De Architectura.*[7]

DORIC AND IONIC

In the history of architecture, however, probably the most significant and long-lasting of Vitruvian classifications is that of the types of column: Doric and Ionic (plus a variant of Ionic, the Corinthian). Although the explanation that Vitruvius gives for the existence of the

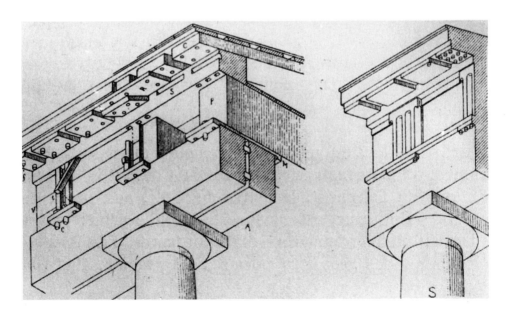

Figure 2.2

The 'manlike, bare and unadorned' Doric order in Auguste Choisy's diagram illustrating Vitruvius' hypothetical carpentry model.

types is a historical one, each of the types has a different character: the Doric shows 'virile strength' compared to the more delicate outline of the Ionic; the ratio of base to height in Doric columns suggests male solidity, whereas the same ratio in Ionic columns suggests feminine slenderness; the volutes of an Ionic capital are like gracefully curling hair with the fluting of the Ionic column hanging like the folds of drapery; the Doric is 'manlike, bare and unadorned', the Ionic 'delicate, adorned and feminine'. A choice between the orders is, therefore, a choice of the character for the building. Doric is appropriate to a temple dedicated to the war-like god Mars, Ionic for the chaste Diana.[8]

Vitruvius' classificatory systems all appear to be Greek in origin; his types have Greek names: Doric, Ionic, Corinthian for columns; prostyle, amphiprostyle, peripteral, dipteral for temple plans; pycnostyle, eustyle and so on for their elevations. Indeed, Vitruvius claims that Hermogenes, a Greek architect working in Asia Minor in the third century BC, invented the eustyle and pseudodipteral schemes, and wrote commentaries on the temples that incorporated them, the temples of Dionysus at Teos and Artemis at Magnesia.[9]

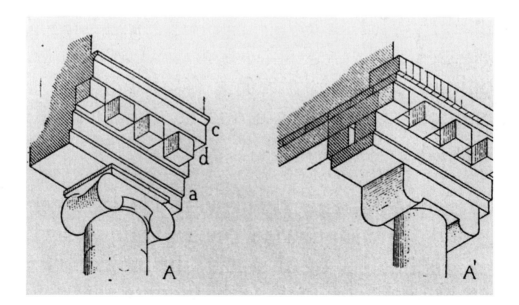

Figure 2.3

The 'delicate, adorned and feminine' Ionic order in Auguste Choisy's diagram illustrating Vitruvius' hypothetical carpentry model.

Hermogenes is a crucial source for Vitruvius' treatise; he is mentioned more than any other author. And it is Hermogenes, Vitruvius tells us, who rejected the use of the Doric order in temples because of what he saw as an insoluble formal problem inherent in the Doric system: the so-called 'corner triglyph problem' described below. Vitruvius follows Hermogenes in this view, so that whereas the choice between the Doric and the Ionic orders that had been (in Book 1 of *De Architectura*) for Vitruvius been simply a matter of propriety – of the appropriateness of the order (masculinity in the Doric, delicacy in the Ionic) to the particular god to whom a temple was dedicated – this choice, when the details of temples are described in Books 3 and 4, weighed overwhelmingly in favour of the Ionic. Vitruvius seems almost to apologize for giving a description of the details of the Doric order, 'but since our plan calls for it we set it forth as we have received it from our teachers.'[10] For Vitruvius the priviliged order is the Ionic. His discussion of temple design (Book 3) assumes the use of the Ionic order, while the details of the other orders are given separately (Book 4). In this Vitruvius follows his sources, the architects of the fourth century BC onward, for whom the normative character of temple building is given by the characteristics of the Ionic order. It had not always been so.

In the earlier Greek world the distribution of the orders had been predominantly geographical: Doric in mainland Greece and the west; Ionic in the Aegean islands and on the coast of Asia Minor. From about 460 BC in Athens and the Peloponnese (the most southerly part of the Greek mainland), however, the orders are mixed, and the choice of order becomes, as Vitruvius described it in Book 1, a matter of appropriateness or *decor*. From the fourth century onward, for temples at least, Ionic is the dominant order. Vitruvius' exposition is a reflection of the situation in the Hellenistic world.

What then were the formal problems inherent in the Doric? Vitruvius tells us that the Ionic entablature is decorated with dentils, the Doric with triglyphs and metopes, and that dentils and triglyphs are both derived from carpentry models imitated in stone: Doric triglyphs from the projecting ends of widely spaced beams, and Ionic dentils from smaller more closely

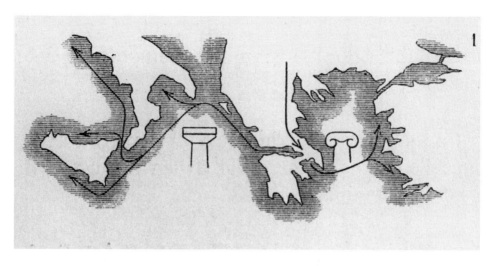

Figure 2.4

Map of southern Italy (left), mainland Greece (centre) and Asia Minor (right) by Auguste Choisy showing the distribution of Doric and Ionic orders.

spaced rafters. It is the large scale and wide spacing of the architectural members that give rise to the corner triglyph problem of the Doric. Each triglyph, representing a beam, sits exactly over (or half way between) the columns that support them, but, at the same time when an external corner is reached the triglyph is expected to cover the corner. This it cannot do without varying either the spacing of the columns or the widths of the triglyphs (and/or the panels, the metopes, between them). Either solution, according to Vitruvius, is faulty.[11]

The problem, if one regards it as one, is not however confined to the spacing of the triglyphs and columns; it extends into the stone beams and coffers that form part of the order. Comparison of the reflected ceiling plan of a Doric temple like the Parthenon with that of an Ionic temple like that to Athena Polias at Pirene makes this clear. The beams and columns of the Doric building do not align; numerous adjustments are necessary. An Ionic ceiling plan, on the other hand, is absolutely regular, undisturbed by the need for any adjustment. The regular beat of dentils is as even as that of the coffering. We see then that the different visual characteristics of the orders are paralleled by a radically different attitude to

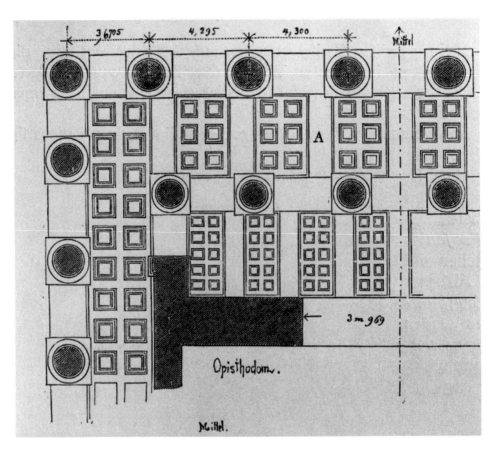

Figure 2.5

The corner triglyph problem in the Doric order: the beams and columns do not align. Parthenon.

architectural uniformity. The differences between the two orders are not simply differences between formal types. The choice of order is not just a choice of an appropriate character but has become one of fundamentally opposed architectural values.

LE CORBUSIER AND AUGUSTE CHOISY

When, in the eighteenth century, Greek architecture became once again a subject of study – visited, drawn, measured and described by generations of travellers and architects – it was the Doric order that, for those

Figure 2.6

Part of a regular Ionic
entablature. Temple of Athena
Polias, Priene (c.334 BC), now
in the Pergamon Museum,
Berlin.

travellers and architects, held a particular power, a
power that can be felt, for instance, in Giovanni Battista
Piranesi's (1720–78) brooding engravings of the temples
at Paestum, and a power that was absorbed by the more
vigorous Greek Revival architects of the nineteenth
century such as Thomas Hamilton (1785–1858). In the
twentieth century, however, the architect who has, more
than any other, given a paradigmatic status to the Doric
is Le Corbusier (1887–1966).

> We shall be able to speak 'Doric' when man, in
> nobility of aim and complete sacrifice of all that is
> accidental in Art has reached the higher levels of the
> mind: austerity.

Figure 2.7

'The higher levels of the mind: austerity.' Le Corbusier, *Towards a New Architecture*, (1923/27). Parthenon, west peristyle from the south. Photograph by Frédéric Boissonas, reproduced in Le Corbusier, *Towards a New Architecture*.

We must realize that Doric achitecture did not
grow in the fields with the asphodels, and that it is
a pure creation of the mind. The plastic system of
Doric work is so pure that it almost gives the
feeling of natural growth. But none the less, it is
entirely man's creation.[12]

These are Le Corbusier's captions to photographs of
the acropolis in *Towards a New Architecture*,
(1923/1927). The details of the order, too, excite his
admiration:

The annulets [of the Doric capital] are 50 feet from
the ground, but they tell more than all the baskets
of acanthus on a Corinthian capital. The Doric state
of mind and the Corinthian state of mind are two
things. A moral fact creates a gulf between them.[13]

For Le Corbusier the Parthenon is *the* key building;
he had first seen it in 1911 and it is central to the
argument in *Towards a New Architecture*, representing
for Le Corbusier a pinnacle of architectural development. He uses images from the Parthenon in three
places in this book. First, a diagram from Auguste

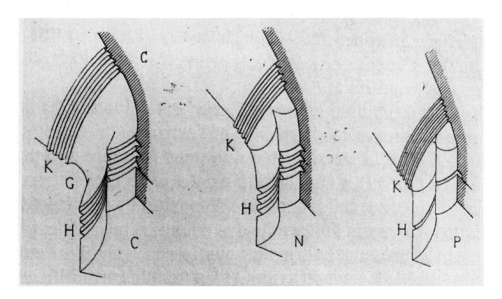

Figure 2.8

Doric annulets (column rings) and necking grooves at Temple C, Selinus, (c. 550–30 BC) (left),
Temple of Neptune, Paestum, (c. 460 BC) (centre), and Parthenon, Athens, (447–32 BC) (right).
Diagram by Auguste Choisy.

Figure 2.9

'Elegant grace.' Auguste Choisy, *Histoire d'architecture*, (1899). Parthenon, north end of west pediment. Photograph by Frédéric Boissonas, reproduced in Le Corbusier, *Towards a New Architecture*.

Choisy's *Histoire de l'architecture* (1899) which presents the layout of the Athenian acropolis as a composition of symmetrical buildings, asymmetrically disposed, offering the visitor to the site a succession of balanced tableaux. Second, there is the famous example of the perfection of a type through evolution demonstrated by comparison of the mid-sixth century BC 'basilica' at Paestum with the mid-fifth century BC Parthenon. This comparison too is borrowed from Choisy. 'The older is distinguished by an excess of force, a certain heaviness; the more recent by an elegant grace' was Choisy's comment on the two temples.[14]

The most extended discussion of the Parthenon in *Towards a New Architecture* occurs, however, in the chapter 'Architecture, Pure Creation of the Mind'. The architecture of the Parthenon, and architecture in its highest sense – whatever its metaphorical relation to construction – is seen as a calculated manipulation,

through visual perception, on the emotions of the
spectator. The mode of this action is through the
artist/architect's control of what Le Corbusier calls
modénature (which his English translator gives as
'profile and contour'). *Modénature*, says Le Corbusier,
is a word found in every page of Choisy's *Histoire*,
'the greatest book on architecture that ever there has
been.'[15] For Choisy *'modénature* properly speaking is
essentially Greek.' Choisy, an editor and translator of
Vitruvius, follows Vitruvius in insisting that mouldings
have their functional origin but for Choisy they
transcend that origin: 'these purely material considerations are far from exhausting the role of *modénature*:
and here enters the analysis of the play of light.'[16]

Figure 2.10

'Everything is stated exactly.'
Le Corbusier, *Towards a New
Architecture*, (1923/27).
Fragments of ceiling
coffering, Parthenon.
Photograph by Frédéric
Boissonas, reproduced in Le
Corbusier, *Towards a New
Architecture.*

Le Corbusier echoes Choisy's concern for visual impact and precision in the details: 'Everything is stated exactly, the mouldings are tight and firm, relationships are established between the annulets of the capital, the abacus and the bands of the architrave.'[17]

These descriptions are, of course, of the Doric order. What for Vitruvius and his Hellenistic sources was 'confusion and inconvenience' became, for Choisy and Le Corbusier in the modern world, a source of power and sensation in architecture. The clues, however, are there in Vitruvius' text; however much he may have followed his Hellenistic sources he did not eliminate all trace of previous values. Choisy was able to extract them, and through Choisy, so was Le Corbusier. The polarity between the architectural values embodied in the two orders as Vitruvius has given them to us – the embodied tension of the Doric, the smooth resolution of the Ionic – remained a vital one.

REFERENCES

1   Le Corbusier, *Journey to the East*, (MIT Press, Cambridge, Mass.) p. 217
2   Nikolaus Pevsner, *An Outline of European Architecture*, (Penguin, Harmondsworth, 1960), pp. 10–11.
3   Plutarch, *Life of Pericles*, 13.3.
4   Vitruvius, 7.praef.10, 12, 14.
5   Vitruvius, 1.1.2.
6   Vitruvius, 1.1, and 1.2.1.
7   Vitruvius, 3.2.1-7, 3.3.1-13, and 6.3.1.
8   Vitruvius, 1.2.5, 4.1.3-10, and 4.2.7.
9   Vitruvius 3.3.8, 3.3.9, and 7.praef.12.
10 Vitruvius, 4.3.1-3.
11 Vitruvius, 1.2.6, 1.3.5, 4.2.2-5, and 4.3.2. See also J.J. Coulton, *Greek Architects at Work: Problems of Structure and Design*, (Granada, St Albans, 1982), pp. 60–4.
12 Le Corbusier, *Towards a New Architecture*, (Architectural Press, London, revised English edition 1946), pp. 188 and 193.
13 Le Corbusier, *Towards a New Architecture*, p. 198.
14 Auguste Choisy, *Histoire de l'architecture*, (Gauthier-Villars, Paris, 1899), v.1, pp. 306–7.
15 Le Corbusier, *L'almanach de l'architecture moderne*, (Crès, Paris, 1926), p. 116.
16 Choisy, *Histoire de l'architecture*, v.1, pp. 290–1.
17 Le Corbusier, *Towards a New Architecture*, p. 197.

BIBLIOGRAPHY

F.E. Brown, 'Vitruvius and the Liberal Art of Architecture', *Bucknell Review*, v.11 n.4 (1963).

Auguste Choisy, *Histoire de l'architecture*, (Gauthier-Villars, Paris, two volumes, 1899).

J.J. Coulton, *Greek Architects at Work: Problems of Structure and Design*, (Granada, St. Albans, 1982).

William Bell Dinsmoor, *The Architecture of Ancient Greece: an Account of its Historic Development*, (Batsford, London, 1950).

Moses Finley, 'The Ancient City: From Fustel de Coulanges to Max Weber and Beyond,' *Economy and Society in Ancient Greece*, (Penguin, Harmondsworth, 1983), pp. 3–23.

Martin Goalen, 'Schinkel and Durand: the Case of the Altes Museum', in Michael Snodin (ed.), *Karl Friedrich Schinkel: a Universal Man*, (Yale University Press, New Haven, 1991), pp. 27–35.

Le Corbusier, *Vers une architecture*, (Crès, Paris, 1923). Translated by Frederick Etchells as *Towards a New Architecture*, (Architectural Press, London, revised English edition 1946)

Le Corbusier, *Journey to the East*, (MIT Press, Cambridge, Mass., 1987).

Robin Middleton, 'Auguste Choisy, Historian: 1841–1909', *International Architect*, v.1 n.5 (1981), pp. 37–42.

Nikolaus Pevsner and S. Lang, 'Apollo or Baboon', *Architectural Review*, v.104 (1948), pp. 271–9.

Nikolaus Pevsner, *An Outline of European Architecture*, (Penguin, Harmondsworth, 1960).

J.J. Pollitt, *The Ancient View of Greek Art*, (Yale University Press, New Haven, 1974).

J.J. Pollitt, *The Art of Ancient Greece: Sources and Documents*, (Cambridge University Press, Cambridge, 1990).

Fritz Saxl and Rudolph Wittkower, *British Art and the Mediterranean*, (Oxford University Press, London, 1969).

Vincent Scully, *The Earth, the Temple and the Gods*, (Praeger, New York, 1969).

Brian Vickers, *In Defence of Rhetoric*, (Clarendon Press, Oxford, 1988).

Vitruvius, *On Architecture*, (Loeb, Cambridge, Mass., two volumes, translated by Frank Granger, 1933–35).

Vitruvius, *The Ten Books on Architecture*, (Dover, New York, translated by M. H. Morgan, 1960).

Dora Wiebenson, *Sources of Greek Revival Architecture*, (Zwemmer, London, 1969).

3

URBAN CLASSICISM AND MODERN IDEOLOGY

Graham Ive

Until recent times, most knowledge about making and doing was preserved and passed from generation to generation through the craft system – meaning artistic, religious and other cultural production as well as the practical trades. But in the modern age the influence of past upon present, though equally powerful, is profoundly different. In matters of technology and ways of making we are accustomed to being revolutionary. No longer is there any presumption that methods of production should resemble those of the preceding period. Instead it is in matters of cultural value that our age is stubbornly conservative. For two centuries – the whole of the 'modern' age – there has been an intense cultural conflict between conservatives and modernists. Not only do cultural conservatives feel the need to preserve old values in the way culture is appreciated, but there has also been widespread invention of traditions for new social identities. As direct relationships gave way to abstractions of class, gender, nation, and ethnicity as the means of understanding society, tradition-myths were invented to identify the timeless and unchanging aspects of belonging.

For the dominant classes of countries such as the United Kingdom, the United States and Italy, the relevant sense of belonging involves the idea that they are the latest bearers of an identity and tradition known as Western Civilization, stretching back to ancient Greece. Such an account views history as starting with the birth of civilization in classical Greece, its development in the Roman Republic and then Empire, a descent into the 'Dark Ages' before the re-flowering of civilization in the Renaissance and onward through the Enlightenment to the present day. The principal characters are rulers, dominant empires and military victors, while little significance is attached to other cultures, other civilizations, or to the mass of people except when they appear as threats to this ruling order. To modernists, by contrast, the traditions important to conservatives are actually nothing but ideological distortions which sit like millstones upon the living. They are historical fictions to be dispensed with. One such dispute concerns the city.

THE IDEA OF THE CLASSICAL CITY

The idea of the classical city is a fusion of political, social and aesthetic elements. If we trace some of the uses of the idea in Britain, the United States and Italy over the last two centuries we can find all of the following.

Firstly, power. A strong, unified state and a centralized ruling class, both located in a capital city, both with effective control of the economic surplus produced in a hinterland – these are the elements of a classical city of power. It is a city based on tribute rather than exchange or urban production, and in its ancient classical form that tribute was threefold: plunder from forcible extension of the state; taxes; and 'rents' (land- and slave-owners' surpluses). The capital city expanded grossly through a flow of surplus from a hierarchy of provincial cities. Thus the apparent stability and order of the classical city was built upon extreme class antagonism between rural producers and urban exploiters, and upon dependence on expansionary warfare.

Politically, it is Athens which has stood for the idea of the autonomous city state, naval imperium and model of popular democracy. Rome, by contrast, has stood both as oligarchic republic of land- and slave-owners, as it did for the newly independent USA, and as a model for empire, as it did for late nineteenth century Britain and, as Jonathan Charley shows in Chapter 18, for Stalinist Moscow.

Socially, the classical city has provided ideas of palace and villa as models for upper class living; technocratic ideas of urban regulation; and, for conservatives and liberals, crucial images of class anxiety and the problem of urban social order. Ancient Rome, remember, gives us the terms 'plebs' and 'proletariat', while the modern conservative term for the those who threaten the urban fabric is 'vandals', after the German tribe who sacked Rome in AD 455.

Aesthetically, it provided a decorative style and a set of rules of proportion and harmony in architecture, a set of principles for building plans, a repertoire of building types and urban spaces, an idea of precincts, the urban grid, and much more.[1]

Let us explore the relationships between these three dimensions – political, social and aesthetic – of the meaning of the classical world in three instances of the urban use of classicism: Trafalgar Square in the United Kingdom; Daniel Burnham's plans for Washington and Chicago in America; and Mussolini's New Towns in Italy.

TRAFALGAR SQUARE

Here we will consider one of the earliest classical schemes in nineteenth century London, Trafalgar Square. The making of this square has been the subject of a detailed study by Rodney Mace on which the following relies heavily.[2]

Although, in general, neo-classicism should not be simply correlated with the emergence in Britain of the idea of the Roman Empire, Trafalgar Square was a direct reference to this ancient source.[3] William Wood, in 1808, published *An Essay on National and Sepulchral Monuments* arguing that monuments must stimulate patriotism, record triumphs and reward military leaders with fame. Referring to two of the most famous Graeco-Persian battles in the fifth century BC, monuments should be in 'that spirit of national devotion which united the Greeks in victory at Marathon and in death at Thermopylae', and, as this alone could excite a sense of public glory, in a classical manner. Wood proposed a pyramid, 250 feet square and guarded by monumental lions, to be a tomb for former admiral of the Royal Navy Lord Nelson and other dead heroes.

Four years later John Nash (1752–1835) proposed a magnificent square for the Trafalgar Square site as part of his grand proposals for the improvement of London. Nothing happened until 1826 when a Commission was established and received a revised proposal by Nash. The Commissioners wanted two things: a new street so that the vista along Pall Mall be terminated by the portico of St Martin's; and the space into which Whitehall opened to be large and 'regular', not 'deformed'. A grand street from Charing Cross to the British Museum was also proposed, which would have left the square from the north east corner. This was never built.

Trafalgar Square itself was to be lined with leading institutions of civil society (such as the Royal

Academy) rather than of the state. The new streets
would reduce carriage congestion and remove the
'unsightly' from a route much travelled by the upper
class, and by 1828 very large sums of money had been
spent on acquisition and demolition. The square was
named Trafalgar in 1830, before official plans for a
monument to Nelson.

In 1832 came William Wilkins' (1778–1839) design
for a National Gallery (1834–8), records office and
Royal Academy. So unmonumental was the original
thinking here that one scheme proposed a ground
floor of shops, while parliament thought it might be
built in brick, not stone, to save money. Wilkins'
design, criticized ever since for lacking grandeur, was
in fact the most neo-classical of the entries. Wilkins
followed up with further plans, with Charles Barry
(1795–1860), to level and pave the square.

Finally, in 1838, a competition was held for a
monument to Nelson. The winning proposal, by
William Railton, was for the highest Corinthian single
column in the world.

What then was the reasoning behind this grand
square, architecture and monuments? Mace implies that
chauvinism is the normal resort of the British ruling class
when under challenge, and in the late 1830s this
challenge was Chartism and trade unionism. The sudden
drive to raise patriotic monuments was the 'natural' self-
assertion of a class which identified deeply with the
nation and its victories. Thus, by 1838, there was no
question of a monument to the dead of Trafalgar or the
Napoleonic wars in general, only to an individual leader.

Figure 3.1

Expression of a dominant
ruling class through
architecture. National Gallery,
London, (1834–8), architect
William Wilkins.

Figure 3.2

A monument to patriotism, war and military leadership, built with strike-breaking labour. Nelson's Column, London, (1838–42), designed by William Railton.

Furthermore, beyond the overt symbolism and assertion through classicism of the dominance of the ruling class, there was to be no question of the square being used for other purposes. To discourage demonstrations taking place, the column and surrounding pools were deliberately designed to break up the space and so facilitate the control of mass assemblies of people.

It is ironic that the construction of this classical monument was itself an arena of the very class conflict it was intended to help resolve. The contractor for the project, Peto, was also at work on the new Houses of Parliament, and 'acts of tyranny and oppression' by the foreman at this site lead to a strike by the Operative Stonemasons Union. As a result, the most famous monument to the British Empire was built by scab [blackleg] labour.[4] The memorial was not completed until 1867, and in a later remodelling of the square by Edwin Lutyens (1869–1944) bronze lions were added. Even Wood might have been satisfied.

The Burnham Plans for Washington and Chicago

Two major schemes for Washington DC – by Pierre L'Enfant (1754–1825) and Thomas Jefferson (1743– 1826) in the 1790s, and Burnham, Senator James McMillan of Michigan (d. 1902), Frederick Law Olmstead Junior (1870–1957) and Charles McKim (1847–1909) in the 1900s – were both explicit demonstrations of the idea that the city be, as McMillan put it, 'the visible expression of the power and taste of the people of the United States' and that only classicism would do for this purpose.[5] We will focus here on the later 'City Beautiful' period. This will enable us to address the commercial as well as the political uses of classicism, and the planning and ordering of whole cities as well as their monumental centres.

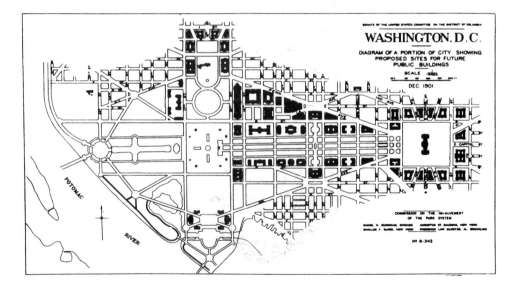

Figure 3.3

'From [the] legacies of aristocrats and nobles, from all these seemingly tireless survivals of departed or decayed societies, they hoped to fashion on the banks of the Potomac an expression of the Republican ideal.' A critic's observation of the Park Commission plan for Washington, (1901–2), prepared by Daniel Burnham et al.

For Daniel Burnham (1846–1912) and his collaborators on the Park Commission plan, the Washington scheme was a political monument equivalent to the 1893 Chicago World's Fair. The formalism of the plan – an emphasis upon order effected by vast axes marked at crossings and terminations by symbolic buildings or monuments – was well researched. At Burnham's insistence, the commission spent months touring Europe, especially Rome, but also Paris, Versailles and Hampton Court. The size of the axes and the scale of the mall mark a shift to the monumental: the mall axis has a width of five generous city blocks, and it took decades for the plan's main elements to be built. Even if it cannot yet be constructed, wrote Burnham, a 'noble, logical diagram once recorded will never die.'

This new approach to the city was the result of the widespread realization in early twentieth century America that even democracy needed plans.[6] Previously it had been thought self-evident that laissez-faire should apply within the city blocks marked out by the strict grid and radials of the plan. A compromise was made between city bosses and building capitalists on the one hand and municipal reformers and their supporters on the other: plan the major streets; leave plot development uncontrolled; reconcile the planning drive for urban order with private property rights; and provide the framework for future business expansion.

However, the small firms and local political bosses of the laissez-faire city were giving way to a new stage in American capitalism. This was the age of the giant capitalist combine or monopoly, the age of imperialism in which architecture and planning were constantly drawn toward a comprehensive model.[7] Here were private clients capable of commissioning vast buildings equal to the public monuments of the neo-classical City Beautiful plans. Burnham's firm itself was responsible for a host of classicized skyscrapers. As one contemporary critic said of Burnham's First National Bank of Chicago (1903), 'To even the average man on the street . . . the exterior of this great building suggests that its interior contains a bank of more than ordinary extent . . . there is a nobility in the conception; a palatial air . . . all in scale and harmony and thoroughly Italian in the best sense, and almost Roman in dignity.'[8] This was just what Burnham's clients wanted to hear.

Figure 3.4

In the age of monopoly capitalism, corporate clients wanted their own classical monuments. First National Bank of Chicago, Chicago, (1903), architects Burnham & Co.

Equally instructive are Burnham's plans for civic beautification, especially the *Chicago Plan* published in 1909. This approach emphasized big plans executed by powerful leaders, and above all, planning based on grand aesthetics rather than social or functional needs. Instead of schemes to improve housing conditions, the working classes were given grand parks and lakeside walks. Moreover, beautification could be good business by improving traffic flow, attracting rich visitors and preparing new districts for commercial development.[9] Faced with the urban crisis produced by competitive laissez-faire period capitalism on the one hand, and on the other by signs of its supersession economically (by giant corporations) and politically (by imperialist and reformist Republicanism under Theodore Roosevelt), Burnham's solutions were typically classicist.

FASCISM AND CLASSICISM IN ITALY

In contrast to this use of classicism to help solve the problems of large American cities, anti-urbanism is also a recurrent theme within the classical tradition. Dreams of an 'ideal' state of free, small property owners, as opposed to a dangerous urban 'democracy of plebs', are as old as Plato and classical Athens.

The New Towns of Mussolini's Italy, despite being called towns, are better understood in this context. As small towns based on agriculture, they provided an alternative location for the rootless poor, saving them from big cities, improper behaviour and socialist political influence. The new towns also drew on an ancient classical precedent. Originally conceived as homes for unemployed veterans of World War 1, they echoed colonies of veterans in ancient Rome.

The best source on this subject is Diane Ghirardo, who also covers the American New Deal new towns of the 1930s.[10] As she puts it, 'Any government architecture has a rhetorical function and . . . tells us what the regime wants us to believe about its nature. . . . In both the public buildings and the new communities the two regimes [Mussolini's Italy and Roosevelt's USA] created, they projected ideal images of sites for human habitation and communal life – ideal cities, in short.'[11] This discrepancy between the reality of Fascist politics and their apparent ideology is borne out by the new towns. Economically, the policies of the Fascist regime favoured large rather than small landowners. But in the 'symbolic politics' of the architecture of the New Towns, and by focusing attention on some exceptional projects aimed at creating small farmers, we are meant to see something else.

Faced with the problems of the inter-war Depression, the Italian dictator Benito Mussolini (1883–1945) needed to promote a feeling of national rather than local pride. To this end he worked on the symbolic level to invoke a noble past with shared traditions, appealing to the ancient Roman Empire to inspire patriotism in a country united only in name. When Mussolini told the Italian Senate that Rome was the source of life, he meant the monuments and the twenty five centuries of history to which they bore witness. In this political scheme, the state conferred special importance on building.[12]

The New Towns also reveal some of the contradictions inherent to Fascism. In particular, while the architecture and planning models were drawn from ancient and medieval types, 'at every point in the physical and social organization of the towns hierarchy emphatically prevailed (over mass participation).'[13] The key features were these: an axial road for parades and grand

Figure 3.5

Hierarchy and control embodied in the fascist headquarters and cinema, (left to right), Sabaudia.

Figure 3.6

Fascist new towns drew on Italian medieval, renaissance and Roman precedents to create a new kind of symbolic politics. Commune, *torre* (tower) and hotel, (left to right), Sabaudia.

Figure 3.7

Classical, imperial and military axiality. Plan of town centre, Sabaudia.

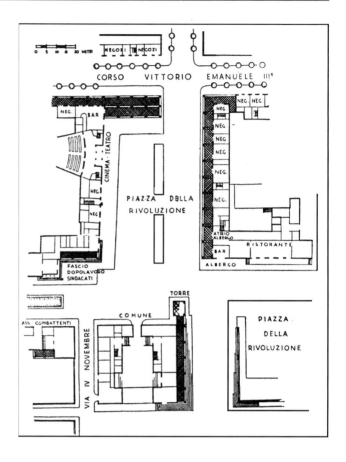

entrances; public buildings arranged along this road, especially at the central piazza; monumentalized buildings for Fascist and corporatist institutions; an oversized piazza for mass demonstrations; fixed spatial and axial relationships; and a unified stylistic language in all buildings. 'From a bird's eye view, then, the planning of the Fascist New Towns corresponded to that of the Roman military and provincial colonies; their layout and purpose mirrored that of imperial programs to a striking degree.'[14] In other words, classical urban models were used to express hierarchy and control.

In the light of this emphasis on hierarchy and control, the idea of internal colonies is also significant. Whereas ancient Rome settled conquered territories with colonies, Fascist Italy's first 'conquests' were internal, confirming dominance over land reclaimed from malarial marsh. In part this reflected a paucity of external conquests, but in part a

conscious pairing of the relations of the state to proletariat and conquered peoples.

CLASSICISM TODAY

Classicism, as an explicit doctrine for the planning of
cities, is today rare and anachronistic – partly because
it gives only a marginal place to commerce, partly
because it implies an interventionist state capable of
founding or reshaping whole cities. But when individual developers seek to impose order on large scale
urban developments it is still to ideas of classical urbanism that they often turn. There are, for example,
elements of classicism, stylistically at least, in recent
office developments at Broadgate (1984–91) in London
and Battery Park City (1983–) in New York, in housing
developments like Le Palais d'Abraxas (1978–83) in the
Parisian new town of Marne-la-Vallé, and in the
pastiche, reactionary designs of architects and town
planners like Ricardo Bofill (1939–), Leon Krier (1946–),
Demetri Porphyrios (1949–), John Simpson (1954–),
Robert Stern (1939–) and Quinlan Terry (1937–).

Nevertheless, postmodernist ideologists tell us that
classicism is finally dead as a serious force (as opposed
to something to be ransacked for ironic, joking reference), killed by the fragmentation and pluralism of
postmodern culture which removes from classicism the
claim to be the superior set of cultural values. We can
see recent events in the bastions of American upper
class education – such as courses in 'Western

Figure 3.8

Ironic, whimsical classicism
bereft of political meaning?
Antigone housing,
Montpellier, (1980), architects
Ricardo Bofill and El Taller de
Arquitectura.

Figure 3.9

The ubiquitous use of classicism represents alternatively the triumph of the barbarians, the arrival of a truly democratic culture, or a bankrupt and anachronistic symbolism. Commonwealth Edison Substation, Chicago, (1989), architects Tigerman McCurry.

Civilization' and canonical 'great books' programmes attacked in Yale and Columbia as racist, sexist and exclusionary – as signs that the ruling class is now prepared not only for polyvalent popular culture to be peddled to others, but to accept the same as its own. To some, this would mark the final victory of the barbarians and philistines and a collapse of all necessary values; to others, the coming-to-age of genuinely democratic and popular culture. Or perhaps we no longer need classicism at all.

REFERENCES

1   See John Summerson, *The Classical Language of Architecture*, (Thames and Hudson, London, revised edition, 1980).
2. Rodney Mace, *Trafalgar Square: Emblem of Empire*, (Lawrence and Wishart, London, 1976).
3   Mace, *Trafalgar Square*, pp. 15–16.
4   Mace, *Trafalgar Square*, pp. 96–7.
5   Quoted in John Reps, *The Making of Urban America: a History of City Planning in the United States*, (Princeton University Press, Princeton, 1965), p. 109.
6   Francesco Dal Co, 'From Parks to the Region: Progressive Ideology and the Reform of the American City', in Giorgio Ciucci et al, *The American City from the Civil War to the New Deal*, (MIT Press, Cambridge, Mass., 1979), pp. 177–8.
7   Mario Manieri-Elia, 'Toward an "Imperial City": Daniel H. Burnham and the City beautiful Movement', in Ciucci et al, *The American City*.

8 Quoted in Thomas S. Hines, *Burnham of Chicago –
   Architect and Planner*, (Oxford University Press, Oxford,
   1974), pp. 296–8.
9 For Burnham's Chicago Plan, see Hines *Burnham of
   Chicago* ch. 14, Richard Foglesong, *Planning the
   Capitalist City*, (Princeton University Press, Princeton,
   1986) ch. 7, and Richard R. Wrigley, 'The Plan of
   Chicago; its Fiftieth Anniversary', *Journal of American
   Institute of Planners*, v.26, (Feb. 1960).
10 Diane Ghirardo, *Building New Communities: New Deal
   America and Fascist Italy*, (Princeton University Press,
   Princeton, 1989).
11 Ghirardo, *Building New Communities*, pp. 9–10.
12 Ghirardo, *Building New Communities*, p. 18.
13 Ghirardo, *Building New Communities*, p. 25.
14 Ghirardo, *Building New Communities*, p. 66.

BIBLIOGRAPHY

Classical Society, Architecture and Urbanism

Perry Anderson, *Passages from Antiquity to Feudalism*, (New
   Left Books, London, 1974).
M.I. Finley, *Ancient Slavery and Modern Ideology*, (Chatto &
   Windus, London, 1980).
N.D. Fustel de Coulanges, *The Ancient City, Study on the
   Religion, Laws and Institutions of Greece and Rome*, (Johns
   Hopkins University, Baltimore, Maryland, 1980).
G. de Ste Croix, *The Class Struggle in the Ancient Greek
   World*, (Duckworth, London, 1981).
John Summerson, *The Classical Language of Architecture*,
   (Thames and Hudson, revised edition, London, 1980).
J.B. Ward-Perkins, *Cities of Ancient Greece and Italy,
   Planning in Classical Antiquity*, (Sidgwick and Jackson,
   London, 1974).

Trafalgar Square, Washington, Chicago and the Italian New Towns

Giorgio Ciucci et al, *The American City from the Civil War
   to the New Deal*, (MIT Press, Cambridge, Mass., 1979).
Richard Foglesong, *Planning the Capitalist City*, (Princeton
   University Press, Princeton, 1986).
Diane Ghirardo, *Building New Communities, New Deal
   America and Fascist Italy*, (Princeton University Press,
   Princeton, 1989).
Thomas S. Hines, *Burnham of Chicago – Architect and
   Planner*, (Oxford University Press, Oxford, 1974).

Rodney Mace, *Trafalgar Square, Emblem of Empire*, (Lawrence and Wishart, London, 1976.)

John Reps, *The Making of Urban America*, (Princeton University Press, Princeton, 1965).

Manfredo Tafuri, *Architecture and Utopia, Design and Capitalist Development*, (MIT Press, Cambridge Mass., 1976).

Raymond Williams, *The Country and the City*, (Granada, St. Albans, 1975).

W.H. Wilson, *The City Beautiful Movement*, (Johns Hopkins University Press, Baltimore, 1989).

Richard Wrigley, 'The Plan of Chicago: its Fiftieth Anniversary', *Journal of American Institute of Planners*, v.26, (Feb. 1960).

4

VERSAILLES – A POLITICAL THEME PARK?

Adrian Forty

The philosopher Ludwig Wittgenstein (1889–1951) once noted, 'Architecture immortalizes and glorifies something. Hence there can be no architecture where there is nothing to glorify.'[1] Wittgenstein's categorical statement suggests architecture is always about something people believe in, whether secular or spiritual; if true, then to understand architecture we need to find out its political or religious subject. This view is not uncommon. A contrary view, however, is that architecture can only ever be about other architecture, and to suppose it can reveal political or religious ideas is a mistake, for forms and spaces have no power to speak on their own. Unlike painting or photography, architecture (apart from its decoration) very rarely directly represents objects from the physical world. Nor, despite what some people have said, is architecture like a book which you can pick up and read to discover ideas previously unknown to you. It cannot itself signify political and religious ideas, and if we have such thoughts in front of a building, it is because we brought them with us.

How are we to choose between these two apparently contradictory ways of thinking about architecture? Does architecture really rely on the glorification of human affairs and beliefs? Can it have a political or religious theme? Or is it concerned solely with the architectonic, with formal and spatial properties? And are these views so incompatible that we must settle for one?

VERSAILLES

Any number of buildings would serve to explore these questions, but let us take the seventeenth century palace of Versailles. Its colossal extravagance makes looking for some sort of meaning irresistible, and from its inception Versailles was always assumed to have a political meaning, although, as we shall see, there have been many interpretations of what that meaning might be. We shall look here at what Versailles represented in the seventeenth century; if we were to look at its meanings in later centuries, we might arrive at different understandings.

53

Figure 4.1

In the enormous palace of Versailles, Louis XIV sought to integrate royal pleasure and political symbolism.

Versailles, seven miles outside Paris, is the largest royal palace ever built in Europe. The enormous house is surrounded by innumerable outbuildings and adjoins a vast park containing a series of smaller gardens, waterworks, sculptural groups and follies. Although much dates from the eighteenth century, it was Louis XIV (1638–1715) who started turning it into a major royal residence soon after he assumed personal rule in 1661. His decision was surprising, for the kings of France were not short of accommodation; apparently suitable palaces were already available in and around Paris, and to the king's advisers Versailles seemed a desolate and unpromising site, ill-suited to major development. Jean Baptiste Colbert (1619–83) – Controller-General of Finance, superintendent of royal buildings and initiator of much French policy – wanted the king to concentrate on extending the Louvre in Paris, and tried to discourage expenditure on Versailles. In a letter to the king in 1665, by when Louis had already spent a large sum on Versailles, with pitiably little to show, Colbert wrote,

> This house at Versailles seems more for the pleasure
> and diversion of your majesty than his glory . . .
> Your majesty knows that after brilliant feats of war,
> nothing shows the greatness and spirit of princes
> better than building. Posterity measures them by the
> great palaces they have built during their lives. Ah,
> what a pity that the greatest king and the most
> virtuous of princes will be judged by Versailles.[2]

Colbert assumed that to build for the king's pleasure was incompatible with the assertion of his greatness. The king, however, had his way, and Colbert, who did not condone expenditure without political purpose, was persuaded that the two aims could be reconciled, and that should be spent not less, but more, money on Versailles.

To understand Colbert's change of mind, we can turn to the official guide book, published in 1674, where we find a succinct account of the early stages of the building of Versailles, telling the story as the state wanted it to be known.

> Of all the royal houses, Versailles had the particular
> fortune to please the King, and in 1661 his majesty
> started works to make it larger and more habitable.
> Because the chateau by Louis XIII had only a single
> corps de logis [central building] with two wings and
> four pavilions, it had to be greatly enlarged. . . .
> However, his majesty was so devoted to the memory
> of the King his father that he would pull down
> nothing he had built, and none of the additions
> were to prevent the old palace from being seen as it
> was before, except that the marble court was paved
> and enriched with fountains and statues, the corners
> of the wings were decorated and the balustrades
> gilded. . . . What makes the house now so
> magnificent, and without doubt one of the most
> beautiful palaces in the world, is that art has not
> only repaired the faults left by nature, but has
> enriched it with things more exceptional and more
> beautiful than are to be found in all the other royal
> pleasure palaces.[3]

In this account, there are several things to notice. In particular, Versailles was chosen for development because it gave pleasure to the king; the palace was an extension of an existing building; and the result demonstrates the superiority of art over nature. Each point calls for comment.

THE KING AND THE STATE

That Versailles was built because the king liked the place is almost certainly true, but why was gratification of his pleasure part of the official programme? In the seventeenth century, to speak of the king's personal pleasure was ambiguous, for the prevalent theory of kingship gave him not one but two persons – his natural, mortal body; and the body politic, an enduring institution. Accordingly, every personal act of the king had also a public dimension: as Louis XIV himself put it, 'The king is not like a private individual; he is entirely public.' The king was like an actor who performs a role in public, but who can never retire to his dressing room, remove his costume and so revert to a private person. The king's private self is public, the embodiment of the state. Therefore to interpret Versailles as the object of Louis' personal delight and amusement is misleading, for the king's pleasure and relaxation were functions of state.

The theatrical dimension of Versailles, often remarked upon, is emphasised by the series of *fêtes*

Figure 4.2

Theatricality pervaded Versailles. Elaborate allegorical *fêtes* were intended to promote the king inside and outside the court.

conducted there, allegorical performances over several days in which courtiers (and occasionally the king himself) had parts; dramatic episodes were interspersed with passages of eating and dancing, again ordered and contrived as a spectacle. Not simply entertainment, fêtes gave the state an appearance that merged with its reality; the events were recorded and illustrated in publications, so their political significance reached beyond the immediate court circle. Fêtes took place out of doors, or in specially built temporary structures, and we can think of the building of the palace of Versailles as an attempt to render permanent these transient settings.

Royal relaxation as a state function also appears in the scheme of decoration. Throughout the palace and grounds, sculptures and decoration express the mythology of Apollo. The guide book explains.

It should be noted that since the sun is the device of the king, and as the poets confuse the sun and Apollo, there is nothing in this superb house that is not related to this divinity. All the statues and ornaments one sees have not been placed at random, but have a relation either to the sun, or to the particular places where they have been put.[4]

Figure 4.3

Allegory was also utilized in sculptural and decorative programmes. Apollo the Sun God stood for Louis the Sun King, and the *Grotto of Thetis* was the most important of many uses of this image.

In the seventeenth century, the most prominently placed of the Apollo sculptures was the *Grotto of Thetis*, just to the north of the house, and important enough to merit a guide book of its own. In mythology, Apollo having driven his chariot through the sky by day, at night sinks beneath the sea, where he and his horses are refreshed and bathed by Thetis and her nymphs. In the grotto this was represented by two group sculptures of the horses, and a third, central one of Apollo himself. Thus the relaxation of the greatest king in Europe, sufficiently important to be state policy, became celebrated by art.

Colbert's 1665 letter had set the pleasure and diversion of the king against his glory, as seemingly incompatible themes. By 1674, a different interpretation had emerged, and the whole purpose of the Versailles programme, it appears, was to make the king's relaxation glorious, to show that two kingly attributes could in fact be one.

Figure 4.4

'Art repaired the faults left by nature.' André Félibien, *Description sommaire du chateau du Versailles*, (1674). La Sal du Bal, Versailles.

To continue with the guide book, Louis XIV wished to remember his father by preserving the existing chateau. This we can again consider either as a sentimental personal whim of the king, or as a decision of state. To the suggestion that the old buildings and additions made to them before 1665 be replaced with a better proportioned building, Louis replied, 'with no little emotion that it could all be knocked down, but it would have to be rebuilt exactly as it was, without changing anything.'[5] If this was the king's personal feeling, Colbert had a political reason for not demolishing what had already been built, for it would make the king appear indecisive, which would 'not at all accord with the great actions of the king.' That keeping the older buildings meant the composition of Versailles would be, as Colbert put it, 'like a small man with big arms and a large head, that is to say a monster of a building,'[6] mattered less than making the king (and the state) seem to be irresolute.

Our third observation from the guide book is that 'art repaired the faults left by nature,' making it more beautiful. This was orthodox seventeenth century aesthetic theory: briefly, nature is the source of all beauty, but is frustrated by accidents from achieving the ideal, so art has to complete what nature never attains. Versailles' gardens provide the exemplar of art's superiority over nature, where living hedges and trees create architectonic effects of spaces and rooms; in their obsessively neat *parterres* (low level gardens), terracing, extravagant sheets and jets of water, artifice completely overwhelms nature. One striking feature is the abrupt transition from the meticulous artificial order within the gardens to the chaos of nature in the wilderness beyond. While an artistic device, this effect was also political, for the gardens are an allegory of the kingdom of France. Just as the landscape artist, André Le Nôtre (1613–1700), created order and beauty from raw nature, so the king was a political artist, whose task was to transform the country into an ordered and effective state. For Louis XIV, this meant extending France to its 'natural' boundaries through war, developing internal resources to release its wealth, and eliminating dissent among citizens. The park at Versailles is France, where good government is contrasted to the dreary wilderness beyond.

ARCHITECTURE, ABSOLUTISM AND THE ECONOMY

To return to our original questions, to what extent does the actual architecture of Versailles convey these political themes? We shall look first not at the building but the regime which Louis XIV represented. Louis instituted what was at the time perceived as a new kind of government, since (but not then) known as Absolutism. He was the pioneer absolutist ruler, and, partly because France was the most powerful state in Europe, absolutist kingship was admired by other, less powerful rulers. To understand absolutism, we must briefly sketch the history of political institutions in Europe from tenth century feudalism.

In feudal kingship, the king gained the allegiance of his vassals through a system of mutual obligation, where money was relatively unimportant. This ran through the social scale: barons received the king's protection, and in return fought for him when required, while serfs received their lord's protection, in return for working his land. In the thirteenth century, feudalism began to break down with lords having to pay serfs to work, and kings having to pay their lords to fight. Kings thus had to raise money, and throughout Europe assemblies were developed to fulfil this task. In France, the assembly was called 'the Estates General'; in England, 'Parliament'. In return for supplying money, these assemblies normally imposed the right to approve royal edicts, though in France this role was assumed by separate institutions known as *parlements*.

During the sixteenth and seventeenth centuries, relations between kings and their assemblies became strained, as kings demanded more money, and assemblies tried to extend their influence over royal authority. In England, relations broke down altogether with the Civil War of the 1640s, and the execution of Charles I. In France at the same time, the authority of the crown was challenged through a series of political disturbances known as the Frondes, though the French crown regained the upper hand.

Significantly, Louis XIV succeeded in ruling without ever calling the Estates General, and rarely seeking the parlements' approval for his edicts. This dramatic break with the past four centuries of European political practice was widely regarded as a new kind of government. How did Louis achieve this apparently remarkable innovation?

The short answer is that wealth was initially accumulated through aggressive military campaigns and sustained through the economic policy of mercantilism, as it was later known, developed by Colbert. Unlike later economic theories where success is measured by volume of trade, in mercantilism what mattered was the quantity of bullion accumulated in the country. France therefore bought very little from abroad, and was made as self-sufficient as possible through domestic industries; strict import controls prevented loss of currency, while special encouragement was given to those producing high value goods for export.

The same applied to artistic products. The outstanding example of this is the East wing (begun 1667) of the Louvre in Paris, which Gianlorenzo Bernini (1598–1680) from Rome was initially invited to design. Colbert, however, decided it was politically inexpedient to use an Italian for the King of France's residence, and it was designed by a Frenchman, Claude Perrault (1613–88). To ensure French artistic products were as good or better than other countries (particularly Italy's), Colbert set up workshops to train French craftsmen and make decorative art – the Gobelins, where all furnishings for Versailles were made, was one such workshop. Similarly, to ensure French art was in the best taste, Colbert set up Academies of Painting, Music, Literature and Architecture to debate the criteria of quality and set explicitly French standards for art.

Colbert's change of heart towards Versailles was in part because he saw it as an opportunity to make it a show piece of mercantilism. Pains were taken to ensure that designs were by French artists and architects, decoration and furnishings by French craftsmen, and all building materials of French origin; for example, the marbles lining the interiors all came from French quarries, some specially opened, and the guide book described the source of each one. In a rather literal way, therefore, Versailles does represent the economic policy of the absolutist regime.

ARCHITECTURE AND THE REPRESENTATION
OF ABSOLUTIST POLITICS

Can we, though, go on to say that Versailles represents the political idea of absolutism? The first problem is that Versailles, like most other buildings, is certainly not a reliable medium of ideas; it may indeed immortalize and glorify something, but what people understand that something to be is all too likely to change. In the seventeenth century Versailles was intended, as we have seen, to signify the absolutist monarchy in its glory, its resolution, its taste and mastery over nature. But by the end of the king's reign in 1715, it was already being understood differently. For the Duc de Saint Simon (1675–1755), writer and courtier of Louis XIV, Versailles no longer enhanced the monarchy, rather the opposite, for 'who could help being repelled and disgusted at the violences being done to Nature?'[7] And the French republican revolution of 1789 gave it further different meanings which largely obscured the original glorification of the king.

The next question is how the architecture of Versailles signified ideas in the seventeenth century? To a visitor knowing nothing of Louis XIV or absolutism, the political meanings of the forms, spaces, planting and water remain hidden. Its differences from other royal palaces and representational sculpture might lead one to speculate, but any comprehensive understanding of Versailles as a political theme park relies upon the presence of the king, whether actual or imagined. Indeed, the king's presence is at the heart of its seventeenth century meaning. The 'image problem' of the absolutist monarchy was the difficulty of making the king appear to be more than an ordinary man, and also the embodiment of the state. Traditionally, kings achieved this by appearing with their parliaments or councils; but the absolutist monarch, having dispensed with these institutions, had to appear alone. While still being a mortal man, the king had to be distinguished from all other men – he had to seem larger, braver, wiser, and his presence felt even where he was not. The quasi-theatrical setting of Versailles (in which it has been remarked 'the king is everywhere, but he is nowhere') provided just such an apparatus to give the

appearance of greatness and omnipresence. Yet the architecture and gardens did not on their own 'immortalize and glorify' the king: just as he needed Versailles to be seen as a king, Versailles needed the presence of the king, actual or imagined, for its political theme to emerge.

Versailles shows that architecture is not a reliable means of conveying precise political messages; liable to a variety of interpretations, only the most generalized political theme survives. On the other hand, architecture can provide a setting against which actions acquire meaning; architecture significantly affects how people are seen and how human relations are understood. (This, it should be stressed, is different to the problematic proposition that people's behaviour is affected by architecture). While architectural spaces and forms cannot themselves speak of a political or religious theme, seen in relation to people, architecture may indeed 'immortalise and glorify'.

Figure 4.5

Architecture on its own has no meaning. Without the presence of the king, the message of Versailles is incomplete. Le parterre du Midi, Versailles.

REFERENCES

1   Ludwig Wittgenstein, *Culture and Value*, G.H. von Wright (ed.), (Basil Blackwell, Oxford, 1980), p. 69.
2   P. Clément, *Lettres, instructions et mémoires de Colbert*, (Paris, v. 5, 1861–2), p. 269.
3   André Félibien, *Description sommaire du chateau du Versailles*, (Paris, 1674), p. 1. Translation by Adrian Forty.
4   Félibien, *Description sommaire du chateau du Versailles*, p. 11.
5   Claude Perrault, manuscript, printed in Clement, *Lettres, instructions et mémoires de Colbert*, v. 5, p. 266.
6   Perrault, manuscript, p. 267.
7   Saint Simon was writing here in 1715. *Saint Simon at Versailles*, translated L. Norton, (London, 1980), p. 231.

BIBLIOGRAPHY

Seventeenth Century France

Perry Anderson, *Lineages of the Absolutist State*, (New Left Books, London, 1974).
Trevor Aston (ed.), *Crisis in Europe, 1560–1660*, (Routledge and Kegan Paul, London, 1965).

Versailles and French Architecture

Philippe Beaussant, *Versailles, Opéra*, (Gallimard, Paris, 1981).
Leonardo Benevolo, *The Architecture of the Renaissance*, (Routledge and Kegan Paul, London, 1978).
Robert Berger, *The Chateau of Louis XIV*, (Pennsylvania State University Press, University Park, Philadelphia, 1985).
Anthony Blunt, *Art and Architecture in France, 1500–1700*, (Penguin, Harmondsworth, Middlesex, 1981).
Peter Burke, *The Fabrication of Louis XIV*, (Yale University Press, New Haven, 1992).
Jean-Marie Pérouse de Montclos, *Versailles*, (Abbeyville Press, New York, 1991).
Guy Walton, *Louis XIV's Versailles*, (University of Chicago Press, Chicago, 1986).

Part Two

INTERPRETATION

5

THE RIB, THE ARCH AND THE BUTTRESS

THE STRUCTURE OF GOTHIC ARCHITECTURE

Francis Woodman

Church building in the West reached new heights after the turn of the millenium with the largest buildings erected since Roman times, such as the cathedrals at Mainz (1009 onward), Speyer (1031–61 and onward) and St Remi Reims (1005–49). These churches were difficult to design, erect and prevent from falling down. Fire too was a problem (candles, votive lights and burning incense played an important role in medieval Christian liturgy) and many churches, including Mainz, were burnt soon after completion which was both expensive and embarrassing. Churches with internally exposed wooden roofs were obviously vulnerable, burning roofs often collapsing onto the wooden furnishings below. In the absence of concrete, a technology previously known to the Romans but lost with the fall of their empire, stone vaulting was the only solution to the twin problems of construction and fire. Stone, however, had its own drawbacks, erecting a high stone vault made from arched elements over a considerable span poses quite different problems from concrete. The trouble with stone is that it will not stick; no 'glue' will fuse stone blocks together in the manner of concrete. Any stone architecture that involves covering spaces greater than the potential of a lintel needs arched or bracketed (corbelled) technology.

All arches are subject to gravitational forces. Their dead-weight pushes the sides (arcs) of an arch outward which must be checked by lateral dead-weight, while the feet of the arch must be secured to prevent spreading. A pointed arch lessens the problem by 'leaning' two arcs against each other, though some risk remains of buckling the individual arcs outward. The problem is usually resolved by the masonry walling (spandrels) carried by the arch, which effectively dead-weights the whole and prevents dislodging. The dead-weight of a pointed arch supporting a masonry structure, expressed as thrust, runs diagonally downward and outward, passing beyond the arcs a little above their feet. These must be dead-weighted into place or countered by an adjoining arch as in an arcade.

ROMANESQUE

A well-built arch is very strong and can carry considerable loading. Around 1100, the designer of Durham
Cathedral (1093–1133) realized that intersecting two
arches at approximately 90 degrees, an immensely
strong combination, would answer the problem of
building high stone vaults. Intersecting the arches from
the angles of an oblong bay creates a relatively
lightweight but strong framework on which it is possible to build small, individual triangular stone cells
(webs) upon the arcs (ribs). The whole thing is then
dead-weighted with a layer of rubble. This system,
known as rib vaulting, has a number of benefits: it
provides a fire-proof barrier between roof and interior;
it is light for its size; and the ribs are dead-weighted
by the webs and rubble against any possible compres-
sive upward movement. Most importantly, the total
weight is transmitted diagonally down the ribs so that
the whole unit is carried upon the angles of the bay,
and because only specific points along the main wall
(elevation) are subject to vault thrust the remaining
wall sections can be pierced by windows, though the
Durham designer did not fully understand or perhaps
dare risk maximizing this benefit. One reason was
undoubtedly the fear that the vault would dislodge the
elevational wall by pushing it outward. How this
problem was solved, as we shall see, lies at the heart
of gothic technology.

Durham Cathedral is a romanesque building. Added
to the massively thick walls of two metres or more used
to dead-weight the structure is the enormous weight of
the roof bearing down upon the elevational walls. Yet
this was no guarantee of structural stability, especially
given unknown factors like the effect of wind gusts on
the upper sections. The particular problem lies in the
basilica plan – a main longitudinal space with upper
windows (clerestory) and side aisles with access
through continuous arcades – which dictates that any
additional support for the main upper elevational wall
has to be built either above the aisle vault, or be
carried over the aisle and dealt with outside. The final
solution achieved at Durham made use of weight and
counter-thrust in a way that was entirely novel.

The first concern was to keep the upper, clerestory
section of the elevational wall perfectly upright. If this

could be achieved then the main vault would stay up as it could not move; its downward diagonal thrust would be absorbed by a thick wall rendered immobile. To this end a series of stone props rise from the outer aisle wall and abut the elevation at the point where the vault thrust must be resisted. The feet of the props are held in place by their own dead-weight plus the inert mass of the aisle wall. Alone, the props would be ineffective (in their original form they were slight enough to explode upward if pressured by outward movement from the elevation) so to counter this, the pent roof over the aisle is manipulated to rest a mid-purlin upon the weak spot of the prop. Leaded oak roofs are very heavy, and resting the roof on the prop creates considerable additional dead-weight. Further, a series of gables was built above the aisle wall, creating dormer roofs whose ridges add their weight to the mid-purlin, thus increasing the overall weight value of the roof. In effect, the aisle roofs prevent Durham's collapse, the props forcing the elevational wall inward, countering the vault which pushes the wall outward. These various thrusts and counter-thrusts should not be seen as active, rather as immobilization. The high vault will stay in place as long as the elevational wall is upright, which in turn will happen as long as the props remain rigid, and this is ensured by the dead-weight of the aisle roof and the stability of the outer aisle wall. If any one element failed, disaster would follow.

FRENCH GOTHIC

An unknown French designer drew a lesson from Durham not seen or at least not exploited by his predecessor. The push and counter-push of Durham's vault support system could be achieved without the massive dead-weight of the intervening elevational wall. True, the Durham scheme depends greatly on the ability of this wall to squash much of the vault thrust, but in doing so the building remains heavy and dark, the glazing forced to the outer plane of the immensely thick walls. Thin the walls and the lighting potential improves as the glass can fit almost flush with the interior. The French proposal was to compensate for the lost elevational dead-weight by increasing the resistance value of the other elements, and this was the

Figure 5.1

The thick-walled English gothic structural system ignored French structural developments. Diagram based on Wells, (c.1180–c.1425), and Salisbury, (1220–58).

achievement of the second master of St-Denis near Paris (c.1135–44). Asked to build a rib-vaulted church with thin walls and huge areas of visible glass, he transformed the technology of Durham and so created Gothic.

Early gothic structures are far lighter in actual weight than their rib-vaulted romanesque counterparts, making possible cheaper, more spacious and better lit buildings and encouraging far more daring feats of scale. The structural principles of the rib vault remain the same; the differences come in how it is maintained. The elevational wall is reduced in thickness by more than half and so contributes less dead-weight to absorb the vault thrust, although it still transmits the dead-weight of the main roof, and in effect exists not for its support value but to frame large windows. The area of wall at the vault springing is now stiffened by means of triangular walls abutting it at right-angles and extending back across the width of the aisle. These triangular walls rest directly upon the transverse arches that divide the aisle vaults. Such stiffening walls do not need to be very thick themselves as they carry directly the whole slope of the aisle roof. Thus, as at Durham, the aisle roof is utilized to dead-weight the vault prop. In order to maximize the window area, the aisle walls are also thinned, their previous dead-weight role taken by buttresses placed beyond and at right angles to the aisle.

The new system still works by immobilization. The high vault thrust is stopped by the resistance of the triangular wall behind the vault springing, which is in turn pinned down by the weight of the aisle roof, and the whole superstructure is prevented from shearing sideways by the dead-weight of the external buttress. Were these buttresses too low or too slight, then there might be the risk of the triangular wall being forced outward by the thrust of the vault, thus 'unlocking' the compression of the vault arches. Getting the correct balance was apparently a matter of trial and error.

Where the designer of St-Denis went wrong – to be followed by a number of other early gothic churches such as Notre-Dame (Paris, 1163–c.1250) and Vézelay (c.1160) – was in the relative heights of the triangular wall and the vault spring, for matching the top of one to the bottom of the other ignores the fact that the vault thrust passes into the elevation somewhat above the level of the actual vault springing. Thus at St-Denis it was soon discovered that the propping devices were too low, and that the clerestory levels threatened to fall outward.

The whole problem arose from a desire to increase the height of the clerestory, the thin walls of St-Denis encouraging larger windows as the glass could so readily be seen. Clerestory windows were limited in size by two factors – the top of the aisle roof and the crown of the vault – and in any system where the aisle roof acts as a major dead-weight to the vault support these two elements are intimately linked. The vault spring cannot be raised without lifting the aisle roof, which would in turn lift the base of the upper windows etc., and, equally, the vault springing level determines the height of the vault crown by simple geometry. Theoretically, had the vault at St-Denis sprung a little lower, all would have been well and the balancing act of thrust and counter-thrust would probably have held. But a lower level of vault spring-ing would have effectively hidden the upper windows while reducing their overall height, and a near fatal step was therefore taken at St-Denis to risk too great a gap between the aisle roof and vault spring. Add to this the decision to arrange the prop wall too low for the real point of thrust absorption and the inevitable

Figure 5.2

St Denis, Paris, the birthplace of gothic architecture. The ambulatory is the only surviving section of the original choir, (1140–3).

happened. All the upper levels had to be taken down and rebuilt.

The designer of Notre-Dame went even further, creating a building so tall (about 30 metres), so thin and with such impractical support systems that failure was almost guaranteed. That the building still stands is due to yet more innovative engineering. The elevational walls were probably slumping outward even before an attempt was made to raise the high vault and, in desperation, the builders did what they still do today, erecting an emergency shoring to support the wall where it was falling. This was an area well above the aisle roofs with their submerged and relatively

Figure 5.3

The extreme height of Notre-Dame, (1163–c.1250), meant structural failure was inevitable. The flying buttresses on the right were originally an impromptu solution.

useless propping devices. Common sense and a loathing to lose more money told both patron and designer that they had done the right thing. Wooden shoring was turned into exposed stone 'flying' buttresses and an engineering breakthrough emerged.

At Notre-Dame it was accepted that buttressing devices are not inseparable from the limits imposed by the wooden aisle roofs. It was not embarrassment at exposing such elements that held them back, but the simple notion that the aisle roof provided the necessary dead-weight. One alternative solution is to allow the vault thrust to continue through the elevation and along a flyer, and to be killed off by the dead-weight of greatly enlarged external buttresses. To this end, the junction between the vault rib and the flying buttress was often cut from a single stone block, while another system is to maintain the idea that the vault is simply held in check by immobile forces, and to allow the dead-weight of the external buttress to fix flyers against the elevational wall, thus checking and absorbing the vault thrust. Doubling the flyers and connecting them by means of open arcading, as happened at

Figure 5.4

The French gothic structural system, lighter and cheaper than Romanesque buildings. Balancing the forces was a matter of trial of error. Diagram based on Beauvais, (1247–1568).

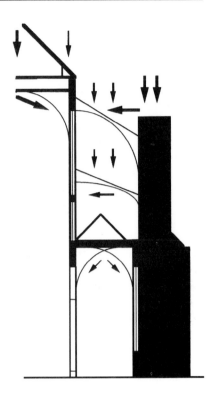

Chartres (1194–1260), increases their own dead-weight while preventing any risk of the lower, vault-supporting flyer from exploding upward. Once the aisle roof ceases to fulfil any structural role it can be eliminated and the resulting elevational space incorporated into an enlarged clerestory, as at Le Mans (nave twelfth century, choir 1217–54, south transept fourteenth century). Because the wall is no longer load-bearing, this classic solution enabled cathedrals like Amiens (1220–88) to be built as tall, slender and lightweight structures with enormous areas of glass.

ENGLISH GOTHIC

The English took little or no notice of such developments. Their early gothic buildings from around 1175 onward had been odd solutions to unique problems, and were almost entirely lacking in mainstream French engineering knowledge. English buildings were traditionally thick-walled and they stayed that way.

Furthermore, the methods of Durham Cathedral were well understood and it seems that no-one was prepared to abandon them. Buildings such as Wells Cathedral (c.1180–c.1425) are merely more sophisticated pointed arch versions of Durham, with stone props weighted down by the aisle roof thus preventing the massive elevation from shifting under the pressure of the high vault. Similar vault support systems recur at Lincoln, (1192–1320), Worcester (c.1217), Salisbury (1220–58) and elsewhere. The walls of the great English churches actually get thicker in the thirteenth century, while at Salisbury the weight of the original aisle roof was so great that it broke down several of the stone props. In some buildings it almost seems that the aisle roof and stone prop combinations are so aggressive that they risk pushing the elevational walls inward, the high vault being used as a strainer to hold the interior walls apart. With such systems, the marriage of aisle roof and vault springing level could never be dissolved. Hence English clerestorys remain low, trapped between geometrical and structural elements. Only around 1300 and beyond did the English accept that their old ways imposed unnecessary limits upon their buildings, yet even then traditions died hard, and the tall, thin-walled clerestory with huge traceried windows remained scarce in England. Westminster Abbey (1245 onward) is a rare example.

What made the French strive for great height and the English rarely bother? Achieving vaulted interiors in excess of 50 metres, as at Amiens, Beauvais (1247–1568) and Cologne (1248 onward), poses enormous technical problems, and that the French tried and the English did not stems from a variety of reasons. Firstly, the French economic base was far stronger than that of England. French cities were larger and their cathedrals were considered civic, that is public property, thus ensuring adequate financial support. English cathedrals on the other hand were considered private and popular support for their reconstruction was consequently rare. In addition, French cathedral chapters seem to have had readier access to funds than their English counterparts. Yet the difference in their churches is not one of scale, for many English cathedrals such as Canterbury (1071–1503), Winchester (1079–1528) and Ely (1198–1349) are far larger, and in particular longer, than those in France. The difference is height and light.

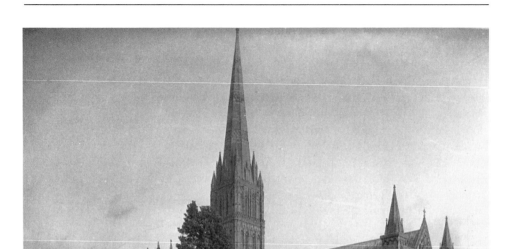

Figure 5.5

Salisbury, (1220–58), from the north-west. The surrounding open land is one reason why English gothic differs from French gothic.

French gothic structure developed in a monastic world. Actual daylight was not the issue, for monks knew their offices by heart. Abbot Suger of St-Denis wanted walls of dark, rich stained glass. In other words, more windows but not necessarily more daylight. Gothic structure offers an efficient style capable of providing spacious stone vaulted interiors with far greater window potential.

But French cathedrals have urban settings. Their towns were more densely packed and their domestic buildings more substantial than their English counterparts with houses of four and five storeys often crowded around their cathedrals, as at Paris and Amiens. A row of such properties, up to 20 metres high, would mask a church and deny almost all direct daylight from the lower aisle levels. If light is required, the clerestory will have to provide it and, to be effective, that clerestory will have to commence above 20 metres. By contrast, English cathedrals nearly all enjoyed open settings, many within private monasteries as at Norwich and Worcester, making side lighting possible and so obviating the need to build high. The only major English cathedrals to be built in the tall French manner were York Minster (13th–15th centuries) and the original St Paul's (destroyed 1666), London. Neither of these then had a 'park' setting, both strove to 30 metres, and both had to adopt French structural technology to do so.

BIBLIOGRAPHY

J.H. Ackland, *Medieval Structure: the Gothic Vault*, (Ontario, 1972).

Jean Bony, *The English Decorated Style: Gothic Architecture Transformed 1250–1350*, (Phaidon, Oxford, 1979).

Jean Bony, *French Gothic Architecture of the 12th and 13th Centuries*, (University of California Press, Berkeley, California, 1983).

John Fitchen, *The Construction of Gothic Cathedrals: a Study of Medieval Vault Erection*, (University of Chicago Press, Chicago, 1981).

Jean Gimbel, *The Cathedral Builders*, (Pimlico, London, 1993).

Cecil Hewett, *English Cathedral and Monastic Carpentry*, (Phillimore, Chichester, 1985).

Henry Kraus, *Gold was the Mortar: the Economics of Cathedral Building*, (Routledge and Kegan Paul, London, 1978).

D. Macaulay, *Cathedral: the Story of its Construction*, (Boston, 1973).

Robert Mark, *Experiments in Gothic Structure*, (MIT Press, Cambridge, Mass, 1982).

Christopher Wilson, *The Gothic Cathedral: the Architecture of the Great Church, 1130–1530*, (Thames and Hudson, London, 1990).

6

THE POWER AND THE GLORY

THE MEANINGS OF MEDIEVAL ARCHITECTURE

Alexandrina Buchanan

From the Norman invasion of 1066 to the break with the Roman Catholic Church in 1534, the most significant form of architectural production in England was church building, in terms of both status and cost. Throughout this period, despite many social, political and economic changes, the erection or modification of a church was one of the most prestigious activities for an individual or community. In the present day, the churches constructed during the Middle Ages are usually the oldest buildings in any settlement, and most have continued to be used for religious purposes. However, over such a long time span, they have functioned and been interpreted in many different ways. It is important therefore to understand the meaning of medieval architecture in its own period. What were the people of the time trying to express, and why?

This question can be only partially answered by direct observation. To begin with, the physical objects are rarely the same now as when first built; even churches which survive apparently intact have been remodelled over the centuries to fit contemporary views on appropriateness and beauty. They might now be almost unrecognizable to their original users, stripped of the many fixtures and fittings required by the liturgy, and gone too are the hangings, many of the wall paintings and sculptures, much of the stained glass and polychrome decoration. Yet they remain rich in possible meanings, while past interpretations of medieval art continue to shape our perceptions.

We shall consider here some of the different ways in which the art of the medieval period might have been understood by different sections of the contemporary population. Rather than using more modern divisions based on economic class, we shall follow the traditional medieval division of society into those who prayed (the clergy), those who fought (royalty and the nobility, or the class of lay patrons) and those who worked (the labourers or laity). We shall also pay special attention to those who worked directly on church design and construction.

THE CLERGY

Medieval intellectual thought was controlled by the Church and derived from two sources: the Bible and classical antiquity, usually interpreted by the Church Fathers. Both contain views on art and architecture but these are ambiguous and at times contradictory. For example, the Ten Commandments forbid the making of graven images, yet the Ark of the Covenant was ornamented with cherubim; Solomon's Temple was a sumptuous building, yet Jesus ordered trust only in the Heavenly Jerusalem, described in all its splendour by the Revelation of St. John. Similarly, classical antiquity vested great importance in temples and cult statues, yet the Greek philosopher Plato (427–347 BC) had condemned art as being but an imitation of an imitation, for, as he conceived it, reality resided only in the world of abstract ideas.

The Middle Ages thus inherited a variety of views on the subject of art which, while differing, could be equally justified. Images were generally more problematic than non-figurative forms, since they conveyed doctrine. From the time of Pope Gregory the Great (AD 590–604), who wrote on the controversial subject of imagery and its role in Christianity, the official defence of figurative art was that it provided education for the illiterate. By contrast, the bare bones of a building formed merely a framework and, except in terms of cost, were less controversial. Nevertheless medieval sensitivity to symbol meant that all churches could be viewed as the Temple and the Heavenly Jerusalem, while existing buildings could also provide a resonance: round or polygonal structures, like the twelfth century nave of the Temple Church, London, and the Lady Chapel (early fourteenth century) of Wells Cathedral, recalled the Holy Sepulchre or the Roman Pantheon (AD 100–25), then dedicated as a church to the Virgin, while the Papal church of St Peter's in Rome was a touchstone for all churches of high ambition.[1] The words of Jesus provided other metaphors: He was both door and cornerstone. Bishop Durandus in the thirteenth century wrote a treatise giving similar symbolic interpretations of every architectural element, turning the entire church fabric into a 'sermon in stone'.

The Church comprized many different religious groups, each with its own architectural identity, so what

Figure 6.1

For some, this kind of Cluniac architecture was too excessively decorated for monastic use. La Madeleine, Vézelay, (c.1104–32). Romanesque

Figure 6.2

Unlike La Madeleine, Vézelay, the nave of Fountains Abbey in Yorkshire, (c.1147 onward), epitomized Cistercian taste for strictly limited decoration. Aisle and nave from south transept, looking west.

was deemed suitable for one was not always acceptable to another. For example, Cluniac architecture such as the romanesque abbey church La Madeleine at Vézelay (mainly 1104–32), was seen by twelfth century reformers such as St Bernard as having imagery and excessive richness of decoration inappropriate for a monastic community. St Bernard for his part belonged to the Cistercians, an order whose buildings were initially of a pared-down severity and international uniformity of plan. Against condemnations such as Bernard's, Abbot Suger, of the ancient Benedictine house of St-Denis near Paris, sought to defend his architectural activity in his writings. Seeking also to refute internal critics who condemned the 1140s rebuilding of the abbey church of St Denis traditionally dedicated by Christ in person, Suger argued that the new choir (1140–44), today hailed as the first work of gothic architecture, was a tool of mystical piety, a means of transporting the viewer beyond worldly beauty to the true light of Christ. Nevertheless, his interest lay more in the stained glass and treasures of metalwork than in the innovatory form of architecture. It is clear that what concerned clerics most were the aspects they could control, such as iconography and the use of materials.

Religious reform was often associated, as with the Cistercians, with simplification of architectural form. It

Figure 6.3

Cult saints were advertised through splendid architecture. 'Nine Altars' transept, (1242–90), Durham.

has been suggested that the linear and non-figurative aesthetic of Early English buildings such as Salisbury Cathedral (1220 onward) are symptomatic of a reformist mood amongst certain bishops after the Fourth Lateran Council in 1215 (at which Pope Innocent III and the church hierarchy attempted to address the issue of lay piety).[2] Nevertheless one English bishop, Richard Poore, who began Salisbury, also initiated the very different thirteenth century 'Nine Altars' transept at Durham Cathedral (1242 onward). Whatever the feelings of some reformers, the role of most great churches as centres of pilgrimage necessitated richness and splendour to advertise the power of the resident saint (for example, Durham's east end housed the relics of St Cuthbert), and many extensions and refurbishments are associated with the initiation of a cult, especially after the martyrdom of Thomas Becket at Canterbury in 1170 and his subsequent enshrinement (1220) in a new luxurious choir.

Figure 6.4

A monument to the power of a private family. Choir, Tewkesbury Abbey, (choir remodelled c. 1331–40).

THE LAY PATRONS

It was impossible for the Church to remain aloof from secular affairs. The views of bishops and abbots were determined by their predominantly noble origins and they were often important statesmen in their own right. The rich laity also influenced the appearance of churches through donations for rebuilding and furnishing. Such gifts were not anonymous: they paid for windows containing glass with heraldry and donor figures, tombs, and private chantry chapels dedicated to the memory of their founders. Tewkesbury Abbey, for example, became the mausoleum of the Despenser family, a symbol of their temporal might as much as their piety. Likewise when Henry III undertook in the thirteenth century to rebuild Westminster Abbey, it was a political as much as a religious move, part of an on-going rivalry with the king of France and

Figure 6.5

A monument to the power of a monarch. Westminster Abbey, (thirteenth century onward).

intended to promote a quasi-priestly view of kingship at home.[3]

Erwin Panotsky has suggested that gothic architecture should be correlated with modes of scholastic thought,[4] but Henry III's motivation for updating Westminster Abbey suggests that an association of new styles with power might be more convincing. The Norman Conquest had led to the erection of new churches throughout England of daunting size and unaccustomed romanesque appearance, a visible proof of the potency and permanence of the new order. Similarly, the rebuilding of St-Denis, which initiated the new gothic architecture, was part of the economic and political resurgence of France. Thereafter Canterbury Cathedral (1174–85), recruited a mason from northern France to honour its murdered archbishop Becket, while Westminster shows detailed knowledge of recent French work.

This much suggests that English churches followed French architectural developments in order to keep up with recent fashion. Nevertheless both Canterbury and Westminster also feature specifically English characteristics of great church architecture. Westminster, for example, has vaults with ridge ribs, an elaborate middle storey and rich mouldings with lavish use of Purbeck marble. Unlike Spain and Germany, where French gothic was imported wholesale, England already had a well established architectural vocabulary which most patrons were disinclined to relinquish in favour of foreign innovation, except where it could be combined with insular pre-occupations. And as Francis Woodman has already pointed out in Chapter 5, the relatively open sites and semi-private origins of English cathedrals also had a part to play in developing the unique character of English gothic architecture.

THE MASONS

Despite the power of the patron, the eventual appearance of the church fabric lay with the mason, whose primary concerns could be very different. Architectural patronage was too infrequent an activity in the life of an individual and the architectural language too ill-formed for non-specialists to play an active role in detailed design. Surviving contracts often stipulate a pre-existing building as model but the subsequent copy is rarely identical to the original, which probably shows a desire to innovate on the part of the masons and an acceptance, even expectation, of this by the patrons. Moreover the impact of gothic architecture, more so than romanesque, depended on technical knowledge and skill in workmanship as much as overall conception and subsequent decoration. The mason thought in terms of the overall frame of the building and had less concern for the fixtures and fittings, which he personally did not produce, and which, as has been suggested, were more open to control by their donors. Nevertheless, one cannot speak of a single 'masonic' aesthetic, for there were many grades of mason. Rates of pay show a rigidly hierarchical organization, and only the master masons had the experience and expertise needed to carry out the design process. The complexity of great church architecture strongly suggests that cathedrals were built according to a pre-existing pattern, devized by a single controlling mind. By at least the thirteenth century these masters were no longer involved in manual work and in the later Middle Ages a few top master masons seem to have been designers at several sites at once, producing drawings for others to interpret, and so were closer to what we today call an 'architect'.

Design was the most prestigious part of the building process, an act which likened the mason to God, who, as is described in the book of Wisdom in the Old Testament Apochrypha, disposed 'all things in measure, number and weight.'[5] Measure and number were of particular relevance to masons. In line with theories of music, to which architecture was sometimes likened by philosophers, each number has a sacred significance: the number three, for example, recalls the Trinity.

Shapes and their mathematical construction, too, were symbolic. The importance of geometry may be gauged by a celebrated debate in the late fourteenth century at the cathedral of Milan (begun 1386) between Northern and Italian masters over whether the design should be governed by the square or the triangle.[6] The few handbooks of masons to survive, all from the last decades of the medieval period, show a similar preoccupation with geometry as the foundation of the art, as do masonic legends. Such knowledge was not

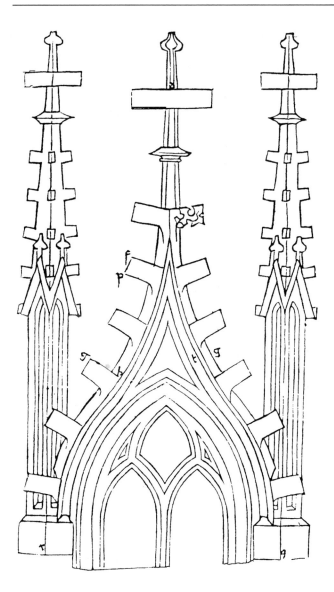

Figure 6.6

Masons kept the design process to themselves, and handbooks on the subject were rare. Illustration by Matthias Roriczer, (late fifteenth century).

particularly academic but nonetheless protected the exclusivity of the design process, and it also gave the freemason the prestige of association, however tenuous, with the liberal arts. Master masons were far from anonymous, and an admired design could bring wealth and status. Geometrical experimentation, as in late gothic tracery and vaults, can be interpreted as master masons showing off to their peers and such innovations moved fast along masonic networks, even internationally. Exactly how they were transmitted, whether by drawings or by personal contact, remains unknown, but the technical nature of some of the elements copied shows the route was via masons rather than patrons.

THE LAITY

If it is hard to detect the thinking of the constructors of the cathedrals, the reactions of their humblest visitors are almost impossible to gauge. The masses have no voice in the historical documents, and the only traces are the often unsympathetic interpretations of their beliefs by the literate observer.

It would be wrong, however, to presume that the place of the laity was not considered with respect to church architecture. When Pope Gregory determined to convert England in AD 596 he advised his emissary Augustine not to destroy pagan temples but to rededicate them to Christian usage to allow a continuity. This meant that churches remained sites of semi-heathen rituals. Although 'popular religion' is too simplistic a term for such practices, in which priests sometimes participated, for much of the population Christian dogma was probably just an overlay on long-standing pagan customs. Since the mass perception of official religion was unorthodox, it seems likely that their view of the trappings of that religion might be equally suspect to the Church authorities. On the other hand, the Church was keen to exploit the beliefs of the ordinary laity in order to increase its power.

Vital to the official view of images as books for the illiterate was that they could be understood. On the one hand, much of the iconography is very complex and may have been incomprehensible even to many of the 'ymagors', the producers of figurative art. On the other hand, subjects carved in churches could include pre-Christian material, like wild men and monsters, given a Christian interpretation by clerics but not necessarily understood as Christian by others. Nevertheless most churches contained conventional scenes such as the Last Judgement. Study of medieval sermons shows that church decorations could be used as illustrations by preachers and were thus explained to the congregation. Canterbury Cathedral apparently had guides for visitors to explain the historiated

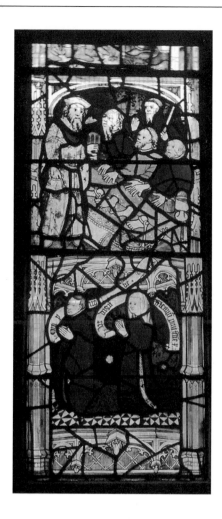

Figure 6.7

Gothic imagery, carefully conceived to produce the right response in the illiterate laity. 'Seven Works of Mercy' window, early fifteenth century, All Saints, York. Detail showing the visiting of prisoners (top), and the donors of the window (bottom).

(containing narrative scenes) glass, and this may have been common practice.

However, more important than the comprehension of images was that they should produce the required effect. Beauty and holiness were frequently equated and a miraculous statue could generate a high income. At the Cistercian Abbey of Meaux in Yorkshire, England, a wonder-working crucifix was erected in the fourteenth century. Their chronicler records the opinion 'that if women had access to the said crucifix, the common devotion would be increased and it would redound to the great profit of our monastery.'[7] Women were particularly associated with such piety, possibly because their nurturing role made them more likely to turn for help in time of family need, or as an outlet for fervour excluded from position in the Church hierarchy, or because, to a clerical writer, they were weak-willed and more susceptible to the sin of idolatry. It must, however, be remembered that for the Middle Ages the sin of idolatry did not mean worshipping through images but honouring those images which had no beneficent power. Statues were considered actively holy, and in the continental Reformation of the sixteenth century they were tried and beheaded, like human criminals, if they failed to fulfil their function.

The ordinary laity had no specific attitude to art; their response was shaped by the controllers of art production, who ignored pagan undercurrents provided they co-existed peacefully with official religion. Their regulation of imagery gave patrons and designers power over the illiterate. We can see the importance of this in the response of the ruling élite to the Lollard movement in fourteenth century England, which sought to give the laity access to the Scriptures by translating them from Latin into the vernacular. The perceived threat to clerical hegemony was such that the Lollards were persecuted as heretics.

Just as today, medieval buildings were frequently described at the time as being 'beautiful'. This adjective was a convention, subsuming many different attitudes, and church beauty related to their function, which was never singular. As we have seen, while the most important role of the church was as the house of God and monument to the piety of the faithful, less spiritual concerns were never far from the surface. Control of the definition and production of artistic beauty could bring temporal power, and in such circumstance aesthetics are never a neutral issue.

REFERENCES

1   Richard Krautheimer, 'Introduction to an Iconography of Medieval Architecture', *Journal of the Warburg and Courtauld Institutes*, v.5 (1942), pp. 1–33.
2   Victoria Jansen, 'Lambeth Palace Chapel, the Temple Choir, and Southern English Gothic Architecture of c.1215–40', in W. M. Ormrod (ed.), *England in the Thirteenth Century*, (Proceedings of the 1984 Harlaxton Symposium, Boydell Press, 1986), pp. 95–9.

3   Christopher Wilson et al, *Westminster Abbey*, (New Bell's
     Cathedral Guide, London, 1986).
4   Erwin Panofsky, *Gothic Architecture and Scholasticism*,
     (Thames and Hudson, London, 1957).
5   *Wisdom*, 11:21.
6   James Ackerman, "Ars sine scientia nihil est.' Gothic
     Theory of Architecture at the Cathedral of Milan', *Art
     Bulletin*, n.31 (1949), pp. 84–111.
7   Michael Camille, *The Gothic Idol: Ideology and Image-
     making in Medieval Art*, (Cambridge University Press,
     Cambridge, 1989), p. 212.

BIBLIOGRAPHY

General Works

Paul Binski and Jonathan Alexander (eds.), *Age of Chivalry:
     Art in Plantagenet England 1200–1400*, (Royal Academy
     of Arts Exhibition Catalogue, London, 1987).
Christopher Wilson, *The Gothic Cathedral: the Architecture of
     the Great Church 1130–1530*, (Thames and Hudson,
     London, 1990).

Patron Aesthetics

Michael Camille, *The Gothic Idol: Ideology and Image-making
     in Medieval Art*, (Cambridge University Press, Cambridge,
     1989).
Paul Crossley, 'Medieval Architecture and Meaning: the Limits
     of Iconography', *Burlington Magazine*, n.130 (1988), pp.
     116–21.
Richard Krautheimer, 'Introduction to an Iconography of
     Medieval Architecture', *Journal of the Warburg and
     Courtauld Institutes*, v.5 (1942), pp. 1–33.
Christopher Norton and David Park (eds.), *Cistercian Art and
     Architecture in the British Isles*, (Cambridge University
     Press, Cambridge, 1986).
Erwin Panofsky, *Gothic Architecture and Scholasticism*,
     (Thames and Hudson, London, 1957).
Erwin Panofsky (ed.), *Abbot Suger on the Abbey Church of
     St-Denis and its Art Treasures*, (Princeton University Press,
     Princeton, second edition, 1979).
Otto Von Simson, *The Gothic Cathedral*, (Princeton
     University Press, Princeton, 1988).
W. Tartarkiewicz, *History of Aesthetics. Volume II, Medieval
     Aesthetics*, (P.W.N., Warsaw, 1970).
Christopher Wilson et al, *Westminster Abbey*, (New Bell's
     Cathedral Guide, London, 1986).

Masonic Aesthetics

James Ackerman, "Ars sine scientia nihil est.' Gothic Theory of Architecture at the Cathedral of Milan', *Art Bulletin*, n.31 (1949), pp. 84–111.

F. Bucher, 'Medieval Architectural Design Methods 800–1560', *Gesta*, v.11 (1972), pp. 37–51.

Douglas Knoop and G.P. Jones, *The Mediaeval Mason*, (Manchester University Press, Manchester, 1933).

Stephen Murray, *Building Troyes Cathedral: The Late Gothic Campaigns*, (Indiana University Press, Bloomington and Indianapolis, 1987).

L.F. Salzman, *Building in England Down to 1540: a Documentary History*, (Clarendon Press, Oxford, 1952).

7

THE PIAZZA, THE ARTIST AND THE CYCLOPS

Iain Borden

What is the relationship between, on the one hand, urban space and buildings and, on the other hand, the artistic and architectural techniques used to represent them? Are the particular kinds of drawings employed the effects or the cause of urban change? To consider such questions, we shall turn to *trecento* and *quattrocento* (fourteenth and fifteenth century) Florence, when parts of the closed irregularity of the walled medieval city were transformed into the open and regular spaces of the renaissance, and when architects such as Brunelleschi and Alberti developed the technique of linear perspective. Was perspective, we might ask, born purely out of artistic and scientific curiosity, or was it an attempt to address the new spatial and architectural form of the nascent renaissance city?

Let us see what we are dealing with. The problem is to show that developments in linear perspective made sense of spatial changes already completed in the fabric of Florence. It is therefore necessary first to assess these urban changes, and then to consider the perspectival experiments of Brunelleschi and Alberti in the light of this urban context. Finally, we shall consider the significance of perspective for art, architecture and conceptions of space in general.

FLORENCE IN THE TRECENTO

The scale of the radical transformations which Florence underwent prior to the renaissance is often underestimated. The last quarter of the thirteenth century witnessed the start of important urban and architectural projects, many under the direction of Arnolfo di Cambio (d. 1302 or 1310), which changed the face of the city. These included the construction of a fifth set of city walls (1284–1333), the church of Sta Croce (1294–1442) and a new square and church of Sta Maria Novella (1278–1350, new façade 1456–70).

Foremost of all was the creation of two great urban squares. The first was the Piazza del Duomo, carved out of the medieval city by the demolition of St Reparta and a palace opposite the Baptistery. With its size, architectural form, sculptural programme and technical innovation the new cathedral in the piazza, Sta Maria del Fiore (1296–1462), dominated not just the square but the whole of Florence. More buildings were pulled down and adjacent roads widened to 22 m so that the cathedral was 'encircled by beautiful and spacious streets.'[1] The second square was 250 m to the south, the Piazza della Signoria. Here the Palazzo del Priori (1298–1314), since the sixteenth century known as the Palazzo Vecchio, was erected as the administrative centre for the new guild republic led by the church priors. Having completed this great public hall, measures were undertaken to create a large and uniform square by paving in 1330, reducing building heights to around nine metres, constructing the Loggia dei Lanzi (1376–82) and further expanding in the 1380s and 1390s by removing buildings on the southern edge. Special

Figure 7.1

New urban spaces, such as the Piazza della Signoria, Florence, enlarged in the fourteenth century, created new problems of representation. Later engraving by Zocchi.

efforts were made to keep the square clean and to prevent carts from passing through. Although, apart from the Palazzo Vecchio, the architecture was not especially grand, the vast piazza dominated by the square tower of the palace created a spatial monumentality as yet unknown in Florence.[2]

Beside their individual importance, the two squares were also related to each other, forming a grand urban plan of a religious centre and political centre joined together by the 200 m straight of the Via dei Calzaioli. An integral part of the plan, this street was widened in 1390 and there were contemporary plans to remodel its building façades along standardized lines.

These constructions were the beginnings of a new kind of urban space, involving not just the formal relationships between buildings, squares and streets but also the ideas with which they were conceived and the contemporary experience of space as an urban phenomenon. Pienza, Parma, Ferrara, Mantua and Bologna, as well as Florence, all underwent similar transformations. And new attitudes to the city were also expressed in commonplace parts of the city; at Florence, wooden structures were replaced with stone ones, streets were widened and straightened, and overhanging *sporti* (upper storeys) were removed. Through such measures rectilinearity, regularity and geometric order became intrinsic elements of the civic improvement programmes. Enough of Florence was transformed in this way to constitute a powerful and dominant presence. Given the close density of the surrounding houses and twisting labyrinth of medieval streets the effect of the new architecture and squares would have been startling. Contrasts between small and large, closed and open, winding and straight served to make the impact even greater.

But the new urban space also required representation, the importance of which was two-fold: adequate depiction required new techniques of representation, and proper understanding and control required equivalent developments in intellectual conceptions of space. Drawing and thinking about space, as we shall see, were precisely the concerns addressed by linear perspective in the following century.

Firstly, how could urban space be shown in painting? To address this problem, artists applied perspective in discontinuous parts of their images in an

Figure 7.2

Early attempts to record the new Italian city used foreshortening, while pictorial space remains conceptually constricted within the painting boundaries. *Christ Opens the Eyes of a Man Born Blind*, artist Duccio. The National Gallery, London.

attempt to record the new Italian cities. Among others, the Florentine Giotto (c.1266–1337), the Sienese Duccio (c.1255–1318), and the Siennese Ambrogio Lorenzetti (active 1319–47) produced external and interior scenes with foreshortened walls, floors and cornice lines. Yet although foreshortening imparts pictures with apparent depth and recession, they remain problematic spatially. Either lines do not all recede to one vanishing point, or relative sizes and distances are difficult to gauge, or the space appears confined to the boundaries of the image.

Secondly, there was the problem of ordering the new urban space, as demonstrated by the various new towns the Florentines founded in the trecento. Anxious to realize in Scarperia, Terranuova, Castelfranco di

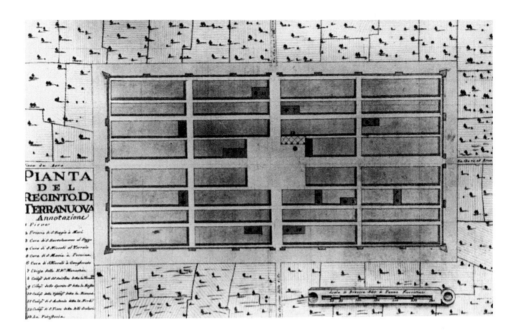

Figure 7.3

The orthogonal composition of the Florentine new towns was dictated by practical as well as aesthetic concerns. Town plan, Terranuova, (fourteenth century).

Sopra and San Giovanni the centralized squares, straight streets, symmetry and regular architecture that were only partially feasible in Florence itself, they were nonetheless limited by the technical descriptions of space available. For example, as David Friedman points out, although straight streets were thought to be beautiful their disposition in grid patterns in these towns was undertaken for purely practical reasons: the exact location of a point on land could only be worked out by considering land as an orthogonally articulated plane of two dimensions crossed with lines at right angles to each other.[3] Although the Florentines had ideas and objectives for the spatial form of cities, they did not yet possess the intellectual and technical means to fully control them; the ability to make accurate maps of irregular landscapes and urban forms did not come until later in the renaissance.

THE RETURN OF PERSPECTIVE

Perspective, of course, existed long before Brunelleschi and Alberti. Democritus and Anaxagoras in fifth century BC Athens used a simple version to create the illusion of recession on painted theatre scenery, and the Roman architectural theorist Vitruvius described the methods of *scenographia*, a form of perspectival sketch of a building showing the sides as well as the façade.[4] After the Byzantine and Romanesque periods of art production, for whose purposes perspective was unnecessary, perspective began to be used again, as we have seen, by such artists as Giotto and Lorenzetti.

Beyond these partial applications of perspective, linear perspective was developed in the humanist fifteenth century as a systematic treatment of space encompassing the entire picture plane. In all probability the first applications of this system were Filippo Brunelleschi's (1377–1446) famous demonstration panels depicting the exterior of the Baptistery and the Palazzo Vecchio, completed c.1416–25 and now lost.

For the Baptistery panel, Brunelleschi stood inside the cathedral portal and painted a perspectively exact representation across the Piazza del Duomo of the octagonal Baptistery and background buildings. The finished panel was small enough to be held in one hand by the spectator, who stood facing the Baptistery in a pre-determined spot, holding the painting at eye level with its back toward her/him. A small hole through the painting enabled one of two things to be seen: either the actual Baptistery or, by holding a small mirror between the painting and the building, the reflection of Brunelleschi's image. Removing and replacing the mirror from the line of sight enabled repeated A–B comparisons, the trick being that no difference could be readily discerned between the two. The second panel focused on the Piazza della Signoria, with Brunelleschi composing his perspective from a point in the north-west of the square and diagonally across to the Palazzo Vecchio in the opposite corner.

In contrast to Brunelleschi's panels which presented the spectator with a finished article, Leon Battista Alberti (1404–72) concentrated on codifying the methods of perspective. In keeping with his learned activities as a humanist scholar, Alberti's achievement was to elucidate linear perspective in terms of logical procedures, and thus to secure its intellectual validity as well as its practical utility. Fundamental to Alberti's explanation is the conception of the world as being perceived through a visual pyramid at the apex of which is the eye of the beholder and which contains all the 'visual rays' or sight lines which connect the eye to the objects to be represented. A painting is then constructed as a plane intersecting the visual pyramid at a position between the eye and objects.

Alberti also provides further detailed information concerning the geometric and optical foundations of perspective, the relative sizing of objects (distance point construction), and the lack of optical distortion for objects whose sides lie parallel to the picture plane. The practicality of the method is underscored by the perspectival net, a mesh screen placed between the artist and her/his scene. Perspective is thus presented as a means by which first to observe to a scene, second to order its spaces and third to construct a representation.

Three significant points arise from these developments in linear perspective for our consideration of urban space in Florence. The first is to do with Brunelleschi's selection of buildings and spaces, for the two panels directed attention at modern projects, not the medieval city. In the case of the Baptistery, although this building was then believed to be Roman (it is in fact a fifth century church converted into a baptistry in the eleventh century), the surrounding Piazza del Duomo had been formed by the demolition of an old palace. Its site and location was the most important single urban square created in Italy since ancient Rome. In the case of the Piazza della Signoria, this too was one of the major urban developments

Figure 7.4

Alberti's perspectival net helped to depict scenes 'objectively'. Sight lines from the figure to the artist's eye intersect the net, and are mapped onto corresponding points on the gridded drawing surface. *Artist Drawing a Reclining Woman*, (c.1525), artist Albrecht Dürer.

initiated by Arnolfo di Cambio, while the Palazzo Vecchio signified the appearance of monumental public architecture. Brunelleschi's diagonal line of sight across the piazza emphasized an oblique view of the palace, its smooth sides receding into the distance from the foremost sharp north corner, and so maximized the sense of open, running space. The two panels therefore provided spatial representations of transformations previously unknown to Florentine eyes, their subject matter most clearly characterizing the newly emerging urban space.

Second, linear perspective was intended not for architectural composition but for observation and

PLATE 20. *(Page 131)*

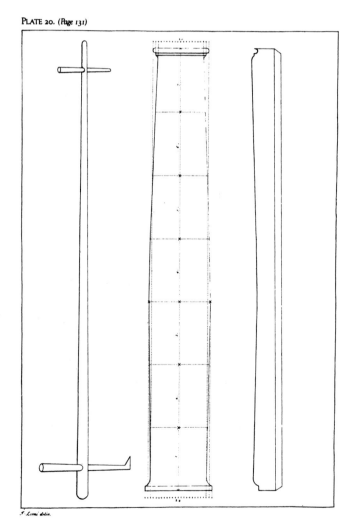

Figure 7.5

Compensating for the physiology of the human eye is the basis of entasis, creating deliberate curves in horizontal and vertical lines. Linear perspective makes no such allowances. L.B. Alberti, *De Re Aedificatoria*, (1452. Illustration from 1755 Leoni edition).

representation. The two Brunelleschi panels were, after all, worked out examples depicting existing buildings, while Alberti chose to set out his views on the subject in his treatise on painting, *Della Pittura* (1436), and in the treatise on architecture, *De Re Aedificatoria* (1452), he simply points out that perspective should not be used in the design process. Indeed, the spatial conception underlying linear perspective is fundamentally at odds with some aspects of classical design. An obvious example is entasis, the slight outward curving or bowing of columns and plinths used to correct the optical illusion of concavity caused by straight lines. Buildings such as the Parthenon (447–32 BC) at Athens and the Temple of Apollo at Didyma (third century BC), or renaissance examples such as Brunelleschi's church of S Lorenzo in Florence and theories of column design like that in Alberti's *De Re Aedificatoria*, adjust building design through entasis to counteract its actual appearance in the human spherical field of vision. By contrast, the geometrical rules of linear perspective require lines to be drawn absolutely straight with no allowance for the physiology of the eye.

Third, as entasis makes clear, as a means of observation and representation linear perspective orders space in a manner quite distinct from the reality of space or actual human perception. It is worth emphasizing this point, for it seems to contradict the notion that perspective was developed to cope with new urban space. In seeking to record, represent and control urban space, perspective requires the artist and spectator to replace direct subjective experience with a systematic objective procedure with powerful operational characteristics. In short, it requires a conceptual abstraction from reality in order to understand it, and, like any abstraction, perspective is subtly different from the reality it is trying to address. It is to these aspects of perspective that we must now turn.

THE WORLD IN PERSPECTIVE

If linear perspective renders perceptual experience rational and so amenable to systematic representation, it follows that our experience of these representations is also rational and systematic. What kind of spatial understanding is then being offered?

In terms of subject matter, perspective prioritizes the geometric, ordered and regular urban space and architecture which, as we have seen, began to emerge in the trecento. Thus rather than an historical accident, linear perspective was developed precisely to represent straight lines and open spaces. The techniques of perspective were worked out with particular regard to the spatial problematic, not by chance, but out of necessity.

And yet soon after the innovations carried out by Brunelleschi and Alberti this relation between the real and the representational was reversed: instead of a necessary device, linear perspective came to dominate representations of space. To give one example, John White points out that while trecento and early quattrocento depictions of the Palazzo Vecchio – including Brunelleschi's own panel – use an oblique view of the palace, from then until the seventeenth century frontal views are used almost exclusively, with the façade turned parallel to the pictorial plane to conform to the axes of the foreshortened square of an Alberti-type perspective.[5]

Once linear perspective became the dominant mode of spatial representation, what were the ramifications for the spectator? Conceptually, the kind of space presented by linear perspective is infinite, (it has no boundaries), unchanging (it is static) and homogenous (it has universally constant characteristics). This is clearly quite different from real urban space which, as Florence shows us, is an historical phenomenon that varies over time and from place to place. Nor are we presented with an accurate picture of what we actually experience – our real encounter with space is of moving around, living over time, using all our bodily senses, intellect and memory. Even if we were static, frozen in time, using only our eyes to perceive, the curved images produced on the two retinae are computed by the brain to produce a spherical, stereoscopic vision quite distinct from the orthogonal, monocular vision of linear perspective. Brunelleschi's peepshow panel of the Baptistery is particularly telling in this respect, forcing the spectator to stand still, in the exact spot prescribed by the artist, and to view both image and the building with one eye. Under carefully prescribed controlled conditions, objective visual geometry dominates subjective spatial experience. The Cyclops replaces the human.

For the spectator, space is represented as a given fixity, defined and immutable, something comprehensible only according to visual rules. It is the place which exists before us, to which we come, rather than the place which we produce and create. Of course, the magic of linear perspective is how it convinces us that what we are looking at is a truthful representation which can stand in for the real, and as Henri Lefebvre has noted, at a unique moment in human history, 'the Renaissance town perceived itself as a harmonious whole, as an organic mediation between earth and heaven.'[6] But from such an all-encompassing understanding, it is but a short and too easy step to grant primacy to the visual experience for our understanding of objects and the world in which they exist. Even scientists can be deluded so. The German astronomer Johannes Kepler's (1571–1630) education in linear perspective led him at first to misunderstand the illusory curves of a comet tail or meteor trajectory; because perspective taught him that what is straight must look straight, conversely he thought that because these phenomena looked curved so they had to be curved.[7]

Perspective encourages us to believe only what we see. On this level, the purpose of linear perspective is not really the representation of objects or buildings themselves, nor is it to mimic a physiological perception of the world around us. Rather it is something more systemic and universal: a system of ordering and understanding space. As such, it was of immense importance to the Florentines and for the rest of the renaissance. And more than five hundred years on, perspective still looks right to us because we are educated and immersed in its ways.

REFERENCES

1   Quoted in Gene Brucker, *Renaissance Florence*, (University of California Press, Berkeley, 1969), p. 31.

2   Richard Goldthwaite, *The Building of Renaissance Florence: an Economic and Social History*, (Johns Hopkins University Press, Baltimore, 1980), p. 6.

3   David Friedman, *Florentine New Towns: Urban Design in the Middle Ages*, (The Architectural History Foundation, New York; and MIT Press, Cambridge, Mass. 1988), p. 51.

4   Vitruvius, *De Architectura/The Ten Books of Architecture*, (Dover Editions, London, 1960), pp. 14 and 198.

5   John White, *The Birth and Rebirth of Pictorial Space*, (Faber and Faber, London, 1987), p. 126.

6   Henri Lefebvre, *The Production of Space*, (Basil Blackwell, Oxford, 1991), p. 271.

7   Erwin Panovsky, *Perspective as Symbolic Form*, (Zone Books, New York, 1991), p. 34.

BIBLIOGRAPHY

Florence and the Renaissance

Giulio Argan, *The Renaissance City*, (George Braziller, New York, 1969).

Eugenio Battisti, *Brunelleschi: The Complete Work*, (Thames and Hudson, London, 1981).

Leonardo Benevolo, *The Architecture of the Renaissance*, two vols., (Routledge and Kegan Paul, London, 1978).

Leonardo Benevolo, *The History of the City*, (Scolar Press, London, 1980).

Anthony Blunt, *Artistic Theory in Italy 1450–1660*, (Oxford University Press, Oxford, 1962).

Gene Brucker, *Renaissance Florence*, (University of California Press, Berkeley, 1969).

Jacob Burckhardt, *The Architecture of the Italian Renaissance*, (Secker and Warburg, London, 1985).

Peter Burke, *The Italian Renaissance: Culture and Society in Italy*, (Princeton University Press, Princeton, 1987).

David Friedman, *Florentine New Towns: Urban Design in the Middle Ages*, (The Architectural History Foundation, New York, and MIT Press, Cambridge, Mass., 1988).

Richard Goldthwaite, *The Building of Renaissance Florence: an Economic and Social History*, (Johns Hopkins University Press, Baltimore, 1980).

Spiro Kostof, *The City Shaped: Urban Patterns and Meanings Through History*, (Thames and Hudson, London, 1991).

Lewis Mumford, *The City in History: Its Origins, Its Transformations and Its Prospects*, (Harcourt Brace Jovanovich, San Diego, 1961).

Peter Murray, *Renaissance Architecture*, (Rizzoli, New York, 1985).

Perspective

Samuel Edgerton, *The Renaissance Rediscovery of Linear Perspective*, (Harper and Row, New York, 1976).

Leonard Goldstein, *The Social and Cultural Roots of Linear Perspective*, (MEP Publications, Minneapolis, 1988).

Martin Jay, 'Scopic Regimes of Modernity', in Scott Lash and Jonathan Friedman (eds.), *Modernity and Identity*, (Basil Blackwell, Oxford, 1992).

Martin Kemp, *The Science of Art: Optical Themes in Western Art from Brunelleschi to Seurat*, (Yale University Press, New Haven, 1990).

Henri Lefebvre, *The Production of Space*, (Basil Blackwell, Oxford, 1991).

Erwin Panovsky, *Perspective as Symbolic Form*, (Zone Books, New York, 1991).

John White, *The Birth and Rebirth of Pictorial Space*, (Faber and Faber, London, 1987).

Lawrence Wright, *Perspective in Perspective*, (Routledge and Kegan Paul, London, 1983).

8

THE PALAZZO TYPE

David Dunster

Nowhere is the puzzle of how we understand architecture clearer than in differing accounts of Florence in the renaissance. Arrayed on one side are those kinds of architectural historians who aim to be precise about buildings, about who built what, where, for whom and under what influences; on the other side are the more sociologically-minded historians who aim to recreate the circumstances of the life of Florence, within which buildings are merely evidence for an over-arching interpretation of Florentine society. Those concentrating purely upon architecture are consistently accused of formalism, of looking solely at the forms, shapes and styles of buildings while ignoring the various social and economic conditions under which they were produced. While those concentrating on society can be accused of being blind, of not looking at the specific forms and spaces of different buildings and tending to see all of them as the product of a general set of conditions and circumstances.

Given these two oppositional camps, how can architecture be understood? Is this question, we might ask, better dealt with from inside architecture as a succession or progression of formal inventions? Or, if it is to be understood at all, must architecture always stand for something other than itself, representing the state of society, conflict between different social classes, or particular historical events? We will examine these contrasting ideas, and suggest that an analysis based on building types will go some way to bridging the chasm.

TYPE

What can the category 'type' mean in architectural terms? We can identify three broad different versions of this concept. Firstly, consider the example of Lincoln (1129–1320), Ely (1198–1349) and Wells (c.1180–c.1425) cathedrals which, it could be argued, all fit neatly into the category, or type, late-gothic cathedral. Here type is not only a distinct use, but also an organization of space with particular forms: a tower over the crossing, an ornate entry porch, separation of nave from choir etc. Such a definition could be called 'functional' because it focuses exclusively on the social functions of the building and on the particular spatial arrangements adopted to accommodate these functions. This is the basis upon which *A History of Building Types*, the last book by Nikolaus Pevsner, was written.[1] Another definition, this time medieval in origin, runs that type is 'that by which something is symbolized.' The concept of type here relates to the attempt to understand scripture, and therefore to decipher the moments when Divine providence is revealed in a physical sign, such as a piece of sculpture or an entire building. In this sense type relates to something material – the sign itself – and to something non-material – the will of God. A third definition of type, and a much more recent one, has disavowed connection to function alone and has instead referred type especially to the fabric of cities. While cathedrals might indeed form a type of building, the ensemble of religious buildings, such as we find in the campo of Pisa, or in Florence in the relationship between the Baptistery, Sta Maria del Fiore cathedral (the 'Duomo') and the surrounding urban square can be argued to constitute a further type.

With this third meaning of type architectural historians tend to contend with sociological interpretations, as it is here that type is extended beyond the physical limits of the building out into the urban field. And yet whatever interpretations are made of this complex type of urban space, one component of it still tends to elude architectural historians, particularly when they consider cities such as renaissance Florence: the buildings which surround religious monuments. Loosely speaking, these buildings are the vernacular, the common speech of the crafts of architectural construction. Certainly in the great urban spaces of northern Italy we never find religious ensembles confronted by private *palazzi* (palaces). In Florence for example, when the richest and most monumental of these palaces were constructed from late in the fifteenth century onward, they were built on sites separate from the Duomo; although it could be argued that the palaces presented an alternative grandeur to that sought by the church, they did not oppose it directly through rivalry in a single piazza (square). If we were to wander around Florence, we would mostly see fourteenth and fifteenth century buildings whose façades form a consistent and recognizable street, and we would be in little doubt as to when we had moved from a medieval quarter into one reconstructed during the nineteenth century. It is these ignored façades and buildings which this essay will discuss, through the category of type.

THE RISE AND FALL OF THE TOWER

The first dramatic physical change in the urban history of Florence occurred in the twelfth century when the construction of a number of stone *torri* (towers)

Figure 8.1

Function and urban image combined in the medieval stone torre. San Gimignano.

erupted. This phenomenon has been attributed to the dominant Guelph party merchants enforcing the Ghibelline party of noble families to migrate into the city from their country strongholds, where they created what amounted to fortified residences within the city walls. By the end of the twelfth century these towers numbered almost 150, and by the middle of the next century some exceeded 60 m in height.

These towers can be considered a type in two of the senses outlined above, in that they possessed both a functionally distinct character of use and form, and a definite relation with the urban realm around them; in particular, the towers transformed the walled city into a city with an image, in other words a city aware of its position and aware of its power against the rivals cities of Parma and Siena.

The towers did not, however, prove to be a lasting feature of the city. After the founding of the Florentine Republic in 1250, a law was passed reducing them all to the height of 29 m, and stone thus recovered from demolitions was used to form the southern bank of the river Arno.[2] Few now remain, and the appearance of medieval Florence can best be judged today from the neighbouring city of San Gimignano.

THE EARLY PALACE TYPE

As trading and textile interests bloomed, the prosperity of a few members of the Florentine population increased beyond expectation, and an identifiably new kind of building emerged which catered for the needs of these new wealthy families. This story, as we shall see, raises the issue of escaping sameness through the creation of the one-off.

During the growth of Florence, the form of the wealthier citizens' residences changed slowly but surely. From the medieval towers evolved a tall narrow house, generally five stories high. But the Florentines, uniquely amongst northern Italians, also retained a covered balcony or terrace on the upper floor, often projecting over the street façade of the lower floors, and thus retaining some of the character of the defensive machicolation – an opening in a parapet – through which boiling oil could be poured onto invaders. Here we see a form, tower-like although now wedged together into terraces, which has lost its spatial isolation but retains, by virtue of the projecting balcony, some of the formal characteristics of its more defence-minded predecessor. The origin of this new urban building type then was not itself urban, being unconnected with the town-based Guelph party of merchants, but rather was rural, being derived from the first countryside residences of the Ghibelline noble families.

It is fairly certain that in the design of these thirteenth and fourteenth century palaces, an architect as we might understand that term today was not employed. In those which remain, such as the Davanzati (late fourteenth century), what architectural order that can be perceived has almost entirely to do

Figure 8.2

An architectural type can persist through a series of transformations. The *torre* transposed into an urban terrace. Palazzo Davanzati, Florence, (late fourteenth century).

with the organization of the façade, and with the decoration of the principal rooms. This does not mean, however, that there have been no architectural developments in the building type. On the contrary, we are presented with an architectural form that has persisted through radical transformations – from rural residence to isolated urban tower to terraced urban palace – and any account of the continued existence of that form cannot simply refer to use or function. Apart from nostalgia what explanations are available?

For sociological historians, the form of the dwelling relates to generalities. How did people live? What were the forces which hindered or helped them to prosper? Martines, for example, sees a homogeneity not in the form of the architecture but in social and economic existence.

> For shopkeepers and the mercantile classes
> generally, domestic life and the money making
> trades had a unified existence. . . . The separation of
> the two functions came later, in the course of the
> 15th century, and then only among citizens of the
> richer sort. The separation presented as a relatively
> novel idea, is clearly seen in Francesco di Giorgio's
> architectural treatise (1470s): family rooms and
> workshop are separated, in part so as to keep
> women and children beyond the purview of
> customers and other merchants. In the 13th and 14th
> centuries, home and workshop were one; so also
> home and counting house, home and warehouse,
> home and the part of it facing the retail outlet.
> Residential quarters on the ground floor gave out
> directly onto the street, while the large windows of
> the floor above also took in the nearby spectacle.
> Home and public world faced each other in a
> relationship that made for a continuous exchange.[3]

Martines here identifies the gradual separation of work and domestic life as the significant factor, rather than any autonomous architectural invention or development.

By contrast, the building-centred architectural historian, looking at the same subject over the same period, will tend to focus on the persistence of the form of the tall narrow building, paying less attention to the arrangement of outbuildings and more to those elements, the façade and principal rooms, upon which the most effort and expense has been lavished.

Despite these contrasting areas of concentration, it is possible to identify an important commonality. In both sociological and the architectural approaches there remains this underlying idea of a spatial arrangement, a type, whose existence and history may be taken for granted. Neither history asks as to why this form persisted. Yet clearly, as Fanelli's study of Florence[4] indicates, there was a remarkable building campaign in which conscious decisions about what to build must have been continuously and repeatedly taken. To answer this question with absolute clarity is impossible, because no documentation survives. Nonetheless, based on the historical development outlined above, we can now speculate that up until the fifteenth century and the emergence of renaissance humanist myths, Florentines built their less monumental buildings according to a formal type which had its origins in the late eleventh century and which now existed in a compressed residual form.

THE HUMANIST PALACE

If we now turn to examine the palaces of the renaissance as they have come down to us today, we can see that no humanist palace from around the middle of the fifteenth century onward contains anything remotely like a tower. From this point on, the design of the entire palace came under the control of one person, the emerging renaissance architect, while the decoration and furnishing would generate an entirely

Figure 8.3

The survival of the palazzo type (1). Aggrandized in Buckingham Palace, London, (1825–47 and 1912–3), architects John Nash, Edward Blore and Aston Webb.

Figure 8.4

The survival of the palazzo type (2). Colliding with brutalism in the Boston City Hall, Boston, (1962–7), architects G. Kallmann, M. McKinnell & E. Knowles.

new set of fine craftswork. And it is at the same historical moment that this architect figure first begins to emerge, that we also find that the tower-derived building type has been expunged from the market of forms. Instead a new building type comes to the fore which, at its best, would allow the rebuilding of a whole city block. This new building type, the palazzo as we now understand it, has been copied throughout the four centuries which separate renaissance Florence from the late twentieth century, and persists as a type denoting a centre of power, whether it be the diminutive White House (1793–1801) in Washington, or the overblown Buckingham Palace (1825–47, remodelled 1912–3) in London.

Consider this new palace type as opposed to the tower. It is everything which the tower is not, broad where the tower form is narrow, and complex in organization where the tower is simple; whereas the tower's relatively small size forbade sophisticated sequences of internal space, rooms within the palace are arranged in a hierarchy of importance. In the palazzo type two features emerge which could never be part of the earlier tower-based type: the staircase as a monumental and theatrical component of processional movement; and a garden, perhaps an internal courtyard, whose existence opened up a whole gamut of symbolic and real relationships between culture and nature. The palace therefore can be seen as the opposite of the earlier dwelling of the well-to-do, but in exactly the same way as the tower could be modified and developed for various rural and urban uses, so the palace type has been used and re-used, whether for museums, universities and offices as well as for residences.

How then, to return to the question raised at the beginning, can the sociological and the architectural be resolved? Martines again throws down the gauntlet.

> Art historians bury the *why* – and hence the sociology – of buildings by their excessive emphasis on questions of form and style. Most of the great building projects of the Italian Renaissance whether commissioned by a Cosimo de' Medici (oligarch-prince), by Stanga counts (Cremonese aristocrats), or by a Pius II, had behind them the urge to exhibit now: to exhibit an identity, to show the power or piety of the man and his family dynasty, and to carve out a space in the city that would belong to that name, that individual and dynasty, for all times.[5]

Figure 8.5

Palazzo Riccardi/Medici, Florence, (1444 onward), contained within the general conception of the humanist palazzo. Architect Michelozzo di Bartolommeo. Engraving by Zocchi.

Martines' formula as to why palaces were constructed in the first place appears convincing, citing the client family's need to represent their identity and power, but fails to answer one question – why were the palaces different? One answer could be that they were different solely in degree, that between, for example, the Palazzo Strozzi (1489–1539) designed by Benedetto da Maiano (1442–97) with cornice by Simone del Cronaca (1457–1508) and the Palazzo Medici/Riccardi (1444 onward) designed by Michelozzo di Bartolommeo (1396–1472), only scale, stone facings and decoration differentiate the two buildings, while their overall form demarcates them as lying within an under-standing of palace building. It is this understanding, their containment within a general conception of the palazzo, which can be characterized through the notion of type.

If we turn finally to the renaissance humanist Leon Battista Alberti (1404–72) we might expect to find in his writings, particularly the *De Re Aedificatoria* (1452) treatise on architecture, some help on the issue of type. Jarzombeck offers a new interpretation in which he emphasizes Alberti the humanist man of letters over Alberti the architect.[6] In particular Jarzombeck doubts whether the buildings we normally think of as being designed by Alberti were in fact done so. Only one palace is circumstantially attributed to Alberti, the Palazzo Rucellai (1446–51) in Florence, and of that palace only the façade. At the Palazzo Rucellai, the right-hand corner abuts an adjoining building in a highly unusual manner, in that the façade here looks to be incomplete or fragmented. This cut-off, Jarzombeck conjectures, may have been purposefully designed.

> I find it unlikely that the carefully crafted unfinished edge of the facade, an architectural delight revealing the individual cross-sections of the various components of the facade (architraves, string courses, moldings, and arches) was accidental . . . Incompletion, facing the future, and fragmentation, facing the past, are the curses associated with the temporal world. Just as Alberti's writings discuss this issue and indeed thematize it (see '*Libri Disvoluti*'), this facade presents this both-and situation as an architectural problem.[7]

Figure 8.6

The palazzo as both structure and decoration, revealed by the right-hand edge of the façade. Palazzo Rucellai, Florence, (1446–51), architect L.B. Alberti.

Employing one concept – 'both-and' – which derives from the theoretical writings of the twentieth century architect Robert Venturi (1925–)[8], Jarzombeck makes the architect, Alberti, into an exterior decorator, albeit one with a profound humanist programme. On the one hand, the greater part of the Rucellai palace façade appears to look structural, but, on the other hand, the unfinished right-hand edge of the façade shows that it is nothing of the sort, and is in fact simply an outer dressing. In other words, the façade appears to be simultaneously both structure and surface.

More importantly, however, the unfinished edge of the Rucellai palace suggests that the façade could continue along the street, re-dressing the neighbouring medieval structures in renaissance make-up. The palace of the family is therefore less significant than the opportunity it presented Alberti to demonstrate a principle of a new architecture: that domestic, even grand, buildings should not be the occasion for virtuosity. The true architect dealt with monumental edifices. For the rest, decorum and elegance would suffice. The type, even if the palatial house of the rich, should not become an occasion for detracting from civic decorum; it required a private humility. Ostentation of architecture should be reserved for the buildings of the church and the state. For the rest, quiet and decorous work with a tradition of building, a tradition dominated by the idea of 'type', should be the highest objective of architecture.

REFERENCES

1   Nikolaus Pevsner, *A History of Building Types*, (Thames and Hudson, London, 1976).
2   E.A. Gutkind, *The International History of City Development. Volume IV Urban Development in Southern Europe: Italy and Greece*, (New York, 1969), p. 334.
3   Lauro Martines, *Power and Imagination: City States in Renaissance Italy*, (Knopf, New York, 1979), p. 99
4   Giovanni Fanelli, *Firenze: architettura e citta*, (Vallecchi, Firenze, two volumes, 1973–75).
5   Martines, *Power and Imagination*, p. 327.
6   Mark Jarzombeck, *On Leon Battista Alberti: His Literary and Aesthetic Theories*, (MIT Press, Cambridge, Mass., 1989).

7   Jarzombeck, *On Leon Battista Alberti*, pp. 175–7.
8   Robert Venturi, *Complexity and Contradiction in Architecture*, (Museum of Modern Art, New York, 1966).

BIBLIOGRAPHY

Giulio Argan, *The Renaissance City*, (George Braziller, New York, 1969).

Leonardo Benevolo, *The Architecture of the Renaissance*, two vols., (Routledge & Kegan Paul, London, 1978).

Leonardo Benevolo, *The History of the City*, (Scolar Press, London, 1980).

Franco Borsi, *Leon Battista Alberti*, (Phaidon, Oxford, 1977).

Gene Brucker, *Renaissance Florence*, (University of California Press, Berkeley, 1969).

Jacob Burckhardt, *The Architecture of the Italian Renaissance*, (Secker & Warburg, London, 1985).

Peter Burke, *The Italian Renaissance: Culture and Society in Italy*, (Princeton University Press, Princeton, 1987).

E.A. Gutkind, *The International History of City Development. Volume IV Urban Development in Southern Europe: Italy and Greece*, (New York, 1969).

Mark Jarzombeck, *On Leon Battista Alberti: His Literary and Aesthetic Theories*, (MIT Press, Cambridge, Mass., 1989).

Lauro Martines, *Power and Imagination: City States in Renaissance Italy*, (Knopf, New York, 1979).

Peter Murray, *Renaissance Architecture*, (Rizzoli, New York, 1985).

9

DEMAND AND SUPPLY IN RENAISSANCE FLORENCE

Graham Ive

What can be achieved by adopting an economic approach to architectural and urban history? We can answer this question by looking at Richard Goldthwaite's *The Building of Renaissance Florence*, a work which justifies extended consideration not just for its contribution to our understanding of an extraordinary episode in the history of architecture, but because of its exemplary demonstration of this kind of approach to understanding architecture and cities in general.[1]

Goldthwaite tries to explain where the wealth to pay for a building came from, why it was spent in a particular way, how the building was produced, and how the city was affected as a result. Architecture is conceived of as an activity, with architects and other kinds of building workers located within a social division of labour, and as a set of building types – the private palace, the hospital, the parish church and so on. This history is 'economic' because it is based upon the concepts of demand and supply. We shall consider demand first.

DEMAND AND TASTE

Demand, in economists' terms, is the need or want for something backed up by the ability to pay for it. Need or want is normally discussed in terms of taste, but taste in orthodox economics is thought to be purely subjective and thus to have little place in its scheme of things. Goldthwaite, however, notes the necessity of taking into account psychology, social conditions and culture in general. 'Buildings have functions and style, and the motives for building them cannot be understood in the usual terms of economic analysis.'[2]

In terms of renaissance Florence, this judgement is supported by two new building types – the private chapel and the large private palace. Neither represented a new need or function, but, nonetheless, more people in fifteenth century Florence wanted and got these things; there also arose the 'desire to give these buildings a certain physical presence, and an interest in new ideas about how to do this ... building was undertaken in a spirit informed by a consciousness of public space and inspired by the desire to make a distinctive mark in it.'³ Furthermore, Goldthwaite argues, it was a collective vision which inspired patrons to see their buildings in a new perspective. Thus taste itself is not seen as individualistic, but formed out of common responses to a shared experience, and shaped by earlier expressions of civic pride.⁴

How then was this collective vision manifested through individual building projects? Goldthwaite's phrase for Florentine upper class demand is 'conspicuous consumption', which he derives, somewhat simplistically, from the American economist Thorstein Veblen (1857–1929). Before the fifteenth century, wealthy Florentines were generally restrained from spending their wealth too conspicuously by religious concerns about the evils of the business world, by Franciscan extremists preaching the doctrine of poverty, and by a desire to avoid hostility among the urban populace or rival political factions.⁵ However, official religion soon bent its doctrines to accommodate the rise of capitalism.

By the fifteenth century, the merchants and bankers of Florence had become the *de facto* ruling class, and their palaces and private chapels are the chief buildings of the period. Seeking to emulate and better the old medieval aristocratic ethos of gaining glory and honour through lavish expenditure, the new class of 'merchant princes' enthusiastically accumulated luxury objects: furniture, paintings, jewellery, clothing, rarities and exotica of all kinds, of which private houses magnificent enough to be called palaces were merely the greatest.

What marks the Florentine families in our eyes today is the 'good taste' which the Strozzi, Medici, Rucellai and Pazzi exercised in their buying sprees. One could say that each simply bought and hired the best artists and architects available, and that Florentine merchant princes were just lucky to have available artists such as the sculptor and goldsmith Benvenuto Cellini (1500–71), the sculptor Donatello (1386–1466), the architect Filippo Brunelleschi (1337–1446), Michelangelo Buonarroti (1475–1564), etc.

Goldthwaite, however, attributes a more active role to the patron, and a lesser role to artists. Firstly, the patrons ensured that their buildings identified them conspicuously and in many different ways: armorial motifs worked into the decorative orders, inscription of names and mottoes, busts, shields, etc. Secondly, the patrons' zeal for building, and in particular their competition with each other, led to the development of new ideas about architecture. Thirdly, intellectual theorists such as Leon Battista Alberti (1404–72), moving in the circles of the richest merchants, articulated for patrons just how their buildings should best bring honour.[6] As a result, patrons could make informed judgements about buildings; members of public building committees did not hesitate to make architectural decisions, while particularly knowledgeable private patrons, such as Lorenzo de Medici and Giovanni Rucellai who collected architectural books and drawings, advised patrons elsewhere on their choice of architect and other architectural matters.

So far, we can partly explain the architecture of specific buildings by learning about their patrons, and about generic architectural types by studying their 'builders' – the patrons responsible for commissioning and financing buildings – as a class. This in turn leads us to a study of the Florentine upper class as a whole.

If we take the example of the Florentine private palazzo type, as described by David Dunster in Chapter 8, we find a number of things. Firstly, nuclear families had replaced extended families among this social group, reducing the amount of domestic accommodation required; even the largest palaces might contain no more than a dozen rooms for living. Their great size was instead achieved by arranging rooms around as large a private courtyard as the site allowed. Secondly, the palace turned only one monumental façade to the outside world. While sides and back could show rubble masonry or brick, the façade was usually the sole public statement, and on this no expense was spared. Thirdly, these palaces were objects of conspicuous consumption, not quasi-investments. No attention was paid to potential rental income, or to future resale or internal division. And in a departure from the residences of earlier European merchants, no space was allocated for the business activities. Fourthly, the palaces housed growing collections of domestic furnishings and other large objects. Thus the size and proportions of rooms had to suit this purpose. Many palaces had more rooms and space than their builders at first knew how to fill.

Veduta del Palazzo del Sig Principe Strozzi, e alla Strada che conduce al Ponte a S. Trinita   xiii

Figure 9.1

The demand side of the equation: the wealth of Florence's merchants and bankers outstripped their way of life. Palazzo Strozzi, Florence, (1489–1539). Engraving by Zocchi.

Florence's palace builders, in other words, were extremely rich businessmen whose wealth had grown faster than their way of life had changed. They could afford big houses, so they had them. They could buy privacy and quiet, in a city where these were the scarcest of commodities, and these they certainly valued. But as yet they lived rather bourgeois lives of private domesticity, with little of the quasi-public and ceremonial use of the building to be found in later, more aristocratic palaces, such as those of Roman cardinals or Bolognan senators.

THE ECONOMIC GEOGRAPHY OF THE RENAISSANCE

Let us turn to a different aspect of Goldthwaite's book: economic geography. Why did the large and innovative building activity of the fifteenth century renaissance occur in Florence, and not in Paris, Antwerp or Naples?

The boom towns of Europe shifted over the centuries. The most important centres of emerging mercantile capitalism in the fourteenth century – those of Bruges, Ghent and Antwerp – soon shifted to Northern Italy, especially Venice. Next, in the late sixteenth century, Amsterdam became pre-eminent; then, in the early eighteenth century, London.[7] As this was also the pattern of changing cultural and artistic innovation and importance, we can conclude that culture followed commerce. More specifically, Florence's economy boomed and grew in the fourteenth and fifteenth centuries; then, by the late sixteenth century it went into a decline. This shows that its renaissance, in general, followed economic events. And to understand the Florentine renaissance then, we have to know more about its economic rise and fall.

No sustained and expensive cultural production such as that of the Florentine renaissance would have been possible without a strong economy and a concentration of great wealth. But by the late sixteenth century all of Italy faced economic decline. New sea routes to the Indies and to America bypassed Italy, while benefiting rival centres of capital on the Atlantic seaboard of Europe. The competitive advantage of manufacturers in Tuscany, the Italian region around Florence, had been their proximity to the centre of trade and banking, and as the latter moved, Tuscany declined. As a result, the capitalists of renaissance Florence soon became *rentiers* – owners of financial assets and land who passively received dividends, rent and interest and consumed most of their incomes.

But why, in their zenith from around 1350 to 1500, did Florentine capitalists not plough their wealth back into their businesses? Why choose local status over a wider sphere of economic operations? Why did they not 'invest their capital in the most productive sector of the economy, the cloth industries, and hope for an industrial revolution'?[8] What would have been the consequences if they had done just that? Goldthwaite's answer to the last question is that it would have resulted in a growth of unskilled, low-paid workers whereas conspicuous consumption permitted the emergence of a better-off, highly skilled artisan class. He also suggests that this may have been preferable to turning Florence into a kind of proto-industrial city, like nineteenth century Manchester.

As to the question why they did not reinvest, even if they had wanted to, it is extremely unlikely that renaissance capitalists could have embarked on such an enterprise, for they faced certain barriers to expansion. As Karl Marx (1818–83) shows, the renaissance capitalists, unlike the later industrial capitalists of the nineteenth and twentieth centuries, were unable indefinitely to self-expand, because they were unable continuously to transform the production and the labour process. Their ability to expand capital instead depended mainly upon geographical boundaries. But their regional hinterland contained only limited natural resources and only a certain number of skilled producers and wage-workers. There was a wider zone of markets for products to which they had good access, but high transport costs limited exploitation of all but a city's most immediate hinterland. Furthermore, the rise of the Ottoman empire restricted Italian capitalists from venturing further to the East, while rising protectionist economic policies across Europe (which favoured nationals over foreign traders) restricted operations outside their own state, as did costly interstate rivalries in Italy. As a result, rather than trying to expand their own operations, renaissance capitalists tried to appropriate other peoples' by wars of territorial expansion.

Capitalists of the Florentine renaissance were thus forced to seek quantitative expansion by carving out larger hinterlands, but the very geography of the Florentine state limited the ways in which its great capitalists could re-invest their profits, and thus made much more likely their diversion into conspicuous display. This helps explain the Florentine focus on urban buildings. Because of geographical constraints, the merchants had little to spend their money on; architecture was simply one of their few available options.

SUPPLY: THE DIALECTIC OF QUANTITY AND QUALITY

Renaissance Florence, as we have seen, experienced a massive step-up in the volume, speed and intensity of high-quality building activity because its urban upper class began to build conspicuously.[9] However, although large by contemporary standards, these were not truly gigantic schemes. Part of the reason for this is that large quantities of unskilled construction labour simply were not available. Wage labour had already become the urban norm, but was strictly regulated by the guilds, whose policy was to guarantee the reproduction of a limited supply of highly-skilled workers through a system of working masters, journeymen and apprentices, while urban policy generally discouraged the growth of a large class of unattached, untrained and unskilled workers.

Renaissance work force requirements, therefore, remained dominated by the need for high skills rather than vast numbers of workers. As a result, construction labour was 'free' rather than dependent (slave or serf) labour, hired in the emergent market for high craft skills. Such skills were in relatively limited supply, and supply could easily have been exceeded had projects been too large; even an important building like the Palazzo Strozzi (1489–1539) probably had no more than a hundred men working on it.[10] Rather than sheer size, patrons could only seek prestige through the quality of their buildings, leading them to seek out not the largest work forces but the best-skilled workers.

Beside the restrictions placed on architectural production by the size and skills of the work force,

Figure 9.2

The supply side of the equation: the construction of the renaissance palace was conditioned by the guild labour system. *Building of a Palace*, (c.1500), artist Piero di Cosimo. The John and Mable Ringling Museum of Art, Sarasota, Florida.

the organization of the work force was also significant. By the *trecento* (fourteenth century), Florence already had a 'conglomerate' guild for all the building crafts – the *Maestri* or masters in stone and wood – dominated by merchants and manufacturers. Active masters each employed several apprentices, with apprenticeships lasting an average of six years. These apprentices were a valuable source of cheap labour, and constituted by far the greatest part of the skilled wage labour force employed by a master. On a large private project, the client would appoint an architect or master-builder, a paymaster and treasurer, perhaps a measurer, perhaps a 'foreman' or supervisor as assistant to the architect, and several small trade-masters.

Some masters worked for clients for wages while others worked on a contract basis. In the former case, the client set the wages paid to master, apprentices and labourers, and the master was in effect only a 'gang-leader'. In the latter, masters could be petty-capitalist employers, pocketing the difference between contract value and the wages they set for their employees.

This kind of guild-based building production is normally characterized as conservative in technique and in social relations of production, as well as limited in quantitative capacity. Goldthwaite broadly concurs, and sees most innovation coming from the formation of architects as a category of professional designers, outside of the pre-existing crafts. In other words, in renaissance Florence, we find a first instance of the separation of the designer from the artisan, and with it the birth of the modern category and concept of the artist.

Although this in itself is a well-known story, Goldthwaite stresses the many opportunities presented to architects, denied to their predecessor master-builders: to undertake several projects at once; to specialize in design, rather than building supervision; to take advantage of competition between patrons for their services to extract better pay, conditions and rights of artistic self-expression. All this originates in changes on the demand side, specifically, in the development through competitive display of demand for novelty within the canons of taste. 'If the architect in the Renaissance began to play with many more of his own peculiar ideas, it was because the market for his services had changed, challenging him to be more inventive and original.'[11]

On the supply side the key change was, Goldthwaite argues, the development at the start of the renaissance of the ubiquitous general artist, prepared to work as goldsmith, jeweller, sculptor, painter or architect – thus transcending the horizontal craft division of labour, where one worker operated in one trade using one material, as well as introducing an extra element into the vertical division of labour, that of the separation of design, supervision and the execution of work. With a few important exceptions, 'the monumental civic buildings of the fourteenth century posed fewer problems of structure and engineering than of decoration; it was therefore natural to turn them over to sculptors and goldsmiths.'[12] By contrast, masons were limited in their opportunity for artistic expression, as they often had to work on just one building for many years. In any case, neither building function nor construction techniques were complex enough to need masons to develop a highly specialized design talent.

Overall, Goldthwaite paints a picture of conservative and imitative craftsmen masons and carpenters, together with innovative architects. The crafts are purely restrictive of building design at this time, setting limits on what architects could imagine and get built; technical limits which most Renaissance architects unthinkingly accepted. However, Goldthwaite is careful to explain that this scope for architectural innovation was created by the growth of a market which permitted and required it.

DEMAND AND SUPPLY

John Summerson's *Georgian London,* is perhaps the single most influential model for writing the history of the building of any city in any period. It uses two key concepts of wealth and taste, both of which are on the demand side of the economic equation.[13] Despite referring to the craftsmen, master-builders, surveyors and architects, Summerson spends few words on the craftsmen, principally because by the end of the eighteenth century in London these workers were firmly subordinated to the master-builder. Summerson's response is to concentrate on the apparent decision-makers, clients and developers.

Goldthwaite, however, is dealing with a society in which no developers stand between the client and the craftsmen and architects. Consequently he goes beyond Summerson's model to consider the supply side of production and work equally with the demand side of need and expenditure; for Goldthwaite, the opposition between demand (clients) and supply (building producers of all kinds) seems evident. It is also a division of social and economic class, and Goldthwaite complements his focus on the upper classes with a study of a cross-section of the Florentine working-class.

By polar contrast with Summerson, Linda Clarke has written a history of the building of London in much the same period, but with the emphasis entirely on the side of supply.[14] Clarke's focus is on the world of the building workers and their employers, and her thesis is that changes in the system of production partly determined the development of demand and the built environment. In her view, developers, builders, clients and architects only appear to have autonomous decision-making capacity. Their decisions are actually constrained by relatively hidden developments in the obscure world of the building labour process.

Goldthwaite's approach can therefore be characterized as falling somewhere midway between Summerson and Clarke. The question we are left with is whether Goldthwaite's methodology is simply the one most appropriate to renaissance Florence, or whether, suitably adapted, it could aid our understanding of the building of later, industrial capitalist cities?

REFERENCES

1   Richard Goldthwaite, *The Building of Renaissance Florence: An Economic and Social History*, (Johns Hopkins University Press, Baltimore, 1980).
2   Goldthwaite, *The Building of Renaissance Florence*, p. 67.
3   Goldthwaite, *The Building of Renaissance Florence*, pp. 68–9.
4   Goldthwaite, *The Building of Renaissance Florence*, pp. 75–6.

5   Goldthwaite, *The Building of Renaissance Florence*, p. 77.
6   Goldthwaite, *The Building of Renaissance Florence*, pp. 87–90.
7   Fernand Braudel, *The Perspective of the World*, (Collins, London, 1984).
8   Goldthwaite, *The Building of Renaissance Florence*, p. 422.
9   Goldthwaite, *The Building of Renaissance Florence*, p. 119.
10 Goldthwaite, *The Building of Renaissance Florence*, p. 123.
11 Goldthwaite, *The Building of Renaissance Florence*, pp. 354–5.
12 Goldthwaite, *The Building of Renaissance Florence*, p. 357.
13 John Summerson, *Georgian London*, Barrie and Jenkins, London, revised edition, 1988).
14 Linda Clarke, *Building Capitalism*, (Routledge, London, 1992).

BIBLIOGRAPHY

Fernand Braudel, *The Perspective of the World*, (Collins, London, 1984).
Linda Clarke, *Building Capitalism*, (Routledge, London, 1992).
Caroline Elam, 'Lorenzo the Magnificent and the Florentine Building Boom', *Art History*, v.1 (1978).
Richard Goldthwaite, *Private Wealth in Renaissance Florence: a Study of Four Families*, (Princeton University Press, Princeton, 1968).
Richard Goldthwaite, 'The Florentine Palace as Domestic Architecture', *American History Review*, v.77 (1972).
Richard Goldthwaite, 'The Building of the Strozzi Palace: the Construction Industry in Renaissance Florence', *Studies in Medieval and Renaissance History*, v.10 (1973).
Richard Goldthwaite, *The Building of Renaissance Florence: an Economic and Social History*, (Johns Hopkins University Press, Baltimore, 1980).
D. Herlihy, 'Distribution of Wealth in a Renaissance Community', in P. Abrams and E. Wrigley (eds.), *Towns in Societies*, (Cambridge University Press, Cambridge, 1978).
Erwin Panofsky, 'Artist, Scientist, Genius: Notes on the 'Renaissance-Dammerung', in W.K. Ferguson et al (eds.), *The Renaissance: Six Essays*, (New York, 1962).
John Summerson, *Georgian London*, (Barrie and Jenkins, London, revised edition, 1988).

Thorstein Veblen, *The Theory of the Leisure Class*, (Penguin, New York, 1979). First published 1899.

C. Wilkinson, 'The New Professionalism in the Renaissance', in Spiro Kostof (ed.), *The Architect: Chapters in the History of the Profession*, (New York, 1977).

10

CITY OF SPECTACLE

RENAISSANCE AND BAROQUE ROME

Jeremy Melvin

For the entire span of the Italian renaissance, generations of Roman patrons and architects attempted to turn Rome into a city of spectacle. They drew both on its glorious, ancient past and its status as St Peter's See, the mother diocese of the western, Catholic Church. If this combination of pagan and Christian precedents seems incongruous, the project of joining together classical civilization with what was seen as the true religion was the central intellectual aim of the renaissance, and was prefigured as early as the fourteenth century in the sixth canto of *Paradiso* by the poet Dante Alighieri (1265–1321). The emperor Constantine's (280–337) conversion to Christianity had set a precedent for the amalgamation of political and religious power to which subsequent popes aspired but rarely achieved. Constantine had been frustrated in his attempts to rebuild Rome around important Christian monuments, deciding eventually to found Constantinople as his new capital.[1] After the split in the empire which this heralded, followed shortly afterwards by the Great Schism between Catholic and Orthodox Christianity, Rome entered a long period of decline. In 1389, at the very dawn of the renaissance, and when the papacy returned from its 80 year exile in Avignon, Rome was an untidy, decayed labyrinth, with little more than ruins to show for its former glory.

Pope Nicholas V (reigned 1447–55), a friend and confidant of Leon Battista Alberti (1404–72), the greatest renaissance architectural theorist, made one of the first and most articulate cases for beautifying the city. On his deathbed he argued that creating spectacles was the only way of reinforcing religious belief among the illiterate masses who were unable to understand religion through reading.[2] However, a combination of political, topographical and artistic factors prevented the fulfilment of the dream, which was to elude many determined patrons and talented architects until the seventeenth century. We will examine here how the papacy, their families and the Roman oligarchy sought to overcome these difficulties.

POLITICS AS A WORK OF ART

Rome's political structure was even more convoluted than most Italian cities of this time. In some ways it resembled a monarchy with the pope as king, but the position was not hereditary and the incumbent often did not come from Rome. Unlike the dukes of Urbino and Mantua or even the Venetian doges (dukes), the pope claimed political primacy over the whole of Europe, including the great monarchies of Austria, France and Spain. This gave the position great significance across the continent, but also invited intervention and influence from powerful foreign forces. Nominally elected by the college of cardinals who wanted to avoid any one clique gaining ascendancy over the others, popes were deliberately chosen from different parties and families to their predecessors. Old age and illness were often to the advantage of a candidate; a young, vigorous pope might live long enough to centralize power. Each new reign heralded a different policy, in building and patronage as well as in politics, even if the intent remained the same. None of this augured well for the emergence of a long-term, coherent building programme necessary to turn Rome into a city of spectacle. Instead various unrelated, incomplete fragments littered the city.

The aristocracy, too, was heterogeneous. There were some families, such as the Colonna and Massimi, with a long lineage and distinguished forbears, but they were interspersed and eventually eclipsed by the *nouveaux riches* families often founded by holders of papal offices. The ideal of a celibate priesthood did not prevent excessive nepotism and the filling of lucrative sinecures with 'nephews' (illegitimate sons), who consolidated the power of these new families. Among this group are many of the most enthusiastic papal builders including Julius II della Rovere (reigned 1503–13), Paul III Farnese (reigned 1534–49), and the three great patrons of the baroque, Urban VIII Barberini (reigned 1623–44), Innocent X Doria Pamphili (reigned 1644–55) and Alexander VII Chigi (reigned 1655–67).

Jacob Burckhardt, the great nineteenth century art historian, argued that this renaissance period saw the emergence of the 'state as a work of art'.[3] This did not mean that the countries physically resembled paintings or statues, rather that each aspect of statecraft was subjected to intellectual scrutiny; this process is exemplified in the demonic pragmatism of the statesman and political theorist Nicolo Machiavelli (1469–1527), author of *The Prince* (1513). While this paved the way for the emergence of absolute monarchies in Spain and France, if the papal state was examined in this way, its *raison d'être*, being dependent on mysticism and tradition, evaporated. The papacy could then not share the benefits of developments in political theory without becoming just another monarchy, one that could never rival the resources of the great European superpowers enriched by the conquest of the Americas.[4]

THE TURN TO ARCHITECTURE

The contrast between Alexander VI (reigned 1492–1502) – from the notorious Borgia family – and his almost immediate successor Julius II marked a turning point in the papacy's attitude to architecture. Under Alexander, Rome did indeed come close to becoming a political 'work of art' in the manner of other states. He almost succeeded in making his position hereditary but his son Cesare died, probably through poisoning, and Alexander did not long outlive him. After Alexander's death Julius was unable to retain control of various territories the Borgias had annexed, and thus also unable to match Alexander's political gains. Julius turned instead to architecture to consolidate his position. He aspired to the arcadian dream of the renaissance intellectual by persuading the artists and architects Donato Bramante (1444–1514), Raphael Sanzio (1483–1520) and Michelangelo Buonarroti (1475–1564) all to work for him, cut several new roads through Rome's tortuous urban fabric, and crucially embarked, in 1506, on the most ambitious project of the renaissance, the rebuilding of St. Peter's.

St. Peter's disobeyed the first law of papal building projects – only attempt what can be completed in your lifetime. Even if its importance was such that Julius' successors could hardly leave it unfinished, they, rather than Julius, would be the beneficiaries of any increased prestige. St. Peter's was not completed until more than a century after Julius' death, having gone through a sequence of major design revisions. In any case its extravagance provoked a reaction across Christendom. When in 1517 Martin Luther lit the smouldering tinder-box of discontent by nailing his 95 Theses to the church door in Wittenberg, the taxes levied by the church for St. Peter's were among his targets. If Julius had a clear end for beautifying Rome, his means were faulty; Luther's action sparked the Reformation, which was irreparably to damage papal power. In 1527 Rome was sacked by a mercenary army with the acquiescence of Charles V (1500–1558), King of Spain and the Holy Roman Emperor; this invasion finally ended any chance of Rome being a major player on the European stage.

Beside his problems with St. Peter's, Julius was also frustrated in his desire for an urban plan for Rome. Rome was a complex topographical artefact, unsuited

Figure 10.1

The centralized plan of buildings such as the Tempietto, Rome, (1502), was considered inappropriate for the city of spectacle. Architect Donato Bramante.

to the contemporary architectural theory which favoured the idea of freestanding buildings on square or circular plans.[5] Bramante, Julius' favourite architect, designed one of the most perfect examples, the exquisite and tiny Tempietto (1502), and the same architect's early designs for St Peter's followed the then fashionable centralized plan form. This approach, however, did not suit the liturgical need, reinforced after the Counter Reformation, for longitudinally planned churches which gave a large space for the congregation and clearly separate space for the clergy. Nor did the centralized plan give much scope for incorporating the existing pieces of urban fabric which were so crucial to Rome's character, as it required regularly-shaped sites which were expensive in a city like Rome where land ownership was complex. Rather than addressing existing cities, renaissance theorists planned new ones, such as Sforzinda (before 1464) by Antonio Averlino Filarete (1400–69). At least one earlier pope, Pius II Piccolomini (reigned 1458–64), had chosen this path, rebuilding his family town of Corsignano and renaming it Pienza in his honour.

Rome's urban fabric is an interwoven palimpsest. Its ancient layout was around the legendary seven hills. Six of these formed the arc of a circle, centred on the seventh. The formation echoes a giant, natural amphitheatre, the arc being the seats and the central hill being the stage. The valley in between forms the orchestra. The ancients organized their city to take advantage of this structure, with residential areas on the arc of hills, focusing on the Capitoline and Palatine hills where the civic government was situated, while the main location of public interchange, the forum, filled the orchestra. When the empire became Christian, this tight structure was exploded. Christian sites had to be incorporated into the urban fabric, but many were martyrdom sites or secret meeting places located away from the existing centre. Rome now was redefined around several centres, each some distance apart – the Vatican where St. Peter was buried, the Lateran which became the mother church of western christianity, and the rest of the seven most important churches. Much ingenuity was exercized in creating rituals and urban monuments to weave these diverse centres together.

At the time of Julius II, the only way of linking these sites was by cutting long and straight streets, super-imposing a diagram over a messy, physical form. Several of his successors began to develop architectonic devices to bring the diagrammatic intention closer to physical reality, notably Sixtus V (1585–90) who erected giant obelisks at important intersections. But these monumental markers came from Ancient Egypt, and contemporary artistic ideas still did not offer a specific way of binding the city together.

ARCHITECTURAL AND URBAN THEORY AT THE SERVICE OF ROME

The evolution of architectural theories particularly suited to Rome's diverse topographical, social and political character was long and tortuous, and can broadly be divided into three stages. We shall look at these in turn, each illustrated by a particular kind of architectural project.

The first stage can be seen by comparing the Palazzo Massimi (1532–6) and Palazzo Farnese (begun 1534, top storey added 1546) where competing families took the renaissance palace type and adapted it to their means. These two palaces are physically close and their periods of construction overlapped, but are otherwise almost as different as they could be. The Massimi family employed Baldassare Peruzzi (1481–1536) as architect and the Farnese family used Antonio da Sangallo (1485–1546). The circumstances of the families was different too, for the Massimi came from an ancient patrician family, claiming descent from Fabius Maximus Cunctator, the great dictator who had defeated the threat from the Carthaginian general Hannibal in the third century BC. The Farnese, on the other hand, were part of the new papal oligarchy, of relatively humble origins and without substantial resources until one of their number became pope as Paul III. The huge sources of wealth which this opened to the Farnese allowed them to build the most perfect example of the ideal renaissance palazzo type in Rome, a graphic demonstration of the usurpation of power. David Dunster and Graham Ive have already described the evolution of the *palazzo* type in Florence, but here the inspiration is taken not just from

a previous building but also from a text: Alberti's *De Re Aedificatoria* (1452). Following Alberti's book, and in contrast to Alberti's own designs for the Palazzo Rucellai (1446–51) in Florence, the Farnese palace is freestanding and entirely fills a rectangular plot. It has a large piazza in front to allow its massive presence to be admired, and there is both an atrium and a garden, all organized regularly and symmetrically about a central axis.

The Massimi, reliant only on inherited wealth, could not compete in such ostentatious terms. Instead the architect Peruzzi had to use considerable ingenuity to fit the Massimi's programmatic needs onto an awkwardly-shaped site. Behind a seductively curved façade are two atria, each giving a separate residence to different brothers of the family, while retaining the maximum possible presence of the public street façade. Illusion is the keynote of the design and decoration, more subtle and more delicate than the bombastic mass which the Farnese's wealth made available to them.[6] If at one level this comparison shows the eclipse of old wealth and power by the new, it was also a harbinger of a more appropriate strategy for achieving the beautification of the whole

Figure 10.2

The massive Palazzo Farnese, Rome, (1534–46), product of the Farnese family's accession to the papal ranks. Architect Antonio da Sangallo.

Figure 10.3

Complex family relations and
limited funds accommodated
in the plan of the Palazzo
Massimi, Rome, (1532–6),
architect Baldassare Peruzzi.
The residence for Angelo
Massimi is on the left, and for
Pietro Massimi on the right.

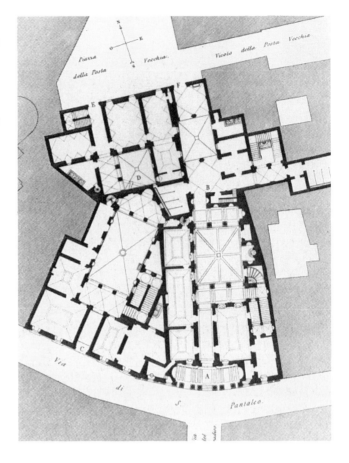

city. Such a departure from orthodox architectural
theory and emphasis on empirical manipulation of
form would inform the urban planning schemes of the
high baroque a century later.

The second stage in the development of an architectural theory specifically suited to Rome can be
disclosed by comparing San Carlo alle Quattro Fontane
(1633–67), designed by Francesco Borromini
(1599–1667), and San Andrea Quirinale (1658–70)
designed by Gianlorenzo Bernini (1598–1680). Church
architecture here responded to the political initiative of
the Counter Reformation, the Roman Catholic church's
reply to the Reformation, and so went right to the
heart of baroque design.

The Counter Reformation initially generated dull
reactionary architecture such as the Gesù church
(1568–84), designed by Giacomo Barozzi da Vignola

Figure 10.4

The first architecture of the Counter Reformation was comparatively uninventive. Gesù, Rome, (1568–84), architects Vignola and Giacomo della Porta.

(1507–73) and completed by Giacomo della Porta (1537–1602). But in the hands of Borromini, Bernini and their contemporary Pietro da Cortona (1596–1669) Rome's architecture took on a new and inspired direction. In short, they developed the kinds of formal innovations exemplified by Peruzzi in accord with political and liturgical demands.

Both San Andrea and San Carlo were commissioned by monastic orders whose roots lay in the struggles of the Counter Reformation. San Andrea was the noviciate church for the Jesuit order, founded by St. Ignatius as the intellectual vanguard of the revized church. San Carlo was built for the Trinitarians, a poor order devoted to raising funds for ransoming Christians captured by Turks. It was dedicated to the Holy Trinity, yet named for San Carlo Borromeo, the cardinal who presided over much of the Council of Trent (1545–64) which codified the precepts of the Counter Reformation. Borromeo's work on the internal reformation of the church was considered to be on a par with Ignatius' work in persuading heretics to recant and St. François Xavier's conversion of the heathens. All three were canonized early in the seventeenth century and were popular dedicatees of new churches. San Andrea and San Carlo therefore had a powerful new doctrinal orthodoxy to which they had to strictly adhere. On the other hand, there were no suitable architectural prototypes available which met these functional requirements, for churches like the Gesù were never seen as satisfactory, and consequently San Andrea and San Carlo offered opportunites to break away from the pedantic church type of the late sixteenth century.

The rivalry between Borromini and Bernini was manifested in different personalities, patronage and approaches to design. Apart from both using variations of an oval plan, the churches could hardly be more different in their search to address the demands of the Counter Reformation. Bernini was not a great formal

Figure 10.5

New religious practices required new architectural forms. San Andrea Quirinale, Rome, (1658–70), began to innovate. Architect Gianlorenzo Bernini.

innovator; he was content with a regular oval plan and on the exterior he merely superimposed a smaller order within a giant one for the portico. For effect Bernini relied instead on a combination of artistic media – he was a great sculptor as well as an architect – using shafts of light and decorative *putti* (cherubs) to imply the Ascension to heaven of St. Andrew, whose crucifixion is depicted in a painting over the altar.

Borromini, brooding, morose and eventually such a depressive that he ran himself through with a sword, depended much more on sophisticated formal devices than did Bernini's dynamic theatrics. Drawing on his background as a mason, a considerable understanding of geometry, and a taste for the more bizarre of ancient classical monuments, Borromini created a sophisticated symbolism in architecture. San Carlo's plan is predicated on a triangle, but this underlying form is about as detectable as, for example, the waltz

Figure 10.6

Architecture, sculpture and light used to maximum effect in the interior of San Andrea Quirinale.

Figure 10.7

San Carlo alle Quattro Fontane, Rome, (1633–67), more sophisticated formally than San Andrea Quirinale. Architect Francesco Borromini.

theme on which Beethoven's *Diabelli Variations* are based. Building up layers of meaning through intersections and interstices of bisecting lines, Borromini interwove a symbolic trinity of formal devices of an octagon, cross and oval. These have been interpreted by Leo Steinberg as having the further symbolism of the See of St. Peter, the world wide rule of Christ, and the Eucharist of the body of Christ, showing how Borromini used purely architectonic form to represent subtle theological concerns.[7]

The third and, for us, the last stage in the development of a suitable architectural theory concerns the evolution of the Piazza del Popolo, and shows how the kinds of innovation already described were finally woven into the Roman urban fabric. Churches so dominate the city of Rome that once problems of church design were tackled, it was a short step to addressing large scale pieces of urban fabric, and, as we shall see, in the Piazza del Popolo individual

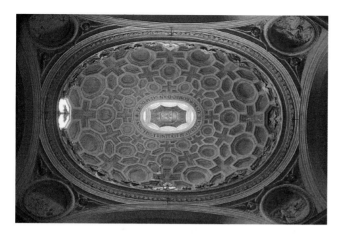

Figure 10.8

Geometry, symbolism and eclectic aesthetics combined in the interior of San Carlo alle Quattro Fontane. The ceiling is a tessellation of octagons, crosses and ovals.

Figure 10.9

A new northern gateway, the Piazza del Popolo, helped turn Rome into an urban work of art.

church buildings play a crucial role in the total urban ensemble.

Although not the grandest piazza in Rome, the Piazza del Popolo is the first to be encountered by those coming in to Rome from the north, the direction of almost all important visitors during this period. In the days of piety the little church of Santa Maria del Popolo had sufficed. Pilgrims could enter it as soon as they were through the city gate, and it had various subsidiary chapels giving a choice of saint from whom to beg intercession at the start of the visit. But as Rome in the seventeenth century became the playground of the leisured rich from across the globe – visitors intent on acquiring cultural kudos – the Piazza del Popolo had become increasingly embarrassing. For them, the Piazza del Popolo had to suggest that in Rome at least, the Pope and the church of which he was head were supreme.

To this end, the old tactic of straight streets was brought to its apogee. Under Alexander VII, in the middle of the seventeenth century, the ancient Via del Corso was straightened for a distance of two miles, and a street on each side (Babuini to the left and Ripiena to the right) also stretched into the distance. But Alexander did not leave it there. The two resulting wedges of convoluted urban fabric were tipped with the twin churches of Santa Maria in Monte Santo and Santa Maria dei Miracoli (1662–79) designed by Carlo Rainaldi (1611–91). Such is the perspective that from the centre of the Piazza del Popolo it appears that the entire fabric is composed of churches. A device borrowed from set design created an architectural illusion which hid uncomfortable political reality even more powerfully than the ensemble of St. Peter's comprising Michelangelo's dome (1546–64), Carlo Maderno's (1556–1629) west front (1607–12) and Bernini's colonnade (1656 onward).[8]

Finally Rome did indeed become a work of art, not as a state but as a city. Developments in palace type, church design and urban planning, among others, helped create an urban fabric suited to the grandeur and importance of the papal state. And so Rome took on its present form, an appropriate setting for Gregory Peck and Audrey Hepburn to frolic,[9] Anita Ekberg and Marcello Mastroianni to sport.[10]

REFERENCES

1   Richard   Krautheimer,   *Three   Christian   Capitals*, (University of California Press, Berkeley, 1983).

2   Paolo Portoghesi, *Rome of the Renaissance*, (Phaidon, London, 1972), pp. 11–12.

3   Jacob Burckhardt, *The Civilization of the Renaissance in Italy*, (Modern Library Editions, New York, 1954, first published 1860).

4   Paul Kennedy, *The Rise and Fall of the Great Powers*, (Random House, New York, 1988); and Fernand Braudel, *The Mediterranean and the Mediterranean World in the Age of Philip II*, (Fontana, London, 1975).

5   Paul Frankl, *Principles of Architectural History: the Four Phases of Architectural Style, 1420–1900*, (MIT Press, Cambridge, Mass., 1968, first published 1914).

6   Portoghesi, *Rome of the Renaissance*, pp. 188–92.

7   Anthony Blunt, *Borromini*, (Belknap Press, Cambridge, Mass., 1979); and Leo Steinberg, *Borromini's San Carlo Alle Quattro Fontane*, (Garland Publishing, New York, 1977).

8   Richard Krautheimer, *The Rome of Alexander VII*, (Princeton University Press, Princeton, 1985).

9   *Roman Holiday*, Director William Wyler, 1953.

10   *La Dolce Vita*, Director Federico Fellini, 1960.

BIBLIOGRAPHY

Leonardo Benevolo, *The History of the City*, (Scolar Press, London, 1980).

Leonardo Benevolo, *The Architecture of the Renaissance*, (Routledge and Kegan Paul, London, two volumes, 1978).

Anthony Blunt, *Artistic Theory in Italy, 1450–1600*, (Oxford University Press, Oxford, 1962).

Anthony Blunt (ed.), *Baroque and Rococo: Architecture and Decoration*, (Elek, London, 1978).

Anthony Blunt, *Borromini*, (Belknap Press, Cambridge, Mass., 1979).

Fernand Braudel, *The Mediterranean and the Mediterranean World in the Age of Philip II*, (Fontana, London, 1975).

Jacob Burckhardt, *The Civilization of the Renaissance in Italy*, (Modern Library Editions, New York, 1954, first published 1860).

Howard Hibbard, *Bernini*, (Penguin, Harmondsworth, 1965).

Paul Kennedy, *The Rise and Fall of the Great Powers*, (Random House, New York, 1988).

Spiro Kostof, *A History of Architecture: Settings and Rituals*, (Oxford University Press, Oxford, 1985).

Richard Krautheimer, *Three Christian Capitals*, (University of California Press, Berkeley, 1983).

Richard Krautheimer, *The Rome of Alexander VII*, (Princeton University Press, Princeton, 1985).

Peter Partner, *Renaissance Rome, 1500–1559: a Portrait of a Society*, (University of California Press, Berkeley, 1976).

Paolo Portoghesi, *Rome of the Renaissance*, (Phaidon, London, 1972).

Leo Steinberg, *Borromini's San Carlo Alle Quattro Fontane*, (Garland Publishing, New York, 1977).

Part Three

THEORY AND PRACTICE

11

THREE REVOLUTIONARY ARCHITECTS

BOULLÉE, LEDOUX, LEQUEU

Richard Patterson

Architectural discourse has always been about the tension between words and things, about the way we describe the things that we build. This difficult, and by no means clear, relationship may be seen in the collision of words, thoughts and buildings in our imaginations. Setting the terms of equivalence between thoughts, words, forms and things is how we generate 'meaning' when we are engaged in debates about architecture. And these debates are never concluded. Briefly, they tend to be characterized by the relative emphasis given to psychological, formal and 'significative' interpretations of architecture. Here we will consider how certain historical changes in the formal basis of architecture had a direct effect on its potential for signification.

In an essay with the provocative title 'Three Revolutionary Architects', Emil Kaufmann opened up such a discussion by pointing out that what is normally thought to have been new in twentieth century modern architecture originated in the eighteenth century and was, as a result, contemporaneous in origin with the modern, western, democratic (bourgeois) state.[1] In order to claim there was something significant in what he saw, Kaufmann had to rethink the way in which the development of architecture had previously been explained. Historians seeking either to support or criticize Kaufmann's claims had to find more and more convincing grounds for explaining why architecture had developed in a certain way. In the end, the issues raised in these kinds of debate have been concerned with the connections between cultural forms and political and economic institutions. They concern the potential of architecture to affect people's lives; that is, such debates are about the relative significance of architecture in general.

On the other side of the coin, as other essays in this book make clear, there is a persistent, recurrent dynamic in the practice of architecture in which the 'language' employed in design is either explored to produce more variety and complexity, or, in contrast, is 'purified' with the intention of returning to a past perfection. In either case, architects were emulating past practice, either as a set of forms from the past, or as what they thought the character of great practitioners to have been.

In the work of the three architects we are about to look at – Étienne–Louis Boullée (1728–99), Claude–Nicolas Ledoux (1736–1806) and Jean-Jacques Lequeu (1757–1825) – we begin to see clear evidence that something different and very new was beginning to happen. We notice that their work challenged not just the forms, composition and expression of the architecture of their age, but the very scope and nature of the discourse that was their legacy. What they were seeking was in fact a radically new vision of authority, an authority that had more to do with 'the light of reason', the logic of function and the articulation of purpose. We might also detect a way in which the physical substance of the building is no longer felt to be an embodiment of sense or meaning, but has become a simple medium, a mere *tablula rasa*, for representing forms, shapes and signifiers that might provoke and 'conduct' sensations, impressions and thoughts. Architecture, for these architects, became a form of 'writing', an arbitrary if useful tool for thinking about and representing something external to itself, something that might be used 'literally' to signify and build a new society, a rational society for which there was no prior model.

Boullée and Ledoux had been profoundly influenced by the ideas of their teacher Jacques-François Blondel (1705–74). From Blondel, as similarly from the *Essai sur l'architecture* (1753) of Marc-Antoine Laugier (1713–69), they had acquired a new meaning for the term 'natural', which, when applied to architecture, instead of implying the imitation of a cosmic or universal pattern, involved greater concern for fitness for purpose and the proper use of materials. It was in such concepts that the beginnings of a departure from baroque architecture lay, for the baroque requirement of organic unity in the whole was superseded by the imperative to express the elements of composition as self-sufficient units. The work of Blondel's students might also be interpreted as a more emphatic form of the tendency in French architecture, in the principle of *dégagement*, to express the 'parts' of a composition.

But through the expression of the larger scale elements of composition as independent volumes without the old sense of continuity in line and gradation of scale, we see a further intention to express the distinct, unique and individual character of each building according to its function.

These transformations in composition and this new use of form also had their counterpart in the way ornament was used. No longer would the formal characteristics of a building be intended to sustain the multiple meanings of metaphorical or allegorical allusions, but to articulate a more explicit, univocal narrative. From our perspective, we might say that meaning was rendered in a more simple and direct way. For example, whereas the desire to imbue composition with content previously might have been accomplished through the use of statuary or symbols drawn from classical mythology (such as the crescent moon or the figure of the goddess Diana as an allusion to feminine morality), in the new context there would be a 'literal' visual depiction of some central aspect of function (such as a horseshoe in a keystone to indicate the occupants of some particular barn) which clearly, 'transparently', and unequivocally represented the meaning of the building.

As the philosopher Giambattista Vico (1668–1744) noted in *New Science* (1744), metaphor (saying something is 'like' something else, such as saying a king is like a lion) was being replaced historically by metonymy (representing something by its attributes, or noting something normally physically adjacent to it, such as 'crown' for 'king') as the predominant means of characterizing objects. In the context of science and linguistics, we note similarly a transformation from symbolism to realism. In architecture, this pursuit of a new mode of representation became conscious as *architecture parlante*, that is as an architecture which 'speaks' and represents its meaning in function.

ÉTIENNE-LOUIS BOULLÉE

In the light of this turn toward metonymic references, we can better understand the monumentality of Boullée's architecture. In his many theoretical and unrealized designs there are severe contrasts in scale,

Figure 11.1

Purified language as *architecture parlante* – the direct communication of emotion and concept through pure architectural form. Cenotaph for Newton, (1784), architect Étienne-Louis Boullée.

and compositions made up of simple, clearly delineated elements, with surfaces only occasionally disrupted by fenestration. There is, moreover, an immediate emotional and conceptual effect achieved purely by architectonic means, normally through a purity of geometrical form set against the raw energy of the sky. The most striking projects are assembly halls, museums, libraries, cenotaphs, towers, gates, and triumphal arches – buildings concerned with activities involving mental concentration, spectacles and performances rather than the vagaries, complexities and contrarieties of everyday life. Such buildings are concerned with very specific purposes, with pure, even univocal meanings.

This does not mean, however, that the primary forms Boullée adopted could not be similarly configured for buildings of different use. Indeed, his architectural geometry was considered as a universally and variously competent mode of articulation, capable of dealing with any building type; a town hall, for example, could, at a diagrammatic level, be identical with a temple or a palace of justice. Nonetheless it would be necessary to signify the component elements of the activities taking place inside through the creation of explicit visual signs.

In the proposal for the Royal Library (1785), an oblong rectangular plan of pronounced linearity is surmounted by a roof, constructed as a coffered barrel vault and supported continuously on an uninflected row of Ionic columns. At the end of the room, both colonnade and roof return towards the axis in order to define a particular limit to the volume. The columns, however, do not close the space; by the size of the opening that remains and a glimpse of additional fabric which can only be incompletely seen, there is a suggestion of further spaces beyond the limit of the room. Light enters both through this opening and through a massive skylight cut into the apex of the vault. The room is open to the sky.

This enigmatic proposal is most curious, for such a structure cannot be constructed in traditional stone masonry. The geometry and the forms it employs, however, provide a neutral basis, a *tabula rasa* upon which is projected a visual 'hieroglyphic' (a sign which actually looks like the thing it refers to), which in this instance is the architectonic use of the shelves of books to create a four-tiered base for the colonnade. The books are the base upon which the fabric of the building rests. The books act as the 'part' representing the 'whole' institution; the books are a metonymic

Figure 11.2

Architecture can be used to signify something outside of itself. In the Royal Library project, (1785), the drawing and the proposed building are both metonymic signs for the institution of the library. Architect Étienne-Louis Boullée.

sign. The institution is further alluded to, signified, by the gesturing figures in Boullée's drawing. There is no use of allegorical or metaphorical reference. The drawing, like the building, is a metonymic reference to the institution. For this reason the representation is given through a selection of details; it need not describe its content exhaustively.

CLAUDE-NICOLAS LEDOUX

Ledoux's architecture, in contrast, was developed with very different objectives. Firstly, in both his real and theoretical projects there are a large number of relatively small scale buildings. Ledoux in fact built more than any other architect of his generation, suggesting that his projects, unlike Boullée's, were all conceived within plausible budgets. Secondly, there is a significant discrepancy between the expression of buildings for individual clients and the expression of theoretical projects. This suggests that the use of architectural language was context specific, rather than an expression of a universal condition or meaning.

The primary elements of Ledoux's architectural discourse are made rational in several ways. Despite his strong formal capabilities, for example, through some very complex distortions of scale many of the works appear to be fragments torn from a larger object. In his later work, when it can be argued that he used a stripped-down geometric architectural language merely derived from classicism, this tendency to treat

Figure 11.3

A small building conceived as part of a larger geometrical system. Barrière de la Villette, Paris, (1785–9), architect Claude-Nicholas Ledoux.

composition in a ludic way is even more pronounced. The elevations and compositional volumes of his *barrières* or toll-houses (1785–9) demonstrate a certain rational ambivalence in the selection of form, which belies a tension between the relatively small-scale 'object' with which he was limited and a sense of yearning for a larger, geometrically systematic context. In trying to meet this challenge, as we shall see, he achieved his most ingenious realizations.

In 1771 Ledoux was appointed inspector of the Royal Saltworks at Arc-et-Senans near the Forest of Chaux in the Franche-Comté. With the backing of a royal administration intent on the reorganization of state industries according to Enlightenment ideas of rational planning and social progress, Ledoux was given here the authority to construct a complete production facility for the manufacture of salt, the Saline de Chaux, (1775–9), in which he developed an architecture which represented the factory both visually, as an institutional concept, and in terms of its functional requirements.

Figure 11.4

Rational expression of a mode of production. Second project for Saline de Chaux, (1775–9), architect Claude-Nicholas Ledoux.

Ledoux produced two schemes for the project, the first of which, while demonstrating a competent awareness of the requirements of salt making, remained largely a formal conception. The second was the more progressive and interesting. Overall, the plan is one of an oblong rectangle separating two semi-circles, only one of which was constructed. In the centre of the rectangle is a pavilion housing administration, visitors' suites and a chapel. Adjacent to this are two identical sheds housing the salt-making activities, storage and distribution facilities. Timber for fuel was stored in the open interior of the semi-circle while secondary accommodation, including workers' housing and the activities of coopers and blacksmiths, is placed on the circumference. A potential for expansion existed in the second semi-circle and along the radiating lines of avenues focused on the director's house.

For the Saline de Chaux the division of space was organized not just to signify, as we saw with Boullée, but according to the actual sequence of tasks and procedures of production. In addition, this co-ordination of parts was not artificially integrated and expressed as a single building, but as a set of discrete entities in the manner of a factory town. This was the first time that a human community had been so comprehensively and single-mindedly designed as the rational expression of a mode of production.

The signs that Ledoux used to indicate the purpose of this factory are metonymic as well. Reference, for example, is persistently made to salt through the depiction of a rather viscous super-saturated salty fluid, in the

Figure 11.5

The building as autonomous element within a logical whole. Director's House, Saline de Chaux, architect Ledoux.

Figure 11.6

Detail of columns, Director's House, Saline de Chaux.

Figure 11.7

Entrance, Saline de Chaux.

Figure 11.8

Metonymic reference to salt, Saline de Chaux.

use of stalactites as ornament and in the oozing surface rustication of the buildings. In this we see an intention not only to represent the institution in a functional and utilitarian way, but also to render its character as a community, as something conscious and natural. Again, the formal structure of this representation is merely conventional and, indeed, subservient to other imperatives. Parts can quite happily be left out. Neither is there any sense in which the totality of the institution need be characterized beyond a selection of strategic details.

Signs are employed in many of Ledoux's projects. For example, those for housing various artisans in his ideal city at Chaux were frequently generated out of the geometry of an essential element with which the artisans worked. Thus the *forestiéres* (woodsmen) and *bûcherons* (charcoal burners) were given houses with log-like forms, while the cooper's house was made up of hoop-shaped circles. This again calls to mind the question of the mode of representation employed. Here again it turns out to be 'realistic' visual metonymy in which, as in referring to 'crown' for king, salt refers to the salt factory and the salt makers, hoops to coopers, logs and pyres to woodsmen and charcoal burners.

Figure 11.9

Dwelling form derived from artisanal practice (1). Charcoal Burner's House and Workshop, Saline de Chaux. The profile refers to the wigwam-like pyres traditionally used to make charcoal.

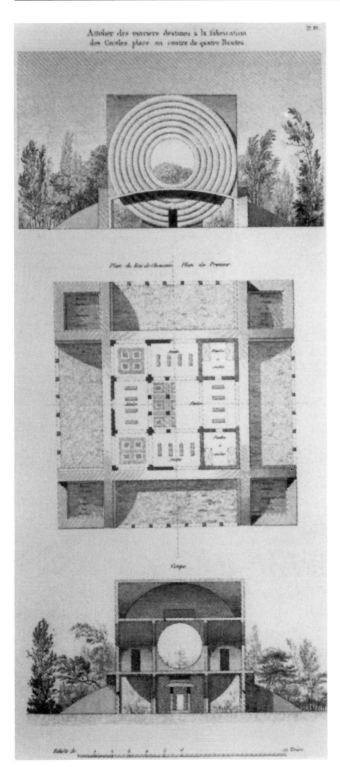

Figure 11.10

Dwelling form derived from artisanal practice (2). Cooper's House and Workshop, Saline de Chaux. The concentric rings are an obvious reference to round barrels and hoops.

JEAN-JACQUES LEQUEU

Although far less well-known than either Boullée or Ledoux, Lequeu is interesting because of the extreme lengths he went to in rejecting the conventions of the past. On one level, his work anticipates a future in which architecture is dominated by the concerns of function and programme to the complete exclusion of any ordering device at all.

Lequeu's projects are often characterized as morbid for their seemingly bitter rejection of the norm, but in this there is also a certain prescience capturing what was to be the future of an architecture given over to the specious objectivity of the programme. In the design for 'The Gothic House' (undated), for example, the composition is entirely governed by a literary text which purportedly describes the ritual spaces of Masonic initiation. To this Lequeu adds quaintly mystical references, but little of known architectural device and nothing of order save the implication of a route. It can barely be

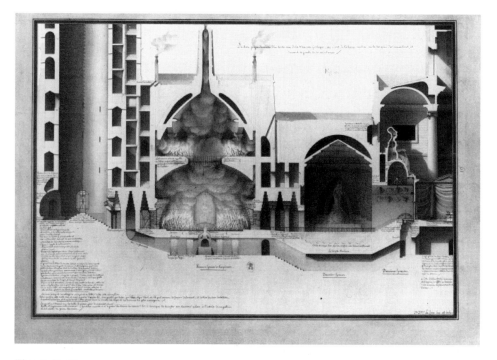

Figure 11.11

Hardly a 'building' at all. Masonic rituals as route in The Gothic House, architect Jean-Jacques Lequeu.

said to be a 'building' in the common sense meaning of the word. Ledoux therefore represents an extreme in the use of a multiplicity of architectural languages for the sake of univocal narrative composition.

REFERENCE

1   Emil Kaufmann, 'Three Revolutionary Architects, Boullée, Ledoux, and Lequeu', *Transactions of the American Philosophical Society*, ns.42/43 (1952), pp. 433–564.

BIBLIOGRAPHY

Edmund Burke, *A Philosophical Enquiry into the Origin of Our Ideas of the Sublime and Beautiful*, (Basil Blackwell, Oxford, 1987, edited by J.T. Boulton). Originally published 1757.

Y. Christ, *Projets et Divagations de Claude-Nicolas Ledoux*, (Éditions du Minotaure, Paris, 1961).

James Curl, *The Art and Architecture of Freemasonry*, (B.T. Batsford, London, 1991).

Philippe Duboy, *Lequeu: An Architectural Enigma*, (MIT Press, Cambridge, Mass., 1987).

Wolfgang Herrmann, *Laugier and Eighteenth Century French Theory*, (Zwemmer, London, 1985).

Emil Kaufmann, 'Three Revolutionary Architects, Boullée, Ledoux, and Lequeu', *Transactions of the American Philosophical Society*, ns.42/43 (1952), pp. 433–564.

Emil Kaufmann, *Architecture in the Age of Reason*, (Harvard University Press, Cambridge, Mass., 1955).

James Leith, *Space and Revolution: Projects for Monuments, Squares and Public Buildings in France 1789–1799*, (McGill-Queen's University Press, Montreal and Kingston, 1991).

Claude-Nicolas Ledoux, *L'Architecture considérée sous le rapport de l'art, des moeurs et de la législation*, (Lenoir, Paris, 1804).

T.A. Marder, 'Context for Claude-Nicolas Ledoux's Oikema', *Arts Magazine*, v.54 n.1 (1979), pp. 174–6.

Helen Rosenau, 'Claude-Nicolas Ledoux', *The Burlington Magazine*, v.88 (1946), pp. 162–8.

Helen Rosenau, *Boullée's Treatise on Architecture*, (Alec Tiranti, London, 1953).

Helen Rosenau, *The Ideal City*, (Routledge and Kegan Paul, London, 1959).

Helen Rosenau, 'Boullée and Ledoux as Town-Planners, a Re-assessment', *Gazette des Beaux Arts*, v.63 (1964), pp. 173–90.

Helen Rosenau, *Boullée and Visionary Architecture*, (Academy Editions, London, 1976).

Edward Sekler, 'Formalism and the Polemical Use of History', *Harvard Architecture Review*, v.1 (1980), pp. 32–9.

Manfredo Tafuri, *Architecture and Utopia: Design and Capitalist Development*, (MIT Press, Cambridge, Mass., 1976).

Georges Teyssot, 'Emil Kaufmann and the Architecture of Reason: Klassizimus and 'Revolutionary Architecture'', *Oppositions*, n.13, (1978), pp. 46–75.

Anthony Vidler, 'The Architecture of the Lodges', *Oppositions*, n.5 (1976), pp.75–97.

Anthony Vidler, *The Writing of the Walls: Architectural Theory and the Late Enlightenment*, (Princeton University Press, Princeton, 1987).

Anthony Vidler, *Claude-Nicolas Ledoux*, (MIT Press, Cambridge, Mass., 1990).

Visionary Architects: Boullée, Ledoux, Lequeu, (University of St. Thomas, Houston, 1968).

12

BUILDING CLASSICISM

SPECULATIVE DEVELOPMENT IN EIGHTEENTH CENTURY PARIS

Maxine Copeland

From the late eighteenth century, the commonest dwellings built in Paris were the purpose-built *immeubles de rapport* or *immeubles* (blocks of rented apartments). Despite a classicist appearance, these immeubles have little in common with the kind of theoretically-informed classicism of architects like Étienne-Louis Boullée and Claude-Nicolas Ledoux that Richard Patterson describes in Chapter 11; they owe more to the operation of the speculative building market than to intellectual aesthetic considerations and monumental architecture. Classicism, as we shall see, suited the market as well as the Academicians.

THE RISE OF APARTMENT LIVING

Parisians had not, of course, always lived in immeubles. The high population density of the medieval city produced streets of tall buildings which filled their sites and were used in many different ways. Because the street was used for manufacture and commerce as well as circulation, the floors closest to the ground were most highly valued, and were generally given over to trade and manufacture. Upper floors contained dwellings.

By the seventeenth century, rooms in five-storey *maisons partagés* (shared houses) were rented in different combinations and for any function. A tenant might have rooms on several floors, living side-by-side with others. The subdivision of houses into self-contained flats, similar to apartments today, first occurred in the mid-eighteenth century in substantial buildings like the *hôtels* (town houses) abandoned by the aristocracy in the overcrowded and unsanitary Saint-Antoine and Louvre areas. When the purpose-built immeuble appeared soon after it was then a relatively new arrangement, with one or more identical flats stacked on each floor, the functions and sizes of the rooms clearly defined and services spatially separated. By the 1760s this was the norm.

How then did this new residential typology take hold, and what part did classicism play? Speculative development is a complex phenomenon, where investors construct buildings not for themselves but for rental or sale to others who are not usually known in advance. Investors gamble – speculate – that the market will repay them. To assess the role of classicism here, we must understand that speculation consists of seemingly isolated factors which together create the right market conditions. We will look at each in turn.

LAND AND FINANCE

When the *Fermiers Généraux* city wall was constructed in 1785, Parisians were still so concentrated in the city core that only one third of the enclosed area was as yet built upon. Much vacant land was of two sorts: aristocratic hôtels with gardens, or horticultural land belonging to religious institutions. Sites were usually sold to clear debt or fund other schemes. For example, the Hôtel de Soissons was sold by the creditors of the Prince de Carignan and eventually became the site of the Halle au Blé (corn exchange) and surrounding housing, and the Prince de Condé promoted his hôtel as the site of the Théâtre de l'Odeon scheme to finance his purchase of the Palais Bourbon.

On the other hand, before the 1789 Revolution, religious communities generally tried to retain land ownership. By only leasing land to speculators they obtained a rental income, with buildings and land reverting to their ownership after 99 years. However, religious property seized by the government at the Revolution was usually sold rather than leased. After 1793, when the whole city covered only 3370 hectares, over 400 hectares of such land was sold off for speculative development.[1] This included the land belonging to the Saint-Lazare house, purchased in 1821 for the laying out of the 'nouveau quartier Poissonnière'.

If land then was readily available, how was it purchased? Small developments, particularly single buildings constructed on sites of older ones, were usually financed by individuals. Such investments provided a regular rental income with owners often living in the best apartment of their building, and this

kind of revenue even tempted some of those commissioning hôtels to set them back from the street behind
rows of shops and flats.

Larger schemes required more complicated financial
arrangements. Many relied on bank loans for the initial

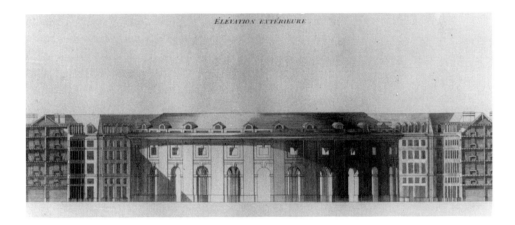

Figure 12.1

Halle au Blé, exterior. Extensive subsidization required for the corn exchange bankrupted the
financiers and architect alike.

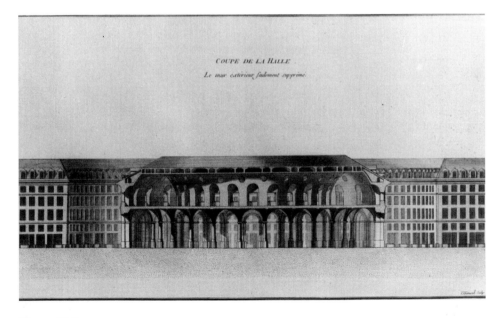

Figure 12.2

Halle au Blé, section.

outlay, but the means of repayment varied. In the Halle au Blé scheme (1763–6) the City Council who owned the site invited the submission of development projects from which they selected financiers Bernard and Charles Oblin, with Nicolas Le Camus de Mézières (1721–93) as architect. The Halle at the centre was to be financed through extra taxes on goods entering the city and the resale of surrounding land (on the assumption that the new development would increase land values). This proved problematic, for the need to raise revenue led to narrow streets, over-tall buildings and high plot prices. Few purchasers came forward and the developers were obliged to buy up most of the plots themselves, bringing ruin to all three.

A similar situation occurred with the Théâtre de l'Odeon project (1767–82) by Charles de Wailly

Figure 12.3

City and Crown financing often had to be rescued by private sector money. Place de l'Odéon, Paris, (1767–82), architects Charles de Wailly and Marie-Joseph Peyre.

Figure 12.4

Théâtre de l'Odéon, Paris, (1767–82). Reliance on private money displaced the theatre to the back of the scheme. Architects Charles de Wailly and Marie-Joseph Peyre.

(1730–98) and Marie-Joseph Peyre (1730–88). Originally to have had joint City Council and Crown funding, and partly offset by selling surrounding immeubles, this scheme eventually relied on a specially formed company using private money. The result was increased emphasis on the *lotissement* aspect of the scheme – the division of land into housing plots and roads – with the theatre given a less prominent site.[2]

Yet another version was the Rue de Rivoli development of 1801, with façades designed by Pierre-François-Léonard Fontaine (1762–1853) and Charles Percier (1764–1838). First initiated by Napoleon and the state, this rather hybrid scheme consisted solely of speculative housing but was intended as a setting for the Louvre and Tuileries. Plot sales were to have helped cover costs but restrictions imposed on prospective purchasers proved an obstacle, and Napoleon eventually had to offer tax concessions on the new houses and even to build on a large plot himself.

By the 1820s the system for financing large developments was clearer. Investors abandoned public buildings and concentrated on making new streets and selling either vacant plots or newly-built immeubles. Speculative companies were established to develop specific sites, as many names indicate: for example, the Société des terrains de Ruggieri et Saint-Georges, or the Société du nouveau quartier Poissonnière. By the time the roads and plots were laid out, however, an economic recession was underway and, unable to sell their sites, most companies were forced into liquidation. It was some 20 more years before the new streets were filled with housing.

DESIGNERS AND BUILDERS

The relationship between investor, architect and builder could be quite varied. For example, in smaller developments many contractors drew up designs themselves. Alternatively, other developments involved both an architect and a contractor, although this did not necessarily mean the architect had attended the Académie Royale, since many had a guild or craft background. Revolutionary and Napoleonic legislation merely codified this situation, since any who paid the

Figure 12.5

Corner of rue de Saintonge
and boulevard du Temple,
Paris, (1778). The architect
here, Samson-Nicolas Lenoir
le Romain, had long-standing
financial relationships with his
backers.

patente (licence) could call themselves architects. Nor
did the lowly nature of the immeuble exclude the
architectural élite, particularly in large developments:
de Wailly, Peyre, Fontaine and Percier were all
Académie trained and Grand Prix winners.

Despite pretensions to being a liberal profession,
many architects, including the best known, acted as
contractors and speculators. Some had a tacit agreement with speculators for mutual benefit, while others
were promoted by certain financiers over a long
period. Samson-Nicolas Lenoir le Romain (d. 1810),
designer of the Rue de Saintonge immeubles (1778)
and many others, was backed not only by his father-
in-law Riboutté, an insurance company director, but
also by the banker Kornmann.[3]

Architects could also belong to speculative development companies. For example, A. Constantin formed
the Société du nouveau quartier Poissonnière with
bankers and the Compagnie Saint-Georges with different individual investors. While building contractors
were rarely members (rather than employees) of these
societies, many used the societies' credit to purchase
plots, thereby achieving some independence and small
scale speculation.[4]

PRESSURES AND CONTROLS ON IMMEUBLE PROPORTIONS

Circulation in medieval Paris was primarily pedestrian,
forming a natural check on the expansion of the city

beyond a two mile range. Coupled with the pressure for a street-side position, this resulted in land being divided into sites as narrow as six metres. These medieval plot boundaries were surprisingly permanent, partly due to the piecemeal replacement of buildings but also because of their continuing suitability for urban life. Thus when land was laid out around the Halle au Blé, the proposed 'maisons commodes' (convenient and comfortable houses) for merchants and craftsmen had relatively narrow plots, when other contemporary developments already had wider street frontages.[5] Large scale development might permit, but did not oblige, changes in the house plots.

There were also legal restrictions. For example, the Généralité de Paris (City Treasury) regulated frontage projection and alignment along public highways, while the Chambre des Bâtiments (Office of Buildings) oversaw safety and structural soundness. More important for façade design were building height controls. Regulations of 1667 had already prohibited gables on street elevations and limited façade height to 15.60 metres. New regulations in 1783 introduced 12, 16 and 20 metre height maxima according to construction method and street width, and in 1784 a maximum height of 17.50 metres was set for the vertical wall of the façade plus 3.33 metres for the roof (which had to be within an imaginary line rising at 45° from the building edge). These regulations were adopted by law in 1791, and codified in 1807 under Napoleon.

THE FAÇADE

So far we have seen how changes in land and building use, finance, development and regulations provided the basic conditions in which the immeuble emerged. We can now turn to consider its design in more detail.

In terms of the façade, the more prestigious immeuble comprises an arcaded basement behind which are ground floor shops and lodgings in an *entresol* (a low storey inserted between two others), while up above are two *étages nobles* (principal floors) and a mansard (double slope) roof containing service rooms. A substantial house door or *porte-cochère* (carriage entrance to an inner courtyard) is sited centrally, often with an oculus (circular wall opening) at entresol level and a balcony above. This arrangement differs little from the street-side *hôtels sur rue* of the later eighteenth century. By contrast, in the most basic immeuble the arcades are replaced by shop fronts with straight lintels, the entresol is omitted, and the ground floor is reduced in height to equal those higher up. The porte-cochère is replaced by a simple doorway, not always symmetrically positioned. Above are four vertical floors, plus attic rooms arranged as flats. Obviously there are variations between those extremes, such as mouldings suggesting basement arcading, or upper floors reduced in height to impart greater status to those below. The 45° roof limit also allows an additional vertical storey, set back above the cornice, forming a kind of classical attic.

Just how these façade arrangements were arrived at, however, presents us with a problem. Firstly, training at the Académie Royale d'Architecture (later the École des Beaux-Arts) provided little help for immeubles design for its competitions addressed nothing less important than a gentleman's residence. And although concerned with more utilitarian matters, the École Centrale des Travaux Publics (which became the École Polytechnique after 1795) seems also to have ignored the humble immeuble.

Secondly, most publications were concerned only with monumental architecture, building materials, construction as a science, or the practicalities of contracting and estimating. Two which did give advice on immeubles were Charles Etienne Briseux's *Architecture moderne, ou l'art de bien bâtir pour toutes sortes de personnes* ('Modern Architecture, or the Art of Good Building for All Classes of People', 1728), and Charles Antoine Jombert's *Architecture moderne* ('Modern Architecture', 1764). Both present plans drawn by the architect Tiercelet in 1726. Jombert's examples include 'those built every day in Paris for leasing to merchants,' but he also makes clear why immeubles were not favoured by prestigious publications: 'For houses of this type there in no need to use the orders. It is much more important to know how to dispose the parts of the building than to be acquainted with the proportion of columns . . .'[6] Thus the Tiercelet plans depict how to fit apartments into difficult sites, while façades are of only secondary importance.

How then were façade designs arrived at? The answer lay close at hand. While the internal arrangements of the immeuble were developed in the eighteenth century, their façades derived from the *places royales* (royal squares) of the seventeenth century, themselves influenced by the Italian renaissance *palazzo* described by David Dunster and Graham Ive. It was only necessary to look around at existing buildings, which thus became the primary source material for many immeubles designers, particularly those with no pretensions to being 'architects'. Rather than a purely intellectual approach to architecture, practised in the rarified realms of the Academy and by its most famous architects, classicism emerged in the immeubles as an almost indigenous style, copied from extant buildings as an appropriate design solution to a new architectural problem.

THE THEORY AND PRACTICE OF SPECULATIVE CLASSICAL ARCHITECTURE

If immeuble classicism was born out of direct, first-hand visual experience of surrounding buildings, how did it differ from academic, theoretical classicism? At the generic level of the style, most immeubles are classical. Even the plainest, the Halle au Blé housing, acquires a classical feel through its regularity and direct association with the classical elements of the Halle itself. However, in other respects immeubles differ greatly from monuments or great private houses produced in the same period.

What of the notions of proportion and harmony in composition, central to any intellectual conception of classicism? The horizontal articulation of the immeuble façade was controlled largely by height regulations, accepted ceiling height minima, and the need to maximize rental income. Similar financial pressures and the traditional narrowness of sites meant that immeubles could not be detached buildings, so designers had no control over façade width and only a limited freedom in its bay divisions, since these were mainly determined by structural and internal arrangements.

The repetition of identical elements across a broad façade, seen in some monumental architecture of the time, might appear to have been consciously applied to the immeuble. Such simplified and geometricized design was however only effective when viewed in its entirety. By contrast, the immeuble, linked to others in a street frontage, was part of a potentially infinite façade. Not for nothing was the street surrounding the Halle au Blé nicknamed 'la rue éternelle' with 'ni commencement ni fin' ('the eternal street', with 'no start and no end').[7] Even when individual blocks, such as 12 rue de Tournon (1777) by Charles Neveu, were given a degree of grandeur through symmetry and enriched decorative detailing, their visual independence melted away when viewed as part of the street.

Neither architects nor critics seemed unduly worried by the potential monotony of the street fronts. In the case of the Halle au Blé, while the architect and theorist Jacques-François Blondel (1705–74) praised the Halle itself he ignored the surrounding streets. Other critical comments on the Halle au Blé likewise focused principally on the narrowness of the streets and not on the immeubles lining them.[8] In schemes which centred on a monument, the role of the surrounding houses was to provide funds and a setting for it; even where the speculative profit assumed greater importance, as with the Théâtre de l'Odéon, the immeubles remained visually subordinate. Only where houses alone constituted the scheme was greater attention given to their appearance, as with 12 rue de Tournon. In Percier and Fontaine's rue de Rivoli designs an important location, a powerful client and the hope of

Figure 12.6

Immeubles were generally not designed to appear distinctive. Napoleon's personal involvement contributed to a rare exception at the rue de Rivoli, Paris, (1801). Architects François-Léonard Fontaine and Charles Percier.

high resale prices resulted in a prestigious *place royale* format with careful detailing.

The exercise of creativity and aesthetic theory was thus severely limited in the immeuble. The building type implied no pretensions to great art, and the market functioned perfectly well without it. And yet classicism was a useful form for the speculative developer. Even in comparatively mean developments it required little detailing to impart a classical feel; around the Halle au Blé, regularity and horizontal banding that echoed the classically detailed Halle were sufficient to impart a certain aura and grandeur. However, the simplicity of the frameless openings was dictated by economy, and any reference to the simplicity of some monumental architecture was purely fortuitous. In fact, the more classical detailing on an immeuble the better, as suggestions of opulence attracted purchasers and tenants.

Perhaps the most important aspect of classicism was its inter-relation with the organizational mechanism of speculative house construction. Although the economic recession stopped the speculative societies from completing their building programmes in the 1820s, the economies of scale made possible, together with the regularity and large scale of developments, rendered the vague application of classicism more attractive. Indeed, these methods aided the continuation of classicism into the late nineteenth century, even when other styles were coming to the fore in monumental architecture. Classicism was part of a winning formula for the design and provision of

Figure 12.7

Rue de Tournon, Paris, (1777), architect Charles Neveu. As an integral part of the speculative house building industry, immeuble classicism like this was repeated throughout the nineteenth century.

residential accommodation, destined to be repeated over the decades to come.

REFERENCES

1   François Loyer, *Paris XIXe siècle: l'immeuble et la rue,* (Hazan, Paris, 1987), p. 19. Translated as *Paris, Nineteenth Century: Architecture and Urbanism,* (Abbeville, New York, 1988).

2   David Rabreau and Monika Steinhauser, 'Le Théâtre de l'Odéon de Charles de Wailly et Marie-Joseph Peyre, 1767–1782', *Revue de l'Art,* n.19 (1973), p. 14.

3   Michel Gallet, *Paris Domestic Architecture of the 18th Century,* (Barrie and Jenkins, London, 1972), pp. 18–9.

4   Michel Lescure, *Les sociétés immobilières en France au XIXe siècle,* (Publications de la Sorbonne, Paris, 1980), p. 69.

5   Françoise Boudon, André Chastel, Hélène Couzy and Françoise Hamon, *Système de l'architecture urbaine. Le quartier des Halles à Paris,* (Centre National de la Recherche Scientifique, Paris, two vols, 1977), p. 61.

6   Quoted in Gallet, *Paris Domestic Architecture of the 18th Century,* p. 63.

7   Quoted in Mark Deming, *La Halle au Blé à Paris, 1762–1813,* (Les Archives de l'Architecture Moderne, Brussels, 1984), p. 79.

8   Emil Kaufmann, *Architecture in the Age of Reason,* (Dover, New York, 1968), p. 149; and Françoise Boudon, 'Urbanisme et spéculation à Paris au XVIIIe Siècle: Le terrain de l'Hôtel de Soissons', *Journal of the Society of Architectural Historians,* 32 (1973), p. 278.

BIBLIOGRAPHY

Louis Bergeron, *Paris: genèse d'un paysage,* (Picard, Paris, 1989).

Françoise Boudon, 'Urbanisme et spéculation à Paris au XVIIIe Siècle: Le terrain de l'Hôtel de Soissons', *Journal of the Society of Architectural Historians,* 32 (1973), pp. 267–307.

Françoise Boudon, André Chastel, Hélène Couzy and Françoise Hamon, *Système de l'architecture urbaine. Le quartier des Halles à Paris,* (Centre National de la Recherche Scientifique, Paris, two vols, 1977).

Allan Braham, *The Architecture of the French Enlightenment,* (Thames and Hudson, London, 1980).

Adeline Daumard, *Maisons de Paris et propriétaires Parisiens au XIXeme siècle, 1809–1880,* (Cujas, Paris, 1965).

Mark Deming, *La Halle au Blé à Paris, 1762–1813*, (Les Archives de l'Architecture Moderne, Brussels, 1984).

Michel Gallet, *Paris Domestic Architecture of the 18th Century*, (Barrie and Jenkins, London, 1972).

Louis Hautecoeur, *Histoire de l'architecture classique en France*, (Picard, Paris, vols. 4, 5 and 6 1943–57).

Emil Kaufmann, *Architecture in the Age of Reason*, (Dover, New York, 1968).

Michel Lescure, *Les sociétés immobilières en France au XIXe siècle*, (Publications de la Sorbonne, Paris, 1980).

François Loyer, *Paris, Nineteenth Century: Architecture and Urbanism*, (Abbeville, New York, 1988).

Pierre Pinon, 'Lotissements spéculatifs, formes urbaines et architecture à la fin de l'ancien régime', *Soufflot et l'architecture des lumières*, (Actes du Colloque Soufflot et l'Architecture des Lumières, Ministre de l'Environnement du Cadre de Vie (Direction de l'Architecture) et Centre National de la Recherche Scientifique, Paris, 1980), pp. 178–91.

Jeanne Pronteau, 'Construction et aménagement des nouveaux quartiers de Paris', *Histoire des enterprises*, n.2 (1958), pp. 8–32.

Daniel Rabreau and Monika Steinhauser, 'Le Théâtre de l'Odéon de Charles de Wailly et Marie-Joseph Peyre, 1767–1782', *Revue de l'art*, n.19 (1973), pp. 9–49.

John Summerson, *The Classical Language of Architecture*, (Thames and Hudson, London, revised edition, 1980).

13

COMMON SENSE AND THE PICTURESQUE

Adrian Forty

In 1837, the American philosopher Ralph Waldo Emerson (1803–82) wrote in his journal,

> Culture. How much meaning the Germans affix to the word, and how unlike the English sense! The Englishman goes to see a museum or a mountain for itself; the German for himself; the Englishman for entertainment, the German for culture.
> The German is conscious and his aims are great. The Englishman lives from his eyes, and immersed in the apparent world.[1]

The pre-occupation with appearance noticed by Emerson has been a characteristic of English (but not only English) attitudes toward culture in general and architecture in particular for the best part of two centuries. In Emerson's time, and ours, it has often been taken for granted that architecture's first and principal appeal is to the eye. A recent but no means unique demonstration of this 'common sense' attitude toward architecture is Prince Charles's television programme and book, *A Vision of Britain* (1989).[2] Why, one might ask, has the experience of the eye counted for so much, particularly in Britain? That there are alternative ways of understanding architecture we need not doubt, and indeed the German tradition to which Emerson referred is one such: in that tradition questions of what architecture is, what it means, have generally been regarded as more important than how it looks. The issue to be discussed here, though, is why the visual has been so remarkably resistant to other modes of understanding, and has been so consistently successful in repelling those other forms of consciousness.[3] Despite successive attempts to direct British attitudes to architecture away from the visual, this mode of understanding has retained its authority, and indeed recent developments – postmodernism as well as the Prince of Wales's interventions into architecture – have each in their own way leant upon it.

The privilege given to the experience of the eye, like some other assumptions lodged in contemporary 'common sense' notions of architecture, carries a strong similarity to ideas first formulated in late eighteenth century Britain by the exponents of what became known as the *picturesque*. This does not mean that present day attitudes in any sense result from eighteenth century theory, only that we should note their resemblance – though this resemblance does offer some insight into the reasons for the lure of common sense and its ability to repel, effortlessly, other modes of thought. To be more specific, there are three particular modern assumptions about architecture that share a similarity with the eighteenth century picturesque: firstly, the notion that reason plays no part in the experience of architecture; secondly, the notion that architecture can be judged and experienced in the same way as painting; and thirdly, that judgements about architecture can legitimately be made from individual experience and personal taste. All these notions, it should be stressed, are at odds with the concepts of architecture developed by modernists in the first half of the twentieth century.

The book generally regarded as the starting point of picturesque aesthetic theory is *A Philosophical Enquiry into the Origins of Our Ideas of the Sublime and Beautiful*, published in 1757 by the English philosopher Edmund Burke (1729–97). Burke's main purpose was to develop an explanation for aesthetics based upon organic sense-experience. He insists that criticism cannot proceed from the study of the works themselves, but only from the understanding of the range of emotions that they produce in ourselves; and that in this process reason or understanding play no part. 'Beauty', says Burke, 'demands no assistance from our reasoning.'[4] A little further on, he expands on the same idea:

> Whenever the wisdom of our Creator intended that
> we should be affected with any thing, he did not
> confide the execution of his design to the languid
> and precarious operation of our reason; but he
> endued it with powers and properties . . . which
> seizing upon the senses and the imagination,
> captivate the soul before the understanding is ready
> either to join with them or to oppose them.[5]

The importance of the idea that the path from sense-experience to aesthetic emotion bypasses reason is clear. For Burke, critics have no need to investigate the object itself, but only the passions it arouses in

Figure 13.1

The human eye as the privileged arbiter of taste and beauty. Drawing by Humphrey Repton.

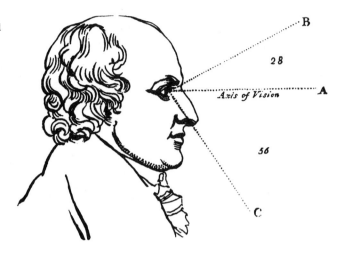

themselves; moreover, he says that aesthetic experiences occur without the mind, or reason, being consulted. This is precisely the ground that common sense likes to occupy in dealing with architecture. As an account of aesthetic experience it is entirely contrary to the tradition of European modernism, where it is assumed that the mind is fundamental to the appreciation of architecture. Consider, for example, a remark by the Swiss-born and modernist-aligned architect Walter Segal (1907–85). Beyond the shapes and arrangements which give pleasure to the eye, he insists there is an essential meaning.

> This is perceived by the mind and not by the eye; and the mind is wont to transfer it into a wider context for testing. Acceptance by the mind is essential for a building to be convincing.[6]

Of the senses with which Burke was concerned, vision was the most important. 'In this discourse,' he writes, 'we chiefly attach ourselves to the sublime, as it affects the eye.'[7] The picturesque, as its name implies, privileges the eye above all other organs. Not only does it concentrate upon the effect of retinal sensations, but it proposes that pictures can enable the eye to find beauty even where, in life, the other senses might be

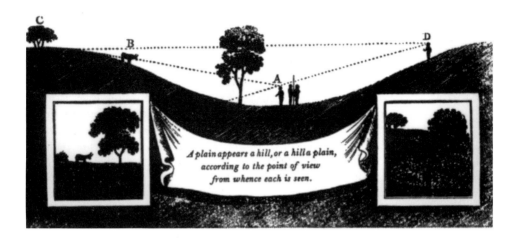

A plain appears a hill, or a hill a plain, according to the point of view from whence each is seen.

repulsed. Richard Payne Knight (1750–1824), theorist of landscape and author of *An Analytical Enquiry into the Principles of Taste* (1806), argued that through painting it was possible to abstract from an object in nature properties that are purely pictorial, and to distinguish these properties from its other characteristics.

Figure 13.2

Analysis of the importance of vision. From the position on the right, the rise of the hill is emphasized. Seeing the same view from the bottom of the valley turns the hill, trees and animal into a flattened plain. Drawing by Humphrey Repton.

> Painting as it imitates only the visible qualities of bodies, separates those qualities from all others; which the habitual concurrence and co-operation of the other senses have mixt and blended with them, in our ordinary perceptions, from which our ideas are formed.[8]

He goes on to explain that many objects in life have visible properties that are beautiful, but also many other properties that are repulsive.

> Decayed pollard trees, rotten thatch, crumbling masses of perished brick and plaster, tattered worn-out dirty garments, a fish or a flesh market, may all exhibit the most harmonious and brilliant combinations of tints to the eye ... but, nevertheless, these objects contain so many properties that are offensive to other senses, or to the imagination, that in nature we are not pleased with them, nor ever consider them as beautiful.[9]

The great ability of the painter is to be able to isolate what is aesthetically satisfying to the eye to the exclusion of all other properties.

For common sense, pictorial abstractions of architecture are alluring. They make architecture easy. They make it possible to experience architecture through a single sense, vision, rather than the many senses that the actual experience of buildings involves; and they offer architecture as a unified, harmonious experience, even though in practice architecture provides a variety of contradictory experiences, by no means all of which necessarily delight. For example, it is significant that in the 1980s and 1990s the architects of various recent controversial schemes in London have resorted to paintings by Carl Laubin to represent their designs: Jeremy Dixon (1939–) with the Royal Opera House in Covent Carden, John Simpson (1954–) for proposals for Paternoster Square next to St. Paul's, and Colin St John Wilson (1922–) for the new British Library beside St. Pancras Station.

Attachment to the visual properties of architecture at the expense of all others leads to the fallacy that what

Figure 13.3

Architecture rendered as a purely visual and delightful affair, while other senses, the intellect and contradictions are ignored. Scheme for Paternoster Square, London, (1992), architects John Simpson and Partners, Hammond, Beeby and Babka, and Demetri Porphyrios Associates. Artist Carl Laubin.

makes a good picture must be good architecture. No
better exponent of this view can be found than Prince
Charles, five of whose 'ten commandments' are
picturesque prescriptions: 'place', 'scale', 'harmony',
'enclosure' and 'materials' are all, as described by him,
qualities assessed by their effect when architecture is
reduced to a picture. He is not alone in being tempted
to simplify architecture in this way. Even the high-tech
architect Richard Rogers (1933–), hardly an ally of the
Prince, uses the image of the late gothic Kings College
Chapel (1446–1515) in Cambridge and the adjoining
range of buildings designed by James Gibbs
(1682–1754) to justify his belief in novelty, arguing that
if the eighteenth century could accept the visual
contrast of two such dissimilar buildings then there is
no case for resisting as 'out of character' the juxtapo-
sition today of modern architecture with older buildings. Such an argument of course neglects other kinds
of experience and knowledge to which architecture
appeals.

Burke's idea that aesthetic experience required no
assistance from reason was, as we have already seen,
qualified by other writings on the picturesque, notably
Knight, who argued that the emotions produced by
sight depended not just upon the pure visual sensation, but rather upon what he called 'improved perception' or 'the association of ideas'. He explained:

> . . . marts thronged with the bustle of commerce,
> seaports crowded with shipping, plains enriched by
> culture and population, all afford pleasures to the
> learned and contemplative mind, wholly independent
> of the impressions, which the scenery makes upon
> the eye; though that, from its richness and variety,
> may be in the highest degree pleasing.
>   All these extra pleasures are from the minds of
> the spectators; whose pre-existing trains of ideas are
> revived, refreshed and re-associated by new, but
> correspondent impressions on the organs of sense.[10]

It might appear from this that Knight brings reason
and understanding into play in his theory. This,
however, is not the case, for Knight's concept of 'ideas'
as a succession of images does not involve reason. In
particular, he makes it clear that the ability to have
such ideas depends upon the cultivation of the mind
through experience of other similar scenes; and he

insists that only those whose minds have been enriched through a large stock of ideas are in a position to enjoy aesthetic experiences to the full.[11] Furthermore, he dismisses all attempts to reduce aesthetics to systems of rules, arguing that it is only through experience that a person is able to make effective judgements. The analogy he makes is a telling one.

> Rules and systems have exactly the same influence upon taste and manners, as dogmas have upon morals. If a person be polite by rule . . . his behaviour will be constrained and formal; and void of all that graceful ease, and ready adaptation to every varying shade of circumstance and situation, which constitute what is called good breeding; and which can only proceed from a just and discriminating tact, cultivated and refined by habitual exercise.[12]

In other words, when Knight talks about that association of ideas, he means 'taste', an ability to form judgements, based upon experience, or 'breeding', rather than the application of any set of concepts or principles to the object under discussion.

We have here the third of the legacies of the picturesque, the notion that taste – the ability to make aesthetic judgements – is a facility possessed only by 'properly' educated people or by those with the leisure to cultivate their sensibility, but not by the large majority. As the landscape gardener Humphrey Repton (1752–1818) wrote in his *Theory and Practice of Landscape Gardening* (1803), 'a knowledge of what is good, what is bad, what is indifferent, whether in actions, in manners, in language, in arts, or science, constitutes the basis of good taste and marks the distinction between the higher ranks of polished society and the inferior orders of mankind.'[13]

The picturesque was a taste-based system of aesthetics, in which judgements of quality appealed not to reason but to experience. It was the stranglehold of taste – its inability to offer judgements beyond the personal and its restriction of aesthetic judgement to a social élite – that nineteenth century architectural thinkers sought to escape from. By setting up ideas such as truth, nature, work or morality as standards against which architecture could be judged, thinkers

Figure 13.4

For some eighteenth century theorists, landscape and architecture could be appreciated only by those few with the right education and innate sense of taste. Illustration from Humphrey Repton, *Sketches and Hints on Landscape Gardening*, (1794).

like the English art critic John Ruskin (1819–1900), French architect and structural rationalist Eugène-Emanuel Viollet-le-Duc (1814–79), and German architect and theorist Gottfried Semper (1803–79), made it possible to discuss architecture in terms beyond that of personal experience. Their ideas, open to reason and argument, were central to the development of modernism.

The 'common sense' attack on modernism has proceeded by invoking the values of the picturesque, presenting them as practical arguments with which all would agree. They are offered, in Prince Charles's words, as the 'popular' alternative to the 'fashionable theories of a professional establishment which has made the layman feel he [sic] has no legitimate opinions.'[14]

But before rushing to agree with this laudable desire to stop the public from being bamboozled by experts, we might reflect that common sense in architecture, as in all walks of life, is not made up of universal truths.

Figure 13.5

Not all architectural theorists are concerned solely with vision. This illustration from Viollet-le-Duc, *Dictionnaire raisonné de l'architecture française*, (1854–68), discloses part of a building's construction invisible to the human eye.

Rather, it consists of ideas that certain groups of people have in the past put forward as truths, and which have been made to seem universal. In the case of architecture, the picturesque secured the values of a social élite, privileged through, among other things, the training of the eye – a class of 'experts' no less than architects trained in the rational analysis of architectural problems, but a class indifferent to the ambitions and pre-occupations of a profession. It is the detachment of the picturesque from matters of professional expertise that have allowed it to be claimed as popular, as common sense, against the rational theories of modernism. We should not, though, be misled into supposing that a scheme of aesthetics deriving from the observer's eye and emotions is any more popular than one founded upon reason: each has been the property of particular groups, the one privileged by its social class, the other by its professional training. Far from offering, as it appears to do, a popular basis for architecture against the authority of experts, the appeal to picturesque values threatens to bring back a taste-based aesthetics more prone to the control of an élite than any system founded on reason.

REFERENCES

1 R.W. Emerson, *Journals*, vol. 4, (London, 1910), pp. 208–9.
2 Prince Charles, *A Vision of Britain: a Personal View of Architecture* (Doubleday, New York, 1989).
3 Some of the material and arguments presented here first appeared as 'The Lure of the Picturesque', *Architecture Today*, n.11 (September 1990), pp. 44 and 47.
4 Edmund Burke, *A Philosophical Enquiry into the Origin of Our Ideas of the Sublime and Beautiful*, (Basil Blackwell, Oxford, 1987, edited by J.T. Boulton), p. 92.
5 Burke, *A Philosophical Enquiry*, p. 107.
6 Walter Segal, 'Beyond Utility. Architecture and the Id', *The Architect*, (March 1971), p. 38.
7 Burke, *A Philosophical Enquiry*, p. 141.
8 Richard Payne Knight, *An Analytical Enquiry into the Principles of Taste*, (London, 1806), p. 69.
9 Knight, *An Analytical Enquiry into the Principles of Taste*, pp. 70–1.
10 Knight, *An Analytical Enquiry into the Principles of Taste*, p. 196.
11 Knight, *An Analytical Enquiry into the Principles of Taste*, pp. 145–6.
12 Knight, *An Analytical Enquiry into the Principles of Taste*, p. 239.

13   Reprinted in J. Nolen (ed.), *Humphrey Repton, The Art of Landscape Gardening*, (Boston and New York, 1907), p. 67.
14   Prince Charles, *A Vision of Britain*, p. 153.

BIBLIOGRAPHY

Edmund Burke, *A Philosophical Enquiry into the Origin of Our Ideas of the Sublime and Beautiful*, (Basil Blackwell, Oxford, 1987, edited by J.T. Boulton). Originally published 1757.

Walter John Hipple, *The Beautiful, the Sublime and the Picturesque in Eighteenth Century British Aesthetic Theory*, (Southern Illinois University Press, Carbondale, 1957).

John Dixon Hunt, *Gardens and the Picturesque: Studies in the History of Landscape Archiecture*, (MIT Press, Cambridge, Mass., 1992).

Christopher Hussey, *The Picturesque: Studies in a Point of View*, (Frank Cass, London, 1967).

Uvedale Price, *Essays on the Picturesque as Compared with the Sublime and the Beautiful, and on the Use of Studying Pictures for the Purpose of Improving Real Landscape*, (Gregg International, Farnborough, Hants, three volumes, 1971, first published 1810).

Richard Rogers, *Architecture: a Modern View*, (Thames and Hudson, London, 1990).

David Watkin, *The English Vision: the Picturesque in Architecture, Landscape and Garden Design*, (Murray, London, 1982).

Part Four

SOCIETY

14

ARCHITECTURE AND PHILOSOPHY

THE CASE OF G.W.F. HEGEL

Jeremy Melvin

Architectural theory shares with philosophy the task of exploring ideas. There has been considerable cross-over between the two disciplines, with theorists adapting philosophical insights to architecture and philosophers borrowing architectural metaphors to elucidate particular points. But it is rare for a practitioner of one to make a significant contribution to the other.

The German philosopher Georg Wilhelm Friedrich Hegel (1770–1831) was an exception. He is best known today as a one of the originators of the notion of historical determinism, where the actions of the individual are seen as being subordinated to the collective will. For this reason Hegel, and other representatives of the German Idealist tradition of thought as ideologically different as Karl Marx (1818–83) and Oswald Spengler (1880–1936), have been roundly criticized by proponents of pluralist societies such as the twentieth century philosopher Karl Popper (1902–94). But as well as being a political philosopher of the first importance, Hegel also devoted great effort to understanding art. During his period as professor of philosophy in Berlin from 1818 until his death, he developed a cycle of lectures dedicated to the philosophy of art, and published from his notes after his death as The *Aesthetics*. Much of this is devoted to architecture.

The great poet T.S. Eliot (1888–1965) may have disparaged The *Aesthetics* when he wrote 'Hegel's Philosophy of Art adds very little to our enjoyment or understanding of art,' but he did acknowledge art's importance in Hegel's thought by adding that 'it fills a gap in Hegel's philosophy.' This kind of judgement opened the door for art historians to criticize Hegel's influence on their discipline almost as vociferously as political philosophers have on theirs. The two best known 'first generation' histories of the modern movement, Nikolaus Pevsner's *Pioneers of Modern Design*[1] and Siegfried Giedion's *Space, Time and Architecture*[2] have been attacked for the historical determinism latent in their assumption that modernism was the culmination of the history of architecture.[3] But it is precisely because Hegel was trying to explain the relationship between individual genius and the role of the collective in artistic creation that his views are worth investigating. He may not have been right, but he attempted to come to terms with a fundamental problem.

Hegel discusses three issues in The *Aesthetics* which are significant in the light of subsequent developments in architectural theory: the importance of function in the generation of architecture, the role of proportion, or symmetry and regularity, and the relationship between structure and decoration. We will investigate how these concepts interrelate in Hegel's philosophy, and suggest why they would be of interest when thinking about architecture in general.

ARCHITECTURE AS MATERIAL ART

Hegel's views on each of these points derive from his basic proposition that architecture is bound by its inherent materiality, and this condition in turn arises from the position he ascribes architecture in relation to other arts. 'Architecture', Hegel argues, 'confronts us as the beginning of art, because, at its start art has not found for the presentation of its spiritual content either the adequate material or the corresponding forms. Therefore it has to be content with merely seeking a true harmony and with an external relation between the two.'[4] If, as Hegel also explains, 'art's vocation is to unveil the truth in the form of sensuous artistic configuration, to set forth the reconciled opposition [between the sensuous and the spiritual],'[5] architecture is an unsatisfactory artistic medium, precisely because its materiality prevents it from being anything but entirely sensuous and physical, with no infusion of spirit.

To understand this further, we should note the role art has in Hegel's overall philosophical system. It shares with religion and philosophy the vocation of expressing the Divine, but differs from the other two by bringing it into the realm of sensory perception. However, only certain stages of human spiritual evolution, such as that achieved in ancient Greece, can be adequately embodied in sensory form. Christianity, for example, is not susceptible to the same means of representation. For Hegel, this makes art an essential, though not the highest, aspect of human intellectual endeavour.[6]

The relationship between form and spirit is, for Hegel, the crux of art. It is art's spiritual content that distinguishes it from, and elevates it above, nature. Art evolves through a dialectical progression between form and spirit through symbolic, classical and romantic categories. Hegel uses these terms to define particular points in the dialectic: symbolic art is marked by a complete separation between form and spirit, classical art brings form and spirit together in discrete forms, while romantic art achieves a complete correspondence between form and spirit and is therefore the highest level of artistic achievement. According to Hegel, architecture is symbolic, sculpture is classical and painting, music and poetry are romantic.

It is then the complete separation between form and spirit which makes architecture a 'symbolic' art. For Hegel, symbolic is the opposite of immanent; the spiritual is never born from within it. What its form indicates as a symbol, as it were in outline, is more significant than the form itself, and for Hegel the meaning of a work of architecture exists before a building is constructed for it: 'the spiritual meaning . . . has already obtained its existence in freedom outside architecture.'[7] This meaning, moreover, is related to purpose of the building. As Hegel explained, 'the architectural work of art is not just an end in itself; it is something external for something else to which it serves as an adornment, dwelling place, etc. A building awaits the sculptural figure of a god or else the group of people who take up their home there.'[8] Architecture, in other words, provides enclosure for some form of religious or social activity which pre-exists the building. Because these activities can exist as social constructs independently of architecture, although architecture exists essentially to serve them, there can then be no complete correspondence between form and idea in architecture. The essence of architecture is what happens inside, lying 'precisely in retaining the spiritual, as something inner, over against its own external forms and thus pointing to what has soul only as to something distinct from these.' So architecture 'does not carry [meaning] in itself but finds in something else, in man and his needs and aims in family life, the state, religion etc., and therefore the independence of buildings is sacrificed.'⁹ This is why, therefore, the symbolic and the architectural are never immanent, for the meaning of architecture is always found in ritualized functions deriving from domesticity, society and religion.

PROPORTION, SYMMETRY AND REGULARITY

Because architecture has to concern itself with 'external things in nature and human affairs'[10] – prosaic, functional matters such as enclosure and protection – it is not a satisfactory artistic medium. This does not mean, however, that its forms are devoid of any kind of regulating principle. Rather, the enclosing forms are by definition external to spirit, and are therefore 'shapeable only according to the laws of gravity [and] bound together regularly and symmetrically.'[11] The constructed form has a discipline which is separate to the functions it encloses.

Symmetry and regularity are, to Hegel, the means whereby architecture can be given the lowly level of artistic expression of which it is capable; they are not, as they are for renaissance and neo-classical theorists, the representation of a divine order. 'The material for [architecture] is the inherently non-spiritual, i.e. heavy matter, shapeable only according to the laws of gravity; its form is provided by productions of an external nature bound together regularly and symmetrically to be a purely external reflection of spirit . . . '[12] Even though 'the ideal work of art must . . . rise above the purely symmetrical . . . this regulation of the unruly and unrestrained is again the sole fundamental characteristic which certain arts can adopt in line with the material for their presentation.' The implication is that there are 'higher' methods of expressing artistic ideas than symmetry and regularity, but they are excluded in architecture, because 'the aim of an architectonic work of art is to give artistic shape to the external, inherently inorganic environment of spirit. What therefore dominates in architecture is the straight line, the right angle, the circle, similarity in pillars, windows, arches and columns, and vaults.'[13]

Although regularity and symmetry were accorded almost divine status in neo-classical architectural theory, the idea that they might not be the absolute culmination of artistic expression was hardly original to Hegel. It was well rehearsed, for example, by the English picturesque theorists of the eighteenth century which Adrian Forty discusses in Chapter 13. But Hegel is unusual in insisting on the pre-dominance of symmetry and regularity in architecture, while also acknowledging their limitations as a mode of artistic expression. Having come to this conclusion, the logical step might have been to follow picturesque architects in freeing architecture from these constraints, but for Hegel this was impossible because if architecture sacrificed regularity for more naturalistic or organic forms, it trespassed on the realm of sculpture. There is therefore, for Hegel, a conflict between the more expressive possibilities of organic form, and the inherently architectural abstractions of regularity and symmetry. This comes out, as we shall now see, in his discussion of the relationship between structure and decoration.

STRUCTURE AND DECORATION

Hegel's contribution to this seminal issue in nineteenth and twentieth century architectural theory is rather different to the moral positions taken by later theorists. Where the art critic and architectural theorist John Ruskin (1819–1900) understood architecture as the presence of decoration on an object, and the Viennese architect Adolf Loos (1870–1933) considered the absence of decoration imperative for modern architecture, Hegel considered decoration to be an integral part in the evolution of architecture, but paradoxically one that could lead to the ultimate eclipse of architecture by a higher art form. In short, decoration could be considered independently of other aspects of architecture, and so its role became problematic.

Decoration was introduced into architecture, says Hegel, because architecture is not limited to providing objects which are socially understood as unifying points. Modifications are made to the form of the objects so that they convey something of their purpose. However, if the modifications are too naturalistic, as when organic animal shapes and human figures are added, the objects 'press on toward a transition to sculpture.'[14] Decoration, therefore, rests on the cusp in the dialectical transition from architecture to sculpture. Again, '. . . architecture may itself attempt to go so far as to fashion in its forms and material an adequate artistic existence for that content; but in that event it has already stepped beyond its own sphere and is swinging over to sculpture.'[15] This, however, only occurs if the spiritual content is sophisticated enough to lend itself to expression in the classical art of sculpture, and if symmetry and regularity are replaced by 'organic' form.

This point is made clear in Hegel's discussion of the arabesque, which, says Hegel, 'falls by its very conception into the transition out of a natural organic form used by architecture to the more severe regularity of architecture proper.' However, architecture is bound to impose certain abstract formal devices which prevent accurate representation. 'But when architecture freely fulfils its purpose it degrades arabesques to a decoration and ornament [bringing them] nearer to the inorganic and geometrical.' Criticism of the resulting stilted forms is misguided as 'this sort of contrariety is not only a right of art as such but is even a duty in architecture, adapted to and made harmonious with the truly architectural style.'[16] So to be truly architectural, decoration should not be too naturalistic or 'organic'; rather it should eschew accurate representation in favour of the stylized effects of geometrically based composition. Again, Hegel's classification system prescribes the formal limits for different arts, and consequently their effectiveness as objects of artistic expression.

The risk of architecture 'swinging over' into sculpture is greatest in its early ancient Egyptian and near Eastern origins, for what Hegel considers to be the relatively unsophisticated spiritual content of these periods – the obsession with death – is more susceptible to being embodied in form than are more advanced spiritual aims. In his discussion of phallic columns, sphinxes and obelisks, revealingly entitled 'Architectural Works Wavering Between Architecture and Sculpture,' the tensions in his conception of architecture are most apparent. Although for Hegel sphinxes are very close to sculpture, because 'they

Figure 14.1

The Egyptian sphinx, occupying the dangerous ground between architecture and sculpture.

were set alongside one another in avenues' they have 'a completely architectural character.' Symmetry and regularity still govern the disposition of the objects, even if such abstractions have been shed in the actual forms. Similarly some Egyptian temples 'might be called a collection of sculptures, yet they generally occur in such a number and such repetition of one and the same shape that they become rows and thereby . . . acquire their architectural character.'[17] Although the line of demarcation between architecture and sculpture is blurred in these examples, Hegel still maintains a distinction between architectural and sculptural ways of manipulating form. Architectural decoration is a problem precisely because it falls between these two techniques. Thus one of the central issues of nineteenth century architectural theory, the relationship between structure and decoration, is also a cornerstone of Hegel's conception of architecture and, indeed, of art in general.

THE DEVELOPMENT OF ART

Although for Hegel all architecture is bound by the condition of being symbolic, he also subdivides the subject of art in general chronologically into symbolic, classical and romantic phases. Slightly confusingly then, the symbolic art of architecture also has symbolic, classical and romantic periods of its history. Each corresponds and gives formal expression to a particular religious sensibility, respectively ancient Egyptian and near Eastern religions, classical religion, and Christianity, and these distinctions are maintained in the examples he uses.

Symbolic architecture, for Hegel, brings the development of aesthetics to a crossroads. So far the evolution of both architecture and aesthetics have followed the same path, but once the possibility offered by sculpture for a closer relationship between form and spirit becomes apparent, the path splits into the line of aesthetic development through sculpture, and the line of architectural development through classical architecture. Classical architecture is not for Hegel a classical art, merely the classical phase of the symbolic art of architecture; and like symbolic architecture, classical architecture is informed by its function. Where symbolic architecture and classical architecture differ is that the spiritual content of classical architecture can only be expressed in its sculpture, such as the statues of gods found in Greek temples, and so the distinction between sculpture and architecture is more clearly demarcated. Accordingly, classical architecture concentrates on its function, 'devizing the substance of its plan and figuration in the light of spiritual purposes . . .'[18] But if the purposes are spiritual, the forms which enclose them are not. 'The beauty of classical architecture consists precisely in this appropriateness to purpose which is freed from the immediate confusion with the organic, the spiritual and the symbolic.'[19] It may be beautiful, but is it art?

In the case of art, as opposed to architecture, we find that with sculpture art enters its classical phase, where there is a complete correspondence between form and idea. At this stage, says Hegel, 'art has reached its own essential nature by bringing the Idea, as spiritual individuality, directly into harmony with its bodily reality . . .'[20] Unlike architecture, sculpture is able freely to embody 'spirit', but this correspondence is also transitory. Art, in the form of sculpture, serves the necessary purpose of giving sensual shape to spirit; once that has been done the absolute spirit develops in ways to which art cannot give adequate expression. Art's later stages can only aspire towards this goal, but by indicating it can facilitate perception of it in another medium. Just as architecture paves the way for aesthetic fulfilment, so aesthetics paves the way for the fulfilment of the absolute spirit.

HEGEL AND CONTEMPORARY GERMAN ARCHITECTURE

The parallels between Hegel's propositions about architecture and those of contemporary theorists and practitioners are intriguing. The great architect Karl Friedrich Schinkel (1780–1841) was working in Berlin at the same time as Hegel and it would be interesting to speculate how far Schinkel was explicitly trying to answer Hegel's implied challenge to his discipline. Gottfried Semper (1803–79), the most important German architectural theorist of his generation, and with John Ruskin and Eugène-Emanuel Viollet-le-Duc

Figure 14.2

Altes Museum, Berlin, (1823–30), architect K.F. Schinkel.

(1814–79) one of the most important of the century, also showed affinities with Hegel. Semper is often cited as a representative of the only significant tradition of artistic thought to have emerged in Germany in opposition to Hegel, but they shared the view that enclosure is a crucial aspect of architecture. He also placed great emphasis on the role of decoration, explicitly stating that decoration and structure, because they were produced by different crafts, were fundamentally different.[21]

But it is not easy to chart the exact extent of Hegel's influence on architecture. This is partly because architectural theory and philosophy are not interchangeable and both are affected by different external factors; practising architects do not need to read Hegel to realize that architecture is bound by its materiality. Furthermore, Hegel is not always original. He is perhaps best treated as a representative of German Idealist thought in general, rather than an isolated thinker. He made frequent allusions to the archaeologist and art historian Johann Winckelmann (1717–68), the poet and historian Friedrich Schiller (1759–1805), the poet and critic Wilhelm (1767–1845) and his brother the critic Karl Schlegel (1772–1829), as well as to the poet, dramatist and scientist Johann Goethe (1749–1832). While he did not always agree with these predecessors and contemporaries, Hegel drew on them and defined his ideas in relation to theirs. As one of the era's most systematic thinkers, he tried to tie together some of the fragmentary ideas of others into a coherent whole.

Herein, rather than in historical determinism, lies Hegel's importance to architectural theory. Almost as a fortuitous by-product of his conception of art, he articulated persistent characteristics of architecture which other theorists could not ignore, and incorporated them into a systematic and influential interpretation of artistic expression.

REFERENCES

1   Nikolaus Pevsner, *Pioneers of Modern Design: from William Morris to Walter Gropius*, (Penguin, London, 1976). First published as *Pioneers of the Modern Movement*, (1936).

2   Siegfried Giedion, *Space, Time and Architecture: the Growth of a New Tradition*, (Harvard University Press, Cambridge, Mass., 1941).

3   See, for example, David Watkin, *Morality and Architecture: the Development of a Theme in Architectural History and Theory from the Gothic Revival to the Modern Movement*, (Clarendon Press, Oxford, 1977).

4   G.W.F. Hegel, *Aesthetics: Lectures on Fine Art*, (Oxford University Press, Oxford, two volumes, 1975, first published 1832–45), p. 624.

5   Hegel, *Aesthetics*, pp. 54 and 55.

6   Hegel, *Aesthetics*, pp. 7–9.

7   Hegel, *Aesthetics*, p. 661.

8   Hegel, *Aesthetics*, pp. 653–4.

9   Hegel, *Aesthetics*, p. 633.

10 Hegel, *Aesthetics*, p. 300.

11 Hegel, *Aesthetics*, p. 624.

12 Hegel, *Aesthetics*, p. 624.

13 Hegel, *Aesthetics*, p. 247–8.

14 Hegel, *Aesthetics*, p. 637.

15 Hegel, *Aesthetics*, p. 84.

16 Hegel, *Aesthetics*, pp. 658–9.

17 Hegel, *Aesthetics*, pp. 640–4.

18 Hegel, *Aesthetics*, p. 662.

19 Hegel, *Aesthetics*, p. 660.

20 Hegel, *Aesthetics*, p. 301.

21 Gottfried Semper, *The Four Elements of Architecture and Other Writings*, (Cambridge University Press, Cambridge, 1989). First published 1851.

BIBLIOGRAPHY

Stephen Bungay, *Beauty and Truth: a Study of Hegel's Aesthetics*, (Oxford University Press, Oxford, 1984).

G.W.F. Hegel, *Aesthetics: Lectures on Fine Art*, (Oxford University Press, Oxford, two volumes, 1975, first published 1832–45).

John Gage (ed.), *Goethe on Art*, (Scolar Press, London, 1980).

M.J. Inwood, *Hegel*, (Routledge and Kegan Paul, London, 1983).

Raymond Plant, *Hegel*, (Allen and Unwin, London, 1973).

Michael Podro, *The Critical Historians of Art*, (Yale University Press, New Haven, 1982).

Gillian Rose, *Hegel Contra Sociology*, (1983).

Mark Swenarton, *Artisans and Architects: the Ruskinian Tradition in Architectural Thought*, (Macmillan, London, 1989).

15

ARCHITECTURE AND THE INDUSTRIAL REVOLUTION

PUGIN AND RUSKIN

Mark Swenarton

In the early nineteenth century people in Britain became aware of enormous changes in the economy and society taking place around them. The phenomenon that became known to historians as the industrial revolution involved fundamental changes in the way goods were made and exchanged and, with that, in the relationships between people, not just in Britain, where the phenomenon first occurred, but across the globe.

We shall consider here the effect that these changes, or rather the perception of these changes, had on architecture in Britain between the 1830s and the 1850s. The approach will be historical materialist, looking at developments in architectural ideas in relation to broader changes in material and social conditions. The focus will be on two major architectural theorists, A.W.N. Pugin (1812–52) and John Ruskin (1819–1900). While the ideas of Pugin will be presented in resumé, for Ruskin, a thinker of enormous richness and complexity, we will concentrate on what he himself considered his most significant achievement: 'the description of the nature of Gothic architecture, as involving the liberty of the workman.'[1]

THE CONDITION OF ENGLAND

In the hundred years between 1750 and 1850 Britain was transformed from a pre-industrial to an industrial economy. With the introduction of new technology, particularly water- and then steam-powered machinery, the locus of production shifted from workshops to factories and the craftsman gave way to the factory 'hand'. Labour productivity was transformed: in 1901 output per head was four times 1801 levels. Thanks to improvements in agriculture, the population sustained by the economy grew in size dramatically, doubling between 1781 and

1841 and again between 1841 and 1901, so that between 1701 and 1901 the population increased from 7 million to 37 million. Much of this increase took place in towns, which assumed a new and central importance in the national economy. Whereas in 1750 only two towns (London and Edinburgh) had a population exceeding 50 000, in 1851 there were 29, and in that year, for the first time, the urban population exceeded the rural. Such towns were made viable by improvements in transport, by which food could be brought in and products sent out. During the eighteenth century the country had been united by a system of canals and greatly improved roads, but the transport revolution received its most striking form with the application of steam-power in the nineteenth century. In 1832 Britain had 166 miles of railways; in 1851; 6 800 miles – in effect a national railway system created in less than 20 years. The railway, the devouring monster of the Romantic imagination, became with the factory the most potent symbol of the new industrial era.

In the first half of the nineteenth century these changes assumed growing importance for the intelligentsia and legislature. From the 1820s, a number of intellectuals commented that Britain had not just changed but, in their view, changed for the worse. In reaction, reformers such as journalist and member of parliament William Cobbett (1763–1855) and writer and poet laureate Robert Southey (1774–1843) constructed the notion of a Golden Age which, they said, had existed in the pre-industrial past, a 'Merrie England' where fairness and contentment reigned. Stopping at Leicester on his *Rural Rides* (1830) Cobbett contrasted this mythical past with the harsh reality of his own day. Leicester, he wrote,

> is well stocked with jails, of which a new one, in
> addition to the rest, has just been built, covering
> three acres of ground! . . . Our forefathers built
> abbeys and priories and churches, and they made
> such use of them that jails were unnecessary. We,
> their sons, have knocked down the abbeys and
> priories, suffered half the parsonage-houses and
> churches to pretty near tumble down, and make
> such uses of the remainder, that jails and tread-mills
> and dungeons have now become the most striking
> edifices in every county in the kingdom.[2]

In the 1830s and 1840s, as the industrial economy experienced its first major slump and political unrest gave birth to the Chartist movement for democratic electoral reforms, concern over the social and moral consequences of industrialization came to a head. The 'Condition of England Question' became the major topic of debate, taken up by reformers such as Lord Shaftesbury (1801–85) and novelists such as Charles Dickens (1812–70). As writer Thomas Carlyle (1795–1881) famously asked in 1839, '[i]s the condition of the English working people wrong; so wrong that rational working men cannot, will not, and even should not rest quiet under it?'[3]

A.W.N. PUGIN

The new attitude to past and present was applied to architecture by Pugin. In *Contrasts* (1836), Pugin followed Cobbett in seeing contemporary Britain as a country where pre-industrial virtues had been driven out by industrial vices. This, Pugin presented in visual rather than verbal form. Pairs of images depicted towns and institutions as (allegedly) they had been in the fifteenth century as against their nineteenth century condition. In 'Contrasted Towns' the new jail has replaced the common land in the foreground and the town is dominated no longer by church spires but by factory chimneys. In 'Contrasted Residences for the Poor', the avuncular regime of the almshouse, in which monks cared for the poor and the discipline was purely spiritual, has been replaced by the rod and manacles of the workhouse. The dissecting table not the burial ground is the final destination for inmates.

A recent and fanatical convert to Catholicism, Pugin equated the virtues of the pre-industrial medieval past with those of his faith, and the vices of the present with the Protestant Reformation implemented by Henry VIII in the sixteenth century. The good old days were good because they were Christian – Catholic – and the bad new days were bad because they were pagan – Protestant. Pugin therefore had no difficulty in equating the architecture of the middle ages – gothic – with Christianity, and the ancient architecture revived in the renaissance – classical – with paganism. For Pugin, the

Figure 15.1

Pugin unfavourably compared
the England of his day with
the England that had
supposedly existed four
centuries before. 'Contrasted
Towns', in *Contrasts*, (1836).

gothic architecture of the middle ages was the only
true and Christian architecture.

The contrast between past and present made by the
critics of industrial society was thus rendered by Pugin
as a contrast between opposing types of architecture.
The classical architecture of his day was rejected in
favour of a return to the gothic. This represented a
marked departure from the prevalent British
picturesque view of architecture; architecture was no
longer to be judged on visual (did it enhance the
landscape pictorially?) but moral grounds (was the
society that produced it Christian or pagan?).

Pugin objected to the picturesque for another, more
conventional architectural reason. Of French extraction
(his father had come to Britain in the 1790s), Pugin
shared the rationalist approach characteristic of the
French tradition which, in contrast to the English

Figure 15.2

'Contrasted Residences for the Poor', in *Contrasts*, (1836).

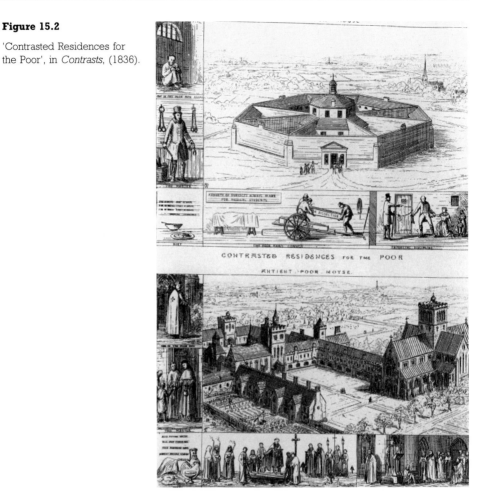

picturesque, thought architecture should be rational and rigorous. In particular there should be a tight, disciplined relationship between form and structure, so that plan and section are deducible from the appearance of the building.

Having proposed in *Contrasts* that gothic was the only valid Christian architecture, Pugin went on in *The True Principles of Pointed or Christian Architecture* (1841) to give architectural grounds for this moral judgement. Gothic buildings, he declared, followed the rule of expressing structure in their appearance. A gothic cathedral was honest and declared its structure by exposing its flying buttresses. By contrast in a classical building like St. Paul's Cathedral designed by Christopher Wren (1632–1723),

Figure 15.3

'Miserable expedient!' –
Pugin's damning verdict on
Christopher Wren's use of
screen walls at St. Paul's,
London, (1675–1709).

Figure 15.4

In *True Principles*, (1841),
Pugin claimed that gothic with
decorated flying buttresses
(left), not classical where the
flying buttresses are hidden
behind a screen (right),
constituted an honest and
logical architecture.

[the] buttresses, instead of being made ornamental, are concealed by an enormous screen, going entirely round the building. So that in fact one half of the edifice is built to conceal the other. Miserable expedient! worthy only of the debased style in which it has been resorted to.[4]

Pugin thus appropriated for gothic what had traditionally been a powerful argument for classical architecture: that it was a logical system in which structure was expressed as architecture. 'The two great rules for design,' he wrote, 'are these: first, that there should be no features about a building which are not necessary for convenience, construction, or propriety; second, that all ornament should consist of enrichment of the essential construction of the building.'[5] The key concept was propriety, which meant that 'the external and internal appearance of an edifice should be illustrative of, and in accordance with, the purpose for which it is destined.'[6]

These principles can be seen in the house and church, St. Augustine's (1846–51), that Pugin built for himself at Ramsgate in Kent. The style is gothic, with the programmatic difference between the church and the house clearly expressed in their external appearance. Ironically, however, the overall result is picturesque, for Pugin showed that such effects were best obtained not by traditional picturesque means but by allowing plan, section and programme to determine massing, that is by following the French structural rationalist approach.

Figure 15.5

Picturesque effects obtained by following rationalist principles. St Augustine's, Ramsgate (1846–51), architect A.W.N. Pugin.

JOHN RUSKIN

As with Pugin, the starting-point for the critique of architecture developed by Ruskin was the social critique generated by the industrial revolution: the contrast between past and present and the notion that virtue was to be found only in the past. Despite personal and religious differences (Ruskin was as virulently anti-Catholic as Pugin was anti-Protestant) we find in both a polarity constructed between good, medieval and Christian and bad, contemporary and pagan. Nonetheless there was an important difference. Whereas for Pugin the contrast was between medieval and nineteenth-century architecture, for Ruskin it was between medieval architecture and nineteenth century industrialism. For Pugin gothic was defined by its expression of structure; for Ruskin, gothic was defined by its expression of the feelings of the craftsmen who made it.[7]

Ruskin was here deploying ideas about art developed over the previous fifty years by Romantic poets and philosophers in Germany and Britain. Ruskin was foremost an art critic – he turned to architecture in the late 1840s in preparing his *magnum opus* five volume *Modern Painters* (1843–60) – and was well versed in art theory. The Romantics conceived of art as being produced by the full creative powers of the human spirit, where the artist was the creative being par excellence. In his architectural writings of the 1840s and 1850s – *The Seven Lamps of Architecture* (1849) and *The Stones of Venice* (1851–3) – Ruskin interpreted gothic architecture in these terms. More importantly, gothic architecture was thus counterposed with the reality of contemporary labour under the factory system.

Ruskin drew on the view, widespread in the 1840s, that workers in factories were little more than slaves or machines. Where craftsman had exercised skill and care in making things, factory hands were alienated from their work, having no say in how it was carried out. In the industrial system the thinking part of work had been taken from the worker and embodied in machinery; all that was left for the worker was to perform mindless repetitive tasks.

Ruskin's innovation was to take the contrast between 'free' creative and 'enslaved' industrial labour

Figure 15.6

For John Ruskin, the inventive carvings of Rouen Cathedral, (1202–30 and onward), were proof of the 'liberty of the workman' in gothic architecture. Drawing by Ruskin of the West porch.

and equate the former with gothic architecture. In the chapter 'The Nature of Gothic' in *The Stones of Venice*, Ruskin states that in gothic architecture the worker carving the stone had been able to express his feelings and character. Just as the personality of an artist like J.M.W. Turner (1775–1851) could be discerned in his paintings, so in the intricate surface of a Gothic cathedral could be read the character of those who carved the stones.

> [G]o forth again to gaze upon the old cathedral front, where you have smiled so often at the fantastic ignorance of the old sculptors; examine once more those ugly goblins, and formless monsters, and stern statues, anatomiless and rigid; but do not mock at them, for they are signs of the life and liberty of every workman who struck the stone . . . which it must be the first aim of all Europe at this day to regain for her children.[8]

Ruskin's contention was that gothic architecture demonstrated that work was not meant to be a mindless task. The 'ugly goblins and formless monsters' of Rouen cathedral (1202–30 and onward) were both proof that forms of creative work were possible and a rebuke to a society that had allowed work to become, in the factory system, a slave-like process.

GOTHIC AND AFTER

Not all architects, of course, read or understood the writings of Pugin and Ruskin. Nonetheless their effect on architectural production was profound, most immediately and visibly in terms of style. In place of those working in the picturesque/neo-classical idiom in the early decades (John Nash (1752–1835), John Soane (1753–1837), Robert Smirke (1780–1867), etc.), in the mid-nineteenth century architects turned *en masse* to gothic not as one style among many, as the picturesque would have it, but as the one true style, and not just in Britain but in the rest of Europe and America as well. In the 1840/50s a generation of architects influenced by Pugin and Ruskin – including Gilbert Scott (1811–78), William Butterfield (1814–1900) and G.E. Street (1824–81) – established gothic

Figure 15.7

The half century after Pugin saw gothic churches constructed across the length and breadth of Britain. Church at Balbersby, Yorkshire, (1855), architect William Butterfield.

Figure 15.8

Gothic architecture applied to the secular requirements of the railway age. The Midland Hotel, London, (1865–71), fronting St. Pancras Station, (1863–7), architect George Gilbert Scott and engineer W.H. Barlow.

Figure 15.9

Architects in America took up Ruskin's teachings in their own buildings. Academy of Fine Arts, Philadelphia, (1872–6), architect Frank Furness.

Figure 15.10

The arts and crafts architect William Lethaby refused to take his fee on Brockhampton Church, Herefordshire, (1900–2), because he felt he had not supervised its construction properly.

in a remarkably short period as the predominant 'Gothic Revival' style. In the 1880s, during the second great downturn of the industrial economy, interest in Pugin and Ruskin revived, developing into what became known as the Arts and Crafts movement, with architects such as W.R. Lethaby (1857–1931), C.F.A. Voysey (1857–1941) and C.R. Ashbee (1863–1942). But long after these two movements had passed, there remained legacies from their thinking – Pugin's structural rationalism, Ruskin's demand for a non-alienated form of architectural production – that architects continued to find fascinating.

REFERENCES

1   John Ruskin, *Lectures on Architecture and Painting*, (1854), and reprinted in E.T. Cook and Alexander Wedderburn (eds.), *The Works of John Ruskin*, (Allen, London, 39 volumes, 1903–12), v. 12, pp. 100–1.
2   Quoted by Phoebe Stanton, 'The Sources of Pugin's Contrasts', in John Summerson (ed.), *Concerning Architecture: Essays on Architectural Writers and Writing Presented to Nikolaus Pevsner*, (1968), p. 136.
3   Thomas Carlyle, 'Chartism', (1839), in A. Shelston (ed.), *Thomas Carlyle: Selected Writings*, (Penguin, Harmondsworth, 1971), pp. 152–3.
4   A.W.N. Pugin *The True Principles of Pointed or Christian Architecture*, (Academy Editions, London, 1973), p. 6.
5   Pugin *The True Principles*, p. 1.
6   Pugin *The True Principles*, p. 50.

7   For a more detailed discussion, see Mark Swenarton, 'Ruskin and 'The Nature of Gothic'' in *Artisans and Architects: the Ruskinian Tradition in Architectural Thought*, (Macmillan, London, 1989).

8   John Ruskin, *The Stones of Venice II*, (1853), paragraph XIV, in Cook and Wedderburn (eds.), *The Works of John Ruskin*, v. 10, pp. 193–4.

BIBLIOGRAPHY

General Culture and Economics

Raymond Williams, *Culture and Society 1780–1950*, (Penguin, Harmondsworth, 1961).

E.J. Hobsbawm, *Industry and Empire: From 1750 to the Present Day*, (Penguin, Harmondsworth, 1968).

Architecture

Michael W. Brooks, *John Ruskin and Victorian Architecture*, (Thames and Hudson, London, 1989).

E.T. Cook and Alexander Wedderburn (eds.), *The Works of John Ruskin*, (Allen, London, 39 volumes, 1903–1912).

Charles L. Eastlake, *A History of the Gothic Revival*, (Leicester University Press, Leicester, second edition 1978). First published 1872.

Christopher Hussey, *The Picturesque: Studies in a Point of View*, (Frank Cass, London, 1967). First published 1927.

Robert Macleod, *Style and Society: Architectural Ideology in Britain 1835–1914*, (RIBA Publications, London, 1971).

Stefan Muthesius, *The High Victorian Movement in Architecture 1950–1870*, (Routledge and Kegan Paul, London, 1972).

A.W.N. Pugin, *Contrasts*, (Leicester University Press, Leicester, 1969). First published 1836; second edition 1841.

A.W.N. Pugin *The True Principles of Pointed or Christian Architecture*, (Academy Editions, London, 1973). First published 1841.

Margaret Richardson, *Architects of the Arts and Crafts Movement*, (Trefoil and RIBA Drawings Collection, London, 1983).

John Ruskin, *The Seven Lamps of Architecture*, (Farrar, Strauss and Giroux, New York, 1981). First published 1849.

John Ruskin, 'The Nature of Gothic' in *The Stones of Venice*, (Faber, London, abridged edition, 1981.) First published as three volumes, 1851–53.

Andrew Saint, *The Image of the Architect*, (Yale University Press, New Haven, 1983).

Phoebe Stanton, 'The Sources of Pugin's Contrasts', in John Summerson (ed.), *Concerning Architecture: Essays on Architectural Writers and Writing Presented to Nikolaus Pevsner*, (Routledge and Kegan Paul, London, 1968).

Mark Swenarton, *Artisans and Architects: the Ruskinian Tradition in Architectural Thought*, (Macmillan, London, 1989).

16

THE POLITICS OF THE PLAN

Iain Borden

Of the standard triad of architectural drawings which describe a building – plan, section and elevation – the plan yields most information: a section depicts volumes and construction, and the elevation suggests external appearance, but the plan tells us most about how the building is arranged and used. In particular, the plan identifies and locates human activities by assigning certain social functions to certain areas of the building. The plan tells us where, and in what size and shape of space, we do what.

A plan is an abstraction, a two-dimensional horizontal slice through the building demonstrating the relative sizes and positions of rooms, circulation, doors and windows. A north point often provides geographic orientation. A series of plans, typically one per floor, add up to a complete functional and spatial inventory of a building, and for this reason plans are one of the principal techniques for designing buildings, performing a key role in how architects perceive and understand them. Indeed, in the work of architects like Hannes Meyer (1889–1954) and Leslie Martin (1908–), a building's design is often generated principally from the plan, with materials, structure and aesthetics relegated to secondary consideration. Yet a plan is quite different from the normal experience of a building – few people visualize a building as a plan unless trained to do so.

This raises a problem. If the plan is a key component of an informed conception of a building, which many have some difficulty in understanding, how do we make sense of this gap between professional technique and public experience? Remembering that the plan is not a real building but only an abstracted representation, does this not imply a disparity between drawings used to design a building and the reality of the building as constructed and used?

One response is that the plan is a purely neutral technique which has a usefulness to the architect inaccessible to others, but whose effects are directly beneficial to them. Architecture in such a view is analogous to the practice of medicine, with the plan equivalent to an x-ray, helping to diagnose the problem and guide the course of action. However, architecture is not the spatial equivalent of medicine. Despite the modernist notion that architecture can cure social ills, architecture is not a scientific process of diagnosis and remedy, nor is it practised with the precision of a surgical operation.

The plan is not a benign technique whose benefits are enjoyed only by the user, rather it facilitates a process of abstraction for designers, allowing the functions, spaces and structure of a building to be mapped out. The important term here is abstraction. In any technique of representation, a process of abstraction is undertaken which simplifies reality to a diagrammatic image. The plan is an architectural abstraction of fundamental social importance, representing where people carry out different actions and how they will be able to interact. The two examples discussed below – the German *existenzminimum* and the Kings Road Studios in Los Angeles – explicate this process in more detail, showing how spaces on the plan are abstractions of the architectural ideas and social relations to which they refer.

THE EXISTENZMINIMUM

In 1929 the second meeting took place in Frankfurt of CIAM (Congrès International d'Architecture Moderne), a principal forum for modernist architects founded one year earlier. The focus here was a particular kind of housing: the *existenzminimum*, or 'minimum dwelling for existence'.

In the aftermath of World War I, marked by political upheavals, economic crises, and by dramatic shifts in population patterns caused by migration and large-scale formation of new family units, European countries faced a deteriorating housing stock and a scarcity of building materials, labour and finance, coupled with an enormous demand for housing. The idea of the existenzminimum was to address such problems through dwellings tailored not to the individual desires of the occupants, but to their actual measured needs and constructed in the most efficient way possible. In order to achieve these aims, the existenzminimum relied on the newly developed techniques of standardized dwelling design, standardized materials and components, and industrialized production, including the use of unskilled labour and production line methods borrowed from Ford automobile factories (and thus often referred to as Fordism).

Figure 16.1

The house as scientific solution to user requirements. Frankfurt, (c.1927), architect in chief Ernst May.

This rationalization of housing provision was accompanied by another modernist tenet, that of functionalism. Just as occupants' individual desires are held to be irrelevant in the existenzminimum, so too are the idiosyncrasies of architects, and 'die neue Sachlichkeit' ('New Objectivity') therefore claimed to subordinate art to the rationality of the machine and to the servicing of public needs. Buildings were to be based on a scientific knowledge of user requirements, transformed into architecture by the application of rationalist methods of design and construction. All this is summed up by the aphorism that 'form follows function', first expressed by the American architect Louis Sullivan (1856–1924) but most commonly associated with German inter-war modernism.

How then was this scientific knowledge of users achieved, and how was it transformed into architectural form? The scientific approach to identifying user needs involves breaking human existence down into basic biological needs and social activities. The contribution made by Walter Gropius (1883–1969), German architect and director of the Bauhaus school, to the 1929 congress provides a precise summary: 'The question of the minimum dwelling is the question of the elementary minimum of space, air, light and warmth.'[1]

Regarding light, research by Walter Schwagenscheidt for the German RFG (Reichsforschungsgesellschaft für Wirtschaftlichkeit im Bau- und Wohnungswesen), the federal agency set up to support experiments in rationalized housing provision, showed the optimum orientation for any dwelling to the sun to be 22.5° off the

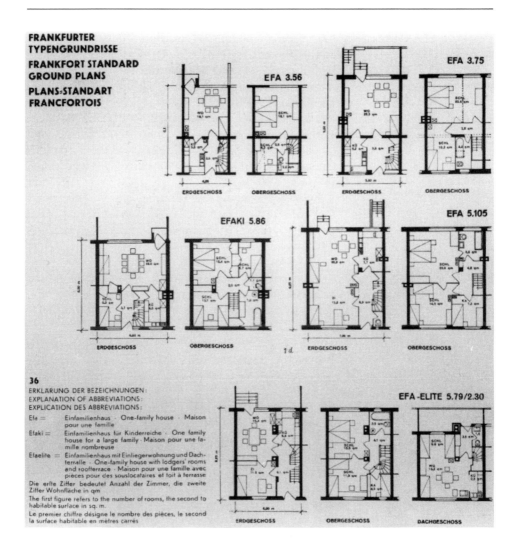

FRANKFURTER
TYPENGRUNDRISSE

FRANKFORT STANDARD
GROUND PLANS

PLANS-STANDART
FRANCFORTOIS

EFA 3.56

EFA 3.75

EFAKI 5.86

EFA 5.105

36

ERKLÄRUNG DER BEZEICHNUNGEN:
EXPLANATION OF ABBREVIATIONS:
EXPLICATION DES ABBREVIATIONS:

Efa =   Einfamilienhaus · One-family house · Maison
        pour une famille
Efaki = Einfamilienhaus für Kinderreiche · One family
        house for a large family · Maison pour une fa-
        mille nombreuse
Efaelite = Einfamilienhaus mit Einliegerwohnung und Dach-
        terralle · One-family house with lodgers' rooms
        and roofterrace · Maison pour une famille avec
        pièces pour des souslocataires et toit à terrasse
Die erste Ziffer bedeutet Anzahl der Zimmer, die zweite
Ziffer Wohnfläche in qm
The first figure refers to the number of rooms, the second to
habitable surface in sq. m.
Le premier chiffre désigne le nombre des pièces, le second
la surface habitable en mètres carrés

EFA-ELITE 5.79/2.30

north-south axis.[2] Air and warmth are supplied by adequate natural ventilation and, in the 1920s Frankfurt social housing provided under the supervision of Ernst May (1886–1970), by central heating.

The most important developments in the existenzminimum deal with the first of Gropius' four criteria, that of space, as demonstrated in radical new arrangements of the plan. Traditional German apartments were typically sub-divided into three or four rooms of roughly equal size, allowing occupants to decide what to do with each. Only the function of the *Wohnküche*, a kitchen large enough for additional living space, is pre-determined by design.[3] By contrast,

Figure 16.2

Standardized plans in a 1930 issue of *Das Neue Frankfurt:* the EFA for one family (top and centre right), the EFAKI for one large family (centre left), and EFA-ELITE for one family with lodgers (bottom). The first number of each plan refers to the total number of rooms, the second number to the total square meterage of habitable space.

the existenzminimum is based on a detailed consideration of each domestic activity, with a specific space being designed and allocated for it on plan. The maximum amount of space is allocated to the living and dining area, around which are minimal rooms for the kitchen, bedrooms and bathroom. Plans illustrated in the congress proceedings show each room not only labelled for its intended function, but with furniture layouts and minimal circulation space to demonstrate that it could work in practice, together with both individual room and overall area figures. This means that where the traditional apartment allowed some flexibility, the existenzminimum designates precisely which room is to be used for what purpose, and provides only the essential space in each case.

The extreme degree of control exercised is particularly evident in the minimal spaces for cooking, washing and sleeping and in the fittings and furniture provided, including built-in fold-away beds and the

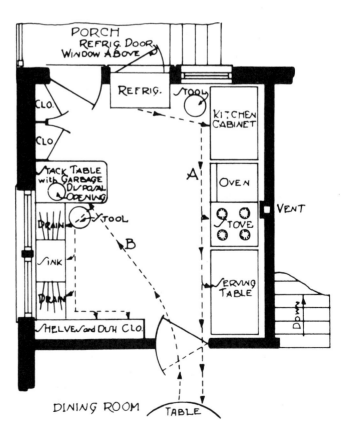

Figure 16.3

Methods of industrial production and management applied to the domestic interior by Christine Frederick. The kitchen as Fordist production line. *Scientific Management in the Home: Household Engineering*, (1920).

THE LIBRARY
GUILDFORD COLLEGE The politics of the plan   219
of Further and Higher Education

famous 'Frankfurt kitchen' (c. 1926–7). Designed by the Austrian architect Grette Schütte-Lihotsky, and based heavily on the ideas of the American domestic expert Christine Frederick about the scientific management of the home and supported by Alexander Klein's research for the RFG, the Frankfurt kitchen brought the techniques and methods of the modern American factory into the home. File records were to be kept of all incoming household goods and food, domestic tasks subjected to time-and-motion studies and broken down into production line steps, and, in contrast to the *Wohnküche*, the kitchen was designed to accommodate solely the preparation of food, clearing away of crockery and related domestic tasks. As a place of domestic work, the kitchen no longer accommodates relaxation and leisure activities.

The attention to detail verges on the body-centric, with each space on the plan reduced down to the smallest possible area for a person to occupy. Exact dimensions for simple actions like sitting and standing are precisely translated into architecture through the plan form. The Frankfurt kitchen involves a highly compact arrangement of furniture and equipment, including a built-in ironing board, easily reached from a swivel stool. Also at Frankfurt, a special register was drawn up listing beds, chairs, lamps and other equipment, much of it specially designed, of the right dimensions for the existenzminimum plan.[4]

The plan had important technical advantages for the architects of the Weimar Republic. It enables the rationalist and functionalist principles of the existenzminimum to be realised by precisely defining and locating different domestic functions, and by allowing minimal spaces to be accurately worked out in advance of occupation. Standardization of dwelling design focused on a strictly limited number of plan-types, and, partly as a result of standardizing plans, materials and construction labour are reduced and costs cut. The overall importance of the plan for the existenzminimum can be seen by its symbolic role, including an appearance as the dominant image on the cover of the Frankfurt CIAM proceedings.

The plan also had a social role, carrying with it a particular model of how people should live. Beside physical constraints on occupants, there is also a less explicit but no less significant social ideology built into

Figure 16.4

Frankfurt kitchen, (c.1926–7). Note fold-away ironing board, adjustable stool, plate racks, double sink, glass fronted cabinets, individual food storage drawers and movable overhead light. Architect Grette Schütte-Lihotsky.

the existenzminimum. In essence, the new dwelling is intended to produce not just new accommodation but a whole new way of living, liberating the family from traditional modes of domestic arrangement into new modes more in keeping with the nascent Weimar Republic.[5] The separation of domestic work from domestic living, modern design and materials, a predetermination of room uses by experts and not by occupants – these things are all part of the rejection of traditional working-class and vernacular living arrangements in favour of a new form of living more appropriate to the urban spirit of the republic. Nowhere is this better seen than in the gender relations implicit in the Frankfurt kitchen, through which women are recast as an active contributor to the new living, providing domestic services without servants in the most efficient, professional and hygienic manner possible. The time a woman saves through new housekeeping methods can then be used for more attentive care for her spouse and children. The intended effect is to create a professionalized identity for women, replacing old models of drudgery and subservience to men with a new model of activity and vocation which emphasizes the unique contributions made by women to the family and the home.

KINGS ROAD STUDIOS

Similar tensions between plan, architectural intentions and social reality may also be discerned in the Kings Road Studios designed by the Austrian-born architect Rudolph Schindler (1887–1953). The Studios, built 1921–2 in the North Hollywood district of Los Angeles, share with the existenzminimum a concern for creating a new way of life, but the exact kind of this new life resulted in a rather different plan form.[6]

The Kings Road Studios was a joint residence for Schindler, his wife Pauline Gibling, and their two friends, Clyde and Marian Chace. It was to be cheap but modern, using all that he and Clyde Chace, an architectural engineer, knew about design and construction. Above all, it was to be a studio-residence, different from a conventional house, with each adult having their own studio-room, drawing on shared spaces and facilities as required. In plan, the building is essentially a squared pinwheel. Beside their individual studio-rooms, each couple has their own wing and entrance hall, and their own garden and patio, with a shared kitchen in the middle at the hub of the plan. Guest quarters, garage and car port are in the third arm of the pinwheel, separated out to the north-west corner. As we shall see, these plan arrangements have to be understood as an exercise in personal artistic identity, in social relations and in gender relations for those who lived there.

The original inspiration was two-fold. On the one hand, Schindler and Gibling had previously lived at Frank Lloyd Wright's (1867–1959) famous Taliesin office and residence community in Wisconsin described by Richard Cándida Smith in Chapter 17,

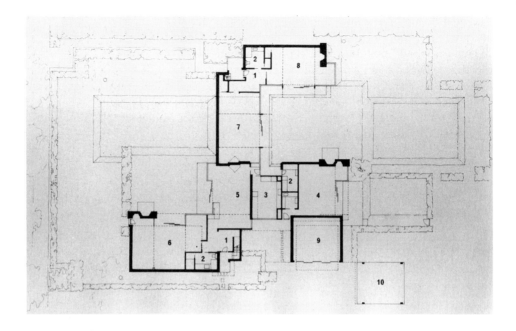

Figure 16.5

The plan is an integral part of the dialectical interaction between the design, conception and everyday inhabitation of architectural space. Kings Road Studios, Los Angeles, (1921–2), architect Rudolph Schindler. 1 Hall 2 Bathroom 3 Kitchen 4 Guest 5 Marian Chase 6 Clyde Chase 7 Pauline Gibling 8 Rudolph Schindler 9 Garage 10 Carport.

where they became convinced of the pleasures of living and working in the same building. As a result, each adult at Kings Road is provided with a studio, connected to the outside via large sliding doors. The house becomes more than a house, an artist's studio where work and pleasure are indistinguishable, where the building and the landscape are in harmony, and where simplicity of design leads to a heightened appreciation of the arts. And the concept of the studio in turn implies that each resident is an artist whose life is on extension of her or his work. The idea of the Studios as a place of art and life, work and play, can be discerned from the many visitors and guests entertained there, including composers John Cage (1912–) and Igor Stravinsky (1882–1971), novelist Theodore Dreiser (1871–1945), Expressionist art collector Galka Scheyer, dancer John Bovingdon, and, after 1925, fellow residents architect Richard Neutra (1892–1970) and his wife Dione Neutra.[7]

The other idea behind the Studios derived from a particular event in the Schindler–Gibling marriage. In October 1921 they went on an extended camping vacation in the Yosemite. Here, deep in the American wilderness, sleeping in tents and beneath the stars, cooking on open fires, Schindler and Gibling felt that

they had experienced a spiritual celebration of life. This is why, rather than the distinct enclosed rooms and gardens of a conventional house, the outdoor spaces of the Studios were conceived not as gardens but as what Schindler called 'outdoor rooms'. The idea is carried through to the minimal shared kitchen and to the fireplaces which face both inward to the studios and outward onto these outdoor rooms. The original intention was for cooking to take place over an open fire or even on the table-top itself, and so transform the burden of cooking into what Schindler called a 'social campfire'. The kitchen itself was merely to be used for food storage, cleaning up, laundry facilities and so on, containing expensive equipment made more affordable when shared by two couples.

In many ways, however, these arrangements are far from perfect. While the plan form is of particular significance in assigning the location, size and relative displacement of different private areas, shared facilities and so on, its final form also discloses some tension between the intended liberatory artistic nature of the living arrangements and the social relations as

Figure 16.6

Part artists' studios, part campsite, the Kings Road Studios residence was intended as new form of living, including sleeping out of doors in roof-top 'sleeping baskets'. Shown here glazed in, these have now been restored to their original state covered only with canvas.

experienced. In particular, the placement of the kitchen next to the women's studios is clearly intended to allow them, and not the men, to perform most of the household chores. As Schindler stated, it allowed them to more easily share and rotate tasks. Nor was this the only inconvenience caused to Pauline Gibling and Marian Chace by the plan form. The only internal circulation in the residence is via the women's own private studios, an arrangement inconsistent with the privacy one would expect to find accorded to all individuals.[8] And although the California climate is good enough for external circulation to be possible most of the time, this cannot always be relied upon.

THE PLAN AND SOCIAL LIVING

As the existenzminimum and the Kings Road Studios both demonstrate, a plan is not a benign technical operation but a particular kind of representation which provides an abstraction of a real building. More than just a useful tool in the design and construction of a building, the plan carries within it both the tenets of architectural theory and a social model as to how people can and should carry out their lives. Disparities thus sometimes occur between the intentions and the social reality of the building designed.

It would however be wrong to talk of an 'error' between the plan and the social reality. A plan is not 'wrong' when viewed against the lives of those who occupy the final building. Rather the plan is a necessary part of the design process – a codified technique of spatial representation – which identifies and locates the intended functions of a building, and through which a rethinking is made of their inter-relationship. History allows us to add a third element to this equation: the social use of a building. We can then see a dialectic at work between the actual social activities of building users, the techniques used to understand and represent them, and those more imaginative representations used to conceive new ways of living. And as in any dialectic, tensions and contradictions necessarily occur. The plan, such as that of the existenzminimum and of the Kings Road Studios, is an integral part of this process.

REFERENCES

1   Quoted in Martin Steinman, 'Political Standpoints in CIAM 1928–1933', *AA Quarterly*, v.4 n.4 (1972), p. 52.
2   Nicholas Bullock, 'Housing in Frankfurt 1925 to 1931 and the New Wohnkultur', *Architectural Review*, v.163 n.976 (June 1978), p. 338.
3   Barbara Miller Lane, *Architecture and Politics in Germany, 1918–1945*, (Harvard University Press, Cambridge, Mass., 1968), p. 99.
4   Nicholas Bullock, 'Housing in Frankfurt 1925 to 1931 and the New Wohnkultur', p. 339.
5   Nicholas Bullock, 'First the Kitchen – Then the Facade', *AA Files*, n.6 (1984), p. 59.
6   I have relied heavily for this account of the Kings Road Studios on Kathryn Smith, *R.M. Schindler House, 1921–22*, (Perpetua Press, Los Angeles, 1987), a booklet produced in commemmoration of the centennial of Schindler's birth and the tenth anniversary of the Friends of the Schindler House.
7   John Pastier, 'Hollywood Classic', *The Architects' Journal*, v. 194 n.20 (13 November 1991), p. 36.
8   Dolores Hayden, *Grand Domestic Revolution: A History of Feminist Designs for American Homes, Neighborhoods, and Cities*, (MIT Press, Cambridge, Mass., 1981), pp. 248–50.

BIBLIOGRAPHY

Existenzminimum

AA Quarterly, special issue on the architecture of the Weimar Republic, v.11 n.1 (1979).

Catherine Bauer, *Modern Housing*, (Houghton Mifflin, Boston, 1934).

Nicholas Bullock, 'Housing in Frankfurt 1925 to 1931 and the New Wohnkultur', *Architectural Review*, v.163 n.976 (June 1978), pp. 335–42.

Nicholas Bullock, 'First the Kitchen – Then the Facade', *AA Files*, n.6 (1984), pp. 59–67.

Giorgio Ciucci, 'The Invention of the Modern Movement', *Oppositions*, n.24, (1981), pp. 68–91.

D.W. Dreysse, *Ernst May Housing Estates: Architectural Guide to Eight New Frankfort* [sic] *Estates (1926–1930)*, (Fricke Verlag, Frankfurt, 1988).

Barbara Miller Lane, *Architecture and Politics in Germany, 1918–1945*, (Harvard University Press, Cambridge, Mass., 1968).

Martin Steinman, 'Political Standpoints in CIAM 1928–1933', *AA Quarterly*, v.4 n.4 (1972), pp. 49–55.

Kings Road Studios

Reyner Banham, 'Rudolph Schindler: Pioneering Without Tears', *Architectural Design*, v.37 (December 1967), pp. 578–9.

David Gebhard, *Schindler*, (Viking Press, New York, 1971).

Dolores Hayden, *Grand Domestic Revolution: A History of Feminist Designs for American Homes, Neighborhoods, and Cities*, (MIT Press, Cambridge, Mass., 1981).

Esther McCoy, *Five California Architects*, (Praeger Publishers, New York, 1960).

John Pastier, 'Hollywood Classic', *The Architects' Journal*, v. 194 n.20 (13 November 1991), pp. 32–9.

August Sarnitz, *R.M. Schindler Architect, 1887–1953: A Pupil of Otto Wagner Between International Style and Space Architecture*, (Rizzoli, New York, 1988).

Kathryn Smith, *R.M. Schindler House, 1921–22*, (Perpetua Press, Los Angeles, 1987).

17

FRANK LLOYD WRIGHT AS EDUCATOR

THE TALIESIN FELLOWSHIP PROGRAM, 1932–59

Richard Cándida Smith

In his 1930 Princeton University lectures, the architect Frank Lloyd Wright (1867–1959) called for American corporations to sponsor 'industrial style centers' throughout the United States. In each forty students under the direction of masters and journeymen would study building design and construction, furniture making, ceramics, textiles, sheet metal work, woodworking, landscaping, dance, music, and a host of allied arts. Equipped with the most modern machinery, these centres would be sources of both technical innovation and artistic expression. American business did not respond, but, two years later, Wright announced that he would accept talented young men and women to work as his apprentices.[1]

In September 1932, the first 23 students arrived at Taliesin, Wright's famous studio, office and residential community at rural Spring Green, Wisconsin. Paying annual tuition, they provided much needed cash and dedicated, unpaid labour for the basic tasks of Wright's practice. Equally important, the students expected that great things would arise from their association with Wright. Having spent the post-World War I years drifting into isolation, Wright found himself in the 1930s the genius of a community. His remaining 25 years would be among Wright's most creative and innovative as he rose to the challenge of training young architects.

LIFE AT TALIESIN

The first students at Taliesin arrived to find neither private rooms nor sufficient work space. Necessity prompted their initial tasks: expanding Taliesin and making it liveable for 40–50 people. Eventually, each apprentice had a comfortable and spacious room, and the group remodelled Wright's Hillside (1902) school building into drafting and work rooms. Wright instructed his students to 'fell trees and saw them into lumber; quarry rock and burn lime; sculpture stone and carve wood; turn sawed lumber into structure and trusses . . . design and make furniture; weave rugs; dig ditches; labour in the fields . . . make roads; prepare meals.' Books and lectures were secondary to intimate daily contact with the 'materials of design' and the 'design of materials.' Taliesin fellows viewed manual labour as a necessary and natural correlate to intellectual work. John Lautner, for one, felt he had learned what wood and stone were 'good for' and was therefore in a better position to exploit the design potential of his materials. While typical architecture graduates made sketches or plans that lacked meaning, he understood that the building processes were guided by practical and aesthetic goals,

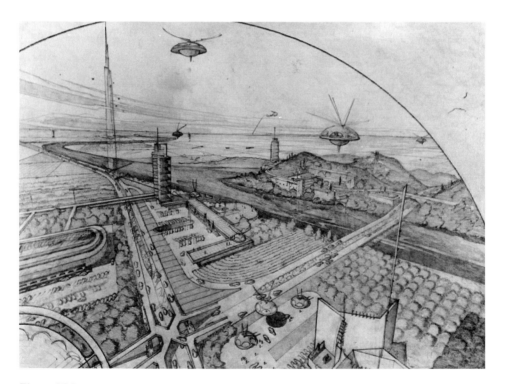

Figure 17.1

'Great roads unite and separate . . . roadside markets, garden schools, dwelling places, each on its acres of individually adorned and cultivated ground.' Frank Lloyd Wright, *When Democracy Builds*, (1945). The Broadacre City project was a technological, automobile-driven version of an anti-urban American tradition reaching back to Thomas Jefferson in the eighteenth century. Drawing by John Rattenbury.

sharpened by possibilities and limitations inherent in the technology available.[2]

A morning bell woke students at six-thirty. Breakfast was served punctually at seven, and anyone late was not allowed to eat. After breakfast, Wright or his senior apprentices assigned duties for the day. Six mornings a week were spent in heavy labour, as the community raised much of the food it ate, and apprentices constantly tended to the farm. They maintained vehicles, prepared roads and parking areas, constructed farm buildings, built walls and fences, and improved plumbing, electrical, and heating systems. Following lunch, apprentices worked on projects related to Wright's practice. For the first two years of the Fellowship, this meant developing Broadacre City – Wright's utopian design for a decentered American society – an activity that required intensive discussion with Wright on his theories of community life, work and culture. Twice a year, on Christmas and Wright's birthday, students gave special presents known as the 'Christmas Box' and the 'Birthday Box'. Generally, Wright let it be known what he wanted: one year their ideas for low cost Usonian concrete block houses; another year, proposals for landscaping Taliesin. Wright went through the schemes and made his comments, as often bitingly critical as appreciative. After the presentations, Wright handed out gifts to each of his apprentices.[3]

After 1935, when Wright began receiving more commissions, apprentices prepared plans and elevations. When there were no such specific assignments, apprentices were free to develop their own projects, while still cooking, serving meals and cleaning up the common areas. Wright believed that cultured people should entertain themselves and encouraged students to form theatre, music and dance groups. Taliesin offered public concerts every Sunday evening. 'Complete living was the training,' Lautner recalled. Wright frequently invited famous guests to stay, usually musicians or writers, but only those architects whose philosophies Wright assumed were compatible with his were allowed to visit. Wright rudely refused both Le Corbusier (1887–1966) and Walter Gropius (1883–1969), but he was pleased to invite the German architect Ludwig Mies van der Rohe (1886–1969) to spend a week working with the Taliesin fellows.

Figure 17.2

Wright allowed only one
official 'architect' at Taliesin –
himself. Wright at Taliesin
with (left to right) Gene
Masselink, Benjamin Dombar,
Edgar Tafel and Jack Howe.

Aside from these occasional visits from Wright's few
architectural allies, apprentices focused almost exclusively on the study of Wright's work. Theory was
provided by Wright's ongoing commentaries on his
own and the students' work. Rather than give
organized lectures, he preferred to stop students in the
middle of a task and discuss the importance of detail
work in establishing meaning and coherence. Detailing
constituted the realm of 'grammar,' he told them, while
stressing that architecture depended upon a single
controlling idea permeating all aspects of a construction; without it, buildings were assemblies of clichés
and façades. Wright encouraged students to develop
their building ideas from their independent observation
of nature, and discouraged imitations of his own buildings. Students considered Wright's frequent comment,
'Hm, looks kind of familiar,' one of the most crushing
they could hear. Wright and his students frequently
toured his buildings, but Wright wanted them to see
how he had solved past problems rather than to adopt
his style as a substitute for their own thinking.

Many students did not like the lack of structure or the exclusive focus on Wright's work. Turnover of apprentices was high, but new students were always ready to join. Others found the programme congenial and stayed for years. Edgar Tafel, having dropped out of the architecture school at New York University, assumed he would be at Taliesin for a year or two. He stayed nine years. John Lautner stayed seven. William Wesley Peters, John Howe and Eugene Masselink stayed their entire lives. Tafel recalled that Wright did not impose himself upon his apprentices; they had to seek him out, but he willingly gave his time to any who came to him with questions. Within the Fellowship a core group formed that was most moved by Wright's philosophy.

WORKING FOR WRIGHT

In 1936, Wright began to receive a series of commissions. In the next four years, he designed, among others, the Johnson Wax Administration Building (1936–9, laboratory tower 1944–50) in Racine, Wisconsin and 24 private residences, including the famous Fallingwater (1937–9) vacation house for Edgar Kaufmann Sr. at Bear Run, Pennsylvania. Those loyal to Wright were amply rewarded by receiving important responsibilities. At Johnson Wax, for example, Wesley Peters, Wright's son-in-law, guided the project, while Tafel supervised the installation of the glass tubing and lighting.

Figure 17.3

Johnson Wax Administration Building and Laboratory Tower, Racine, Wisconsin, (1936–9 and 1944–50), architect Frank Lloyd Wright.

Figure 17.4

Johnson Wax Administration
Building and Laboratory
Tower, interior of
administration building. The
mushroom shaped columns
defy usual constructional
rationality by being thinner at
the bottom than at the top.

Figure 17.5

Fallingwater, Bear Run,
Pennsylvania, (1937–9),
presented apprentices with
impossible constructional
problems. The house
continues to suffer from
structural failings in its
cantilevered concrete decks.
Architect Frank Lloyd Wright.

Apprentices in charge of a project prepared the plans and then went to the site to ensure that contractors adhered to Wright's vision. Wright himself remained in almost daily contact, determining progress and sending detailed instructions. Wright's use of materials was often idealistic, motivated by a desire for striking visual effect, so that when inexperienced apprentices attempted to implement problematic ideas, difficulties were compounded. Robert Mosher had to be removed at Fallingwater after the client Kaufmann lost faith in his technical abilities. Tafel supervised the construction of the second floor, but similarly found himself unable to mediate the conflicts between Wright's vision and the client's concern for structural stability. In fact, these conflicts were unresolvable because the floating cantilevers over the waterfall tested the limits of building technology. Cracks have continued to appear and reappear after repair, while deflections of the cantilevered terraces have been visible to the naked eye.[4]

By the beginning of 1942, only a dozen apprentices remained at Taliesin; most had left to begin personal careers or to join the war. A tight-knit group consolidated around Wright as they spent the war years developing future projects. Wesley Peters, Howe, Masselink and others determined that they never wanted to leave Taliesin; it was not only an education but a community, in which service to Wright's architecture gave them the emotional satisfaction they required.

After 1945, the apprentice program resumed, but with students having much less direct contact with Wright than their predecessors. Most assignments and supervision came from the apprentices turned journeymen, while Wright himself was busy travelling, lecturing, and visiting his many buildings under construction. Construction supervision was usually handled by the older apprentices, and the primary duties of students were maintenance of the Taliesin estates and handling the increased demands for sketches and plans.[5]

This post-war period saw an explosion in the amount of work given to Wright. He designed and built 112 residences and nine commercial projects including doctors' offices, stores, a restaurant, a filling station and a school. He completed the Florida

Figure 17.6

Solomon R. Guggenheim Museum, New York, (1943–6 and 1956–9). Architect Frank Lloyd Wright. The infamous spiral ramp deployed internally as the gallery was an idea first mooted for the Gordon Strong Planetarium project, (1925).

Southern College campus in Lakeland, Florida and expanded the Johnson Wax buildings. The period also brought several of his most monumental creations, including the Guggenheim Museum (1943–6 and 1956–9) in New York, the Price Tower (1953–6) in Bartlesville, Oklahoma and the Beth-Shalom Synagogue (1958–9) in Elkins Park, Pennsylvania. Beyond this, Taliesin was engaged in a constant production of sketches and proposals for unrealized projects. The volume of work was phenomenal, considering that Wright insisted that he could be the only architect in the practice, and that he was already 78 years old in 1945.

In actuality, the Taliesin community was not a one-man firm. The practice depended upon his spirit, but much of the work, including design, was done by journeymen and apprentices. Old plans were recycled in new projects, so that Tafel's plan for the St. Mark's-in-the Bouwerie project in New York became the floor plan for the Price Tower. The volume of work may also have accentuated repetitiveness of design features. Wright increasingly used circles, spirals, and ellipses in order to accentuate separation from the environment – breaking away from his poetic ideal that design organically reflected site, materials and function – and thus to allow the incorporation of abstract motifs in a variety of situations.

Such standardization of ideas was essential if a variety of hands were to work on projects. Journeymen told their apprentices that their drawings were only rough concepts; no matter how fine in execution and conception, Wright's final touches would transform their work into masterpieces. Wright signed all sketches and plans.

WORKING AFTER WRIGHT

The ideology of service to an incomparable master kept Taliesin running but did little to promote a Wrightian architecture that could survive him. In 1939 and 1940, many of Wright's most valuable apprentices were already leaving to set up on their own, many because of Wright's insistence that he was the only architect. While few went on to achieve internationally distinguished careers, many established successful local practices and influenced the course of domestic architecture in the United States and Europe.

A paradox in Wright's teaching method was that by stressing the uniqueness of every building and the importance of developing individual taste, Wright could swallow up students who had come to find their own individuality. Lautner and Donald Hoppen, a British architect apprenticed in the 1950s, both noted that few apprentices were able to develop an individual architectural philosophy. Wright did not impose his aesthetic, but most were so overawed by the completeness of his vision that they adopted his perspective instead of making their own observations.

Furthermore, Wright had a long history of appropriating discoveries of his students without crediting them. For example, Walter Burley Griffin, a former apprentice from the early 1900s, successfully developed the 'Knit-Lock' textile block system in Australia in the 1910s, and later had an acrimonious dispute with Wright over its authorship. Wright used the textile block system for his California homes of the 1920s and claimed, with little justification, that its design principles uniquely reflected his philosophy that building materials should grow out of local resources.[6]

Such bitter arguments were, however, not typical. Lautner and Tafel accepted Wright's personal limitations as the price of learning their craft from a singular teacher. Tafel noted that most apprentices who left to begin their own practices could not work in an overtly Wrightian style, mainly because of its inherently high cost. Instead, they adapted to the sparser language of the prevailing modernist architecture but with greater attention, Tafel felt, to the expressivity of materials and the potential of the site.

After Wright's death in 1959, the journeymen formed Taliesin Associated Architects (TAA), which completed several of Wright's masterpieces, including the Guggenheim, Beth-Shalom Synagogue, and the Marin County Civic Center (1957–66) in northern California, Gammage Auditorium (1959) at Arizona State University, and many residences. Lacking Wright's constant evaluation, such buildings constructed after his death could only approximately reflect his intentions. TAA did develop buildings from original designs, but these, such as the Lincoln Income Life Insurance Company Building (1966) in Louisville, Kentucky, are unsuccessful pastiches of Wrightian effects, lacking a single controlling idea.

The Wrightian tradition has been more effectively carried on by individuals who studied in the Fellowship programme, as well as by the numerous others influenced by his writings and published designs. Paolo Soleri (1919–), an apprentice from 1947 to 1949, and Lautner have become among the best-known examples of the 'poet' architect. Soleri's work in some respects can be considered a parody of Wright's. Having returned to Wright's conception that a building should be an organic outgrowth of its site, Soleri's earth houses and his fantastic city Arcosanti

Figure 17.7

Not derived from a Frank Lloyd Wright design, but an original creation. Lincoln Income Life Insurance Company Building, Louisville, Kentucky, (1966), architect William Wesley Peters of Taliesin Associated Architects.

Figure 17.8

Once they left Taliesin, few of Wright's students found it easy to either innovate or remain close to his ideas. Arcosanti, Arizona, (1970–), architect Paolo Soleri, is closer in theory than many others who tried to develop Wright's organic architecture.

(1970–) in Arizona have been constructed out of compacted desert soil and designed to masquerade as rock formations.[7]

Yet Wright's original ideas on the relation of building and site were at best metaphors, and in many cases Wright's dictums on siting just described possible ways of looking at his buildings. His theories were post-rationalizations that attempted to explain his practice after the fact. Lautner was one of a handful of students who understood this, and decided to ignore Wright the philosopher and follow Wright the practitioner. While at Taliesin, Lautner paid little attention to Wright's general discussion of architecture, nor did he seek to engage Wright with theoretical puzzles. Instead, Lautner was most fascinated with how Wright defined and solved specific problems.

As a result, although Lautner borrowed many of Wright's characteristic design elements for his own buildings, these took on very different meaning and function as Lautner's work developed. Having been sent to supervise the Sturges House (1939) in Los Angeles, Lautner decided to remain, and the Lautner House (1939–40) he designed for himself reflects the tension between Wright's design principles and his philosophy that every artist starts from personal vision. The exterior presents a modified version of the Sturges House's projection over a hillside. But Lautner had already begun to root his building more firmly on the ground, while allowing the roof to detach itself from the structure and soar. Internally, the space is opened up vertically to allow more light than in a typical

Figure 17.9

Just as Rudolph Schindler was sent by Wright to Los Angeles to oversee construction of the Barnsdall ('Hollyhock') House, (1917–20), and stayed on to build the Kings Road Studios, so John Lautner designed for himself this Lautner House, Los Angeles, (1939–40), after supervising the Sturges House.

Wright residence. There is also less roof overhang and more window area. Similarly, the opposition of hearth (protective shelter) and window (environmental integration) that characterized Wright's residential designs quickly disappeared in Lautner's work. Yet Lautner has placed the inspiration for his residential work in the first building he constructed for Wright, Deertrack (1936) in Michigan. 'In the wintertime,' he noted, 'when you'd go in that living room, in a woods full of snow, and you're just right in the middle of it. All spring, summer, and autumn, it's just magnificent, because you're just part of the woods.'[8]

In the transition from Wright to Lautner, an important progress in twentieth-century modernism can be seen. Residences did not lose coherence when they lost functional centres such as the hearth because that functionality had been largely poetic, even fictional, in the first place. In this Wright was not alone, and the quest for organic roots to social phenomena can be found in the writings of Americans as diverse as the philosopher John Dewey (1859–1952), urban reformer Jane Addams (1860–1935), poet and philosopher George Santayana (1863–1952) and politician Theodore Roosevelt (1858–1919). As Lautner's generation matured in the decades following World War II, the social character of the imagination could be faced squarely. Elements of building design could be treated as artist and client wanted, for no other justification than their own pleasure and sense of aesthetic refinement.

This transformation is one reason why Wright's successors have had difficulty dealing with him as an

Figure 17.10

Sturges House, Los Angeles, (1939), architect Frank Lloyd Wright.

educator, despite testimonials from many architects affirming his importance for their visual thinking. Wright has been accepted as the pre-eminent 'poet-architect' of America, who showed the viability of individual achievement in a century dominated by bureaucratic structures. Wright has become pure, shimmering symbol. Yet the achievement was based on a ruthlessness unthinkable in most corporations. Wright the man may not be as romantic as Wright the symbol, but ultimately may even be more meaningful. His late career is unimaginable without the Fellowship and the hard work of his students. Just as modern architecture was an unforeseen movement towards building as pleasure, its adventure was based on men and women working together as a team even when they believed that great artistic achievement was always singular and individual.

REFERENCES

1   Frank Lloyd Wright, *Modern Architecture: Being the Kahn Lectures for 1930*, reprinted in Frank Lloyd Wright, *The Future of Architecture* (Horizon Press, New York, 1953), pp. 108–11.

2   John Lautner, 'Responsibility, Infinity, Nature,' interviewed 1982 by Marlene L. Laskey, Oral History Program, University of California, Los Angeles, pp. 33–4, 38 and 53; and Frank Lloyd Wright, *Letters to Apprentices*, (The Press at California State University, Fresno, Fresno, 1982), pp. 38–9 and 53–4.

3   Edgar Tafel, *Apprentice to Genius: Years with Frank Lloyd Wright*, (McGraw-Hill Book Company, New York, 1979), p. 19; Donald Hoppen, 'A Journey with Frank Lloyd Wright into Architecture,' *UIA International Architect*, n.6 (1984), p. 51; Wright, *Letters to Apprentices*, p. 110; and Brendan Gill, *Many Masks: a Life of Frank Lloyd Wright*, (G. P. Putnam's Sons, New York, 1987), pp. 326–34.

4   Gill, *Many Masks*, 348–54.

5   'Frank Lloyd Wright – durch drei seiner Schüler gesehen, interviews mit Roland von Rebay, Frank Sidler, und Ernst E. Anderegg,' *Bauen und Wohnen*, 33 (March 1978), pp. 113–6; Hoppen, 'A Journey with Frank Lloyd Wright into Architecture,' pp. 49–59; Wright, *Letters to Apprentices*, pp. 123–84; and Robert C. Twombly, *Frank Lloyd Wright: An Interpretive Biography*, (Harper & Row, New York, 1973), pp. 167–76.

6   James Birrell, *Walter Burley Griffin*, (University of Queensland Press, Brisbane, 1964), pp. 14 and 143–9; Gill, *Many Masks*, pp. 238–9 and 267–8; and James Weirick, 'The Griffins in Australia,' *Transition*, n.24 (1988), pp. 4–43.

7   Paolo Soleri, 'How Things Look to Me,' *Stolen Paper Review*, n.1 (1963), pp. 37–8; and Peter Blake, 'Paolo Soleri's Visionary City,' *Architectural Forum*, (March 1961), pp. 111–18.

8   Pierluigi Bonvicini, *John Lautner: architettura organi-cosperimentale*, (Dedalo libri, Bari, 1981), pp. 7–12; and Lautner, 'Responsibility, Infinity, Nature,' pp. 45–6 and 67–8.

BIBLIOGRAPHY

H.A. Brooks (ed.), *Writings on Wright: Selected Comment on Frank Lloyd Wright*, (MIT Press, Cambridge, Mass., 1981).

Giorgio Ciucci, 'The City in Agrarian Ideology and Frank Lloyd Wright: Origins and Development of Broadacres', in Giorgio Ciucci et al *The American City: From the Civil War to the New Deal*, (MIT Press, Cambridge, Mass., 1979), pp. 293–387.

Arthur Drexler, *The Drawings of Frank Lloyd Wright*, (Horizon Press, New York, for the Museum of Modern Art, 1962).

Robert Fishman, *Urban Utopias in the Twentieth Century: Ebenezer Howard, Frank Lloyd Wright and Le Corbusier*, (MIT Press, Cambridge, Mass., 1977).

Brendan Gill, *Many Masks: a Life of Frank Lloyd Wright*, (G.P. Putnam's Sons, New York, 1987).

Henry Russell Hitchcock, *In the Nature of Materials, 1887–1941: the Buildings of Frank Lloyd Wright*, (Da Capo Press, New York, 1975).

Donald Hoppen, 'A Journey with Frank Lloyd Wright into Architecture,' *UIA International Architect*, n.6 (1984).

Vincent Scully, *Frank Lloyd Wright*, (Braziller, New York, 1960).

Meryle Secrest, *Frank Lloyd Wright*, (Chatto, 1992).

John Sergeant, *Frank Lloyd Wright's Usonian houses: the Case for Organic Architecture*, (Whitney Library of Design, New York, 1975).

William Allin Storrer, *The Architecture of Frank Lloyd Wright: a Complete Catalog*, (M.I.T. Press, Cambridge, Mass., 1978).

Robert Sweeney, *Frank Lloyd Wright: An Annotated Bibliography*, (Hennessey and Ingalls, Los Angeles, 1978).

Edgar Tafel, *Apprentice to Genius: Years with Frank Lloyd Wright*, (McGraw–Hill Book Company, New York, 1979).

Edgar Tafel, *About Wright: An Album of Recollections by Those Who Knew Frank Lloyd Wright*, (John Wiley and Sons, New York, 1993).

Robert C. Twombly, *Frank Lloyd Wright: An Interpretive Biography*, (Harper & Row, New York, 1973).

Morton White and Lucia White, *The Intellectual Versus the City: from Thomas Jefferson to Frank Lloyd Wright*, (Harvard University Press, Cambridge, Mass., 1962).

Frank Lloyd Wright, *Modern Architecture: Being the Kahn Lectures for 1930*, reprinted in Frank Lloyd Wright, *The Future of Architecture* (Horizon Press, New York, 1953).

Frank Lloyd Wright, *Letters to Apprentices*, (The Press at California State University, Fresno, Fresno, 1982).

18

MODERNISM AND THE USSR

Jonathan Charley

On the last day of 1999 an army of authors, pen in hand, are waiting for the clock to strike midnight. This is the cue for a shower of popular histories of the twentieth century, carefully sanitized, sold as commodities in the department store realm of magic and mystery. In these accounts, time suffers intense compression; events, individuals and classes have to jostle for attention. In particular, history is cleansed of human agency, those struggles and labour processes which transform the world and the built environment, and a great mask is thus invented that buries the history of people under a history of things. We are delivered a tale of the Russian revolution, perhaps the greatest modernist project of all, as a naïve and childish experiment destined from birth to become a monster, and worthy of no more than a footnote in the 'real' history, that of the television and the motor car.

This is more than idle speculation. Now that capitalism is being proclaimed as victor and standard bearer of social justice, it is important to reclaim those attempts to build a society and an architecture that aspire to values different from those of capitalist institutions and practices.

THE RUSSIAN REVOLUTION

The German philosopher G.W.F. Hegel (1770–1831) characterized world history as 'the progress of the consciousness of freedom'[1] and thus largely concerned with the deeds and sufferings of people. Similarly, Karl Marx (1818–83), his colleague Friedrich Engels (1820–95), and the Russian revolutionary leader Vladimir Ilich Lenin (1870–1924) were concerned with the material basis of exploitation, and how a class society such as capitalism could be overthrown and transcended.

Engels and Marx considered that social justice could not be achieved through the utopian speculations of early thinkers such as Duc de Saint Simon (1675–1755), Charles Fourier (1772–1837) and Robert Owen (1771–1858), but only through a class struggle. In capitalist society, this struggle would take place between the capitalist classes (those who owned facto-ries, machinery, property and had money to invest) and the working classes (those who owned little and therefore had to sell their labour to survive) and would inevitably involve the workers wresting power from the capitalists. Ushered in would be fundamental changes in the organization of political, economic and social life. This then is what makes Russian architec-ture of the 1920s so unusual; uniquely in history, the revolution which followed the events of 1917 created the pre-conditions for buildings which were part not of capitalism but of a system whose ultimate goal was emancipation from exploitation.

But why did the revolution occur in Russia? During the late nineteenth and early twentieth century, forms of property ownership and class rule began to impede Russian society, which became polarized between a repressive autocratic regime in alliance with a reactionary class of capitalists and landowners, and a property-less impoverished mass of workers and peasants. The security of working class and peasant life could no longer be guaranteed, and the break-down of any widespread social contract between rulers and the ruled exploded in the first Russian revolution of 1905. However, in the following decade, later known as the 'years of reaction', many of the new social gains, such as the right to join trades unions, were undermined.

The First World War exacerbated the situation, and Russia plunged into a deepening crisis. In 1917, under the leadership of the Bolsheviks (members of the Marxist Russian Social Democratic Labour Party that included Lenin), the Tsar and the Duma (the parlia-ment founded after 1905) were replaced by a new form of government that declared the mass of workers, peasants and soldiers, through representatives in the Soviets (councils), as the new ruling class.

However, the country they inherited was hungry, decimated by war and industrially underdeveloped. In 1917 the urban working class, upon whose shoulders rested the success of the revolution, constituted only 9% of the working population (the rest were rural peasants), and were concentrated in a few areas such as St. Petersburg, Moscow and the Donestk basin. The construction sector itself was scarcely an industry in the modern sense, being dominated by seasonal workers of peasant origin, still steeped in the traditions of guild-type building organizations and the religious customs and prejudices of rural life.

Nevertheless, the revolutionary government forged ahead in their plan to change the structure of society, advocating long-term programmes which included the nationalization of land, a socialized construction sector, and social ownership of banks and factories. This helped plunge the Bolshevik government into war not only against forces within Russia opposed to the revolution, but against Western imperialist countries panic stricken at the Bolshevik desire to spread the proletarian revolution throughout Europe.

THE NEW ECONOMIC POLICY

After the havoc of the civil war and the enforced nationalizations of War Communism, Lenin considered that the continuing revolution depended upon maintaining the Soviets' authority and the immediate introduction of an electrification programme to stimulate economic growth and industrial productivity. However, he also believed this was achievable only by the controversial re-introduction of elements of the capitalist market. In the new state-owned building industry, capitalist work and payment practices were therefore re-established, and workers had to compete with re-emerging capitalist building contractors.

This period became known as the New Economic Policy (NEP), running from 1921 to 1927. It was also the era of a cultural revolution unprecedented in the way it touched all areas of creative activity, whether architecture, film, ceramics, painting, sculpture or textiles.

Abstract speculations of the kind in the paintings of Lyubov Popova (1889–1924) and Kasimir Malevich (1878–1935) had been a pillar of the early modern movement, and were now incorporated into an exploration of forms and techniques suited to the dynamic tasks of revolution. Such explorations can be seen in the use of photomontage in the films *Strike* (1924) and *Battleship Potemkin* (1925) of director Sergei Eisenstein (1898–1948) in the red and black abstract covers for the journal *New Left*, in the functional furniture and clothing of Alexander Rodchenko (1891–1956), and in

Figure 18.1

After years of capitalist economics and culture, innovative forms of imagery and communication were considered imperative for the social programme of the Russian Revolution. Still from *Strike*, (1924), director Sergei Eisenstein.

the collage and text compositions of poet and playwright Vladimir Mayakovski (1894–1930). It is precisely because artists were required to fulfil new social functions, to convey slogans, ideas, and knowledge to the proletariat and peasantry, that innovative forms of language and communication were invented. This is one reason why Russian modernism differs from its counterpart in Western Europe.

But just as there was no blueprint for how to organize a socialist economy, neither was there a clear idea on how art and architecture should develop. At the most extreme, groups of artists and intellectuals like Proletkult considered it essential to build a new proletarian culture untainted by art of the bourgeois epoch. On the other hand, Lenin and Leon Trotsky (1879–1940) argued that the achievements of both capitalist technology and capitalist culture should be harnessed.

It is essential to grasp the contradictory nature of this period. Because of the attempt to reconcile objectives of freedom and democracy with the immediate tasks of reconstruction, much of life was characterized by the clashing of opposing forces. Consequently, the architecture and art of the Russian avant-garde should not be evaluated in terms of right or wrong, but understood in the context of conflicting interests and arguments.

REVOLUTIONARY ARCHITECTURE AND PLANNING

During the NEP and under GOELRO, the plan for the electrification, most construction was for factories, power lines and railways. Nevertheless, this did not prevent a vibrant stream of innovative ideas for settlements, housing, workers' clubs and factories.

Although pre-revolutionary classicists like the neo-renaissance architect Ivan Zholtovski (1867–1959) and the theorist of 'proletarian classicism' Ivan Fomin (1872–1936) were to dominate Soviet architecture after the fall of the avant-garde in the 1930s, during the 1920s the two most influential groups in the race to capture revolutionary aspirations in built form were the Constructivists, centred around Moisei Ginzburg (1892–1946) and the Vesnin brothers Aleksandr (1883–1959), Viktor (1882–1950) and Leonid (1880–1933), and the Rationalists, led by architect Nikolai Ladovski (1881–1941). Both groups taught at the Moscow VKhUTEMAS, The Higher Artistic Technical Studios founded in 1920 to co-ordinate architectural and art education.

Despite acrimonious disputes between the two – Constructivists being labelled as 'functionalists' for focusing on social issues, and the Rationalists as 'formalists' for concentrating on aesthetics – in terms of building form, there are more similarities than differences. Both use simple geometric shapes combined with a machine aesthetic where the building structure is often clearly expressed. But what makes architecture of this period not only modern but truly avant-garde is the interdependence of this formal experimentation with a revolutionary social programme.

Beside a struggle over time, the Russian revolution was also concerned with how historical processes occur in space. The importance of space, and control over it, is evident not only in the erection of street barricades, in armies claiming territories, but in the antagonistic relationships between town and country, and in the spatial distribution and organization of production, resources and people. At the heart of the modern movement in the USSR was an attempt to spatialize democracy, to find a theory of urban development and building design commensurate with socialism.

Among a mountain of projects, the majority never built, a few are of special importance for two reasons. Firstly, they represent new ways of thinking about materials, technology, and form, thus departing from the dominant tendencies of pre-revolutionary Russian architecture, neo-classicism and the *Russki Moderne* movement, the Russian equivalent of Art Nouveau headed by Fedor Shekhtel (1859–1926). Secondly, and more generally, they document a society in transition where new building needs and functions were being produced. Their designers believed that a fundamental transformation of daily life had taken place at home, work and school, and which required a new built environment at the levels of the world, the settlement and the building. We shall look at each in turn.

In the first years of the 'Workers State' before it was transformed under Joseph Stalin (1879–1953), many Bolsheviks believed it was impossible to build socialism in just one country, and that success depended on an International Revolution. The tower project designed by Vladimir Tatlin (1885–1953) was not only a monument but the headquarters of such a world-wide movement. In the Monument to the Third International (1919), three volumes, a cube, cylinder and pyramid, in which the world's socialist and left-wing groups would meet, are suspended and revolve inside a spiralling steel and glass structure some 300 m high. A synthesis of orbital motion and primary solids produce a powerful metaphor of the global aspirations of the communist movement and of the permanent necessity of struggle. But, as we shall see, criticisms of this and other projects for lack of available resources and technology disguise far deeper contradictions within the revolution. The tower's real impossibility lay not in its complex technological vision but in the abandonment by Stalin of internationalism.

Figure 18.2

Monument to the Third
International, (1919), both a
functional and metaphorical
manifestation of the global
aims of the Bolsheviks.
Designed by Vladimir Tatlin.

At the level of the settlement, the schemes of Leonid
Sabsovich and Mikhail Okhitovich (1896–1937) are but
two of many concerned with urban development.
Others include a version of Ebenezer Howard's
(1850–1928) garden city, cosmic and vertical cities, the
Magnitogorsk (1930) linear city project by Ivan
Leonidov (1902–59), and a radial city by Ladovski.
Sabsovich envisaged a web of transport and communication routes across the entire country, linking what
were effectively production units: compact settlements
of a similar size, each with a core of collective social
and cultural facilities. Okhitovich proposed a similar
communication and transport network, but with
mobile settlements; people would live in houses along
communication lines containing not only motorways
but telephones and radios. Although Sabsovich was
labelled 'urbanist' and Okhitovich 'disurbanist', this
obscures their similarity. Both believed in rational
planning and expressing in physical and spatial terms
the egalitarian, even and uniform distribution of
resources. Although these ideas may have been

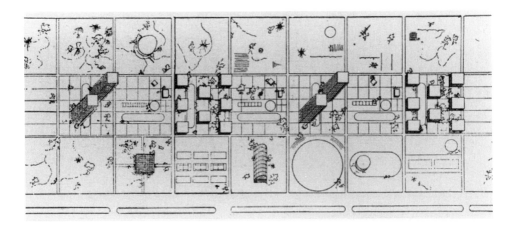

Figure 18.3

Revolutionary politics translated into an urban project. Magnitogorsk, (1930), incorporates parallel linear zones of industry, roads, residences and public institutions. Architect Ivan Leonidov.

utopian, this is not because all other Russians disagreed with their vision, or indeed because of the paucity of motor cars. Rather there was a contradiction between those who believed in the inevitability of the end of exploitation, and the emergence of a new group of exploiters, a Communist Party bureaucracy slowly usurping the democratic goals of the revolution. Democratic aims were no longer shared by the new ruling class.

As with these urban projects, the Constructivist 'social condenser' was premised on the belief in the inevitable and necessary transformation of daily life. Part or all of a building, the social condenser encouraged a new co-operative way of life and, in particular, sought to liberate women from the burdens of domestic labour. Such a theory stressed the transformative and educational possibilities of architecture; collective laundries, child care establishments, housing communes and workers' clubs were thus all social condensors.

The most sophisticated attempt to realize the social condenser was the Dom Narkomfin in Moscow (1928–30) designed by I. Milinis and Ginzburg, author of the seminal book *Style and the Epoch* (1924).[2] The Narkomfin block was a 'transitional' housing commune with both individual and collective facilities to ease individuals into the new social relationships. Formally, it lay within the modernist paradigm with ribbon windows, internal street, pilotis and split level flats. The Russakova workers' club by Konstantin Melnikov (1890–1970), one of five he designed in Moscow, was equally revolutionary, not only as an early leisure and

Figure 18.4

The 'social condensor' as dwelling. The Narkomfin apartment block, Moscow, (1928–30), prepared people for full collective living through shared kitchen and dining room, library, nursery and recreational facilities. Architects I. Milinis and Moisei Ginzburg.

Figure 18.5

The 'social condensor' as club. Russakova Workers' Club, Moscow, (c.1927–9), architect Konstantin Melnikov.

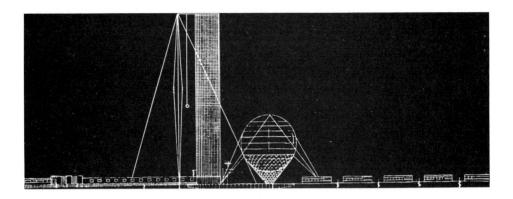

Figure 18.6

As with other revolutionary artistic practices that integrated form and content, architectural form could be rendered inseparable to the function of the building. Project for Lenin Institute of Librarianship, (1927), architect Ivan Leonidov.

educational centre but because of the explosive use of technology where the building form is dominated by three cantilevered auditoria separated by vertical steel windows. Comparable in technological and social vision is Leonidov's Lenin Institute of Librarianship (1927), a student project for a vast book and information depository connected to Moscow by aerial tram and to the world by a radio station. A glass, steel and reinforced concrete structure houses a library, reading rooms, research facilities and auditoria; dynamic form and geometry are inseparable from the primary social function of democratizing and disseminating knowledge. What distinguishes these projects is that they proclaim the new epoch of workers' democracy, freedom, collective organization and internationalism. And this is also why they are so contradictory, being conceived in an era when these principles were being gradually veiled in a blanket of deception.

SOCIALIST REALISM

By the 1930s industrial productivity had passed its pre-war levels. But behind this achievement, the political authority of the Soviets and the working class had been smashed by a ruling élite within the Communist Party; instead of worker control of production, a new bureaucracy, while not formally owning industry, nevertheless directed it and benefited from it most. On building sites and in factories, essentially capitalist forms of work practice were introduced such as one-man management, piece rates and 'Taylorism' – the scientific, rational management of production named after its American intiator Frederick Winslow Taylor (1856–1915). All these practices were designed to maximize output at the expense of worker conditions, control and remuneration. Critics such as Trotsky consequently argued that, despite certain progressive features, the Soviet Union could not be characterized as socialist but more as a workers' state that had degenerated.

One way the new dictatorship manifested itself was through an attack on the modern movement and the heady egalitarian vision of early urban and housing design. The modernist aesthetic was considered bourgeois, and ideas concerning disurbanism and communes were considered naïve, utopian and even dangerous. Architects and artists had to yield to forms of cultural activity acceptable to the new ruling élite, or become marginalized. For painters this meant returning to idealized figurative works, for architects an heroic decorative monumentality often deeply influenced by classicism. In the early 1920s Malevich, leader of the Suprematist painting movement, was renowned for geometric abstractions like *Red Square* (1915); by 1933, at the height of the Russian famine, he was depicting rosy cheeked peasants. Similarly, Melnikov's humanist architecture for the Russakova club became the triumphalist despotism of the People's Commissariat of Heavy Industry (1934).

Figure 18.7

Red Square: Painterly Realism of a Peasant Woman in Two Dimensions, (1915), artist Kasimir Malevich. Extreme modernist abstractions like this were considered unacceptably bourgeois by the party dictatorship lead by Stalin in the 1930s.

Figure 18.8

Female Worker, (1933), artist
Kasimir Malevich. Socialist
Realism in art favoured
images and messages readily
comprehensible to the
masses.

Two competitions in the early 1930s for a development plan for Moscow and a Palace of the Soviets
marked the turning point in architecture, and the
emergence of what became known as Socialist
Realism, a concerted and conscious attempt to exploit
the ideological possibilities of architecture. The
winning Moscow plan, inspired more by Imperial
Rome than Russian socialism, and Boris Iofan's
(1891–1976) winning Palace of the Soviets design
(1930–4), a terrifying edifice that would have dwarfed
the city, were both conceived at the very point when
the bureaucracy was concentrating all economic and
political power in the capital, delivering the death
blow to the democratic structure of the Soviets.
Prestigious neo-classical housing schemes reserved for
party officials replaced communes and egalitarian
urban development. Instead of Leonidov's project for
a library that aspired to universally available knowledge, the neo-classical Lenin library as built had
restricted access to books and information.

Figure 18.9

Melnikov's competition entry for the People's Commissariat of Heavy Industry, (1934), the architectural equivalent of Malevich's peasants, but fiercely attacked for drawing too freely on classicism for its imagery.

Figure 18.10

Palace of the Soviets, (1934), architect Boris Iofan. Intended to be the most important piece of architecture in the world, the competition winner merges classicism, modern compositions, new technology and a 100 m statue of Lenin. Work started in Moscow on the construction of this monumental enaction of Socialist Realism but was never finished.

The schemes of the 1920s were threatening because they advocated democratic ideas in direct contradiction to the regime developing under Stalin. It is this antagonistic relationship that led to attempts to mask the betrayal of the revolution. Consequently the search for an architecture aspiring to a socialist democracy became utopian not because it was impossible, but because it conflicted with the ruling élite, with the negation and atomization of democracy.

REFERENCES

1   G.W.F. Hegel, 'Realisation of Spirit in History', in *Lectures on the Philosophy of World History*, (Cambridge University Press, Cambridge, 1988), pp. 54–5.
2   Moisei Ginzburg, *Style and the Epoch*, (MIT Press, Cambridge, Mass., 1982). First published 1924.

BIBLIOGRAPHY

Soviet History

E.H. Carr, *The Russian Revolution: Lenin To Stalin (1917–1929)*, (Macmillan, London, 1980).

Maurice Dobb, *Soviet Economic Development Since 1917*, (Routledge and Kegan Paul, London, sixth edition, 1966).

Boris Kagarlitsky, *The Thinking Reed: Intellectuals and the Soviet State*, (Verso, London, 1989).

Architecture, Art and Planning

John E. Bowlt (ed.), *Russian Art of the Avant Garde: Theory and Criticism, 1903–1934*, (Thames and Hudson, London, revised and enlarged edition, 1988).

William Craft Brumfield, *The Origins of Modernism in Russian Architecture*, (University of California Press, Berkeley, 1991).

Catherine Cooke, *Russian Avant Garde*, special issue of *Architectural Design*, v.53 n.5/6 (1983).

James Cracraft, *The Petrine Revolution in Russian Architecture*, (University of Chicago, Chicago, 1988).

Andrei Ikonnikov, *Russian Architecture of the Soviet Period*, (Raduga Publishers, Moscow, 1988).

Magomedov Khan, *Pioneers of the Soviet Avant Garde*, (Thames and Hudson, London, 1987).

Anatole Kopp, *Constructivist Architecture in the USSR*, (Academy Editions, London, 1985).

Alexei Tarkhanov, *Stalinist Architecture*, (Laurence King, London, 1992).

19

PATCHING THE FUTURE

THE EVOLUTION OF A POST-WAR HOUSING ESTATE

Joe Kerr

As architects of the ultimate human and material scenes of the new order, we are not so much concerned with the formal elements of 'style' as with an architectural solution of the social and economic problems of today . . . As creative architects we are concerned with a Future which must be Planned, rather than a Past which must be Patched up.[1]

This bold pronouncement by the British modernist architect Wells Coates (1895–1958), can be read as both a poignant relic of the utopian face of pioneer modernism and an example of the kind of statement held up today to illustrate the dangerously naïve thought which condemned British architecture to the fifty-year dark night of modernism. The vision of an ordered future dictated by a technocratic élite provokes in us a feeling of sublime horror, although we are now safely protected from this spectre by the passing of the era and the death of the modern movement itself.

With the political transformations of the last decade the corpse of modernism has been eagerly picked over, in particular by those who see modern architecture as synonymous with welfarism and the rotting tower block as icon for the collapse of the post-war ideological consensus. As Patrick Wright puts it, an image has been created of 'the tower block as tombstone not just of council housing but of the entire Welfare State.'[2] Throughout the 1980s and 1990s, as Wright reveals in

Figure 19.1

An experiment in new living for the nomadic intelligentsia, the Isokon apartments, Lawn Road, London, (1933), combined the social programme of the Narkomfin housing with *existenzminimum* planning. Architect Wells Coates. The 'Isobar' club room was originally designed by Marcel Breuer.

A Journey Through Ruins, the 'New Right' has successfully exploited the close association between the architecture of mass social housing and socialism to discredit them both. However, this assault is based only on a general assertion that these two sets of ideas – political ideas which advocated the comprehensive transformation of society and architectural principles which promised to achieve this through intervention in physical fabric – were inevitable fellow-travellers.

There is therefore good reason to question this interpretation, not least because empirical evidence suggests a much more complicated chain of events. For example, many people now believe that a vast state-sponsored social housing programme must necessarily have been rigorously controlled from central government, whereas, as we shall see, this was not always the case. Refocusing on the particular rather

Figure 19.2

'The tower block as tombstone of the entire Welfare State.' Hutchestown-Gorbals Area C Development, Glasgow, (1962), architect Basil Spence. When the building was demolished in 1994, an unfortunate witness to the demise of this icon of welfarism was killed by a flying lump of debris.

than the general therefore allows us to question received interpretations, and to avoid drastic, erroneous simplification of an intricate subject.

We will concentrate here on the planning and construction of a single, large public housing scheme – the Regent's Park Estate built by the Metropolitan Borough Council of St. Pancras, London. This project is particularly revealing about two key themes: firstly, the estate's early planning illuminates links between politicians and architects at the birth of post-war reconstruction; and secondly, the realization of the estate speaks eloquently of the problems of actually implementing social transformation within the material constraints of the post-war world.

THE REGENT'S PARK ESTATE

Two events within the history of the Regent's Park Estate scheme help to locate these two themes in the narrative. In October 1945, at a public meeting held at the RIBA (Royal Institute of British Architects) in London, a visionary plan was presented for an enormous public housing scheme on the bomb-damaged land east of Regent's Park. Among the audience were Charles Reilly (1874–1948), President of the RIBA, and Patrick Abercrombie (1879–1957), author of the County of London Plan published that same year. Both spoke warmly in favour of the scheme, and congratulated the borough for being the first to exploit and make use of the local facilities at their disposal. Some 18 years later, the new Labour Party leader Harold Wilson (1916–95) ceremoniously opened the borough's 5 000th post-war flat in a new block on the Regent's Park Estate, thereby attracting considerable publicity in the run-up to the forthcoming general election, and capitalizing on an ideal opportunity to emphasize Labour's commitment to housing.

Taken in isolation, these two events are plausible metaphors for the creation and execution of the whole post-war housing programme, from conception as the central plank of Welfare State policy under the Labour government (1945–51) of Prime Minister Clement Attlee (1883–1967), through its realization by successive Conservative and Labour administrations over the next quarter of a century. But what happened in between was not smooth straightforward progress, for the estate visited by Wilson in 1963 was very different to that originally proposed in the new dawn of 1945. In this disjunction between plan and built reality we can see the massive institutional failure of the whole post-war housing drive.

The story actually begins in the last year of the war, when the government was gearing itself to the task of peacetime rebuilding. Significantly, although financing of building programmes remained within central government control, their implementation was almost wholly in the hands of local councils, who had to draw up plans, commission architects and secure tenders. With little common ground between the various reconstruction proposals produced during the war (although architects, planners and politicians alike generally believed in rehousing people in suburban cottage estates, and not in high-density inner-city estates), these local authorities were offered no central Whitehall consensus on planning or architectural guidance. There was no vision of what a future replanned society might look like, only the political desire to effect it.

The Conservative-controlled St. Pancras Borough Council had already drawn up its own modest plan for a post-war housing programme. But late in 1944, a local Labour Party activist, Eric Cook, started an extraordinary campaign to redevelop the land east of Regent's Park, originally the working-class residential and commercial components of John Nash's (1752–1835) great plan for the park (1811 onward), but now badly bomb-damaged and in danger of redevelopment with luxury apartments. Local political support

Figure 19.3

Cumberland Terrace, Regent's Park, London, (1826), architect John Nash.

was quickly gained, notably from another local party official, Evelyn Denington, whose involvement in the plan subsequently led to a distinguished career in social housing and town planning.

Cook's was a visionary political conception of the future for bomb-damaged cities. His intention was to create the modern equivalents of Nash's elegant, élitist terraces: great, white blocks of worker's flats surrounding a broad swathe of park land designed to open up the exclusive, rich man's park to the ordinary people of St. Pancras. He wrote of the 'inspiration it would be for the hundreds and thousands who come to Regent's Park every year if they saw, instead of a restricted number of luxury flats for the very wealthy, right round the 'outer circle' of the Park a magnificent sweep of modern flats where people like themselves, service couples and families, had their homes.'[3]

Were it not for the peculiar nature of local politics in the borough, this would have remained a seductive dream. The north-west part of London above Regent's Park had long been home to both radical politics and a strong artistic culture. In the 1930s, Hampstead, two miles north of the park, had been the most important centre of modernist architecture in England, where many advocates of modernism lived and engaged in local politics. Because of these local connections, Cook rapidly acquired support from influential architectural figures, most significantly E.J. Carter, the Librarian of the RIBA. Throughout the 1930s, when the RIBA was generally held to be a traditionalist influence within British architecture, Carter had openly used his position to promote modernism, most famously by helping to rescue the German modernist architect Walter Gropius (1883–1969) from Nazi Germany and supplying him commissions during his few years in London. Later, during the war, Carter was operating almost as a fifth columnist for modern architecture within the RIBA – whose official wartime concerns were with straightforward professional issues and not with design ideologies – running an informal advisory service for local authorities, to whom he invariably recommended modernist architects. An active campaigner for the 1944 County of London Plan, a modernist blueprint for dealing with the damaged city, he later wrote *The Future of London* (1962) in further support of modernist planning principles.

It was Carter who introduced the Regent's Park campaigners to a young architect, Peter Shepherd, godson of Abercrombie under whom he worked on the County of London Plan, who was first to give form to Cook's idea. Working anonymously because he was a government employee, Shepherd prepared a perspective and plan for the site, displaying massive white five and ten storey slab blocks organized on a rigid grid-plan. The scheme was thus heavily influenced by the modernist social housing programmes of 1920s Germany, which Shepherd had visited before the war. In effect, it was a realization of the theoretical neighbourhood model prescribed by the Abercrombie Plan; the sheer size of the site – 25 hectares – made it not so much a housing estate as a comprehensive redevelopment plan for whole area. This was to be largely its downfall.

In October 1945 a landslide victory in the local elections swept the Labour Party into power in boroughs across Britain, including St. Pancras where Cook and Denington moved onto the council. Within a short time they and Shepherd had their scheme adopted as official council policy, and sent to the London County Council (LCC) for planning assent.

From here on delays and compromizes increasingly diverted the scheme from the clarity of the original idea. Most of these subsequent problems stemmed from the sheer size and ambition of the plan, which was calculated on a perception of future need and not on any ability to build. St. Pancras became increasingly in conflict with higher authorities, for the leadership of the Labour Party of 1945 did not share the socialist fervour of its grass roots.[4] The housing programme, alone among

Figure 19.4

German social housing in the 1920s proved of widespread and lasting influence. Apartment block at the Weissenhof housing exhibition, Stuttgart, (1927), architect Ludwig Mies van der Rohe. Organized by the Deutscher Werkbund under the direction of Mies van der Rohe, this exhibition included contributions from Le Corbusier, Walter Gropius, J.J.P. Oud, Hans Scharoun and Mart Stam.

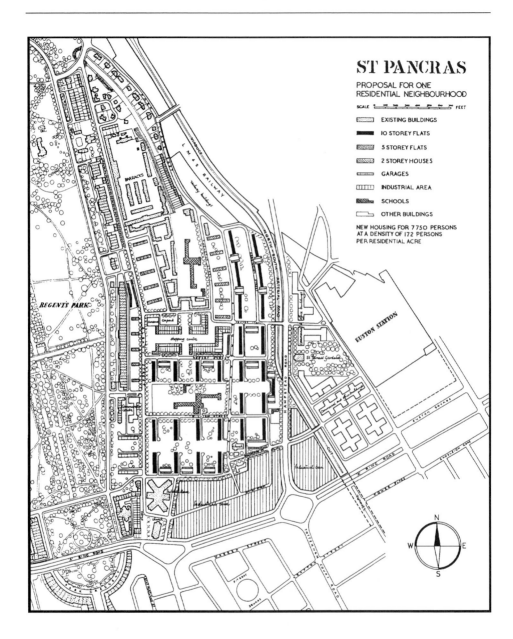

Figure 19.5

Peter Shepherd's original design for the Regent's Park Estate, with a *zeilenbau* arrangement of parallel blocks typical of inter-war German modernist site planning.

the welfare initiatives of the Attlee government, remained without adequate targets or administrative structures. Furthermore, early central government ambitions to ensure the high quality of post-war housing designs were quickly replaced by a desire for quantity above all else, fuelled by a cynical numbers game played by both major parties on the issue of state housing in successive general election campaigns of the 1950s and 1960s.

Back at the local level, difficulties in gaining planning assent, which even necessitated the Mayor of St. Pancras making a personal appeal to Health Minister Aneurin Bevan (1897–1960), created considerable delays, and by 1948 it became clear that the original comprehensive plan needed to be replaced by a gradual, phased development. Shepherd had by now moved on to work on the state New Town programme, and so architect Frederick Gibberd (1908–84) was selected to draw up a new plan. Gibberd's proposals called for as many as six phases of development, eventually designed by several different architects, including Arnold & Davies, Armstrong & MacManus and Gibberd himself. Construction was to continue for nearly twenty years.

Figure 19.6

The final design of social housing projects was often dictated as much by local political interests as by the State or the architects. The Combe 19-storey point block, (1960), on the Regents Park Estate, architects Edward Armstrong and Frederick MacManus.

Today, a walk through the estate reveals an interesting progression of designs for high-density housing, but there is no sense of coherence to what is often little more than a piecemeal arrangement of individual blocks, weakly following the pre-existing road pattern. The result is the familiar lack of adequate delineation of the public and private realms, characterized by large areas of neutral open space. The failure to achieve a neighbourhood identity was compounded by the LCC's insistence in the 1960s that the southern boundary of the site bordering the Marylebone Road was developed not with social housing but with more profitable commercial office towers.

Politicians involved with Regent's Park today express their disappointment with the architectural quality of the estate. But for several of the participants, the experience of initiating this grand scheme was highly influential on their later careers. Thus the problems of form and scale encountered here led Shepherd to revise his design ideas, making him an early convert to the notion that high densities in housing could be achieved without recourse to high-rise blocks. For Denington it was the first step toward a long involvement with state housing, as a member of the LCC and GLC (Greater London Council), and most famously at Stevenage New Town where she became Chairperson of the Development Corporation.

MODERN ARCHITECTURE AND POLITICS

What does Regent's Park Estate tell us about post-war modern design in general? Firstly it allows us to recon-

Figure 19.7

In direct opposition to the neighbouring Alton East Estate, (1952–5), the Alton West Estate, Roehampton, (1955–9), shown here used a more extreme modernism derived from Le Corbusier's Unité d'Habitation, Marseilles, (1947–52). London County Council Architects Department, chief architect, J.L. Martin.

sider the relationship between architecture and politics at the dawn of post-war reconstruction, showing this link was achieved at the local level where effective executive power resided. Central government and national institutions – Whitehall and the RIBA – played a relatively smaller part. Secondly, and most importantly, the estate highlights the causes of failure of the post-war programme, showing that, despite optimism from the early collaborators and the assumptions of later critics, the convergence of modernist architecture with the interventionist politics of mass state housing was neither inevitable nor particularly comfortable. Although within a decade the LCC's great projects at Loughborough Road, Brixton (1955–7), Alton East Estate (1952–5) and Alton West Estate (1955–9), Roehampton, had successfully promoted modernism as the appropriate image for public housing, by then the chance to develop a comprehensive strategy for post-war reconstruction was submerged in a political debate which increasingly concentrated on simple statistical success. Wilson, we should remember, was invited to St. Pancras not to celebrate the planning vision commended two decades earlier at the RIBA but to underline the quantitative achievements of the housing drive.

The lack of coherent planning was compounded by the failure to create a system adequate to foster radical urban restructuring, and the local problems and ultimate failure of the Regent's Park plan were thus the consequences of the larger inadequacies of the welfare state. Insufficient state guidance, planning delays and other practicalities necessitated a programme based entirely on the existing urban fabric,

Figure 19.8

Loughborough Road Estate, Brixton, (1953–7), London County Council Architects Department, chief architect, J.L. Martin.

however damaged, and so prevented the kind of comprehensive replanning central to the utopian ideologies of architects and politicians addressing the challenge of a new Britain. We should not therefore see the short-comings of the post-war housing programme as proof of the disasters of centralized state planning and the unchallenged authority of an unaccountable professional élite. Rather this failure, as Regent's Park Estate shows us, arose from the inadequate apparatus provided for comprehensive planning. To return to our first quotation, far from being the realization of Coates' vision, the future failed because it was 'Patched' and not 'Planned'.

This does not absolve architects and planners from responsibility for the acknowledged failure of the whole housing programme. Indeed it is hard to condone the lack of consultation with future tenants in the design process, for the design of mass-housing architecture generally reflects the concerns of its producers rather than those of its inhabitants. On the other hand, those involved in reconstruction schemes such as the Regent's Park Estate could not have realistically solicited the opinions of prospective tenants still dispersed by evacuation or wartime service.

Given the complexity of the situation, we should be wary of making over-simplistic judgements of architects, planners and of the buildings themselves. Recognizing this, English Heritage, the government body responsible for preventing the demolition and disrepair of important buildings in Britain, has campaigned to include a selective version of post-war architecture in the listings process:

> As the thirty years from the end of the Second
> World War to the oil-price crisis of the mid 1970s
> dissolve into history, things begin to look different.
> Far from being uniform and monotonous in
> character, we start to realize that post-war
> architecture was of unsuspected, often bewildering
> variety, richness and inventiveness. We can once
> more value the courage and drive of post-war
> reconstruction and now acknowledge what was good
> as well as what was bad in the period's
> unprecedented social building programmes.[5]

But we need to do more than just separate those 'good' buildings from the general disasters of the era

Figure 19.9

The conservation of post-war modernist buildings, and the reasoning behind it, is frequently controversial. English Heritage have protected the 'cluster' block Keeling House, London, (1959), architects Denys Lasdun and Partners. The block has been listed despite serious concerns about its operation as social housing.

of social engineering, while decisions must depend on more than the connoisseurship of the government's appointed experts. In understanding the relationship between modern architecture and the welfare provision, we must recognize the conditions under which this link was formed and give due credit to those who attempted to deal with its problems. Only then can useful lessons be learned and applied about the proper use of architecture as a tool of urban intervention; only then can the gradual transformation in public perception be understood, from post-war utopian optimism about modern architecture to contemporary disgust and despair; and only then can modernism be understood as a complex phenomenon, and not simply used as a justification for the dismantling of the institutions of the welfare state.

REFERENCES

1   Wells Coates, in Herbert Read, (ed.), *Unit One: The Modern Movement in English Architecture, Painting and Sculpture*, (London, 1934), p. 108.

2   Patrick Wright, *A Journey Through Ruins: The Last Days of London*, (Radius, London, 1991), p. 92.

3   *North London Press*, (24 November 1944). Among a number of enthusiastic replies was one from the local prospective Communist Party candidate, who compared the scheme to the pre-war housing programme in Vienna.

4   Stephen Merrett, *State Housing in Britain*, (Routledge and Kegan Paul, London, 1979), p. 235.

5   Royal Commission on the Historical Monuments of England, and English Heritage, *A Change of Heart: English Architecture Since the War, A Policy for Protection* (London, 1992) pp. 3–5.

BIBLIOGRAPHY

Politics and the Welfare State

T.O. Lloyd, *Empire to Welfare State: English History 1906–1985*, (Oxford University Press, Oxford, 1986).

Rodney Lowe, *The Welfare State in Britain Since 1945*, (Macmillan, Basingstoke, 1992).

Architecture

Patrick Dunleavy, *The Politics of Mass Housing in Britain, 1945–1975: a Study of Corporate Power and Professional Influence in the Welfare State*, (Clarendon, Oxford, 1981).

Lionel Esher, *A Broken Wave: the Rebuilding of England 1940–1980*, (Allen Lane, London, 1981).

Brian Finnimore, *Houses from the Factory: System Building and the Welfare State, 1942–1974*, (Rivers Oram Press, London, 1989).

Miles Glendinning and Stefan Muthesius, *Tower Block: Modern Public Housing in England, Scotland, Wales and Northern Ireland*, (Yale University Press, New Haven and London, 1994)

Anthony Jackson, *The Politics of Architecture: a History of Modern Architecture in Britain*, (Architectural Press, London, 1970).

Stephen Merrett, *State Housing in Britain*, (Routledge and Kegan Paul, London, 1979).

Patrick Wright, *A Journey Through Ruins: The Last Days of London*, (Radius, London, 1991).

20

FORM AND TECHNOLOGY

THE IDEA OF A NEW ARCHITECTURE

Andrew Higgott

The ideal of making an architecture for the people, of forging a new relationship to society, was first articulated, as we have seen, in the early modernist theories of the 1920s. Le Corbusier's books *Towards a New Architecture*[1] (1927) and *City of Tomorrow and its Planning*[2] (1929) gave such ideas their clearest expression, seeing the existing forms of the city as inefficient and unhealthy, and urgently in need of replacement, while the belief that architects should incorporate new technology and new materials was central. Yet it was not until the 1960s that the ideas and forms of modernism were truly realized, when tower blocks serrated city skylines, comprehensive development schemes re-shaped every centre, new housing replaced old terraces and new roads cut through existing city patterns. Cities around the western world were transformed by large scale redevelopment into a version of the modernist city first envisaged by Le Corbusier.

This was far from the dream city of the future, often adopting only the appearance of modernism bereft of its more radical social and technical propositions. Consequently, at the same time as extensive redevelopment was underway, an avant-garde of young architects was reinventing modernism while remaining inspired by similar principles of the necessity of a new architecture, rejection of traditional forms, response to new technology, and a belief in a new synthesis of architecture and society.

TECHNOLOGY AND THE NEW ARCHITECTURE OF THE SIXTIES

As David Greene (1937–) noted in the first edition of *Archigram*, modernist architecture had become successively debased and abandoned.

> A new generation of architecture must arise with forms and spaces which seems to reject the precepts of 'Modern' yet in fact retains these precepts. We have chosen to bypass the decaying Bauhaus image which is an insult to Functionalism.[3]

With this reference to the Bauhaus – the experimental and influential school of architecture, art and crafts in inter-war Weimar Germany first run by Walter Gropius (1883–1969) – Greene reaffirmed a commitment to functional and technical architecture, to a renewal of the revolutionary spirit of modernism. The 'new architecture of the sixties' is concerned with this renewal, bringing forth radically new ideas and building forms still evident today.

This new architecture was principally formulated in Britain, a country which had, prior to World War Two, been particularly slow in applying the avant-garde notions of architecture from continental Europe. But during the 1950s, the Independent Group of artists and architects centred on the ICA (Institute of Contemporary Art) in London and, in particular, historian and critic Reyner Banham's text, *Theory and Design in the First Machine Age* (1960), helped furnish an intellectual pedigree for this new movement. The history of the modern movement was redefined to include Futurists, Expressionists and technologists like Buckminster Fuller, and so to undermine Le Corbusier and the hegemony of CIAM (Congrés International d'Architecture Moderne).

Central to modernism was the belief in the need to respond to new technology. Buildings no longer had to be stone or brick, for steel and concrete could create a new architecture unrestricted by tradition, and which could thus contribute to the modernist vision of the city. Two of the most important figures in the application of technology to modern architecture were Jean Prouvé (1901–84), first trained as a metal-craftsman, and Buckminster Fuller (1895–1983), an American engineer. Prouvé's work developed from the mid-1930s with such projects as the Maison du Peuple at Clichy in France (1939, architects Eugène Beaudouin and Marcel Lods). Made entirely of sheet steel and a steel frame, with panels for cladding, sliding roofs and moveable floors, its construction represented a fundamentally new way of making architecture. Fuller's early projects embodied a true functionalism that went far beyond aesthetics. His Dymaxion House, (1927), closely followed by a Dymaxion Bathroom and Dymaxion Car, created an entirely new house form. A hexagonal dwelling space is suspended from a duralumin mast housing all the mechanical services. Both light metal and plastics are used in the cladding, adapting current aircraft industry methods. The Dymaxion House was light, cheap, expendable and, moreover, meant for mass production. Le Corbusier had asked why a house should not be more like a car, and Fuller's project provided a radical response, prefiguring experimental work of the sixties. Of Fuller's later projects, the Geodesic Dome (patented 1954) is seminal: a self-supporting lightweight triangulated structure covering maximum internal volume at minimum cost. In 1985, there were 300 000 such domes in existence,[4] and a three kilometre diameter example (1962) was even projected for Manhattan.

Technology, rapidly developing in the sixties, was thus the source and the inspiration for the new avant-garde. Most optimistically, technology was seen as liberating, freeing human beings from drudgery and routine; travel would be easy and frequent, and machines would enable people to achieve far more than they had dreamed possible. The built environment would be not only sleek and efficient, but would facilitate this way of life. As Banham concluded in his book, such technology was both a challenge and a necessity to architecture.

> The architect who proposes to run with technology knows now that he will be in fast company, and .that, in order to keep up, he may have to emulate the Futurists and discard his whole cultural load, including the professional garments by which he is recognized as an architect, If, on the other hand, he decides not to do this, he may find that a technological culture had decided to go on without him.[5]

Technology was indeed developing at an unparalleled rate. Computers, for example, promised to be increasingly useful. Yet it was upon materials that most architects' attention was directed. Frequent reference was made to the aircraft industry and the developing space technologies, particularly as a source for lightweight, high performing metals. But, as Prouvé pointed out, if aeroplanes were manufactured in the same way as buildings, they would never fly; by implication, rather than just using new materials, the whole building process required a radical overhaul.

NON-ARCHITECTURE AND THE ENABLER

Following the centralized government planning and controls of World War Two, architects had become increasingly involved in strategic planning, transport planning and even economic issues. As a result, comprehensiveness in scope and scale of projects became central to their thinking, as typified in the multi-functional Cumbernauld Town Centre (1966), chief architect-planner Hugh Wilson (1913–85). Thus just at the moment Banham was encouraging architects to discard their 'cultural load', a new conception of architecture emerged, a 'non-architecture' where design was no longer the most important priority.

Non-architecture was far more concerned with solving problems than with appearances. Systematization of the working method was crucial, leading to a systematized product within a larger system. Above all, experimental architects were uninterested in architectural precedents for a particular problem, preferring a scientific spirit of enquiry. But an 'information explosion', as a contemporary writer termed it, rendered the process problematic: increasingly bewildering amounts of social, scientific and technical information made certainty elusive. Therefore, as we shall see, the paradigmatic architectural projects of the period are deliberately indeterminate and open-ended, the equivalent of scientific experiments where final results are left in question.

We should also note a philosophic influence: the Situationist International, a contemporary French Marxist-revisionist group debating the role of urbanism and creativity in a post-revolutionary future. Principal among them, Guy Debord and Constant Nieuwenhuys envisaged an environment for *homo ludens*, man at play, in an advanced society where work has been abolished by technology and where flexibility transcends functionalism.

> Every element would be undetermined, mobile and flexible. For the people circulating in this enormous social space are expected to give this space its ever-changing shape: to divide it, to vary it, to create its different atmospheres, and to play their lives in a variety of surroundings. The sector . . . is a spatial system of levels . . . the sector floors are primarily empty. They represent a sort of extension of the

earth's surface, a new skin that covers the earth and multiplies its living space. Any logical subdivision is senseless. We should rather think of a quite chaotic arrangement of small and bigger spaces that are constantly mounted and demounted.[6]

In such a society, all that is left are play, constant change and re-creation; there is no need for 'home'.

An exemplary architectural manifestation of such unfixed and flexible spaces is the Fun Palace (1961), designed for a site in East London by Cedric Price (1934–). Commissioned by theatre director Joan Littlewood, the Fun Palace is cultural in the broadest sense, embracing 'jam sessions, popular dancing, science playgrounds, teaching of film, drama therapy, music stations' and film and drama presentations. Price's design is revolutionary in that, rather than each activity being allotted a particular space, the building could be constantly changed; in fact, no configuration was likely to be used twice. Furthermore, users controlled their environment, as appropriate for a building dedicated to participatory activity. 'Building', indeed, may be not be an appropriate description of what was effectively a kit of parts: flooring panels, projection screens, lighting baffles, nylon tensioned canopies, cubes with panel infill, and other elements

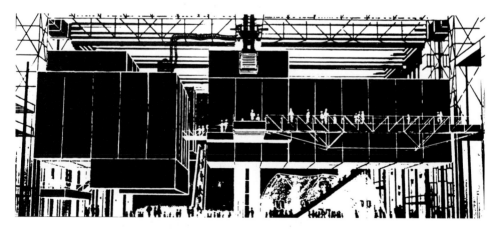

Figure 20.1

'Planning must allow for ordered increases but not suggest the direction of appetites.' Cedric Price, 'Planning for Pleasure', (1964). Enabling structure of the Fun Palace project, London, (1961), shown here with high-level access platforms and two suspended auditoria, each with its own air conditioning supply.

could be disposed within the frame, serviced by a gantry crane. Neither did flexibility end there.

> The whole complex, in both the activity it enables and the resultant structure it provides, is in effect a short-term toy to enable people, for once, to use a building with the same degree of meaningful personal immediacy that they are forced normally to reserve for a limited range of traditional pleasures.[7]

Technological change was envisaged as being so rapid, that within a decade the whole project would be abandoned as obsolete.

Another Price project, embodying similar principles, is the Potteries Thinkbelt (1964). A critique of the contemporary state university building programme, 20 000 science and technology students are dispersed on a series of sites spaced over North Staffordshire (centre of the declining pottery industry) and connected by existing railways. Faculty areas are temporary in nature and located in mobile units on the tracks themselves; housing integrates accommodation for students, local residents and workers. Central to the project is the absence of separation between students and community, but along with the implicit agenda of 'education for the people' is that of an immediately responsive and indeterminate architecture. Such projects propose non-architectural solutions, and so present the architect as enabler, helping people find appropriate

Figure 20.2

'Madeley Transfer Area', Potteries Thinkbelt, (1964). A road and rail interchange in a decentred university, with a linear zoning of cranes and gantries, smaller cellular workshops, public facilities and staff accommodation. Architect Cedric Price.

vehicles for their activities with architecture always as support rather than a fixed element to be negotiated. Flexibility, adaptability and expendability are the key principles.

The most memorable and startling projects of the period come from a group working within a similar discourse to Price: Archigram. This avant-garde group consisted of six young architects – Warren Chalk (1927–88), Peter Cook (1936–), Dennis Crompton (1935–), David Greene, Ron Herron (1930–94) and Michael Webb (1937–). Using their eponymous magazine *Archigram* (architecture/telegram) for publicity, they espoused no specific manifestos yet nevertheless through graphic style and editorial irrev-

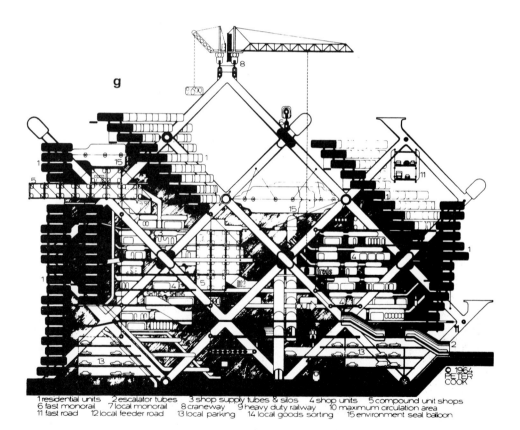

1 residential units   2 escalator tubes   3 shop supply tubes & silos   4 shop units   5 compound unit shops
6 fast monorail   7 local monorail   8 craneway   9 heavy duty railway   10 maximum circulation area
11 fast road   12 local feeder road   13 local parking   14 local goods sorting   15 environment seal balloon

Figure 20.3

Plug-In City, (1962–6), a hierarchical system of residential units, shops, escalator tubes, local monorail, heavy duty railway, local and fast roads, cranes, telescopic handling devices and 'environment seal balloons'. The project included a proposal to turn all of Britain's cities into one giant megastructure. Architects Archigram/Peter Cook.

erence promoted a radical programme; architecture was to cheerfully disregard precedent, embrace space-age technology and emphasize flexibility and temporality. Cook's Plug-In City, (1962–6) posits a giant megastructure into which removable elements can be plugged, thus programming the whole city for change. Each city component has a given lifespan, ranging from three years for bathrooms and kitchens, fifteen years for the location of house units, to forty years for the megastructure itself.

The pre-cast serviced capsule was used in several Archigram projects including the Capsule Homes Tower (1964) designed by Chalk. However, a series of projects of an entirely different scale and applicability radically extended the principle. These began with Greene's Living Pod (1965) – 'the house is an appliance for carrying with you, the city is a machine for

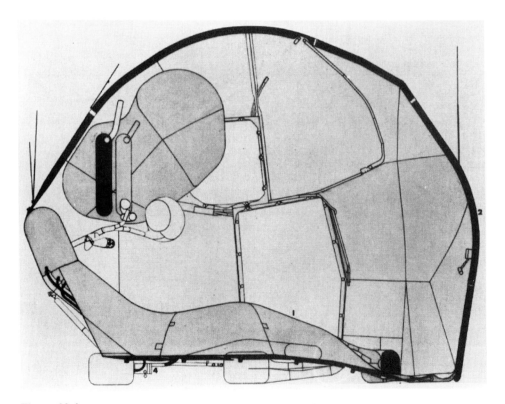

Figure 20.4

Cushicle, (1966–7), with spinal chassis and outer inflatable envelope. Transportable on a person's back, food and water are in pod attachments, radio and television in the helmet. The unit opens out to form a complete dwelling environment. Architects Archigram/Michael Webb.

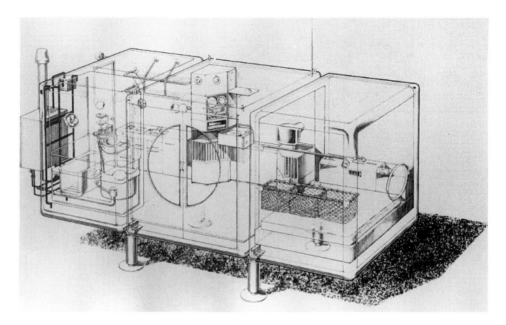

Figure 20.5

Capsule Village Project, (1972). A 'Metabolist' project in part influenced by Archigram, the 3 × 6 metre capsule has three mechanical, living and sleeping sections, and was attached to a lattice beam structure. Architect Kisho Kurokawa.

plugging into'[8] – while two projects by Webb, the Cushicle (1966–7) and Suitaloon (1968), evolved even more minimal and portable systems of shelter and servicing. Clearly based on a Situationist future of human beings roaming the world with no need of structured cities or fixed base, these projects posit an 'architecture' nearer to the servicing of human needs provided by a car or even an overcoat.

THE ARRIVAL OF HIGH-TECH

Although Archigram themselves never realized their projects (the group formally ceased existence in 1976), their influence as the *enfants terribles* of the architecture was world-wide. While the serviced capsule can be seen in the Bathroom Tower (1968), by Terry Farrell (1938–) and Nicholas Grimshaw (1939–), where a cluster of plastic pods are inserted into a London Victorian terraced house, the notion of a serviced and neutral enclosure was seen first in the Reliance

Figure 20.6

Bathroom Tower, London, (1968), architects Terry Farrell and Nicholas Grimshaw. A service zone added on to the back of an international students' club, individual bathroom pods spiral around a structural core.

Figure 20.7

Reliance Controls Factory, Swindon, (1967), architects Team 4. Intended as a modifiable and ultimately disposable structure, the architects consequently welcome the fact that it may now have come to the end of its useful life and be demolished.

Figure 20.8

Minimal glazed skin of the IBM Advance Head Office, Cosham (1970), architects Foster Associates.

Figure 20.9

High-tech reaches the masses. Pompidou Centre, Paris, (1971–7), architects Renzo Piano and Richard Rogers. Office partitions can be moved in one minute, gallery partitions in one hour and firewalls in one day.

Controls Factory, Swindon (1967) designed by the Team 4 practice of Norman Foster (1935–) Wendy Foster (1938–89), Richard Rogers (1933–) and Su Rogers (1939–). This building was the first of the 'well serviced sheds' which became the norm in the later 1970s and 1980s; constructed of lightweight steel panels and distinguished by thin steel cross-bracing and a lack of internal structure, it paved the way for a new kind of flexible and adaptable industrial architecture. Further projects extended the concept, including the Foster temporary IBM Office at Cosham (1971), and Renzo Piano's (1937–) Italian Pavilion for the Expo '70 at Osaka, Japan, where a plasticized enclosure is surrounded by a minimal steel frame.

But it is the building of the Centre National d'Art et de Culture Georges Pompidou (1971–7) in Paris, commonly known as the Pompidou Centre, which launched the new architecture into public consciousness.

Figure 20.10

Lloyds Building, London, (1986), architects Richard Rogers Partnership. Because they require more frequent maintenance and eventual replacement, all services are located on the external periphery of a central office floor and atrium core, enabling easier access.

Figure 20.11

Sainsbury Centre for Visual Arts, University of East Anglia, (1978), architects Foster Associates. Despite ideas about being a flexible shed, a later addition, also designed by Foster Associates, was built underground in order to preserve the original external profile.

The subject of a major international competition for a multi-functional cultural centre, the winning Piano and Rogers design covered only half of the available site, while each floor was a 50 m space fitted with demountable wall hanging panels and enclosures. Most extraordinary was the exterior, where, due to the intention to keep the interior uninterrupted, were placed not only the structure, lifts and escalator but all the services: plumbing, air conditioning and so on became brightly coloured external features. Projection screens, electric newspapers and other gadgets were to make the main façade a constantly changing surface. As Rogers wrote,

> We want our building to be adapted and changed by the people who use it. We want to stop the architecture being a straight-jacket inhibiting ideas. We want the outside to reflect the activities inside – big projections, moving walls, technical gadgetry that aids change – and we want to encourage the maximum possible participation by the public with the specialist users and the things on display. Things change all the time. Maybe one day our museum might become a supermarket.[9]

In the event, the building which opened in 1977 had façades capable of little modification, and the rest of the site, left for spontaneously-generated activities, was largely unused. Nevertheless it looked like nothing built before, and it quickly became the most visited attraction in Paris. However, the indeterminacy of the plan – the library, for example, is identical to a gallery for large works of art – is less than ideal, and huge

Figure 20.12

Hongkong and Shanghai Bank, Hong Kong, (1986), exterior. Architects Foster Associates.

Figure 20.13

Hongkong and Shanghai Bank, interior view of atrium.

amounts of wall space have been provided to create enclosure as hanging space. It can even be argued that the building is not flexible enough; unlike the Fun Palace, the floors cannot be moved.

Despite some discrepancy between intention and realization, the Pompidou Centre opened the way for a new 'style' commonly known (but not by the architects concerned) as 'high-tech'. Along with Richard Rogers, the architect most associated with this is Norman Foster whose Sainsbury Centre (1978) at the University of East Anglia, Norwich, is a huge flexible shed for the exhibition of art. A smooth aluminium skin, with services enclosed within the trussed steel frame, provides an alternative model to the complexity of the Rogers and Piano exterior, and this distinction has continued in subsequent projects by the two practices, notably the Lloyds Building (1986) in London

Figure 20.14

High-tech in a traditional setting. Mound Stand, Lord's Cricket Ground, London, (1987), architects Michael Hopkins and Partners.

by the Richard Rogers Partnership and the Hongkong and Shanghai Bank (1986) by Foster Associates. Others, notably Piano, Grimshaw and Michael Hopkins (1935–) have also continued in a similar use of new technology to create innovative forms.

Ultimately, evaluating the new architecture of the sixties two or three decades later is problematic. While the forms of the architecture first projected by Price and Archigram are visible in most British cities and around the world, in most cases the results are largely stylistic, albeit perhaps with some notion of flexibility. Some, such as the Ladkarn Haulage building (1985) by Grimshaw, have even been successfully dismantled and moved to a different site, and, since the Pompidou Centre, such structures have been popular with many not otherwise stimulated by architecture. However, the radical social programme – to liberate people from an

Figure 20.15

Because of the development of London's Docklands, the owners of the Ladkarn Haulage building, (1985), were persuaded to move it to another location. Architects Nicholas Grimshaw and Partners.

architecture of permanence – has never been achieved. Perhaps such idealism must await larger changes in society. But subsequent developments have also shown that the principles of flexibility and expendability cannot supply an entire philosophy of design, and the continuing emphasis on functionalism, however different from the early modernists, remains an inadequate synthesis of what architecture needs to be.

REFERENCES

1   Le Corbusier, *Towards a New Architecture*, (The Architectural Press, London, 1927). First published as *Vers Une Architecture*, (1923).
2   Le Corbusier, *City of Tomorrow*, (The Architectural Press, London, 1929). First published as *Urbanisme*, (1925).
3   David Greene, *Archigram*, n.1 (May 1961), p. 8.
4   Muriel Emanuel (ed.), *Contemporary Architects*, (St. James Press, Chicago, 1985), p. 307.
5   Reyner Banham, *Theory and Design in the First Machine Age*, (The Architectural Press, London, 1960), pp. 329–30.
6   Constant Nieuwenhuys, 'New Babylon: an Urbanism of the Future', *Architectural Design*, v.24 n.6 (June 1964), p. 304.
7   Cedric Price, 'Fun Palace', *Link*, (June 1965).
8   David Greene, 'Living Pod', in Peter Cook (ed.), *Archigram*, (Studio Vista, London, 1972), p. 52.
9   Quoted in *Architectural Design*, v. 42 n.7 (July 1972), p. 407.

BIBLIOGRAPHY

Architectural Design, (United Kingdom), particularly after 1964.

Reyner Banham, *Megastructure: Urban Futures of the Recent Past*, (Thames and Hudson, London, 1976).

Peter Cook (ed.), *Archigram*, (Studio Vista, London, 1972, new edition 1991).

Peter Cook, *Experimental Architecture*, (Studio Vista, London, 1970).

Colin Davies, *High Tech Architecture*, (Thames and Hudson, London, 1988).

Benedikt Huber and Jean-Claude Steinegger (eds.), *Jean Prouvé: Prefabrication, Structures and Elements*, (Praeger, New York, 1971).

Royston Landau, *New Directions in British Architecture*, (Studio Vista, London, 1968).

Robert Marks, *The Dymaxion World of Buckminster Fuller*, (Anchor Press, Garden City, N.Y., 1973).

Cedric Price and the Architectural Association, *Cedric Price*, (Architectural Association, London, 1984).

Elisabeth Sussman, *On the Passage of a Few People Through a Rather Brief Moment in Time: Situationist International 1957–72*, (MIT Press, Cambridge, Mass., 1989).

Part Five

CITIES

21

THE BIRTH OF A MODERN CITY

FIN-DE-SIÈCLE VIENNA

David Dunster

During the nineteenth century, in 1830, 1848 and 1870, three periods of revolution changed the face of Europe. Of these, the bourgeois and anti-aristocratic revolutions of 1848 most affected the future development of cities, not so much for any subsequent attempt to remove the traces of the previous era but for the concern to prevent any upset to the newly-dominant power of the bourgeoisie. In particular, unruly oppositional forces, especially those of the working classes, were perceived as being able to hide within the complex medieval structures which baroque city planning had framed, but not eradicated. If the bourgeoisie were to be able to exercise its forces of suppression, these older urban areas had to be regulated.

The most famous city restructuring is that of Paris undertaken by the French emperor Louis Bonaparte, Napoleon III, (1808–73) and Baron Georges-Eugène Haussmann (1809–91) between 1850 and 1870, and which greatly influenced American cities like Washington, Chicago and Cleveland.[1] Another such restructuring, that of Vienna, was equally dramatic and influential, being widely copied in European cities like Frankfurt and Milan. What happened in Vienna could not have been adopted in America, where no city had fortifications dating from the seventeenth or eighteenth century. But in Europe, where fortifications often constrained the growth of cities, the ramparts, ditches and other machinery of war could be transformed into public space; the word 'boulevard', for example, is said to derive from the word 'bulwark' for a rampart or earthwork.

THE CREATION OF THE RINGSTRASSE

In the old Austro-Hungarian empire the aristocracy alone could staff the army who in turn held sway over the old Vienna fortifications. After the revolution of

Figure 21.1

After the bourgeois revolution of 1848, and the rising power of the Viennese liberals from 1860, the Ringstrasse became an expression of middle class values. Materialist public programmes of hospitals, clean water and parks were matched by overtly ideological buildings such as the Reichsrat Parliament, (1883), architect Theophil Hansen.

1848 the emerging commercial and mercantile classes sought control of this fortified area – the *glacis* – which separated the medieval core of Vienna from the growing suburbs. From 1857 onward, this zone was rebuilt into the Ringstrasse, a monumental circumferential street which followed the course of the old fortifications while placing a public building in the centre of each side. Land around each of these new buildings was sold to pay for the constructions, creating an area ripe for the development of apartment buildings. On the Ringstrasse itself, grandiose buildings like the Rathaus town hall (1884), the Reichsrat parliament building (1883), a University (1885) and an Opera House (1861 onward) were installed as symbols of the new political power; each building's purpose – municipal autonomy, national government, higher learning, liberal culture and so on – contributed to a vision of a new democratic power.

The creation of the Ringstrasse and the development of its neighbouring residential sectors helped give physical form and identity to the new city life. By the *fin-de-siècle* (turn of the century), Vienna dominated Budapest and Prague as the cultural capital of Mittel Europa, the region roughly conceived as covering what we now think of as eastern Germany, the Czech and Slovak republics, the Balkan states, Austria and parts of Poland. To Vienna, as to Berlin farther north, flocked intellectuals in the arts and sciences, although they were attracted more by each others' company than by the conventional Viennese middle classes.

Often the Viennese intelligentsia came from solid bourgeois stock. Karl Krauss (1874–1936), editor of the satirical journal *Die Fackel*, lived from private means. Around him and *Die Fackel* congregated the free spirits who sought to transform Mittel Europa out of the complacent environment of the post-revolutionary era. Richer and altogether grander than Krauss, the Wittgenstein family played host to musicians and artists running salons modelled on those of pre-revolutionary French aristocrats. From the family came Ludwig Wittgenstein (1889–1951), the philosopher of language and meaning who also had a limited activity as an architect, designing a house for his sister. And from the Freud family came Sigmund Freud (1856–1939), who developed the theory and practice of psycho-analysis from case-histories of patients suffering mental instability. Krauss, the iconoclast of society, Wittgenstein, the radical logician, and Freud, to whom the twentieth century owes an entire vocabulary of illness, represent the texture of Viennese intellectual life, and as far as we know that life was so varied that they never met.

If these men stand for intellectual freedom, then the Ringstrasse stood for political freedom. Within these two interdependent contexts, what of architecture? In the transformation of the glacis into the Ringstrasse architectural styles were adopted as thought appropriate for each purpose: Greek for the Reichsrat parliament building because of its associations with Athenian state democracy, gothic for the Rathaus town hall because of is associations with medieval municipal autonomy and freedom from aristocratic power, and neo-classical for the University because of its associations with renaissance secular learning. Architectural aesthetics were considered as something like a book of patterns, from which a selection could be made by educated reading. Each example of a style stood for a larger cultural or historical idea.

THE BIRTH OF MODERN ARCHITECTURE

The view of architecture demonstrated in the public buildings of the Ringstrasse was overtly simplistic, being dependent on a tradition of representational architecture, and as a result architectural education and

Figure 21.2

Majolica House, Vienna, (1899), architect Otto Wagner. Majolica – glazed or enamelled ceramic – is used for the decorative elements of the façade.

practice often consisted of little more than choosing and copying the right buildings from the past. Against this unsophisticated thought-process some architects questioned the dogmas of propriety in the same rational spirit which animated Krauss, Wittgenstein and Freud.

Of these, Otto Wagner (1841–1918), who in 1895 published a book entitled *Modern Architecture*, stands out as a complex figure: a property speculator, architect and city planner who began to break the mould of architectural conformity. In his own work, and in his teachings, Wagner held to the belief that all buildings should be symmetrical but progressively shed any ornament which was based upon precedent.[2] His own houses collapse the classical vocabulary into a formalized experiment with colours and forms, while the urban buildings for shops, apartments and offices employ steel frames covered with stone or tile whose decoration, as on the façade of the Majolica House (1899), often relates to plant forms. His most enduring contributions at the urban scale were the designs for the Danube canal, and for the railway lines, one underground in the city and the other above ground, the so-called Gürtel Line which girds the expanded city in an transportation arc.

Wagner also completed the Ringstrasse's seventh side with his design for the Postal Savings Bank (1904–6 and 1910–12), one of the earliest buildings in Europe to use aluminium. Here the metal is employed externally to bolt stone panels to a reinforced concrete frame, and thus creates decoration in the Ruskinian

Figure 21.3

Contradictions in modernity are replicated in architecture. While architect Otto Wagner responded to metropolitan anonymity and democracy, the Postal Savings Bank, Vienna, (1904–6 and 1910–12), and bust of Georg Coch in front are also anti-Semite monuments. Set up by Coch in the 1880s, the PSB attracted Christian investors wishing to avoid Jewish bankers and liberals.

Figure 21.4

'The whole basis of the views of architecture prevailing today must be displaced by the recognition that the only possible point of departure for our artistic creation is modern life.' Otto Wagner, *Modern Architecture*, (1895). Postal Savings Bank, interior.

sense of being a necessary part of the structure rather than as applied ornament. Sculptures above the cornice, by Othmar Schimkowitz (1864–1947), were also cast from aluminium, though the most dramatic use of the material is reserved for the public banking hall where heat arrives through machine-like tubes. This room, in the original design to have had a suspended double-glazed roof, is flooded with light sitting as it does at the bottom of the light well. Below it, the glass block floor transmits light down into the vaults. Glass, metal and stone were used here in an innovative way, and the fascination with modern materials that we encounter here is typical of fin-de-siècle architecture.

In an opposite direction, architects like Josef Hoffmann (1870–1956) were working with craftsmen-artisans in the Wiener Werkstätte, the craft group which he helped found in 1903, to produce domestic objects lacking conventional decoration but nonetheless precious and elegant in appearance. Hoffmann's glassware, still in production, uses stems so thin and fragile that the user hardly dares to lift them. Of his buildings, the Palais Stoclet (1905–11) in Brussels best represents the union of arts and crafts to which the Werkstätte aspired. Originally commissioned for a site in Vienna, the clients had to move cities in order to look after their banking interests. An exterior of white cubic volumes edged in black tile conceals a room for small concerts, as well as the usual wealthy bourgeois requirements. Each room is treated as a distinct piece and was entirely designed by Hoffmann and executed

Figure 21.5

Unlike the use of aluminium and other modern materials by Wagner, Josef Hoffman and the Wiener Werkstätte focused on older artistic and craft traditions. Palais Stoclet, Brussels, (1905–11).

Figure 21.6

'To the Age its Art, to Art its Freedom.' *Ver Sacrum* (Holy Spring). The Secession movement aimed to regenerate art in Austria and to regenerate Austria through art. Secession Building, Vienna, (1898), architect Joseph Olbrich.

by Viennese craftsmen, the dining room, for example, carrying a mural by the artist Gustav Klimt (1862–1918).

The Palais Stoclet adopts a certain ease of planning from the English nineteenth century tradition of Richard Norman Shaw (1831–1912) and Edwin Lutyens (1869–1944). In contrast to the propriety of this aspect of Hoffmann's design, and to the rationalism of Wagner, the Secession (f. 1897) alignment of artists and architects, which soon was to include both Hoffmann and Wagner, saw Viennese social formalities as things to be decorated and transformed into a mystic experience. The Secession Pavilion (1898) designed by Joseph Olbrich (1867–1908), with its giant gilded globe sitting on top of an otherwise undistinguished stone building, repeats the pattern observable elsewhere in Paris, with Hector Guimard (1867–1942), and in Brussels, with Victor Horta (1861–1947), of a fin-de-siècle fascination with making buildings look more biological, using the forms of ferns, lilies, and pansies in cast iron and stone. Art Nouveau, in either city, sought to infuse nature into building craft, but as such could never compete with the emerging rationale of mass-production.

ORNAMENT AND CRIME

Vienna in the 1900s was still not a modern city in the sense that, unlike Berlin, Paris or London, it possessed no serious manufacturing industry living; its economy was instead based on the service industries of the state. It is unsurprising then that inspiration for its new architecture should also come from elsewhere.

Adolph Loos (1870–1933) travelled in America between 1893 and 1896, where the hygiene, scale and efficiency of its cities impressed upon him the how primitive Vienna was in comparison. He returned with a sceptical voice and a critical eye. Writing for Krauss' *Die Fackel*, Loos developed a theoretical position on the future of architecture almost before he began to receive commissions. Passionately fond of American plumbing, English tailoring and intellectual conversation, he moved widely within a cultural milieu which included, apart from Karl Krauss, the composer Arnold Schönberg (1874–1951) who would in the 1920s change the basis of music from tonality to the twelve tone theory, and the painter Oscar Kokoschka (1886–1980) whose experiments with dense, thick and impassioned expressionism opened a new field of painting.

Not surprisingly Loos remodelled three cafés where the intelligentsia met, of which now only the American Bar (1907), known also as the Kärntner Bar or Loos Bar, remains. This, the smallest and the most luxurious of the three, depends upon mirrors to create a feeling of an endless space within which the bar and tables hide. A marble coffered ceiling is reflected infinitely in the mirrors which line the walls above head height. Loos' writings on architecture come as something of a surprise after this. In his most famous essay, 'Ornament and Crime' (1908), he argues that only savages tattoo themselves, and that the quality of a civilization can be read from its graffiti. A twentieth century man should refuse such primitivism as ornament, and instead seek only objects that are well-made.[3] Such a position was in clear opposition to the stylistic tendencies of Olbrich and the Secession.

How then are we to reconcile Loos' stated predilection for austere aesthetics with his evident use of rich materials such as marble, with decoration such as coffering, and with classical references such as columns? In the building now known as the Loos House but constructed as the Goldman and Salatsch Store (1909–11), Loos scandalized Vienna through his suppression of ornament. At shop level, however, marble covered Ionic columns support a string course

Figure 21.7

'Every material possesses a formal language which belongs to it alone . . . No material permits any intrusion upon its own repertoire of forms.' Adolf Loos, 'The Principle of Cladding', (1908). In the Kärntner Bar, Vienna, (1907), Loos used mahogany, onyx, marble, leather, glass and brass.

Figure 21.8

Goldman and Salatsch Store, Vienna, (1909–11), architect Adolf Loos. Construction halted temporarily when the severely restrained façade decoration provoked the city planning authorities into demanding an alternative design. The addition of flower baskets was the eventual compromise.

above which a rendered façade is articulated only by simple window reveals. On either minor façade the two-storey shop has bays which ape the windows of the Art Nouveau Glasgow School of Art (1898–1909), designed by Charles Rennie Mackintosh (1868–1928), while the internal courtyard is lined with white glazed brick and industrial steel windows. How could these devices be used by an architect who was later to condemn ornament as crime?

To answer this question, we should consider the physical and intellectual context of Vienna. Loos, unlike the iconoclastic Krauss, but like Schönberg and others, worked in the positive. Any building can be seen as a criticism of its predecessors, but only because it proposes something new to replace what has been attacked. Much of Loos' early commissions were public buildings like cafés and shops in which he could counter the traditions of Vienna with a simpler, more austere architecture. These are not the most minimal of buildings, but nonetheless denote a change to good manners, urbanity, and *politesse*; in other words to a kind of banality which unlike the Werkstätte or the Secession did not call attention to itself, in the way that tattoos call attention to the skin of the wearer.

Only in interiors such as those of the Villa Muller (1930) in Prague, or of the house he designed in 1926 for the dadaist poet Tristan Tzara (1896–1963) in Paris, did Loos produce architectural spectacle, the kind of spaces in which a visitor is delighted or shocked. For the exterior, Loos in general adopted techniques which are so calm and quiet that it is sometimes hard to see why he has any importance in the twentieth century. It is his attack on ostentation in 'Ornament and Crime', and the morals behind it, for which Loos is famous. For Loos himself, what an architect did was mostly

Figure 21.9

According to Adolf Loos' *raumplan* concept, the height as well as floor area of each room is adjusted to suit its function. Complex sections and staircase arrangements are produced as a result. Villa Muller, Prague, (1930), interior view of living room.

Figure 21.10

Pure architectural minimalism in the bronze skin of the Seagram Building, New York, (1954–8), architects Ludwig Mies van der Rohe and Philip Johnson.

Figure 21.11

New National Gallery, Berlin, (1962–8), architect Ludwig Mies van der Rohe. Cruciform column supports, set back from the corners, are treated as isolated objects.

building, doing a craftsman-like, intelligent and rational job; architecture was for monuments, tombs and memorials. But theoretically, the logic of his American experience and his hatred of the Viennese bourgeoisie combined into a positive attitude, which we might think of as one of restraint, not minimalism. The development of that latter idea would have to wait for the work of Ludwig Mies van der Rohe (1886–1969), and later Aldo Rossi (1931–); only then would the idea that architecture could exist entirely without ornament be explored in actual constructions.

Loos established a new path for architecture, and this role was recognised by both Walter Gropius (1883–1969) and by Le Corbusier (1887–1965) in the 1920s. His quiet, almost ordinary architecture now seems to lack the pyrotechnics of modern movement inventiveness, the expressionisms of the post-World War II period, and the historicism and bravura of self-styled postmodernism. Yet we should not lose sight of the radical character of its intentions. The tense context in which Loos' ideas emerged, that of an anxious battle between an established bourgeoisie and an avant-garde prepared to overturn even those mechanisms by which the arts were financed, is the same context as that of Freud, Wittgenstein and Schönberg whose writings and compositions equally exhibit a searching, almost tortured desire for change.

REFERENCES

1   David H. Pinkney, *Napoleon III and the Rebuilding of Paris*, (Princeton University Press, Princeton, 1972).

2   Otto Wagner, *Modern Architecture*, (Getty Centre for the History of Art and the Humanities, Santa Monica, 1990). First published 1895.

3   Adolf Loos, 'Ornament and Crime' (1908), in L. Munz and G. Künstler, *Adolf Loos: Pioneer of Modern Architecture*, (London, 1966).

BIBLIOGRAPHY

General History

C.A. Gulick, *Austria: From Hapsburg to Hitler*, (1948, two vols).

B. Jelavich, *Modern Austria: Empire and Republic, 1815–1986*, (Cambridge University Press, Cambridge, 1987).

Architecture and City Planning

Kenneth Frampton, *Modern Architecture: a Critical History*, (Thames and Hudson, London, 1992).

Heinz Geretsegger and Max Peintner, *Otto Wagner 1841–1918: the Expanding City and the Beginning of Modern Architecture*, (Academy Editions, London, 1979).

Benedetto Gravagnuolo, *Adolf Loos: Theory and Works* (Idea Books, Milan, 1982).

Adolf Loos, *Spoken Into the Void: Collected Essays 1897–1900*, (MIT Press, Cambridge, Mass., 1982).

Adolf Loos, 'Ornament and Crime' (1908), in L. Munz and G. Künstler, *Adolf Loos: Pioneer of Modern Architecture*, (London, 1966).

L. Munz and G. Künstler, *Adolf Loos: Pioneer of Modern Architecture*, (London, 1966).

Donald Olsen, *The City as a Work of Art: London, Paris, Vienna*, (Yale University Press, New Haven, 1986).

Vera Pintaric, *Vienna 1900: the Architecture of Otto Wagner*, (Studio Editions, London, 1989).

Camillo Sitte, *Der Städtebau*, (1889), translated as 'City Planning According to Artistic Principles' in George Collins and Christina Collins, *Camillo Sitte: the Birth of Modern City Planning*, (Rizzoli, New York, revised edition, 1986).

Carl Schorske, *Fin-de-Siècle Vienna: Politics and Culture*, (Cambridge University Press, Cambridge, 1981).

Peter Vergo, *Art in Vienna 1898–1918: Klimt, Kokoschka, Schiele and their Contemporaries*, (Phaidon, Oxford, 19881).

Otto Wagner, 'The Development of a Great City', reprinted in *Oppositions*, n.17 (Summer 1979), pp. 102–16.

Otto Wagner, *Modern Architecture*, (Getty Centre for the History of Art and the Humanities, Santa Monica, 1990). First published 1895.

Robert Waissenberger (ed.), *Vienna 1890–1920*, (Alpine Fine Arts, London, 1984).

22

THE CITY WITHOUT QUALITIES

Adrian Forty

How do you tell you are in a *modern* city? Is it by what goes on in the buildings – shopping malls, hotels, banks and apartment blocks? Or is it by their appearance – large, spacious and glassy? Is it the broad straight roads with flyovers and underpasses? Or is it the people hurrying past without looking at you?

These sorts of questions very much concerned architects and planners who from the early twentieth century onward tried to envisage what a truly modern city might be like. We might recall here the Cité Industrielle (1904) of the French architect Tony Garnier (1869–1948), the Città Nuova (1913–4) of the Italian Futurist architect Antonio Sant'Elia (1888–1916), the Ville Contemporaine (1922) of the Swiss–French architect Le Corbusier (1887–1965), Magnitogorsk (1930) by Russian architect and town planner Ivan Leonidov (1902–59), and Broadacre City (1932–58) by American architect Frank Lloyd Wright (1867–1959), and also books like *Der Städtebau* (1889) by Austrian architect and town-planner Camillo Sitte (1843–1903), *Garden Cities of Tomorrow* (1902) by English town planner Ebenezer Howard (1850–1928), *Die Schonheit der Grossen Stadt* (1908) by German architect August Endell (1871–1925), and *Town Planning in Practice* (1912) by English architect and town planner Raymond Unwin (1863–1940). All have in common the pursuit of the modern, but there are also many differences between them. We will concentrate here on one particular theme that divides them: some aimed to create a city where everyone could potentially know everyone else, but others accepted the idea that the inhabitants would remain forever unknown to each other.

The illustration of the village street at Dunster in Somerset, from Unwin's *Town Planning in Practice*, shows a scene where a stranger, should he or she appear, would immediately be spotted. One purpose of Unwin's book – which it shares with many other urban schemes and writings on the city from Sitte to Radburn, the garden city built outside New York in 1928, to Jane Jacobs' book *The Death and Life of Great American Cities* (1961) – was to break the great city down into a series of neighbourhoods, each distinguished by squares, monuments, greens or shops, and small enough for all the inhabitants to recognize one another. This

Figure 22.1

The Futurist Città Nuova, (1913–4), envisaged by Antonio Sant'Elia, combines proto-fascist politics with a utopian celebration of the technological metropolis.

Figure 22.2

'The city of today is dying because it is not constructed geometrically.' Le Corbusier, *The City of Tomorrow*, (1929). Ville Contemporaine, (1922), one of Le Corbusier's first attempts to design the modern city afresh.

Figure 22.3

Absence of anonymity in Dunster village. Raymond Unwin, *Town Planning in Practice*, (1909), illustration by C. Wade.

notion, that a city should be a community who can all know each other, is as old as the ancient Greek philosophers Plato and Aristotle, so why should an idea first developed in ancient cities should suit modern ones? Why try and turn a city into a place where everyone might get to know everyone else? This seems especially strange when we consider that since the middle of the nineteenth century intellectuals have been saying that the main characteristic of modern cities is that their inhabitants do not know each other, and, because they are so numerous, can never do so. Unlike the provincial market town where a stranger would at once be noticed, in the modern city everyone is a stranger.

FEAR AND AMBIVALENCE

We will look here at the history of the idea that modern cities are places full of people who do not and never expect to know each other, and see how this has been expressed architecturally. When this feature of cities was first noticed in the 1840s, the

Figure 22.4

London's teeming streets, as depicted by Gustav Doré in *London: A Pilgrimage*, (1871). Doré was escorted on his journeys into London's East End by a plain-clothed policeman.

reaction was fear, revulsion and horror. The Prussian Friedrich Engels (1820–95) wrote in his first book *The Condition of the Working Class in England* (1844),

> A town, such as London, where a man may wander for hours together without reaching the beginning of the end, without meeting the slightest hint which could lead to the inference that there is open country within reach, is a strange thing. This colossal centralization, this heaping together of two and a half millions of human beings at one point, has multiplied the power of this two and a half millions a hundredfold; has raised London to the commercial capital of the world . . . But the sacrifices which all this has cost become apparent later. After roaming the streets of the capital for a day or two . . . one realizes for the first time that these Londoners have been forced to sacrifice the best

qualities of their human nature . . . The brutal
indifference, the unfeeling isolation of each in his
private interest becomes the more repellent and
offensive, the more these individuals are crowded
together, within a limited space. And, however
much one may be aware that this isolation of the
individual, this narrow-self-seeking is the
fundamental principle of our society everywhere, it
is nowhere so shamelessly barefaced, so self-
conscious as just here in the crowding of the great
city. The dissolution of mankind into monads of
which each one has a separate principle and a
separate purpose, the world of atoms, is here
carried out to its utmost extreme.[1]

Engels did not find wandering around the streets of
London pleasurable; a similar perception of London,
dark and crowded with strangers, appears in Gustav
Doré's engravings of London published in 1872.

The first person to really appreciate the crowds of
large cities and write about the experience was the
French poet and critic, Charles Baudelaire (1821–67).
Running throughout Baudelaire's work is an attack on
the eighteenth century idea that nature is the source
of all beauty. 'Nature', he says, 'can produce only
monsters.'[2] Beauty comes not from nature, but from
imagination; he writes, for example, about make-up,
which creates beauty because it is artificial and
counteracts nature. The other main aspect of
Baudelaire's aesthetic theory was what he called 'correspondences', the imagination's ability to perceive 'the
intimate and secret connections between things' that
are otherwise independent.

Baudelaire's excitement about the city was partly
because it was unnatural and partly because it offered
infinite possibilities for the occurrence of 'correspondences'. Baudelaire was fascinated by crowds of
strangers and by the experiences of the *flanêur*, the
individual who strolled through the city as a discon-
nected observer.

For the perfect *flâneur*, for the passionate spectator,
it is an immense joy to set up house in the heart
of the multitude, amid the ebb and flow of
movement, in the midst of the fugitive and the
infinite. To be away from home and yet to feel
oneself everywhere at home; to see the world, to
be at the centre of the world, and yet to remain

hidden from the world . . . Any man . . . who can yet
be *bored in the heart of the multitude*, is a
blockhead! a blockhead! and I despise him![3]

Baudelaire, then, reversed Engels horror of the crowd,
and made it into an aesthetic experience.

The artist usually credited with representing this
characteristic of the city in paintings is Baudelaire's
French contemporary, Edouard Manet (1832–83). A
painting like *Exposition Universelle* (1867) shows a
group of Parisians who are curiously distracted; they
co-exist in the space of the picture, but they do not
relate to each other by any principle of perspective or
composition. The peculiar effect is, it has been
suggested by the art historian T.J. Clark, a depiction
of urban *anomie*.[4]

Another product of the piling up of strangers in the
city was the detective story, a genre which relies for
its effect upon the existence of a city into which
people could disappear and become invisible. The
skill of Sherlock Holmes or any other detective is in
being able to discover from the minutest traces the
identity of people otherwise lost in the crowd. This
sort of detective story would make no sense in a
world in which everyone is potentially knowable, and
in this respect the genre was a product of the modern
city.

Figure 22.5

'No one knew me, no one
looked at me, no one found
fault with me; I was an atom
lost in that immense crowd.'
George Sand, *Histoire de ma
vie*, (1831). *Exposition
Universelle*, (1867), artist
Edouard Manet.

CULTURE AND THE MODERN CITY

So far we have considered writers ambivalent about the experience of the city, who enjoyed the anonymity of being in a crowd of strangers but at the same time showed signs of anxiety about being swallowed up and disappearing into it. One of the first people to articulate wholly positive ideas about the modern city was the German sociologist Georg Simmel (1858–1918), in an important and original essay called 'The Metropolis and Mental Life' first published in 1903.[5] Simmel's argument is that the intensity of life, the emotional experience of the city is so great that city dwellers develop a blasé attitude toward all things. Their only measure of things is in terms of quantities, primarily of money, and they lose any sense of qualities. Out of this indifference comes a deep reserve, and an aversion to contact with others. By never showing emotions, each person makes themself invisible in the city. However, this reserved behaviour contains opportunities for individual intellectual freedom, and may cover substantial intellectual differences, such as would never be found in small towns. At the same time, conditions in the metropolis allow ever increasing opportunities for contact with wider groups of people, and for the spread of ideas. Together, these circumstances are favourable to the development of a rich and varied urban culture. Moreover, Simmel argues that, beside providing unprecedented opportunities for the development of culture, the modern city lets culture thrive independently of any great individual; modern metropolitan culture is thus distinguished by being depersonalized. Simmel's essay is significant because it attempts to identify the positive attributes of modern urban life, of 'the city without qualities'. While all previous writers had seen the effect of the modern city as destructive, Simmel argued that even if the city was unpleasant, modern culture depended upon it, and was inconceivable without it.

The interdependence of the modern city and modern culture was to obsess artists and intellectuals in the early decades of this century, reaching its height in the 1920s with novels like Marcel Proust's *Remembrance of Things Past* (1922–31) and Robert Musil's *Man Without Qualities* (1930), in Berthold Brecht's poems, and in the writings of Berlin intellectual Walter Benjamin. Of all these, it is perhaps Benjamin (1892–1940) who expresses more completely than any other the sense of the city as a great mass of people living in apparent chaos, but in the process creating a culture from which he would not for one moment want to be parted. Benjamin wrote endlessly about cities, but his best known work on urban culture is his never completed history of nineteenth century Paris, often referred to as the 'Arcades Project', which exists only in various outlines and fragments.[6]

ARCHITECTURE AND ANONYMITY

What did all these ideas about the city as a crowd of strangers, as a place of discontinuous experience, and of individual intellectual freedom mean for modern architecture? How, if at all, did they affect attempts to articulate the forms of a modern city? We find two kinds of reactions. One, as with Unwin, Radburn and its garden city successors, is the attempt to redefine the city as a number of small units, where everyone becomes knowable again. The opposite reaction is to argue that any attempt to reduce the enormity of cities would destroy those very aspects responsible for modern culture. If everyone was condemned to life in garden suburbs, modern culture would be finished. Furthermore, no traditional or historical model of cities could be expected to sustain the unique culture that has grown up in the great cities of the present: cities in the form of English market towns or Italian medieval city states are unlikely to suit a culture whose richness lies in anonymity and indifference.

It was all very well to argue this, but there remained the problem of how to represent such an abstract idea in architectural terms. For the modernists of the 1920s, and successive generations, this has been a recurrent question. One of the first to acknowledge the issue was the Viennese architect and city planner Otto Wagner (1841–1918), whose ideas for the extension of Vienna assumed a uniform regularity, deriving from the standardized character of the large number of apartment blocks required. Decorative features on the buildings or picturesque variations in the street line were, Wagner argued, out of place in a metropolis.[7]

Figure 22.6

Design for Chicago Tribune Tower, (1922), architect Ludwig Hilberseimer, as shown in *Grosstadtbauten* (1925).

Of people who explored the architectural expression of anonymity and indifference in the 1920s, one of the most interesting, because the most extreme, was the Berlin architect Ludwig Hilberseimer (1885–1967). Hilberseimer's design for the Chicago Tribune tower – the international competition of 1922 for a Chicago newspaper – was the blandest, dullest of the entries. This was not, however, through lack of architectural talent; rather, Hilberseimer was pursuing the idea that the life of a great city is in the crowd, in the masses; the culture of the modern city does not depend upon individuals, so monuments, the products of individuals' aspirations, are redundant. It is not the job of the architect to create values or impose them upon the city, but instead to allow the life of the city to take its own form. Hilberseimer's design attempted to create a

very large building that was not a monument, and which celebrated no individual or group of individuals. It is utterly anonymous, and that is its quality.

The concept of the city as a place without values is even clearer in *Grossstadtarchitektur*, (1927), Hilberseimer's scheme for a large city. In drawings for this project, which represents just about everything now most disliked about modern architecture, people scurry about like ants beneath blank curtain walled slab blocks. The buildings are crudely geometric, because aesthetics would only get in the way of the life of the mass. Hilberseimer explained that he was dealing only in generalities, for city planning is an abstraction, and does not deal with individuals. This 'involves a reduction of architectonic form to its most modest, necessary and general requirements: a reduction that is to cubic geometric forms, which represent the fundamental elements of any architecture.'[8] Architecture, in its conventional sense of creative form, is made to disappear, and instead is concerned only with organization. According to Hilberseimer, the architecture of the city is determined by two factors only: the design of the individual room to give the best possible conditions, thus influencing the arrangement of the dwelling and so ultimately the form of the city; and, conversely, the city layout optimized to reduce transport and increase production, thus affecting everything down to the arrangement of the single room.

Figure 22.7

Project for a high-rise city. Ludwig Hilberseimer, *Grossstadtarchitektur*, (1927). The layering of two cities – businesses and automobiles below, residences and pedestrians above – was intended to reduce congestion by bringing work and home closer together.

Hilberseimer's project is an attempt to give an image to such an analysis of urban architecture. When the drawings appeared in the 1920s, people were quick to complain, and they have gone on complaining ever since. When people object that the city it shows is impersonal and lifeless, they are of course right; but they are missing the point, for these are precisely the qualities that Hilberseimer wanted to represent. Alienation, lack of identity and discontinuity were the acknowledged features of urban life, out of which modern culture was understood to have emerged, and Hilberseimer was consequently trying to conceive a form that would best accommodate modern cities, where people would not aspire to know each other. It was not the business of architecture to put identity, community and continuity back into the life of the city, because not only would this make the city look like something it was not, but it would undermine the very conditions which had created modern culture. For a city to be a place where people could remain unknown to one another indefinitely, the architecture of the city had to be neutral, anonymous and without value.

It has to be said these are not comfortable ideas, but they cannot be swept aside or ignored as so many people have tried to do. Whether we like it or not, alienation and anonymity are an intrinsic part of urban life. One way or another, we have to find room for them in our thinking about modern cities.

REFERENCES

1   Friedrich Engels, *The Condition of the Working Class in England*, (Panther Books, St. Albans, 1974) pp 57–8. First printed 1844).

2   Charles Baudelaire, 'Further Notes on Edgar Poe', (1857), in *The Painter of Modern Life and Other Essays*, (Phaidon, London, 1964), p. 99.

3   Charles Baudelaire, 'The Painter of Modern Life', (1863), in *The Painter of Modern Life and other Essays*, pp. 9–10.

4   T.J. Clark, *The Painting of Modern Life*, (Thames and Hudson, London, 1985), pp. 65–6.

5   Georg Simmel, 'Die Grossstädte und das Geistesleben', (1903), translated as 'The Metropolis and Mental Life' in Donald Levine (ed.), *George Simmel On Individuality and Social Forms*, (Chicago University Press, Chicago,

1971), pp. 324–39 and in Richard Sennett (ed.), *Classic Essays on the Culture of Cities*, (Prentice-Hall, Englewood Cliffs, 1969), pp. 47–60.

6   Walter Benjamin, 'Paris – Capital of the Nineteenth Century', in *Reflections: Essays, Aphorisms, Autobiographical Writings*, (Harcourt Brace Jovanovich, New York, 1978).

7   Otto Wagner, 'The Development of a Great City', (1912), reprinted in *Oppositions*, n.17 (1979), pp. 102–16.

8   Ludwig Hilberseimer, *Grossstadtarchitektur*, (1927), quoted in Manfredo Tafuri, *Architecture and Utopia: Design and Capitalist Development*, (MIT Press, Cambridge, Mass.), p. 106.

BIBLIOGRAPHY

Urban Culture

Charles Baudelaire, *The Painter of Modern Life and Other Essays*, (Phaidon, London, 1964).

Walter Benjamin, 'Paris – Capital of the Nineteenth Century', in *Reflections: Essays, Aphorisms, Autobiographical Writings*, (Harcourt Brace Jovanovich, New York, 1978).

Marc Blanchard, *In Search of the City: Engels, Baudelaire, Rimbaud*, (Stanford French and Italian Studies/Anma Libri, Saratoga, 1985).

Friedrich Engels, *The Condition of the Working Class in England*, (Panther Books, St. Albans, 1974). First printed 1844.

David Frisby, *Fragments of Modernity: Theories of Modernity in the Work of Simmel, Kracauer and Benjamin*, (MIT Press, Cambridge, Mass., 1986).

Francis Haskell, 'Doré's London', *Architectural Design*, v.38 (December 1968), pp. 600–4.

Andrew Lees, *Cities Perceived: Urban Society in European and American Thought, 1820–1940*, (Manchester University Press, Manchester, 1985).

Richard Sennett (ed.), *Classic Essays on the Culture of Cities*, (Prentice-Hall, Englewood Cliffs, 1969).

William Sharpe and Leonard Wallock (eds.), *Visions of the Modern City: Essays in History, Art and Literature*, (Columbia University, New York, 1987).

Carl Schorske, 'The Idea of the City in European Thought: Voltaire to Spengler', in Oscar Handlin and John Burchard (eds.), *The Historian and the City*, (MIT Press, Cambridge, Mass., 1963), pp. 95–114

Georg Simmel, 'The Metropolis and Mental Life' in Donald Levine (ed.), *George Simmel On Individuality and Social Forms*, (Chicago University Press, Chicago, 1971), pp.

324–39 and in Richard Sennett (ed.), *Classic Essays on the Culture of Cities*, (Prentice-Hall, Englewood Cliffs, 1969), pp. 47–60.

Elizabeth Wilson, *The Sphinx in the City: Urban Life, the Control of Disorder, and Women*, (Virago, London, 1991).

Architecture and City Planning

Peter Hall, *Cities of Tomorrow: an Intellectual History of Urban Planning and Design in the Twentieth Century*, (Basil Blackwell, Oxford, 1988).

Barbara Miller Lane, *Architecture and Politics in Germany 1918–1945*, (Harvard University Press, Cambridge, Mass., 1968).

Richard Pommer et al, *In the Shadow of Mies. Ludwig Hilberseimer: Architect, Educator and Urban Planner*, (Art Institute of Chicago and Rizzoli, New York, 1988).

Camillo Sitte, *Der Städtebau*, (1889), translated as 'City Planning According to Artistic Principles' in George Collins and Christina Collins, *Camillo Sitte: the Birth of Modern City Planning*, (Rizzoli, New York, revised edition, 1986).

Anthony Sutcliffe (ed.), *Metropolis 1890–1940*, (Mansell, London, 1984).

Otto Wagner, 'The Development of a Great City', (1912), reprinted in *Oppositions*, n.17 (1979), pp. 102–16.

23

GENDER AND THE CITY

Iain Borden

Of all the social characteristics of cities, one of the most significant is gender. Indeed, gender rivals class to be seen as the single most important issue which structures not just our cities but our whole way of life.

But what are gender relations? At their simplest, gender relations are the ways people socially interact where the gender of men and women is thought to be significant. Such gender relations have had an enormous influence on many aspects of life, ranging from what jobs men and women do to what clothes they wear. Gender relations are then part of the social reproduction of life – the way society is continually sustained, not just through the biological reproduction but through the continual invention and reinvention of social rules and conventions.

What have gender relations to do with cities? As both are needed for society to survive and develop, it follows that, on the one hand, gender relations and ideas about them influence the way cities evolve, and, conversely, that cities help sustain gender relations. This essay looks at three areas where this process occurs: the division between domestic and wage-earning work, particularly in the suburbs; the architectural and planning professions; and the experience of urban space.

WORK AND THE SUBURBS

The most general division between men and women, historically, has been what they do everyday and where they do it. Particularly for the past two centuries, there has been a classic division between the industrially productive activities which men do and the socially reproductive activities which women do. Men have tended to work for industry or in the management, government, or service systems which regulate it, and they do this in a workplace separate from the home. They gain remuneration as wages, receive recognition by society that they do 'real' work, and obtain overall financial and social control of what is consequently a patriarchal society. Women on the other hand have customarily worked as a service to men and children in the home. Even when women have gained employment outside of the home, this has usually been as an addition to their domestic duties. And their remuneration is less tangible, coming, supposedly, as a secure position, a 'personal' sense of achievement, and some social recognition of their role as wife and mother. Women were frequently dependent on men for both income and social status, praised not for being themselves but for their support to men and their families. Like it or not, this is the historic division of labour by gender which has dominated in the West.

One of the most pronounced features of cities is how their spatial arrangement accurately reflects this situation, with male-dominated work areas, often in the city centre, separated away from the female, domestic realm of residential suburbs. This public/private division is not new, and is apparent even in the first city suburbs. Thus in eighteenth century Clapham in south London, the religious middle class residents deliberately isolated themselves from the dense city core, and so separated domestic life

Figure 23.1

A suburban site of female reproductive labour. No. 113 Clapham Common, North Side, London, (late eighteenth century).

from work. The residents here, William Wilberforce (1759–1853) and other members of the Evangelical movement, viewed the city as a man-made evil in contrast with the godly virtues of the country. As a result, the coffee houses, plays, balls, and social visits of London were replaced in Clapham with family life and direct contact with nature: libraries, family rooms and gardens, with numerous places for women to knit, crochet, do fancywork stitching, converse and raise children.[1] Rather than the busy comings and goings of the city residence, the Evangelical suburb is the place of very careful definition, control and exclusion. And at the heart of it all are women, continually present, responsible primarily for the continued education and servicing of the family in an entirely god-fearing way.

The confinement of women to the home was to be repeated over the centuries to come. While wartime exigencies have occasionally shown that women are quite capable of doing industrial work, the gender division of labour more usually prevails.

Figure 23.2

Wartime conditions often disprove the notion that women cannot work in industry and other productive enterprises. In 1942, 61 000 British women formed the Land Army to boost agricultural and forestry output.

Figure 23.3

'The woman's intellect is not for invention or creation, but for sweet ordering, arrangement and decision. By her office, and place, she is protected from all danger and temptation. The man must encounter all peril and trial. This is the true nature of home – it is the place of Peace.' John Ruskin, 'Of Queen's Gardens'. Illustration from Robert Shoppell, *Modern Houses, Beautiful Homes*, (New York, 1887).

In the late nineteenth century, a more secular version of Evangelical ideas about women, nature and family life developed into a 'cult of domesticity'. For example, in the new American middle-class suburbs outside Boston, Chicago, Los Angeles and Minneapolis women were confined to the domestic hearth. But, in contrast to their Evangelical predecessors, the underlying reasoning was economic and social more than religious. Women provided an essential support service to their wage-earning men folk, and therefore the same trams and trains that carried the men to the city to work also carried women there to shop. Nevertheless, women's essential role remained tied to the home and family; while men existed in order to work, women existed to allow men to work, to provide a domestic refuge on their return. Women made the home beautiful, luxurious and relaxing, creating a private retreat from the city where men and children benefited from the more uplifting activities of refined education and proper morals.[2]

When lovely women vote

Figure 23.4

The image and caption used in a 1930s advertisment for toothpaste. The manufacturer implies that a woman's choice of dentifrice is equally important as her political vote. *American Magazine*, (October 1932).

From around the 1910s onward, there gradually emerged greater realization that women's domestic work was necessary for society. For example, as I show in Chapter 16, the 1920s German *existenzminimum* modernist dwelling was partly intended to recast women as professionals, thus explicitly recognizing the domestic work they did, albeit still without much financial or social independence.

In the 1930s and 1950s, during the great suburban booms of the United Kingdom and the United States, the same pattern continued of men going to work while women stay largely at home to run the house and raise the children. The difference here was that women were increasingly thought of not just as the creator and manager of the household but as responsible for the consumption of goods. Buying the right food, clothes and appliances, even the right house, became part of the gender division of labour, for while men earned money, women were responsible for spending it effectively and properly. Women's national duty was to select the best goods at the best prices, and thus to ensure that only the best manufacturers and retailers survived.

Furthermore, once identified with making consumer choices, women were targeted for the marketing of all manner of domestic goods, with traditional gender roles and stereotypes deployed to persuade them. In particular, advertisers exploited the idea of women as natural mothers, with innate desires to look after children, to powerful effect. Advertisements for cleaning materials, soap powders, clothes, kitchen equipment and all manner of domestic supplies combined fundamental ideologies about parenthood with some

Figure 23.5

'You, as a conscientious mother, buy the best food for your children and cook it correctly. Yet you may be giving your children food which is possibly dangerous! There is only one way to be sure that your children's food is fresh and healthful – correct refrigeration.'
Saturday Evening Post, (21 September 1929). Woman's role as consumer underlined by appeals to her role as wife and mother.

very banal, if necessary, household routines. They
show how capitalism in the twentieth century has
intensified, becoming a deeper and more intimate part
of everyday life.

So far we have seen how gender relations are implicated in conventional social arrangements in cities. The
system whereby men undertake waged labour and
women perform duties to do with social reproduction
is made possible by defining the home as women's
place of work and the suburb as their place in the
city.

But what happens in deliberately unconventional
approaches to living, where people have seemingly
tried to change gender relations? As I show in Chapter
16, one attempt at alternative living took place at the
Kings Road Studios in 1920s Los Angeles, and Jonathan
Charley identifies another in the Narkomfin housing
commune of revolutionary USSR. Indeed, over the past
two centuries there have been a large number of such
domestic experiments on both sides of the Atlantic.[3]
One such was the Homesgarth (1909–13) co-operative
housekeeping quadrangle built in the English garden
city of Letchworth under the direction of Ebenezer
Howard (1850–1928). Here a mixture of private apartments arranged around a central kitchen, communal
dining room and shared gardens was promoted as a
solution to the 'Woman Question', freeing women
from the drudgery of running a home. However, the
scheme was little more than a country hotel, allowing
its middle class residents to employ servants more
cheaply. Nor were the women, once liberated from

Figure 23.6

Architecture may raise the
profile of class and gender
issues, but can never provide
the solution on its own.
Homesgarth, Letchworth,
(1909–13), architect Harold
Clapham Lander.

household management, expected to do much more than converse politely and potter in the garden.[4]

Residences like Homesgarth demonstrate that gender relations are conceptual and ideological, and that just changing the physical fabric of the domestic realm is not enough. If gender relations are to be transformed, ideas about what women and men do and how they interact must also be addressed. But such alternative living schemes are not intended to make drastic transformations, and ultimately simply aid in the continual process of social reproduction. On the other hand, such schemes explicitly recognize that gender relations do exist, and thus make people conscious of them. Unlike suburbia, gender relations are not presented here as natural.

THE URBAN DESIGN PROFESSIONS: PLANNING AND ARCHITECTURE

The existence of dominant conceptions about what women can and cannot do is obvious in the role they have had in the design of cities and buildings, now and in the past. There have been some very famous and influential female architects like Jane Drew (1911–), Eileen Gray (1879–1976), Wendy Foster (1938–89), and Denise Scott Brown (1931–), and female planners like Jane Addams (1880–1935), Edith Elmer Wood and Catherine Bauer (1905–64). Such professions are, at least notionally, equally open to men and women.

Nevertheless, these professions are not bastions of sexual equality. For example, less than 10% of architects and 30% of architectural students in the United Kingdom, 12% and 40% in the United States, are women.[5] For those who do become professionals, in all fields and not just architecture and planning, women generally expect to be less 'successful' in terms of fame and corporate status, and face more difficulties in getting the most prestigious work.

Even when they do become successful, there are still problems. For example, Denise Scott Brown, architect and personal and professional partner of Robert Venturi (1925–), has described what she calls the invidious 'Star System' in architecture, which prefers to recognize male individuals as the heroes personally responsible for the buildings which their large office actually designs.[6] Thus, despite their practice's pleas for accuracy, even projects like Philadelphia Crosstown Community (1968) for which she had primary responsibility and Venturi virtually none, are often described by critics and historians as being 'by' Venturi. Clients, students and acquaintances similarly refuse to believe that she too is a significant figure in the office.

Such appropriation by men of what women have done is also evident in the origins of the professions, particularly in planning, where much early activity in social planning and housing reform was instigated by women like Octavia Hill (1838–1912) and Henrietta Barnett (1851–1936) in England, and by Jane Addams (1860–1935) in Chicago. Here, in the philanthropic activities of groups like the Charity Organization Society, which decided which of the poor deserved charity, women first addressed issues central to early urban planning: hygiene, sanitation, health, housing, class relations, morality and sexuality.

However, after some 20 years of concentrated female activities, in the 1900s the nascent predominantly male planning profession took over, ordering and 'professionalizing' them in order to gain control; at national conferences on housing and other planning issues, women stopped giving papers and attending. Planning activity, as a set of concerns first addressed by women, had been appropriated by men as the planning profession.

URBAN SPACE

If the spatial division of the workplace and the residential suburbs demonstrated the confinement of women to the home, and their predominant association with family life, what then of the non-residential, public parts of the city?

Arguments about the nature of urban space and its relation to women can be divided into three groups: those that concentrate on a functional critique, those that adopt a more experiential or personal standpoint, and lastly a highly conceptual approach frequently focusing on different representations of gender. We shall look at each in turn.

Figure 23.7

Pornographic sexism in the streets or an empowerment of female sexuality? Part of the controversial 'Wonderbra' campaign, Caledonian Road, London, (1994).

One of the most pervasive ideas about cities and women, as we have seen, is that cities are bad places, unsuitable for women in general and nice women in particular. Curiously, despite patriarchal implications that women should behave differently to men, the same kind of reasoning underlies functional gender critiques of cities. These argue that if cities are indeed bad for women, then one way of making them more equitable, less sexist, is to eradicate those bad places. For example, in the work of the American feminist planner and historian Dolores Hayden, we find proposals to replace inhospitable streets, sexist symbolism and outlets for pornography with child-care facilities, safe houses, better public transport and so on.[7]

Although these are laudable aims, and would no doubt ameliorate city streets and public spaces, they touch only on the surface of things. In particular, by assuming that changing the physical city will result in a more equitable society, such arguments tend toward architectural determinism – the idea that buildings and cities have in themselves the power to change and control the way people live. It would be wrong, however, to reduce the arguments of people like Hayden to this level of crudity. In effect what they are doing, in promoting things like collective houses designed to allow mothers to retain a paid job, is to say that these are ideas, visions of what a non-sexist city might be like.

We must, however, be cautious of saying what should and should not be allowed in cities, for what one person sees as bad and unwanted another may see as inviting and desirable. Censorship, however well meant, runs the risk of promoting the views and interests of only one section of society.

Thus while art historian Griselda Pollock and sociologist Janet Wolff have argued that the 'public' sphere has largely been a male domain,[8] others have been more enthusiastic about women's experiences in the city. Kathleen Adler has interpreted middle class suburbs such as Passy in late nineteenth century Paris, far from being zones of confinement and social sterility, as areas where women could work, relax and enjoy the city.[9] Nor should women be necessarily excluded from city cores. In *The Sphinx in the City* (1991) Elizabeth Wilson argues that while cities undoubtedly present very real dangers, so also they potentially offer women excitement and personal liberation. Nineteenth century Paris, for example, yielded individual anonymity, bohemian lifestyles and sexual liberation, especially for lesbians and gays, plus new urban realms for women to enjoy: cafés, restaurants, the opera, theatres, hotel foyers, department stores and even, for prostitutes, the city streets themselves.[10]

Of course much that Wilson describes was the exceptional rather than the normal experience of women. This then is almost the opposite of what people like Hayden are trying to do. Instead of trying to change the fabric of the city according to a set of rules or provisions, Wilson articulates very personal ideas about what living in cities is like, a more libertarian idea that the individual should revel in those parts of the city that they most like.

This brings us closer to the third, conceptual approach to the urban realm, which often seems to be only tangentially related to cities in their physical form. A good example of this kind of thinking is *Sexuality and Space*, edited by Beatriz Colomina, in which, for example, essays on the renaissance Leon Battista Alberti (1404–72) and the twentieth century modernist Le Corbusier (1887–1965) try not just to understand these architects were actually saying, but to speculate upon the meaning and representations of gender. For example, Colomina notes the continual absence of women in many photographs of Corbusier's architecture, while the presence of men is enigmatically suggested by a few male objects, like a hat, a pair of

Figure 23.8

Villa Savoye, Poissy
(1929–31), architect Le
Corbusier. An image
analysable through theory for
the construction of
masculinities, absence of
women, domesticity, the act
of looking, and the associated
role of the photographic
medium in the creation of
architectural identity.

sunglasses, a lighter and a pack of cigarettes.[11] Gender,
even if not immediately obvious, is nevertheless a part
of the photographic representation of the buildings.

This tactic of taking major buildings and figures –
canonic features of mainstream culture – and re-inter-
preting them in radically new ways, is a very particular way of dealing with dominant conceptions of
gender, gender relations and sexuality. We see this also
in someone like the singer k.d. lang, who plunders the
overtly sexist music and imagery of country and western
music to transform it into her own perspective of what
it means to be female and lesbian. Appropriating things
like country and western music, or Le Corbusier, lets
their original meanings be discarded, even destroyed,
making them symbolic not of what they originally
meant but of what they can be made to mean now.

REFERENCES

1   Robert Fishman, *Bourgeois Utopias: the Rise and Fall of
    Suburbia*, (Basic Books, New York, 1987).

2   Gwendolyn Wright, *Building the Dream: a Social History
    of Housing in America*, (MIT Press, Cambridge, Mass.,
    1983), pp. 96–113.

3   Dolores Hayden, *Grand Domestic Revolution: A History
    of Feminist Designs for American Homes, Neigborhoods
    and Cities*, (MIT Press, Cambridge, Mass., 1981); and

Lynn Pearson, *The Architectural and Social History of Co-operative Living*, (Macmillan, London, 1988).

4 Iain Borden, 'Social Space and Co-operative Houskeeping in the English Garden City', *Journal of Architectural and Planning Research*, forthcoming.

5 Ellen Perry Berkeley, 'Introduction', in Ellen Perry Berkeley and Matilda McQuaid (eds.), *Architecture: a Place for Women*, (Smithsonian Institution Press, Washington, 1989), p. xv.

6 Denise Scott Brown, 'Room at the Top? Sexism and the Star Sysem in Architecture', in Ellen Perry Berkeley and Matilda McQuaid (eds.), *Architecture: a Place for Women*, (Smithsonian Institution Press, Washington, 1989), pp. 237–46.

7 Dolores Hayden, *Redesigning the American Dream: the Future of Housing, Work and Family Life*, (W.W. Norton, New York, 1984); and 'What Would a Non-Sexist City Be Like? Speculations on Housing, Urban Design, and Human Work', in Rachel G. Bratt, Chester Hartman and Ann Meyerson (eds.), *Critical Perspectives on Housing*, (Temple University Press, Philadelphia, 1986), pp. 230–46.

8 Griselda Pollock, 'Modernity and the Spaces of Femininity', *Vision and Difference: Femininity, Feminism and Histories of Art*, (Routledge, London, 1988), pp. 50–90; and Janet Wolff, 'The Invisible *Flâneuse*: Women and the Literature of Modernity', *Theory, Culture & Society*, v.2 n.3 (1985), pp. 37–46.

9 Kathleen Adler, 'The Suburban, the Modern and 'Une Dame de Passy'', *The Oxford Art Journal*, v.12 n.1 (1989), pp. 3–13.

10 Elizabeth Wilson, *The Sphinx in the City: Urban Life, the Control of Disorder, and Women*, (Virago Press, London, 1991).

11 Beatriz Colomina, 'The Split Wall: Domestic Voyeurism', in Beatriz Colomina (ed.), *Sexuality and Space*, (Princeton Architectural Press, Princeton, 1992), pp. 73–128.

BIBLIOGRAPHY

Kathleen Adler, 'The Suburban, the Modern and 'Une Dame de Passy'', *The Oxford Art Journal*, v.12 n.1 (1989), pp. 3–13.

Judy Attfield and Pat Kirkham (eds.), *A View from the Interior: Feminism, Women and Design*, (The Women's Press, London, 1989).

Ellen Perry Berkeley and Matilda McQuaid (eds.), *Architecture: a Place for Women*, (Smithsonian Institution Press, Washington, 1989).

F. Bonner et al (eds.), *Imagining Women: Cultural Representations and Gender*, (Polity Press, Cambridge, 1992).

Iain Borden, 'Social Space and Co-operative Houskeeping in the English Garden City', *Journal of Architectural and Planning Research*, forthcoming.

Beatriz Colomina (ed.), *Sexuality and Space*, (Princeton Architectural Press, Princeton, 1992)

Dolores Hayden, *Grand Domestic Revolution: A History of Feminist Designs for American Homes, Neigborhoods and Cities*, (MIT Press, Cambridge, Mass., 1981).

Dolores Hayden, *Redesigning the American Dream: the Future of Housing, Work, and Family Life*, (W.W. Norton, New York, 1984).

Dolores Hayden, 'What Would a Non-Sexist City Be Like? Speculations on Housing, Urban Design and Human Work', in Rachel Bratt, Chester Hartman and Ann Meyerson (eds.), *Critical Perspectives on Housing*, (Temple University Press, Philadelphia, 1986), pp. 230–46.

Jo Little, Linda Peake and Pat Richardson, *Women in Cities: Gender and the Urban Environment*, (Macmillan Education, London, 1988).

Linda McDowell and Rosemary Pringle (eds.), *Defining Women: Social Institutions and Gender Divisions*, (Polity Press, Cambridge, 1992).

Matrix, *Making Space: Women and the Man–Made Environment*, (Pluto, London, 1984).

Griselda Pollock, 'Modernity and the Spaces of Femininity', *Vision and Difference: Femininity, Feminism and Histories of Art*, (Routledge, London, 1988), pp. 50–90.

Daphne Spain, *Gendered Spaces*, (University of North Carolina Press, Chapel Hill, 1992).

Catherine Stimpson et al (eds.), *Women and the American City*, (University of Chicago Press, Chicago, 1981).

Judith Williamson, *Consuming Passions: the Dynamics of Popular Culture*, (Marion Boyars, London, 1986).

Elizabeth Wilson, *The Sphinx in the City: Urban Life, the Control of Disorder, and Women*, (Virago Press, London, 1991).

Janet Wolff, 'The Invisible *Flâneuse*: Women and the Literature of Modernity', *Theory, Culture & Society* v. 2 n.3 (1985), pp. 37–46.

Gwendolyn Wright, *Moralism and the Model Home: Domestic Architecture and Cultural Conflict, 1873–1913*, (The University of Chicago Press, Chicago, 1980).

Gwendolyn Wright, *Building the Dream: a Social History of Housing in America*, (MIT Press, Cambridge, Mass., 1983).

24

THEORIZING EUROPEAN CITIES

ALDO ROSSI, O.M. UNGERS AND ROB KRIER

David Dunster

The cities of Europe experienced unprecedented expansion in the nineteenth century, making the city of a million people a commonplace, and creating much of the physical form of the cities in which we live today. The poverty, disease and degradation visited upon the mass of the population spurred efforts to reform and to revolutionize the cities, but application of the remedies by planners and reformers was both patchy and ineffectual, while novelists and artists were fascinated through a mixture of awe and horror.

The first attempt at physical reform, the Garden City movement inspired by Ebenezer Howard's little book *To-Morrow*,[1] denied that centralized cities had any validity, and instead proposed removing people to a kind of pseudo-countryside. To this movement, the world owes the first extended conception of suburbia, notably in the garden cities of Letchworth (begun 1903) and Welwyn (begun 1920) in the United Kingdom. For the full arrogance of the near feudal ideal behind this movement, consider the suburb of Hellerau outside Dresden where a factory for making furniture is housed in what appears to be a converted castle, the shops mimic the high street of a village, and the wooded common land includes a fake flowing stream.

The birth of the Modern Movement in architecture and planning in the 1920s promised a means to improve cities without imposing feudal forms upon peripheral urban land. But it was only in the post-World War II era that rebuilding on the scale advocated by the early modernists was undertaken, and only then, as Joe Kerr shows in Chapter 19, in a piecemeal fashion. As a result, the rational, health-giving, and systematic proposals of modernist city planning and urban architecture have never been properly tested, while the legacy of what was constructed has now passed into history as a myth, that of the failure of modernism.

Northern European countries exhibit this process in various ways. It was they who suffered the worst bombing and devastation during World War II, and consequently it was they too who had to rebuild fastest, and when least economically prepared. Southern Europe, notably Spain and Italy faced rather different problems; although they had largely escaped destruction (with the exceptions of Florence and Bari), they encountered enormous pressure to expand as the agricultural workforce sought better conditions in the cities. The problem in Italian cities was compounded by their historic centres, often based upon the plans of Roman *castrae* (military camps), which contained a consolidated urban fabric dating at least through a millennium. Furthermore, buildings had been adapted over time, so that the simplistic principles of urban zoning which made some sense in the newly built cities of America were clearly irrelevant to the complex patterns of use in these historic city centres.

URBAN THEORY IN SOUTHERN EUROPE

All of this means that theories of urban form developed from the precepts of modernism found no hold within southern European cities, and that while they might be applied to the burgeoning suburbs, they offered no clue as to what to build, or where to build it, within the historic cores. The urban theories we shall deal with here – those advanced by the Italian Rationalist architect Aldo Rossi (1931–), the Luxembourgeois Rob Krier (1938–) and the German Oswald Ungers (1926–) – therefore return to a pre-modern set of terms, although they also depend upon concepts derived from twentieth century geography and linguistics. Although not all southern European in origin, these three nonetheless address exactly the kinds of problem presented in historic cities. Their aim is to provide a means by which the city can be understood as a living organism, heterogeneous and changeable, in which the effects of history are encrusted upon and within the fabric of the city.

These historical effects could be thought of as simply those great monuments which have been produced over a thousand years. By contrast, Rossi, Krier and Ungers offer insights into the entire city fabric which make little distinction as to the importance of one building over another; in this lies the organic nature of their ideas. Put briefly, they argue that both monuments and the matrix of ordinary buildings are essential to the city, and indeed enjoy a powerful reciprocal relationship. Beyond the rhetoric of public versus private space, or the preference for a rectilinear geometry over meandering streets, or indeed beyond any description predicated upon a pre-existing set of categories, the theories of Rossi, Krier and Ungers work instead from the relationship between the monumental and the ordinary.

ALDO ROSSI

Aldo Rossi's book *The Architecture of the City* first appeared in 1966.[2] His readings of archaeologists, urban geographers and planning theorists here leads him to expound a novel theory of urban form and change dependent upon the idea of type. Rossi's direct architectural source for this concept is the French classical architect Antoine Quatremère de Quincy (1755–1849). A type, following Quatremère de Quincy,

Figure 24.1

Trans-historical persistence of architectural types in the city of collective memory. *The Analogous City*, (1977), collage by Aldo Rossi.

is a built form which recurs over time and has no specific function attached to it. Thus an arcade is one very particular urban form, which can be found in Northern Italy in Bologna, Padua, Milan and elsewhere. Another example of a type is the window, divided into four panes by horizontal and vertical bars. And a further example is the continuous urban terrace. In none of these cases do the purposes to which the arcade, window or terrace are put – whether housing, administration, manufacture, storage or shopping – make any difference to the persistence of the type over time. This is then an overtly formalist definition of type, based on physical appearance and composition rather than on technical or social function. Rossi, however, extends this concept by arguing that the various historic architectural types have become embedded in the sub-conscious 'collective memory' of the citizenry, a term which he derives from the twentieth century urban studies of Maurice Halbwachs, from the structuralist anthropology of Claude Lévi-Strauss (1908–), and from the nineteenth century French cartographer and geographer Paul Vidal de la Blache. As part of this collective memory, architectural types make up the notion of the city which the citizens continuously possess and discontinuously change. Indeed the ability of a particular building form to facilitate changes in purpose, the persistence of that form over time through the accommodation of modifications, is an important part of Rossi's theorization.

Many of these ideas are incorporated in the Analogous City (1977) collaged drawing, but it is in the San Cataldo Cemetery extension at Modena (1971–6, begun 1980), designed in collaboration with Gianni Braghieri, that Rossi gives the most concrete exposition of his theory of urban types. The cemetery is interpreted here as a city of the dead. A long portico/arcade separates the existing cemetery from the extension, while next to this extended gateway stands a city wall, within which are three floors of tombs. The wall divides on the shorter axis to allow a further gateway building, facing the city of Modena but inaccessible from it. In the centre of the cemetery stands a red cube, punched with windows and open to the sky; close to it will rise a chimney. These are the 'monuments' of the cemetery. Between them and enclosing them are the city streets, fanning out from

Figure 24.2

Categorizing building types from the city of the living provides the elements for the city of the dead. San Cataldo Cemetery, Modena, (designed 1971–8, begun 1980), architects Aldo Rossi and Gianni Braghieri.

Figure 24.3

San Cataldo Cemetery.

a rectangle, aligned with single storey housing which contains space for more tombs. Thus the principal types of building – wall, street, house, gateway, arcade – which Rossi has reduced analytically from the city have been repeated; types are copied from the city of the living for use in the city of the dead.

O.M. UNGERS

For O.M. Ungers, the notion of type has somewhat different connotations. Although he shares Rossi's notion that the type is something which persists over time, for Ungers the forms which compose cities are primary forms of three-dimensional geometry,

Figure 24.4

'A basic model for an integrated environment, characterized by a multiplicity of forms. A microcosm, in which the complexity of the macrocosm is reflected, almost as a model for a pluralistic city'. The plan of the Student Residence Hall, Enscede, (1964), interpreted by O.M. Ungers in *Sieben Variationen des Raumes über die Sieben Leuchter der Baukunst von John Ruskin*, (1985).

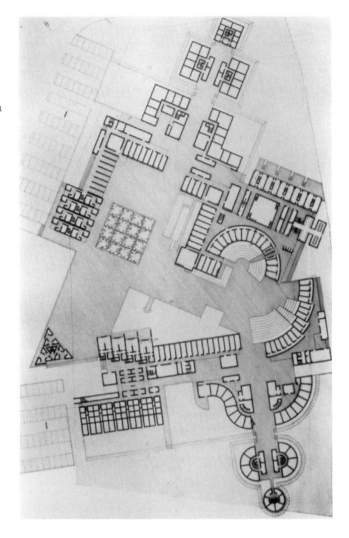

especially as found within the buildings of the Holy Roman Empire in Aachen, Cologne and Trier. A scheme for a Student Residence Hall in Enschede (1964) shows these forms assembled in an apparently haphazard fashion. But although these forms appear to be randomly composed, over them Ungers draws a grid. This grid is an ordering framework, both abstract, in the sense of the grid on ordinance maps which is simply used to aid in the identification and location of geographic features, and material, in the sense in which all buildings can be laid out or measured according to its lines. The grid-framework not only operates over the city, but also in the building as an analogue, as a securing device or lock which then permits the expression of those ideas which allow a more surreal perception of the city. As a result, the juxtapositions which are to be found in a city like Frankfurt, such as those between an older suburb of separate bourgeois villas and the modern commercial towers interspersed among them, can be incorporated into a theory of the city which accepts such diversity.

In the Gleisdreieck Tower (1984) for the Frankfurt Messe exhibition grounds Ungers designed what

Figure 24.5

The modern building as analogy of historic gateway – three massing components. Gleisdreieck Tower, (1984), Frankfurt, architect O.M. Ungers.

Figure 24.6

Gleisdreieck Tower, view of
interior.

appears to be a completely glazed solid extruding from
a concrete base. In the base of the tower, a large hole
further suggests the analogy between the building and
a gateway. In these ways the theory of the forms
which constitute the city are transposed into the building which, through analogy with pre-existing forms, is
both new and old; by interpreting the historic structure of the city it contributes to the re-structuring of
the twentieth century city. What makes the building
somewhat surreal is of course the scale which the
gateway analogy takes, a scale that allows the Messe
tower to be seen from all over the city.

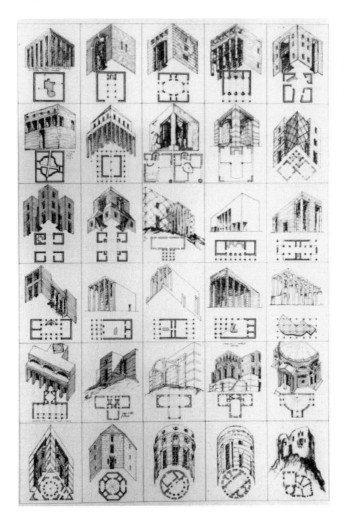

Figure 24.7

Scale, façade and aspect emphasized in one of Rob Krier's numerous analytical studies of typologies for urban buildings and spaces.

ROB KRIER

In both Ungers' and Rossi's theories of urban forms, the shapes of past buildings recur analogically, that is without being directly copied exactly from historical precedents. In the urban theory of Rob Krier, who worked for Ungers in Cologne at one point in his career, urban form is described by geometric patterns of construction, by the continuation of existing scale, and apparently therefore by a return to eighteenth century and early nineteenth century forms of urban development such as might be found in Regent Street and Regent's Park terraces (1811 onward) in London, in the rue de Rivoli (1801) in Paris, or in the urban centre of Nancy. In his theoretical text *Urban Space* Krier analyzes the core of historic European cities in order to uncover the rules by which these cities are formed.[3] Particular attention is paid to a precise formal analysis of the patterns of entry into urban squares, the ratios of building heights to street widths, and the variety of possible façade treatments. Like Ungers and Rossi, Krier is not particularly interested in the functions which these formal features can house, and undertakes, as do the others, a complete break with the modernist dogma which asserts that the exterior of a building should reflect or express the functions which carry on behind the façade.

Krier's major contribution has been to restore the forms of the historic city according to principles which survive through time: those to do with scale, building forms and the layout of buildings in the landscape. The most extended test of his theories is in the Masterplan for South Friedrichstrasse in Berlin, developed from 1984 onward. Here Krier re-instated the street patterns prior to the bombings of World War II, laid down the ground rules of building height and shape, and then invited a multitude of architects, including Rossi, to contribute single buildings or parts of terraces to this overall plan. His proposition is clear: that within an orderly framework, precise architectural expression can vary enormously once a framework of types of building, their positions and overall scale has been established by a master plan. In this way, a monotonous architecture, the curse which systems-building brought to urban centres and fringes everywhere in the 1960s, is avoided. And while monotony is side-stepped, a larger urban pattern emerges for the inhabitants; because an historically-derived framework is deployed, people can understand it and so, the argument continues, they will produce all of those good qualities of architecture which modernism has tended to eradicate from cities by its concentration upon individual, isolated and object-like buildings.

URBAN THEORY AND THE TWENTIETH CENTURY CITY

How far can these theories be judged successful? At the level of theory, all depend upon a leap of faith, accepting as self-evident that urban dwellers do indeed carry deep inside their subconscious minds memories of the pleasures of cities before they were attacked by the various forces we bracket under 'the twentieth century'. There can be no disproof of this axiomatic belief at the level of theory, and indeed at the level of day-to-day evidence its plausibility does seem to be supported by the obvious interest the leisured public take in the historic centres of European cities. But beyond such simple observations, it is impossible to gauge the truthfulness of the proposition. Because the effects of historical memory are presumed to lie buried behind our consciousness, the statistical techniques of consumer satisfaction, for example, will not seriously assist in answering the question.

Even if these theories cannot be proven, we should nonetheless stress their contribution to a new approach to urban planning. True, some of the ideas, especially Krier's, can be found in the writings of the Austrian architect and city planner Camillo Sitte (1843–1903), some of Rossi's can be found in Otto Wagner (1841–1918) and in Adolf Loos (1870–1933), and some of Ungers' stretch back to the German architect Karl Friedrich Schinkel (1781–1841). What is new is the emphasis upon an architecture and a form of building within cities which is uninterested in the precise dictates of function and new functional requirements, and which instead bases the search for building form upon an abstraction from the forms which already exist.

We should also note that the analysis of forms passes through the filter of surrealism, an aesthetic philosophy which enables opposite reactions to coexist. Hence Rossi's sketches of buildings as coffee pots and coffee pots as buildings, and the trickery of scale already noted in Ungers' Gleisdreieck Tower. In using this kind of surrealist tactics, both Rossi and Ungers distance themselves from questions of taste, with which Krier can unfortunately become so deeply involved, and accept that the twentieth century city is a confusing, possibly alienating environment. And they can simultaneously argue that the twentieth century city can be read, can be understood, not by attending to its individual symbols but by seeking the deeper structures of urban construction, and then by employing these structures within a complex story about the sustenance of the best within the urban frame. Theirs is no revolutionary position; but rather like jets waiting to land at a busy airport, these theories circulate in a holding pattern waiting for the signal from society that will establish the possibility of radical changes into some as yet unspecified but new form.

REFERENCES

1   Ebenezer Howard, *To-Morrow: a Peaceful Path to Real Reform*, (Swan Sonnenschein, London, 1898), re-issued with some changes as *Garden Cities of Tomorrow*, (1902).
2   Aldo Rossi, *L'architettura della città*, (Padua, 1966), published as *The Architecture of the City*, (MIT Press, Cambridge, Mass., 1982).
3   Rob Krier, *Urban Space*, (Academy Editions, London, 1979).

BIBLIOGRAPHY

David Dunster, 'Oswald Mathias Ungers: the Romance of the Grid', *Architecture Today*, n.7 (April 1990), pp. 38–43.

Keneth Frampton (ed.), *O.M. Ungers: Works in Progress*, Exhibition catalogue, New York, 1981).

Vittorio Gregotti, 'O.M. Ungers', *Lotus*, ns. 11/12 (1976), pp. 14–41.

Rob Krier, *Urban Space*, (Academy Editions, London, 1979).

Rob Krier, *Architectural Composition*, (Academy Editions, London, 1988).

Rob Krier, *On Architecture*, (1982).

Rob Krier, Urban Projects 1968–1982, (Rizzoli, New York, 1982).

L'architecture de Rob Krier a Vienne-Bruxelles, (Archives d'Architecture Moderne, 1987).

The Work of Rob Krier, special issue of *Architecture and Urbanism*, (June 1977).

Rafael Moneo, 'Aldo Rossi: the Idea of Architecture at the Modena Cemetery', *Oppositions*, n.5 (Summer 1976), pp. 1–30.

Rafael Moneo, 'On Typology', *Oppositions*, n.13 (Summer 1978), pp. 22–45.

Francesco Moschini, *Aldo Rossi: Projects and Drawings*, (Academy Editions, London, 1979).

Carlo Olmo, 'Across the Texts: the Writings of Aldo Rossi', *Assemblage*, n.5, (February 1988), pp. 90–121.

Aldo Rossi, *The Architecture of the City*, (MIT Press, Cambridge, Mass., 1982).

Aldo Rossi, *A Scientific Autobiography*, (MIT Press, Cambridge, Mass., 1981).

Aldo Rossi and 21 Works, special issue of *Architecture and Urbanism* (November 1982).

John Summerson, 'Urban Forms', in Oscar Handlin and John Burchard (eds.), *The Historian and the City* (MIT Press, Cambridge, Mass., 1963), pp. 165–176.

O.M. Ungers, *Architecture as Theme*, (Electa, Milan, 1982).

25

INDUSTRIALIZATION AND THE CITY

WORK, SPEED-UP, URBANIZATION

Jonathan Charley

The open gates of the New Tower of Babel, the machine centre of Metropolis, threw up the masses as it gulped them down.

Metropolis, directed Fritz Lang.

The industrial revolution brought mesmerizing visions of heaven and the abyss to people still tuned to agricultural life. Of all the great art projects of the nineteenth and early twentieth century that attempted to grasp the mad frenzy of urbanization and industrialization, perhaps the film *Metropolis* by Fritz Lang (1926) captures best the contradictory social character of the modern revolution which pitted wage workers against capitalists, vernacular houses against the apocalyptic city, and raised the spectre of the tyrannical machine that would one day subordinate us all. Yet more than a machine, industrialization is the violent force that propels us from the mystic uncertainties of the feudal world into the rationalist bliss of the modern. It drags us from the field to the factory, from the cottage to the housing estate, from the rural market to the shopping mall. As we shall see, industrialization in cities starts with the transformation of the labour process, and brings in its wake the wholesale revolution of everyday social life and its spaces. We shall look at each of these in turn – the labour process, space and everyday life.

TRANSFORMATION OF THE LABOUR PROCESS

At the heart of history lies the labour process, where men and women produce useful things, transform nature and reproduce the means of human life. Not surprisingly, the labour process has been the terrain on which social classes and interest groups have battled to fashion the world according to their own aspirations. This is quite simply because successful control over the labour process, and therefore economic development, is the key test on which all social systems ultimately flourish or flounder. Consequently, industrialization has as much to do with the maintenance of patterns of political and economic power as it has to do with the satisfaction of human need and desire. Within the capitalist world this is revealed in the contradiction between the satisfaction of people's biological and social requirements, and the capitalist imperative to continue making profits.

One of the ways in which historians have periodized history is by distinguishing different epochs by the changes that occur within the labour process. Probably the most profound transformation in the labour process has been the development of industrialization, which begins with the transition from feudalism to capitalism and sees the journeymen and apprentices of medieval handicraft building production replaced by the wage worker harnessed to more mechanized forms of manufacture and production. In looking at this development we need to be wary of believing too readily in the inexorable march of scientific and technological progress. Images of the victorious machine should be tempered by the knowledge that for all its promises, modern industrial society has been characterized by antagonistic forces. The transformation of the construction economy is part of the general history of capitalist industrialization, and thereby mirrors struggles that have occurred throughout its two hundred and fifty year history to transcend and direct productive activity along different lines.

While the initial revolutions in productivity in the eighteenth and early nineteenth centuries had largely been achieved with human labour power, within the industry of the nineteenth century this revolution was heightened still further with the use of machines. Furthermore, in the twentieth century the new machine technologies were combined with management principles concerning the organization of the labour process, resulting in enormous increases in the productivity of labour, such that workers were able not only to produce more, but at ever increasing speed.

Nowhere in this development is the dialectic of hope and despair more clearly articulated than in the shift from manufacture (making by hand) to machino-facture

Figure 25.1

Fordist system of production line machino-facture, Highland Park Plant, near Detroit, (c.1913).

(mass-production by machine processes). This opened up the possibility of liberation from poverty and hardship, but also the threat of subordination to a new set of dictated needs. If we have any single person to thank for this, then it was Henry Ford (1863–1947), who applied Frederick Winslow Taylor's (1856–1915) ideas on time, motion, and work organization to the production of cars. Under the 'Fordist' regime non-skilled and semi-skilled workers were ranged along an assembly line, each performing a single task over and over again, each adding to the construction of an automobile according to a detailed and finely controlled procedure.

In terms of building production, this meant that work which had previously been conducted by skilled

craftsmen with hand tools became increasingly mechanized and, in some cases, automated. If in the late
feudal era a single carpenter could make all the doors,
windows, and trusses a building might require, the
modern world saw a new division of labour: each
aspect of the labour process became fragmented into
many parts, each presided over by a different worker.
The location of the process also changed, shifting from
the building site and small workshop with hand saws
and chisels, to the factory, and to the machinery of
lathes, routers, and bench drills. Within three centuries,
tasks that had previously needed a thousand labourers could now be accomplished by two machines and
two operators. At last the unshackling of the human
subject from heavy manual labour seemed a real possibility. Yet the capitalist condition of private ownership
was to temper and contradict this dream.

Within manufacture, production was absolute in
that there were limits to the length of the working
day. But in modern industry it is the speed of the
machine that dictates the amount any single worker
can produce. The growth in the scale and speed of
production was also mirrored in the expansion of a

Figure 25.2

Fordism as building
construction at Precasting
Combine No. 2, Obuhov,
Leningrad, (c.1965). The
ribbed strips of concrete
joined together as wall
sections of 'Lagutenko'
system-built large-panel
buildings. Versions were
used in France and Britain as
the 'Camus' system.

managerial bureaucracy, whose task was to supervise the increasingly complex division of labour, ensure labour discipline, and maintain efficiency and profits. The outcome was a situation where the direct producers were divorced from the products of their own labour, creating commodities in a process over which they had very little control.

As a result, the automated machines which dominate modern building production appear to the worker not as the results of human labour and thought, not as things which make life easier, but as objects that are remote and alien. And instead of being the inventors and controllers of technological inventions, workers are treated as organs scattered within mechanical systems. Rather than the means of emancipation, the machine 'confronts labour as a ruling power and as an active subsumption of the latter under itself.'[1] Herein lie the origins of the technological tyranny of the twentieth century and one of the cornerstones of modern alienation.

Furthermore, such contradictions have manifested themselves on building sites and factories throughout the cities of the industrial world. Indeed, life for a worker on the automated line producing concrete panels often differed little whether it was inside one of the great Soviet house building combines, or in a concrete plant outside London, or San Francisco.

LABOUR PROCESS IN SPACE

Industrialization, as a material entity, cannot exist independently of space or time. As matter is transformed, so is space. This would suggest that the transformation of the labour process is mutually interdependent with urbanization and the rapid physical transformation of cities. The space of work (the factory) and the space of home life (such as the mass housing schemes of the twentieth century) represent revolutions in the spatial organization of social life that are inseparable from the revolution within the labour process itself.

Similarly, at a more general level, industrialization of building not only involves the rationalization of the labour process, but is accompanied by the rationalization of space through urban design – both processes demonstrate the desire for order and control

Figure 25.3

In the intersection of industrialization and urbanization, work space, domestic space and urban space alike are rationalized through fragmentation and socio-spatial control. Boulevard St. Germain, Paris, (c.1853–70), laid out under the direction of Georges-Eugène Haussmann.

with all the discipline a ruling class can muster. This truly gets underway with the nineteenth century re-planning of Paris, Budapest, Glasgow, and indeed of virtually every other major European city. Even at this early stage there is an inescapable correspondence between the rationalization of space through the boulevard, public square and urban grid, and the increasing division of labour. Both urban space and labour become fragmented into easily controlled and packaged parts, a process which gathers pace in the transition to the zoned city of the late twentieth century, with its mass-produced middle class suburbs and working class estates, and reaches its apogee in the globalization of capitalism. As the truly international character of communications, travel and capitalism increases, the world appears to shrink, and we experience an increasing convergence of scientific knowledge and of economic and political practice. And we witness the simultaneous construction of almost identical built environments, be they in New York, London or Tokyo, whether as office developments, out-of-town residential sectors or the enclosed world of the shopping mall.

If this is one of the most important features of the modern industrialized landscape, the spatial segregation of society along class, gender and ethnic lines is another, and is similarly replicated wherever capitalist urbanization gathers pace. Historically this has been reinforced by the class disparities in the quality of building, and in this respect the *barriadas* and *favelas* of twentieth century Latin American cities are merely the

Figure 25.4

House improvements in an informal *favela* settlement, Rio de Janeiro, (1986).

Figure 25.5

Industrialized building production (1). Tower blocks in the micro-regions on the outskirts of Moscow, (1970s and 1980s).

latest version of the speculative housing developments such as those of London's nineteenth century East End.

But without doubt the most celebrated examples of the industrialization of building are the seas of housing blocks that punctuate the peripheries of virtually every metropolitan centre, whether it be Manchester, Berlin or Paris, and which continue to be built in Latin America, the former USSR and Africa. This aspect of urbanization sharply reveals the contradictory character of building production. On the one hand, we can see a quantitative expansion in building production brought about by technological innovation. Faced with periodic destruction through war, and the associated pressures of migration and population growth, governments everywhere had a moral, social and political imperative to build as much and as fast as possible.

But there were clearly other forces at work. Post-war Fordist building production offered hitherto unimagined opportunities, not just for solving the housing crisis, but for the rapid accumulation of capital and surpluses. Within the west, peoples' needs were met with a state-regulated building industry where the land and technologies of construction lay in private hands. In the Soviet bloc, needs were met through a centrally-planned and completely state-owned industry.

Despite their differing patterns of ownership, the speedy realization of the housing programme was vital for the ruling classes and state bureaucracies in both kinds of society to maintain their ruling class hegemony. The housing and welfare needs of subject peoples were ultimately subordinate to financing the arms race, propping up the military industrial complex, and lining the coffers of capitalists, bureaucrats and Communist Party hacks.

It is precisely during this classic post-war industrialization that the Soviet building industry became almost completely dependent on the prefabrication of concrete components, employing thirteen million workers and operating over two thousand concrete factories. Similarly in Britain, construction output tripled between 1948 and 1964 and doubled between 1955 and 1970, allowing the giant construction firms of Wimpey, Laing and Taylor Woodrow to consolidate their position at the forefront of the British building industry, a position that they still enjoy, not least because of the speculative mass production of new housing suburbs in the late 1980s and early 1990s.

Figure 25.6

Industrialized building production (2). Moriarty Place, London, developers Wimpey, (1991–2).

Figure 25.7

International news coverage for the opening of the Moscow McDonald's hamburger franchise. Such events signify both the world-wide replication of standardized buildings and the commodification and homogenization of global culture.

When we think of industrialized building, it is often the concrete panel housing project that comes to mind. Although many countries have now ceased this kind of system-built production, the process of industrialization is accelerating rather than slowing down. Indeed, almost all contemporary buildings use factory pre-fabricated building components. It is simply that the process has changed to using more sophisticated machines and computer-based technologies, and to the production of building types that differ in appearance from those normally associated with industrialized building. The timber-framed house, the populist Wimpey and Barratt home in the United Kingdom, the Levittown suburb of America, the speculative office block, the McDonald's fast food outlet, the supermarket store, and the light industrial factory unit are all heavily dependent on factory prefabrication of components. All are equally reliant on a site labour force that is mobile, and has been largely retrained with 'fitter' type skills – building workers who do not so much make buildings, as assemble them. Buildings and space can now be produced and transformed with ever increasing speed in a situation where capital turns over with equal rapidity.

THE INDUSTRIALIZATION OF EVERYDAY LIFE

The industrial revolution not only helped redefine the human subject as an assistant to the process of mass production, it also remade us as mass consumers. This

Figure 25.8

CNN helped turn the Gulf War of 1991 into a global media event and news into a mass commodity.

process is achieving new heights with the profusion of do-it-yourself stores where we buy the products of industrialized production, and thereby mass produce our own domestic spaces. Such familiar changes have been accompanied by perhaps the most important contemporary innovations of all, those connected with mass communication and information systems. The massive increase in the production of information as a commodity – such as global media conglomerates and 24-hour television news stations – and of pleasure devices in the form of new technologies – such as televisions, radios, videos, personal computers, satellite receivers and CD players – are all part of the armoury and fabric of industrial society. It would be easy to see such improvements in the quality of life as wholly positive and democratic. However, this would presume that such new technologies develop autonomously, beyond the limitations set by political and economic interest groups.

Ultimately, it is impossible to discuss industrialization in the abstract. Within the history of Western Europe, industrialization not only marks the inauguration of the modern, but of the two great classes of the modern world – the bourgeoisie and the industrial proletariat – and it has been primarily the unfolding relationship between these two classes that has guided the development of industrialization. Unsurprisingly, rather than the Enlightenment promise of the glorious and uninterrupted march of science and reason, industrialization has continued to display all the strengths and weaknesses, creative might and ruthless destruction that

Figure 25.9

Capitalism is intensifying, seeking to commodify and regulate everything. Surveillance and notions of exclusive privacy are part of this condition. Photography prohibited at the Yaohan Plaza shopping mall, London. Photograph 1994.

one would expect from a process predicated on the antagonistic relationship between capital and labour.

Authors like Herbert Marcuse (1898–1979), Theodor Adorno (1903–1969) and Henri Lefebvre (1901–91) have argued that the process of capitalist industrialization has, in place of prosperity and freedom, given birth to a tyranny that extends beyond the workplace, and which seeks to regulate all aspects of everyday life. What we think of as our freedom to consume the products of industrialization is no more than the unfreedom of suffocating under a limited range of false needs; the possibilities of self-determination, of enjoying non-administered free time, and of occupying non-regulated space, becomes ever more elusive. The antithesis of freedom and progress, industrialization is but one aspect of a near terroristic rationality where we enter into the 'technological community of the administered population'. Under the rule of non-elected private interest groups and monolithic state dictatorships, the liberation from need, want and poverty that industrialization had promised becomes eternally shattered by the monstrous waste and destruction of not only nature but of human life itself.

Such a view of the world for many is either unpalatable or simply wrong. One way out of this dilemma has been to proclaim that the age of Modernism, of industrial society, is at an end. According to commentators like Daniel Bell and Jean-François Lyotard, we have moved into a 'post-industrial' era where homogeneity, mass production, large unwieldy enterprizes and unresponsive bureaucracies have been

Figure 25.10

'The triumph of effect over cause, of instantaneity over time as depth, the triumph of surface and of pure objectivization over the depth of desire.' Jean Baudrillard, *America*, (1988). Trump Tower, New York, (1978–84), architects Der Scutt and Swanke, Hayden, Connell and Partners. Interior view of atrium.

replaced by heterogeneity, choice and flexibility. No doubt the debate will continue as to whether this postulated shift actually corresponds to the realities of global change, or whether it is simply a desire to escape, at least within the written text, the inevitability of the total commodification of social life. Either way, we must conclude that industrialization and urbanization have compounded the contradictions of a society to such an extent that we are now faced with a social world based on the culture of the commodity, dominated by passive shoppers and spectators, increasingly unable and unwilling to become conscious of our own oppression.

REFERENCE

1   Karl   Marx,   *Grundrisse*,   (Pelican,   Harmondsworth, Middlesex, 1981), pp. 693–5.

BIBLIOGRAPHY

Capitalist Development

Theodor   Adorno   and   Max   Horkheimer,   *Dialectic   of Enlightenment*, (Herder and Herder, New York, 1972).

Harry   Braverman,   *Labour   and   Monopoly   Capital: the Degradation of Work in the Twentieth Century*, (Monthly Review Press, New York, 1974).

Michael Burawoy, *The Politics of Production: Factory Regimes under Capitalism and Socialism*, (Verso, London, 1985).

Maurice Dobb, *Studies in the Development of Capitalism*, (Routledge, London, 1981).

David Harvey, *The Condition of Post Modernity*, (Basil Blackwell, Oxford, 1989).

Rodney Hilton et al, *The Transition from Feudalism to Capitalism*, (Verso, London, 1984).

Eric Hobsbawm, *The Age of Capital 1848–1875*, (Weidenfeld and Nicolson, London, 1975).

Henri Lefebvre, *Everyday Life in the Modern World*, (Transaction Books, New Brunswick, 1984).

Craig Littler, *The Development of the Labour Process in Capitalist   Societies: a   Comparative   Study   of   the Transformation of Work Organization in Britain, Japan and the USA*, (Heinemann Educational, London, 1982).

Wajcman Mackenzie et al, *The Social Shaping of Technology*, (Oxford University Press, Oxford, 1988).

Herbert Marcuse, *One-Dimensional Man: Studies in the Ideology of Advanced Industrial Society*, (Ark, 1986).

Karl Marx, *Grundrisse*, (Pelican, Harmondsworth, Middlesex, 1981).

Guy Debord, *The Society of the Spectacle*, (Black and Red, Detroit, 1983).

Industrialization of the Building Industry

Marion Bowley, *The British Building Industry: Four Studies in Response and Resistance to Change*, (Cambridge University Press, Cambridge, 1966).

Marion Bowley, *Innovations in Building Materials: an Economic Study*, (Duckworth, 1960).

R.M.E. Diamant, *Industrialised Building*, (Iliffe Books, London, three vols, 1967–8).

Brian Finnimore, *Houses from the Factory: System Building and the Welfare State, 1942–1974*, (Rivers Oram Press, London, 1989).

Gilbert Herbert, *The Dream of the Factory-Made House: Walter Gropius and Konrad Wachsmann*, (MIT Press, Cambridge, Mass., 1984).

Ludwig Mies van der Rohe, 'Industrialized Building', in Ulrich Conrads (ed.), *Programmes and Manifestoes on Twentieth Century Architecture*, (1970), pp. 81–2.

Part Six

PRESENT FUTURE

26

WHAT IS GOING ON?

Richard Patterson

Something funny is going on. In some as yet unclear way, the world has been opened up and it isn't behaving as it ought to, as predicted. This is not just a recent event. This has not just happened. It has been going on for some time and any number of commentators have been trying to come to terms with it, to describe it, in some sense to get to the bottom of it, to reveal the mechanisms, the shifts in form and modes of production – to reveal the paradigm shifts that might enable us to control what is going on, at least to affect it, at least to have commented upon it.

But somehow it has broken free of all our conceptual apparatus, and if one thing is at all certain, it is simply that we no longer believe that we can clearly understand what is going on. We no longer believe that our concepts and language represent 'transparently' and unproblematically what is going on.

SCIENCE, LANGUAGE AND COMMUNICATION

In science this began as a form of systematic doubt, in the observation of an irruption – a violent invasion – of analytical and descriptive activity into the very phenomena, the very objects of study themselves. In his 'Uncertainty Principle', the great German physicist Werner Heisenberg (1901–76) set a boundary to the character of the 'knowable'. He pointed out the reflexivity that haunts the grounds of our knowledge. He pointed out the limits to the 'objective' character of observation. And with physics unable to lead the way, with mathematics unable to provide us with the totality of possible calculations, things have got much worse. Attempts to describe and understand human behaviour, the economy, the weather, the environment, desire, addiction and so on, suffer profoundly from the effect of investigation, from the effect of human agency in the very act of describing, conceptualizing or representing.

In what has been called the 'linguistic turn', attention has focused ever increasingly on the role played by language itself on what were previously thought to

Figure 26.1

What is going on? (1) Postmodern play, the parking facility that looks like a car. 60 East Lake Street, Chicago, (1986), architects Tigerman, Fugman, McCurry.

Figure 26.2

What is going on? (2) The ocean-side Slow House, North Haven Point, (1989–91), provides both a real view out to sea and a simulation via a video monitor. Architects Elizabeth Diller and Ricardo Scofidio.

be our 'concepts', and on our understanding and perception of the world. Beginning with the philosopher Friedrich Nietzsche (1844–1900) and developed by the philosopher Martin Heidegger (1889–1976), this linguistic turn was no mere lament for the loss of belief, but a vision of the way language creates the world in its own image. Deconstruction, the mode of philosophical literary criticism associated with the French philosopher Jacques Derrida (1930–), is a kind of rear-guard action to confound the potency of this dehumanizing insight.

In the past, however, it had been possible to map a conventional or common context of debate. We

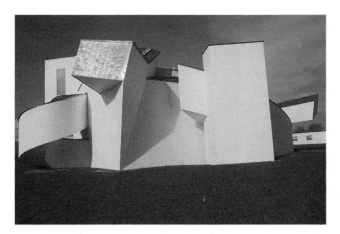

Figure 26.3

The translation of values as formal systems (1). Vitra Design Museum, Weil am Rhein, (1989), architects Frank O. Gehry and Associates.

might refer to it as the framework which enabled us to generate a sense of focus. This framework, or common context, was variously articulated as 'History', the 'Spiritual Realm' or 'Nature'. Within it were various subdivisions separating certain groups of people, certain disciplines, certain intrigues and certain professional or technical languages – each of which tended to produce certain realizations, configurations and certain structural similarities more or less simultaneously. And this was held to be what was going on. 'Ages' were conceived as having characters, the Age of Iron, the Industrial Age, the Age of Reason. Such characters were specific, marked by an internal logical consistency, albeit masked by obscure, mystical, supernatural origins. At present it would seem that it is this very agreement concerning a common context which is somehow up for grabs.

As a result, terms such as 'expertise' and 'competence' have become highly problematic. Certainty is seen more and more consciously as a rhetorical gloss masking simple familiarity with practice, simple obsessive practice; we have no certainty concerning how we know or even how we do things. But nonetheless we accept that we know that we do things and we know what it feels like to do things; that somehow there is simply more to being alive than merely noting and mapping our existence in an abstract way. Additionally, within this sense of being and within our sense of confidence in daily achievement, there is also our desire to 'communicate', to transform our mode of

Figure 26.4

The translation of values as formal systems (2). Vitra Fire Station, Weil am Rhein, (1991–3), architect Zaha Hadid.

Figure 26.5

The translation of values as formal systems (3). Vitra Conference Centre, Weil am Rhein, (1993), architects Tado Ando and Associates.

being into a mode of expression, to translate, to agree on what is shared or common, or, if nothing we can put our fingers on, to agree a surrogate for things common or shared. Even if we no longer feel we know what is going on.

In architecture this problem surfaces as the translation of values, principles and meanings as formal systems. The list of things to be translated has no certain boundaries, no ending, and no universal model. Each instance, each project, each situation determines its own schematic, its own references and its own image. This is what is going on. It is becoming more and more difficult to evoke the feeling of the familiar; to elucidate 'the eternal return of the same' beyond the haunted iteration of certain figures.

ARCHITECTURE AND THE ORGANIZATION OF KNOWLEDGE

What is architecture? A dictionary will say it is something about the design and construction of buildings. Under 'architectonic' it will refer to something like a 'structure of knowledge within a philosophical system' or a 'constructive systematization of knowledge'. Such definitions refer to an older and broader use of the term 'architecture', where one might think about architecture in the same way as one might think about anything: about things in general, about important things, about Real things. This concept, of organized information or knowledge, is fundamental to what is meant by 'thought' in the West. Accordingly, what is considered to be 'thought' is only possible – can only happen – within the context of organized information. The way that information is organized and the structure of the way it is managed could be called its 'architecture'. This we accept as a matter of faith. But when we look at the ways in which information or knowledge have been organized in the past we note that there have been historical differences, and that our faith might therefore be radically misplaced.

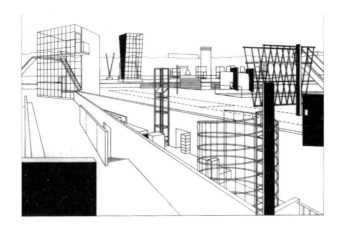

Figure 26.6

Architecture and the organization of knowledge. Porta Vittoria project, Milan, (1986), architect Stephen Holl. The traditional design sequence of plan to section, elevation and perspective is reversed; perspective sketches lead to plan fragments, recast in an overall site layout.

The origin, stability, nature and dynamic of historical differences in both 'thinking' and 'architecture' have been articulated on various grounds: tradition and ritual, the division of labour, the structure of the human mind, the concept of limited and specific reciprocal obligations (a contract), trade, and constructional practice. In the *De Architectura* treatise (c. 25 BC) by the Roman architect and theorist Vitruvius, classical rhetoric was used as a model for the elaboration of a conscious, systematic practice of building which, more importantly, could be translated into a form of discourse accessible to all learned persons. The principle which Vitruvius introduced to building was that of *ratiocinatio*, a rhetorical figure meaning to reason calmly by means of a syllogism; in other words, to present a rational argument and to design a building according to the articulation of efficacious and proper connections or associations. And these connections or associations could be made between all kinds of things: religious, medical, formal, climatic, social, or practical things, (not to mention the physical connections between the elements of a building). Architecture marked an advance over esoteric building practice in that it made the practice of building subject to the criteria of open debate and of the legal process.

It is in this sense, as the organization of discourse or knowledge, that computing science uses the term 'architecture' to describe the configuration of the elements of a computer. The way the computer is wired up is the way in which we might say it 'thinks'. But as computers are limited to binary language – to saying either 'yes' or 'no' through combinations of '0' or '1' – their choice of allowable inferences is extremely restricted. But this is why computers do not make mistakes. Human beings, in contrast, are not limited in this way. Their range of allowable inferences is more varied. As noted above, this varies in history. It also varies between cultures and across disciplines and schools. The study of the range of the possible modes of inference is undertaken in the classical art of rhetoric in the theory of 'tropes'. But the grounds of this study are fairly uncertain. As a result, no one can ever be entirely certain of how or why we think exactly as we do – or of how or why we produce a certain kind of 'architecture'.

ARCHITECTURE AND TECHNOLOGY

At one time, architecture as the profession or science of constructing buildings attempted to embody the totality of human events, to embody what we call meaning and to demonstrate the use of allowable inferences with the purpose of making all knowledge and feeling legible and shared. But as time wore on, the site of legibility and of human sharing has changed. On the one hand this has had something to do with changes in modes of inference, modes of production, the maturity of economies and forms of reciprocity. On the other it has had something to do with the invention of printing and of electronic information technology. Nothing, after all, happens as the result of any one thing.

This brings us to the verge of saying what it is that is going on, for there seems to be a conspiracy abroad, confounding the very grounds of any paradigmatic set of allowable inferences. It may be that we are no longer constricted to think spatially; that is, it may be that we may come to deny the philosophical principle of non-contradiction. What are your terms of reference when pondering these issues? It may be that your architecture is somewhat idiosyncratic. It may be that you are secure in your beliefs. Good luck.

Technically, architecture goes back a long way. Technically speaking, much of what goes on in architecture as a science or profession is of very recent provenance. 'Technology', on the other hand, is where the set of allowable inferences for our age is presumed

Figure 26.7

'Architects play a dialectical game with science.' Stadelhofen Train Station Extension, Zurich, (1988), architects and engineers Santiago Calatrava Werner Rueger.

to be most clearly and comprehensively shown. What we have come to call 'science' is the testing of allowable inferences at the limit of instrumentation. 'Scientists' we call those people who are not constricted by the allowable set of normal inferences, who play at the boundaries of what is technically allowed. Architects play a dialectical game with science.

TEXT

Each technology, each professional or technical language, each language, each discourse creates its own community. Each confounding of the purity of

Figure 26.8

Architecture and text (1) Housing for *Internationale Bauausstellung* exhibition, Berlin, (1987), architect Peter Eisenman. The façade patterning is a superimposed vertical projection of Eisensman's double analysis of the site next to Checkpoint Charlie: the local grid and the global Mercator grid.

discourses – through application, trade, war, election, plague, translation – confronts us with the failure of once seemingly coherent aspirations and, in contrast, (amazingly, sometimes), a multiplicity of hopeful possibilities of transformation. Some have called it chaos, but it is the simple discovery of the violence of origins, of violation, of dialogue, of the end of discourses.

Texts do not end. Texts are work. 'Concepts' and 'principles' are reifications – relations treated as if they were objects. Texts genuinely exist. Texts can be commented upon, exchanged, destroyed, made into wallpaper, read, observed, reflected upon. Texts are the plenitude of those obsessively reiterated fragments, figures and tropes, violently reconfigured for the sake of a sentimental moment of coherence. Beneath this

Figure 26.9

Architecture and text (2). Wexner Center for Visual Arts, Columbus, Ohio, (1989). The red brick castellated structure is conceived as a memory-trace of an old armoury formerly on the site. Architects Peter Eisenman and Richard Trott.

there is but an obsessive reiteration of idiosyncratic syntax, and of ethnicity. A rough and ready digestion, some might say, of other discourses; grumpiness. In other words, a deepening suspicion of smug coherence.

The imagination is dialogical. The essence of the dream-work is syntax.

What is going on?

(This seems to be what is coming to the surface.)

Who speaks?

Who judges?

BIBLIOGRAPHY

Roland Barthes, *Elements of Semiology*, (Jonathan Cape, London, 1967).

Roland Barthes, *Mythologies*, (Jonathan Cape, London, 1972).

Georges Bataille, *Visions of Excess: Selected Writings, 1927–1939*, (University of Minnesota Press, Minneapolis, Minn., 1985).

Jean Baudrillard, *Fatal Strategies*, (Pluto, London, 1990).

Marshall Berman, *All That Is Solid Melts Into Air*, (Verso, New York, 1983).

Jonathan Culler, *On Deconstruction: Theory and Criticism after Structuralism*, (Routledge and Kegan Paul, London, 1983).

Neil Denari, 'Four Statements on Architecture', *Architecture and Urbanism*, (March 1991), pp. 11–45.

Jacques Derrida, *Writing and Difference*, (Routledge and Kegan Paul, London, 1978).

Jacques Derrida, *Positions*, (Athlone Press, London, 1981).

Terry Eagleton, *Literary Theory: an Introduction*, (Basil Blackwell, Oxford, 1983).

Hal Foster (ed.), *Postmodern Culture*, (Pluto, London, 1985). Previously published as *The Anti-Aesthetic*.

Sigmund Freud, *The Interpretation of Dreams*, (Penguin, London, 1991).

Martin Heidegger, *Basic Writings*, (Routledge, London, 1993).

Max Jammer, *The Conceptual Development of Quantum Mechanics*, (American Institute of Physics, 1989).

Julia Kristeva, *The Kristeva Reader*, (Basil Blackwell, Oxford, 1986).

Jean-François Lyotard, *Post-Modern Condition: a Report on Knowledge*, (Manchester University Press, Manchester, 1984).

Tom Mayne, *Morphosis: Connected Isolation*, (Academy Editions, London, 1993).

Friedrich Nietzsche, *Twilight of the Idols*, (Penguin, Harmondsworth, 1968).

Christopher Norris, *Deconstruction Theory and Practice*, (Routledge, Chapman and Hall, London, 1982).

Christopher Norris, *Derrida*, (Fontana, London, 1987).

Paul Shepheard, *What is Architecture? An Essay on Landscapes, Buildings and Machines* (MIT Press, Cambridge, Mass., 1994)

George Steiner, *Heidegger*, (Fontana Press, London, revised edition, 1992).

M.P. Vitruvius, *De Architectura*, (Loeb, Cambridge, Mass., 1931).

Mark Wigley, *The Architecture of Deconstruction: Derrida's Haunt*, (MIT Press, Cambridge, Mass., 1993).

27

COMMERCIAL ARCHITECTURE

Graham Ive

During the 1980s, in the United States, the United Kingdom and many countries throughout the world, the construction sector of the economy underwent dramatic shifts. One of these was the boom of commercial construction, either office or retail buildings for large corporate firms or property developers. This increase occurred both as an absolute magnitude and as a percentage of total construction. Despite the end of this commercial construction boom, these events have had profound consequences for the practice of architecture, which promise to shape its future in the 1990s and beyond.

The impact of modern business forces on the practice of architecture has left it with two, apparently contradictory, scenarios. On the one hand architects are being increasingly constrained by clients who measure architecture by its economic value, and by heightened competition between architectural firms. On the other hand, as they give up their responsibility for the management of building projects, architects are increasingly gaining autonomy as design originators, as creators of spatial concepts. Depending on the view taken, architects are acting either less or more in the traditional role of the artist.

THE CHANGING WORK OF THE ARCHITECT

Ever since the emergence of the traditional contracting system in nineteenth century England, the architect had been responsible to the client for large elements of project management, overseeing other participants in the contract, especially building contractors, and simultaneously arbitrating in disputes between client and builder.

This was necessary because although, on the face of it, contracts turn the relationship between client and builder into a clear, legally-binding form, life, especially life in the building world, is not like that. Contracts are only promises (which clients and builders may not intend to fulfil), and the building process is uncertain. Furthermore, contracts were awarded on the basis of competitive tendering, in which each builder looked at the project drawings and decided what economic amount they could build it for. In practice, these drawings were rarely either complete or final, nor useful for clarifying any problems arising during construction.

For these reasons, therefore, someone had to be appointed to supervise the construction of a building – the architect – who not only designed the building but had a duty to the client. Eventually, in Britain, this range of tasks was codified in the RIBA *Plan of Work*, along with a schedule of payments for each task.[1]

In the last twenty years or so, this range of tasks has been systematically reduced. On the one hand, clients – particularly commercial clients – have appointed project managers or other specialists to co-ordinate the design-team and to manage the building contractors. Not only does this reduce the role of the architect, it also leads to the architect losing their position as project 'leader'. On the other hand, again especially with commercial clients, the later stages of design are normally left to the contractors; architects are appointed as the client's advisor, helping to translate requirements into a brief, while subsequent design is done by the 'design-and-build' contractor. More widespread still, is the use of partial contractor-design on what is otherwise a traditional type of contract. In Britain for example, by the late 1980s, design-and-build and management systems each had around 20% of the total building market.[2]

The kinds of buildings being put up have also had an effect on the architect's role. 'Shell and core' projects – where the developer supplies the basic structure, skin and fabric of the building but leaves the tenant to supply everything else – further restrict the architect's work by excluding all design of services, finishes and fittings. The rise of highly-serviced commercial buildings likewise reduce the proportion of total project design performed by the architect. Building services and structural engineering have never been part of the architect's role, but with these complex and difficult structures the work of the structural engineer often expands to embrace the basic design of the building, while, similarly, the rise in work performed by the services engineer necessarily leaves less work for the architect.

The role of the commercial client in all this has also been significant, for, while in the post-war period the dominant type of client for architects was the public sector, in the 1970s this shifted to corporate clients or commercial developers, such that, in Britain, the British Property Federation, for example, introduced its own new procurement system and form of contract. A few years later, individual property developers, such as Stanhope plc, also began to impose innovative forms of project organization. In the early 1980s, with the public sector still wedded to traditional practices, 60% of private sector projects used either design-and-build, two-stage tendering, project or construction management, or management contracting.[3]

Partly in response to these kinds of changes, some architecture practices have become businesses, with strategies for achieving growth and profitability in a competitive business environment.[4] Those that succeeded in establishing a competitive advantage over other architectural practices in the fast-growing commercial building market of the 1980s quickly grew in size. But what has this meant for those involved?

Part of this concerns the employment conditions of individuals. As architectural firms grew larger, so did the difficulty of managing the practice, and firms with large overhead costs found they needed a continuously high volume of work and cash flow. As a result, most turned fixed costs, such as permanent salaried staff, into avoidable costs by sub-contracting and by changing the nature of employment contracts.

Another change has occurred in the way architecture firms relate to their clients. The public sector, until the 1980s, had been willing to conduct its relations with architecture firms through government agencies and professional institutions. By contrast, private commercial clients generally prefer to negotiate with each firm separately, creating the opportunity to respond to the changing fortunes of the building cycle. 'Sellers' markets', where there is more demand for architectural services than architects can supply, favour architects, whose incomes are likely to rise faster than they would if centrally bargained. In 'buyers' markets', the reverse is true, so that during the downswings in the building cycle, as in the early 1990s, not only do practices' workloads fall but so does their fee income per project. However, as we shall see, the architect's role, particularly when dealing with commercial clients, is shifting ever further from construction management, and ever nearer to the marketing and sales of building.

ARCHITECTURE AS MARKETING

Commercial clients have been persuaded – usually by builders, surveyors or building economists – that architects are poor project managers and uninterested in cost-effective design. If given a free hand, it is argued, architects will cost their clients money. However, few clients are yet prepared to hand over design management to non-architects and, as a result, many architectural firms have in fact created niches as experts in the management and co-ordination of the design phase of the building process. But the emphasis on design management expertise is not the only way that architects have dealt with the challenge from project managers. Some have offered a quite different kind of business service: how to make buildings saleable or add to their market value, and how to create flagship buildings to boost a whole district or city.

For a property developer who provides a building speculatively, without knowing in advance who will occupy it, building design can have a crucial influence on its saleability, price and, hence, on the developer's profit.

Until the 1970s, the conventional wisdom of the property world was that, for offices and shops, building value depended overwhelmingly on location and very little on architecture. It was assumed that, in the right location, there was a virtually inexhaustible demand for standard new office space, despite its often cramped and cost-cutting design. The architects' role was therefore simply to maximize the lettable space on the site, within the limits set by the planners and cost-effective technology. In Britain, the acknowledged experts at this task included such firms as Richard Seifert and Partners.[5]

But this was not the only way of approaching things. Profitability of any property project always depends on the ratio between market value and cost of the project. In some circumstances, profit is best increased by reducing cost; while in other situations, it is better for the developer to accept greater costs if market value

Figure 27.1

Indomitable logic of location and lettable area. John Hancock Tower, Boston, (1972–5), architect I.M. Pei.

Figure 27.2

Centre Point, London, (1963–7), architects Richard Seifert & Partners. Complex planning negotiations allowed maximum space to be squeezed out of the site, yet, once built, the building remained unlet for over a decade.

can be raised as a result. It is this latter strategy that architecture-as-marketing adopts.

In the 1980s, the market for commercial property in cities like New York, Chicago and London changed and matured. While there was roughly the right amount of office space, developers tried to segment the market into different kinds of office space, and to create niche markets for their operations. Architectural reputation and publicity was one valuable means to achieve this end; for example, 'high-tech' commercial building space was heavily marketed by property firms as a distinct product, commanding a premium price. For such marketing claims to be credible, developers employed well-known 'high-tech' architects, or at least those capable of closely imitating the 'style'. Other

Figure 27.3

'If initially the world market sterilizes local sources, in a second moment it revitalizes them'. Edgar Morin, *Sociologie*, (1984). A niche market in the global city, Stockley Park, near London's Heathrow airport, targets prestige offices of high-tech and science businesses. W3 Building, (1991), developers Stanhope, architect Eric Parry.

marketing campaigns made their own differentiations, such as 'atrium' buildings and 'science parks'. Marketing cannot create demand out of nothing; the product must really be different, as must be the wants of the buyer. Nonetheless, marketing can persuade the buyer to 'see' their needs in a certain way, and then to perceive the marketed product as the ideal means of meeting those needs.

This was not the only way architecture could be used as a marketing device. Outside established office districts, another process was at work, that of 'urban regeneration'.

Architectural boosterism – the promotion of a particular city or district by special building projects – is of course not new, and the term 'boosterism' originates from the late nineteenth century United States. In its late twentieth century variation, what have become known as 'flagship' developments are single projects which are supposed to have major external effects, beyond the boundary of their own site, on restoring demand for property in a district or city.[6] They therefore bridge the two levels of 'single development' and 'place'. The idea is that, by being the first of their kind in a particular place, they reveal the latent capacity of the place to meet other demand, and thereby create the demand that will make follow-up projects viable. If the flagship projects are very large, such as the International Convention Centre in Birmingham, England, a further idea is that, by their very scale and presence, they transform the 'attractiveness index' of nearby space, either because everyone else 'wants to

Figure 27.4

Flagship projects frequently promote location and identity through dramatic architectural forms and semi-public spaces. 'Winter Garden', World Financial Center, Battery Park, New York, (1988), developers Olympia & York, architect Cesar Pelli.

be associated with them', or because they permit and obtain massive infrastructure investment in the locality.

In large flagship projects, marketable architecture is a prime requirement. Unless such buildings succeed in transforming the locality, construction costs will always exceed their market value. There is therefore no point in having a 'quiet' low-cost design, because here cutting costs can never guarantee financial viability. From the private developer's viewpoint, the profitability of the flagship project depends on its ability to conjure up market value. For example, the developers at Canary Wharf in London's Docklands needed a

Figure 27.5

'Docklands is the Thatcher government's showpiece, a model being applied to all urban redevelopment programmes.' Peter Dunn and Loraine Leeson, 'Digital Highways', (1991). Canary Wharf Tower, London Docklands, (1991), developers Olympia & York, architect Cesar Pelli.

unique selling point to overcome what was otherwise just a lot of anonymous, badly located office space; as a result, the Canary Wharf tower was designed to be marketed as 'the tallest office building in Europe'.

FASHION EFFECTS AND TECHNOLOGICAL IMPROVEMENTS

Design in general, as we have seen, can be a marketing tool, where the role of the architectural profession is to raise the general desirability of new buildings to potential buyers. This can be done by creating 'fashion effects' where new styles are highly desired precisely because they are new, while simultaneously reducing the relative attractiveness of older buildings. Alternatively, potential buyers can be persuaded that new buildings embody important technological advances that give them improved performance characteristics relevant to those buyers' needs. We shall deal with each of these in turn.

Fashion requires leaders. In conventional fashion systems, including architecture, styles are set by leaders of 'high fashion'. Cheaper, derivative versions of the 'high style' are then spread through increasingly broader markets. In order for this to happen, a new fashion must be simplified to a limited number of features – to a style – and must be capable of being supplied, at least in imitation, in cheap scaled-down versions. At the same time, each seller and buyer will look for 'uniqueness' and differentiation from other examples of the same style. The most profitable fashions, we might suggest, are those which permit wide variation upon an easily recognizable theme, using features which are cheap to produce under small batch processes.

The architectural fashion system has undergone two very important changes since its origins in the nineteenth century. The first of these concerns the switch from the leadership of high fashion by patrons to leadership by architects. Whereas, in the past, certain individuals and institutions might exercise leadership by virtue of their social pre-eminence, such that even the most fashionable of architects would, for the right patron, agree to work in a given style, today it is certain architects who set the fashion, once their reputation has been confirmed in the relevant fashion media.

The second important change concerns the mechanisms of diffusion. Fashion leaders do not face direct competition from other architects and can therefore charge much higher fees. However, styles can be readily copied, and fashion followers can therefore only expect to make normal profits. Conversely, the economic importance of the most fashionable architects is not to be judged from the market value of their own projects; the style and rationale of their designs are spread through the market place by the works of other architects.

Buyers can be attracted by technological innovations as well as by architectural fashions. Innovation in this context refers to the idea that new buildings are capable of enhanced performance compared to older buildings, or of similar performance but at lower cost.

Figure 27.6

'I'm for sale, I'm a whore. I'm a practicing architect. I work for money for whoever commissions a building from me.' Philip Johnson's own view of his role as an architect. The AT&T Building, New York (1978–84), architects Philip Johnson and John Burgee.

Figure 27.7

The architect as fashion leader. A member of the avant-garde 1970s 'New York Five' (with Peter Eisenman, Charles Gwathmey, John Heyduk and Richard Meier), Michael Graves turned in the 1980s to large-scale commercial architecture. Public Services Building, Portland, Oregon, (1980–2).

Some cases of construction innovation are clearly led by a demand from construction clients, such as where a technical or social failure in existing buildings leads to a technological search for a marketable solution. On the other hand, some construction innovations may stimulate demand, although this depends on whether building owners decide to sell or replace existing buildings, and to invest in new buildings to meet new demands. It is helpful to distinguish the case of replacement from other cases. Marketing of 'superior' performance characteristics can only succeed if these are a high priority to buyers.[7] Marketing of cost-reduction can only succeed if it accords with the way buyers actually calculate their costs. Of course, in order to favour their product, sellers will also attempt to influence the way buyers do such calculations. Such marketing efforts may be frustrated, however, by the fact that measurement of cost is the subject of firmly established conventions. In property investment, for example, the success of trying to persuade buyers to choose designs that are initially more expensive but cheaper to run will depend, crucially, on the buyer's investment appraisal technique.

ARCHITECTURE FOR SALE

The marketing activities of firms are aimed at increasing total sales. Selling, on the other hand, involves

Figure 27.8

'The main task for the administration would be to provide service for the front line, and to develop and formulate visions, strategies and goals. We wanted to put all this into the architecture.' Jan Carlzon, chief executive of Scandinavian Airline Systems, explaining some of the complex briefing requirements for their bespoke headquarters building, Stockholm, (1988), architect Nils Torp.

actual sales of individual items to specific customers. The design of a specific building may play an important role in making that sale.

In orthodox economists' accounts of buying and selling, there is first a 'subjective' process, in which buyers become aware of and express their needs, and a later 'objective' process in which they appraise products in relation to these requirements. In this scenario, the client independently generates a building brief as a complete statement of their requirements but without referring to any particular products or designs. The architect selects from the range of possible products the one which best meets the client's requirements, and then by inspection of the design the client establishes what value-for-money it offers. However, this creation of a bespoke building presupposes that buyers can articulate their wants, analyse and break products down into a set of 'features', and identify how they might use each feature and at what 'cost'.

An alternative view proposes that consumers do not really know what they want until they see it, that products are viewed holistically as 'objects of desire', and that commodities are actually part of the psychic world of consumers. In this scenario, the client has rather unarticulated wants which they believe can perhaps be met by a new building. The architect then tries to design a sufficiently enticing 'object of desire', which a quantity surveyor then prices, and which the client decides whether to buy at that price. The architect is here the salesperson of the construction industry. To improve the chances of a sale the architect may

Figure 27.9

The building as corporate object of desire. Broadgate office development, London, developers Rosehaugh Stanhope, architects (Stage 1 1984–88) Arup Associates and (Stage 2 1988–91) Skidmore, Owings and Merrill.

offer a range of options, and of financing and after-sales service packages. To do this, and to improve parts of their sales pitch, they may bring in other associates such as a building contractor or specialist designer. Alternatively, for some kinds of client, it may be a surveyor who takes the lead in selling the customer the idea that they should build.

In this second approach, where construction professionals sell schemes to customers, they do not frequently advise clients that a new building is inappropriate, or that they should spend less money; in this scenario, the professionals' income is usually tied to the value of sales they make, rather than taking the form of a fee for advice, and then a separate fee for other services if the client does decide to build. In a significant number of cases, of course, a design is produced but the client nonetheless decides not to build; although professionals usually try to approach those with potential sites and/or funds, they are sometimes rebuffed. Clients, for their part, do not usually produce detailed briefs. Instead we find substantial numbers of design competitions, and much sales effort in the form of expensive architectural models and presentations. If, on the other hand, the first model of the rational, informed customer with architect as technical advisor is correct, we would expect to find the reverse of all the above, with clients rather than professionals taking the lead. Relatively little systematic research has as yet been conducted to test either of these formulations.

As yet it is uncertain whether commercial architecture will indeed become more an activity subordinated to project management, and whether architectural practices will become increasingly involved in the marketing and sales of buildings. No matter which course the construction sector now takes, architects will want to preserve their control over the design process, but how they will do so is not clear. The future of architecture as a commercial activity, and of architects as professionals, hangs in the balance.

REFERENCES

1   Royal Institute of British Architects, *Plan of Work for Design Team Operation*, (RIBA, London, 1983).

2   J.W.E. Masterman, *An Introduction to Building Procurement Systems*, (Spon, London, 1992), p. 19.

3   Patricia Hillebrandt, *Economic Theory and the Construction Industry*, (Macmillan, Basingstoke, 1985); and Masterman, *An Introduction to Building Procurement Systems*.

4   Graham Winch and Eric Schneider, 'The Strategic Management of Architectural Practice', *Construction Management and Economics*, v.11 (1993), pp. 467–73.

5   Oliver Marriott, *The Property Boom*, (Hamish Hamilton, London, 1967).

6   Hedley Smyth, *Marketing the City*, (Spon, London, 1994).

7   Peter Earl, *The Economic Imagination: Towards a Behavioural Analysis of Choice*, (Wheatsheaf, Brighton, 1983).

BIBLIOGRAPHY

Judith Blau, *Architects and Firms*, (MIT Press, Cambridge, Mass., 1984).

Marion Bowley, *The British Building Industry: Four Studies in Response and Resistance to Change*, (Cambridge University Press, Cambridge, 1966).

British Property Federation, *A Manual of the BPF System for Building Design and Construction*, (BPF, London, 1983).

Weld Coxe et al, *Success Strategies for Design Professionals: Superpositioning for Architecture and Engineering Firms*, (McGraw Hill, New York, 1987).

Dana Cuff, *Architecture: the Story of Practice*, (MIT Press, Cambridge, Mass., 1991).

Peter Earl, *The Economic Imagination: Towards a Behavioural Analysis of Choice*, (Wheatsheaf, Brighton, 1983).

Robert Gutman, *Architectural Practice: a Critical Review*, (Princeton Architectural Press, Princeton, 1988).

Patsy Healey et al (eds.), *Rebuilding the City: Property-led Urban Regeneration*, (Spon, London, 1992).

Patricia Hillebrandt, *Economic Theory and the Construction Industry*, (Macmillan, Basingstoke, 1985)

Spiro Kostof (ed.), *The Architect: Chapters in the History of the Profession*, (Oxford University Press, New York, 1977).

D. Maister, 'Balancing the Professional Service Firm', *Sloan Management Review*, (Spring 1982).

Oliver Marriott, *The Property Boom*, (Hamish Hamilton, London, 1967).

J.W.E. Masterman, *An Introduction to Building Procurement Systems*, (Spon, London, 1992)

Royal Institute of British Architects, *Plan of Work for Design Team Operation*, (RIBA, London, 1983).

Andrew Saint, *The Image of the Architect*, (Yale University Press, New Haven, 1983).

Hedley Smyth, *Marketing the City*, (Spon, London, 1994).

Graham Winch and Eric Schneider, 'The Strategic Management of Architectural Practice', *Construction Management and Economics*, v.11 (1993), pp. 467–73.

CITIES, CULTURAL THEORY, ARCHITECTURE

Iain Borden

Thinking about architecture and cities can involve subjects as diverse as construction methods or aesthetics, economics of production or building patronage, personal politics of architects or the fine arts, and land policy or the experience of city streets. Explaining just why Chartres cathedral was built or the Vienna Ringstrasse looks the way it does is never easy simply because there is so much to consider. In practice, no account of architecture can realistically hope to include everything of value, and in any case the aim surely cannot be to recreate on paper all that has gone before. Even if the 'definitive' history was possible, there would be little value in finding, having finished the last page, there is nothing else to explore or think. There is then no single 'proper' way to understand architecture, and certainly no way to understand it all.

UNDERSTANDING EVERYTHING

Yet some texts, even if they do not try to say everything, do attempt to present a complete framework in which architecture and cities can be understood. This totalizing objective has been attempted in three ways, which we might call the historical, the purposeful, and the theorized.

The historical approach is most obviously characterized by the 'survey', those encyclopaedic volumes which range from Egyptian pyramids to twentieth century offices, from ancient graves to Michael Graves. Such works conduct a long journey through history, presenting what the author considers to be the most significant works from each period in one long narrative. The resulting enormous body of material, often supported by detailed scholarship and a plethora of visual material, is at once impressive and numbing, for the thud-factor, that serious weighty sound as the book lands on the table, can produce intellectual inertia as well as valuable sources of reference. In particular, surveys tend to establish an immutable canon of important buildings which alone, it is implied, stand as the monuments of civilization. And as stone becomes metaphorically inscribed in stone, other things get left out: common-place buildings, buildings in non-Western countries, buildings distant from international airports or freeway systems, or simply buildings which have always been accidentally or deliberately ignored. The canon has an overpowering authority which tends to freeze criticisms of it, making it difficult to change.

The purposeful approach achieves its totality not by wide-ranging historical references but by an explicit process of prescription and proscription. I call this approach 'purposeful' because it is frequently used when there is an axe to grind. Books like Le Corbusier's *Towards a New Architecture* (1927)[1] and *Learning from Las Vegas* (1972)[2] by Robert Venturi, Denise Scott Brown and Stephen Izenour are intended to justify the author's opinion as to what the present or immediate future should be like. For example, in Le Corbusier's text ancient Greek buildings are included while gothic ones are not because they better exemplify the kind of modernist principles being advocated. What the book prescribes here is not a canonic set of buildings (although a canon may be implied), but a very particular way of understanding buildings so that, far from rendering criticism ineffective, the reader is motivated into active agreement with the author. The reader is enlisted in support of the crusade being waged by the author.

More sophisticated than the two described above is the third kind of approach, to which the remainder of this essay is given over. Theorized history and criticism, as we shall see, have valuable attributes in relating buildings to a wider range of knowledge.

The theorized approach can be described as a critical framework, developed largely at a theoretical level, used to understand the world in general. Specific human activities or events are not important in themselves but for the degree they fit in the framework. What theorized accounts share in common is a sense that things can to be understood in terms of what might be described as a global condition, or in architectural terms that the specific characteristics of individual projects and buildings can be understood in terms of broad processes – economic, political and social – that affect the world in general. In short, to understand buildings we have to look at the big picture, and to understand the big picture we have to model it.

Furthermore, far from reducing architecture to a small bit part on the world stage, since the 1970s onward theorized accounts, while invariably springing from outside architectural circles, have made increasing reference to it. We can mention here Manuel Castells and Henri Lefebvre (1901–91) in urban sociology, Jacques Derrida in philosophy, David Harvey and Edward Soja in urban geography, Fredric Jameson and Jean Baudrillard in cultural theory, and Michel Foucault (1926–84) in historical theory. While the architectural and building professions may now be under attack, as Graham Ive shows in Chapter 27, buildings themselves are playing a more important role in terms of how we might understand the world.

FREDRIC JAMESON AND POSTMODERNISM

We will consider here the writings of the American literary critic and cultural theorist Fredric Jameson. The task is not to summarize everything Jameson has said, or to outline all of the possible objections to his work (of which there are many), but to consider some of its consequences for architectural history and criticism. We will explore the kind of theorization offered and the kinds of things learned through it, and so suggest the relevance of a totalized critique to those interested in buildings.

The reputation in architecture of Jameson's work stems largely from an essay first published in the journal *New Left Review* in 1984. That essay, 'Postmodernism, or, the Cultural Logic of Late Capitalism', and its much expanded book version of the same title, set out to engage from a marxist perspective with the burgeoning debates about postmodernism.[3]

Jameson's understanding of postmodernism is conceived in the context of multinational 'late' capitalism, a concept which he derives from the marxist economist Ernst Mandel. As capitalism exploits nuclear power and other highly sophisticated technologies from the 1940s onward, capital encroaches into previously uncommodified areas. For example, all of Nature

Figure 28.1

The cultural logic of late capitalism? Westin Bonaventure Hotel, Los Angeles, (1978), developer and architect John Portman.

becomes colonized through the destruction of pre-capitalist Third World agriculture, while the unconscious regions of the individual human mind become increasingly dominated by the media and advertizing industry.[4] Nothing is left unconsidered or untouched, be they far-flung regions of the world or intimate territories of the individual's mind and body. Postmodernism is the cultural concomitant, the 'logic', of this process: not just a set of stylistic descriptions of buildings and art, a condition of existence or a way of thinking but all of these things. It is the reality, experience and critique of culture under capitalism in the late twentieth century.

How then do we recognize and experience postmodernist culture? Jameson identifies five key characteristics: commodification of aesthetics, depthlessness, historicity, emotional intensities, and technology. The first term, commodification of aesthetics, refers to the way the production of art has become absorbed into the production of commodities in general. In other words, images are produced not for their use but for their economic value, and are bought and sold like any other goods.[5] Architecturally, we can see this in the appropriation of modernist architecture for corporate offices and in the stylistic pastiche described below.

The second term, depthlessness, refers to the way modern art – Vincent Van Gogh's *A Pair of Boots* is the example – responds to the stark physical conditions and attenuated emotions of real life, while postmodernist art – Andy Warhol's *Diamond Dust Shoes* – treats its subjects as images, using a flat or 'depthless' style to convey the impression that the world is just images and commodities devoid of social meaning.[6] Depthlessness in architecture is seen in the flat curtain wall facades of city centre skyscrapers which reveal nothing about the rooms or activities of those working inside. This removal of social meaning then leads to the third term, a reduction in historicity, or a weakening of historical traditions in favour of parody and pastiche. Stylistic references which recall the appearance of the past without engaging in its real conditions or meanings are, as Jameson recognizes, what architectural historians call historicism – the 'random cannibalization of all the styles of the past, the play of random stylistic allusion.'[7]

The fourth term, 'intensities', refers to how we perceive and experience postmodernism. This new 'emotional ground tone' is the terror and awe we feel when confronted with something outside of our known and controllable society, and is also our incapacity to represent it.[8] And this something other is the fifth term, technology, or the 'Third Machine Age' explosion of nuclear power and esoteric sciences in the late twentieth century already referred to above. The problem is that unlike the turbines, trains and grain elevators of the 1920s the new technology offers little scope for representation: computers, televisions and satellites are machines of reproduction and communication, not production, and demand a response based on intellect rather than imitation. Buildings designed to look like stacked music cassettes seem at best humorous.[9]

POSTMODERN ARCHITECTURE

What has postmodernism to do with architecture and cities? Each of the five terms described above have their architectural manifestations, as we have already briefly seen. But what of the experience of postmodernity and our possible responses to it, as hinted at in the identification of a new emotional ground tone? How might the global condition be represented in a single building and made manifest through our experiences of it? It is in his dealing with these questions that Jameson makes his most explicit references to architecture and some of his most revealing comments about postmodernism in general.

The building Jameson chooses to exemplify his account of postmodern culture is the Westin Bonaventure Hotel in Downtown Los Angeles, designed by the developer-architect John Portman (1924–) and opened in 1978. A kind of multi-purpose hotel, conference centre and retail complex, the Bonaventure's five mirrored towers and monolithic concrete base occupy an entire block of the Bunker Hill section of Downtown. Despite the aesthetic references to corporate modernism, the building easily satisfies typical characteristics of postmodern architecture: it is popular with locals and tourists (at least with white middle class ones); it creates a distinct alternative to the city rather than a contribution to it; and it provides internally a fairground of commodity consumption, where visitors choose from a bewildering variety of boutiques and restaurants.

In experiencing the Bonaventure, pleasure is paramount; an express ride in a transparently-glazed elevator pod launches from the pool-covered atrium floor to burst out of the main body of the concrete plinth onto the outside wall of the towers and up into the revolving restaurant at the hotel summit. Undertaking such journeys means a series of reversals: from exclusion on the outside of the building with no sense of way in, to a penetrative entry into

Figure 28.2

Westin Bonaventure Hotel, dialectical heightening. *State 1* The building 'content to let the fallen city fabric continue to be in its being'. Jameson, *Postmodernism*, (1991).

Figure 28.3

Westin Bonaventure Hotel, dialectical heightening. *State 2* The 'lateral and backdoor affair' of the high level entry.

Figure 28.4

Westin Bonaventure Hotel, dialectical heightening. *State 3* The trajectory of the elevator cab. Inside the atrium, looking out through the glazed roof.

Figure 28.5

Westin Bonaventure Hotel, dialectical heightening. *State 4* Roof-top restaurant, overlooking Los Angeles.

the building through narrow walkways and hidden entrances, to a sudden immersion into an unexpected and incomprehensible interior, to movement along escalators, to an explosive elevator journey, to a return to the building roof-top restaurant and bar, to a view across the expansive cityscape. In the Bonaventure the conventional sense of a building unfolding itself as a narrative, disclosing its functions as you walk around, is replaced with a 'dialectical heightening' whereby escalators and elevators do not just replace pedestrian movement, but become its emblem. How you move, whether by foot or machine, is incidental to the experience and idea of moving at all.

Space and our experience and understanding of it thus emerge as one of the central features of Jameson's theorization of postmodernity. Postmodernism, through characteristics such as the dialectical spatial experience, demands a new form of spatial understanding – which Jameson calls 'cognitive mapping' – in order to comprehend it. The problem is that most of us do not have the intellectual and perceptual apparatus by which to achieve this understanding; dominated as we are by the spaces of modernism, and educated as we are by the spatial perceptions that go with them, we are unable to understand or locate ourselves in the spaces around us. Whether visitors to the hotel or residents of any late twentieth century city, we are without signs, without maps and without radar. We are lost in space.

The architecture transcends the ability of the individual human body to locate itself in space, to organize with one's senses the immediate surroundings, and to cognitively map the external world. From here Jameson makes a huge interpretive leap, stating that the Bonaventure is in this sense a symbol of a far greater intellectual and social problem, 'the incapacity of our minds, at least at present, to map the great global multinational and decentered communicational network in which we find ourselves caught as individual subjects.'[10] For the Bonaventure as for the world, we know not where we stand. And we have finally come full circle from the global condition, to cultural production in general, to a specific building, to an individual's experiences of it, and back again.

Figure 28.6

'Postmodern hyperspace has finally succeeded in transcending the capacities of the individual human body to locate itself, to organize its immediate surroundings perceptually, and cognitively to map its position in a mappable external world'. Jameson, *Postmodernism*, (1991). Westin Bonaventure Hotel, interior.

THE VALUE OF THEORIZATION

In Jameson's critical understanding of postmodernism and late capitalism, architecture and the city serve to provide glimpses of a larger totality. The urban realm is nothing in itself, except as existing within a global-scale reality and being understood through cultural theory. The value of architecture is to demonstrate some of the material and experiential characteristics of postmodernism, and to do so in a particularly direct and spatialized manner. And understanding this much allows us to comprehend the reality of the postmodern world, to navigate between our immediate consciousness and the global context in which such experiences take place.

To return to our question regarding the value of theorizations in general, we can see that abstract totalizations of the kind practised by Jameson promise to let us understand the world at its most profound level – we can see those broad sweeps of economics and culture which cause global shifts in the way people live. And references to individual cities or buildings offer direct evidence for the why these global shifts are relevant to everyday life and experiences.

Yet other questions remain problematic. Firstly, we might ask whether the Bonaventure really justifies what Jameson says about it. What are the historical connections between the Bonaventure and our incapacity 'to map the great global multinational and decentered communicational network'? Do these connections actually exist, and can they be shown to exist; or is the building just a metaphor for this global condition, supported by some highly personal recollections by Jameson? Secondly, if there is indeed some connection, how far is the Bonaventure a good example of Jameson's theoretical propositions? Is it a better one than other buildings, or is it typical of a general condition? Thirdly, must architecture always represent something else; can it not be experienced and understood for itself? Alternatively, fourthly, we might ask as to social, political and racial issues not considered by Jameson. As Mike Davis has shown in *City of Quartz* (1991),[11] the Bonaventure is part of a concerted (largely white) middle-class and corporate attempt to control Downtown to the detriment and exclusion of others.

This kind of knowledge is then useful but difficult. When used carefully, theorizations disclose things which otherwise would remain hidden or impenetrable. They allow us to look outside of what appear to be the most immediate issues, to communicate with those engaged in other fields, and to do so in a overtly critical manner. But there are also caveats to be heeded and substantive commitments to be made. One of the main problems with any theorization is understanding exactly what is being discussed. Is the subject the buildings referred to, interpretations suggested by the theoretical model, or the theory itself? These things are frequently unclear, and demand considerable knowledge about both the subject matter and the intellectual traditions of the theorization. Understanding Jameson, for example, requires knowledge about literary criticism, marxist theory and a wide range of history as well as about the buildings and art forms he discusses.

Of course such things are not impossible, simply that complicated texts may need to be read and re-read over a number of years. In any case, changing ideas and interpretations are not only inevitable but the whole point of the exercise. In the last analysis a theorized history or criticism is like any piece of writing; not an end in itself, but a tool for thinking with.

REFERENCES

1 Le Corbusier, *Towards a New Architecture*, (The Architectural Press, London, 1927). First published as *Vers Une Architecture* (1923).

2 Robert Venturi, Denise Scott Brown and Stephen Izenour, *Learning from Las Vegas* (MIT Press, Cambridge, Mass., 1972).

3 Fredric Jameson, 'Postmodernism, or, the Cultural Logic of Late Capitalism', *New Left Review*, n.146 (July/August 1984), pp. 53–92, and Fredric Jameson, *Postmodernism, or, the Cultural Logic of Late Capitalism*, (Verso, London, 1991).

4 Jameson, *Postmodernism*, pp. 35–6.

5 Jameson, *Postmodernism*, pp. 4–5.

6 Jameson, *Postmodernism*, pp. 6–14.

7 Jameson, *Postmodernism*, pp. 16–18.

8 Jameson, *Postmodernism*, p. 34.

9 Jameson, *Postmodernism*, pp. 35–7.

10 Jameson, *Postmodernism*, pp. 38–44.

11 Mike Davis, *City of Quartz: Excavating the Future in Los Angeles*, (Verso, London, 1991). See also Mike Davis, 'Fortress Los Angeles: the Militarization of Urban Space' in Michael Sorkin (ed.), *Variations on a Theme Park: the New American City and the End of Public Space*, (Noonday Press, New York, 1992), pp. 154–80, and Mike Davis, 'The Infinite Game: Redeveloping Downtown L.A.' in Diane Ghirardo, (ed.), *Out of Site: A Social Criticism of Architecture*, (Bay Press, Seattle, 1991), pp. 77–113.

BIBLIOGRAPHY

Fredric Jameson

Mike Davis, 'Urban Renaissance and the Spirit of Post-modernism', *New Left Review*, n.151 (1986), pp. 106–13.

Fredric Jameson, 'Postmodernism, or, the Cultural Logic of Late Capitalism', *New Left Review*, n.146 (July/August 1984), pp. 53–92.

Fredric Jameson, 'Architecture and the Critique of Ideology', in *The Ideologies of Theory, Essays 1971–1986. Volume 2: The Syntax of History*, (Routledge, London, 1988), pp. 35–60, and in Joan Ockman (ed.), *Architecture Criticism Ideology*, (Princeton Architectural Press, Princton, 1985).

Fredric Jameson, *Postmodernism, or, the Cultural Logic of Late Capitalism*, (Verso, London, 1991).

Colin MacCabe, 'Preface' in Fredric Jameson, *The Geopolitical Aesthetic: Cinema and Space in the World*, (Indiana University Press, Bloomington, 1992), pp. ix–xvi.

Donald Preziosi, 'La Vi(ll)e en Rose: Reading Jameson Mapping Space', *Strategies* (UCLA), n.1 (Fall 1988), pp. 82–99.

Postmodernism

Steven Connor, *Postmodernist Culture: an Introduction to Theories of the Contemporary*, (Basil Blackwell, Oxford, 1989).

Hal Foster (ed.), *Postmodern Culture*, (Pluto, London, 1985). First published as *The Anti-Aesthetic*, (1983).

David Harvey, *The Condition of Postmodernity: an Enquiry into the Origins of Cultural Change*, (Basil Blackwell, Oxford, 1989).

Edward Soja, *Postmodern Geographies: the Reassertion of Space in Critical Social Theory*, (Verso, London, 1989).

Downtown Los Angeles

Reyner Banham, *Los Angeles: The Architecture of Four Ecologies*, (Penguin, Harmondsworth, 1971).

Mike Davis, *City of Quartz: Excavating the Future in Los Angeles*, (Verso, London, 1991).

Mike Davis, 'Fortress Los Angeles: the Militarization of Urban Space' in Michael Sorkin (ed.), *Variations on a Theme Park: the New American City and the End of Public Space*, (Noonday Press, New York, 1992), pp. 154–80.

Mike Davis, 'The Infinite Game: Redeveloping Downtown L.A.' in Diane Ghirardo, (ed.), *Out of Site: A Social Criticism of Architecture* (Bay Press, Seattle, 1991), pp. 77–113.

INDEX

Numbers in italics refer to illustrations

Aachen, 336
Abercrombie Plan (London), 260, 263
Abercrombie, Patrick 260, 263
Absolutism, 60–3, 133
Académie Royale d'Architecture, 167–8, 170–1
Academies, 61, 163, 167–8
Academy of Fine Arts (Philadelphia), 210, *15.9*
Addams, Jane, 239, 324–5
Adler, Kathleen, 327
Adorno, Theodor 6, 354
Advertising, 322–3, 390
Aesthetics, 4, 5, 25, 39, 45, 86, 90, 143, 149–61,
    163, 177–9, 181–2, 185, 189–98, 214, 239,
    247, 272, 293, 298, 309, 313, 341, 387, 391
Aesthetics, 12, 189–98
Africa, 350
Agency, 14, 243, 260, 354, 361
Agri-business, 15
Agriculture, 46, 164, 200–1, 228–9, 332, 344, 390
Aircraft, 273, 342
Airports, 342, 377, 388
Alberti, Leon Battista, 9, 20, 93, 97–102, 115–7,
    121, 131, 137, 327, *7.5*, *8.6*
  De Re Aedificatoria, 100–1, 115, 117, 137, *7.5*
  Della Pittura, 101
  Palazzo Rucellai, 9, 115–7, 137, *8.6*
Alexander VI, 133
Alexander VII, 132, 144
Alienation, 314, 341, 348
All Saints (York), 89, *6.7*
Allegory, 56–7, 59, 151, 154
Almshouses, 202
Altes Museum (Berlin), 197, *14.2*
Althusser, Louis, 6

Alton East Estate (London), 266–7
Alton West Estate (London), 265–7, *19.7*
Aluminium, 284, 294, 296
Ambivalence, 307–11
America, 355
American Magazine, 321, *23.4*
Americas, *see* United States
Amiens, 74–6
  Amiens Cathedral, 74–6
Amsterdam, 123
Analogous City, 333–4, *24.1*
*Analytical Enquiry into the Principles of Taste,
    An*, 179, 181–2
Anaxagoras, 97
Ando, Tado, and Associates, 364, *26.5*
  Vitra Conference Centre, 364, *26.5*
Anonymity, 295, 304–14, 327
Anthropology, 334
Anthroposophy, 13
Anti-Semitism, 295
Anti-urbanism, 46, 110, 228–9, 249, 253, 304,
    306, 311, 319–20, 331
Antigone housing (Montpellier), 49, *3.8*
Antwerp, 122–3
Apartments, 163–75, 217, 250, 259, 262–3, 292,
    294, 304, 311, 323
Apollo, 57–8
Appropriation, 325, 328
Arabesque, 194
Arc-et-Senans, 155–9
  Royal Saltworks 155–9, *11.4*, *11.5*, *11.6*, *11.7*,
    11.8, *11.9*, *11.10*
Arcades, 311, 334–5
Arcades Project, 311
Arch, 67–75, 152, 192
Archaeology, 333

Archigram, 15, 271, 277–9, 285, *20.3*, *20.4*
  Cushicle, 278–9, *20.4*
  Living Pod, 278
  Plug-In City, 278, *20.3*
  Suitaloon, 279
Architect, role of 2, 17, 24–5, 61, 85–7, 112–3,
    115, 117, 119–21, 124–8, 167–8, 171, 185,
    214–6, 227–40, 253, 262, 273–9, 300, 302,
    312, 372–84, 389
Architectural determinism, 63, 259, 268, 324, 326
Architecture and the City, 333
Architecture moderne, (Briseux), 170
Architecture moderne, (Jombert), 170
Architecture parlante, 151–2
Arcosanti (Arizona), 236–8, *17.8*
Aristotle, 306
Arizona, 236–8
  Arcosanti, 236–8, *17.8*
Arizona State University, 236
  Gammage Auditorium, 236
Arms race, 351
Armstrong, Edward, 265, *19.6*
  Regent's Park Estate, 265, *19.6*
Arno, River, 109
Arnold & Davies, 265
  Regent's Park Estate, 265
Arnolfo di Cambio, 93, 100
  Florence city walls, 93
  Sta. Croce, 93
  Sta. Maria Novella, 93
Art galleries, *see* Museums
Art history, 6, 114, 132, 189, 198, 207, 327, 398
Art Nouveau, 248, 297, 299
Artistic identity, 17, 126–7, 221–3, 227, 233, 235,
    238, 240, 372, 379–82
Arts and Crafts, 211, 296–7
Arup Associates, 383, *27.9*
  Broadgate, 49, 383, *27.9*
Ashbee, C.R., 211
Assembly halls, 152
Association of ideas, 181–2, 366
AT&T Building (New York), 381, *27.6*
Athena, 23–4, 29
Athens, 23–4, 29–30, 32–4, 39, 46, 97, 101, 293
  Parthenon, 23–4, 29–30, 32–4, 101, *2.1*, *2.5*,
    2.7, *2.9*, *2.10*
Atria, 282, 284, 355, 377, 378, 392, 394
Attic, 169–70
Attlee, Clement, 260, 264
Attractiveness index, 377–8
Attribution, 13, 325
Auditoria, 252, 275
Australia, 236
Austria, 16, 132, 193, 221, 291–302, 304, 311,
    341, 387

Automobiles, 19, 215, 221–2, 228–9, 243, 250,
    272–3, 279, 313, 346, 362, *1.14*
Avant-garde, 14, 247, 271–3, 302, 381
Avignon, 131

Balbersby (Yorkshire), 210, *15.7*
Balkan states, 292
Banality, 300, 312–4
Banham, Peter Reyner, 272–4
  Theory and Design in the First Machine Age,
    272–3
Banks and banking, 44–5, 120, 123, 165–6, 168,
    245, 285, 294–6, 304
Baptistery (Florence), 93, 98–9, 107
Bari, 332
Barlow, W.H., 210
  St. Pancras Station, 210
Barnett, Henrietta, 325
Barnsdall House (Los Angeles), 238
Baroque, 131–44, 150, 291
Barratt, 352
Barriadas, 349, 350
Barricades, 248
Barrière de la Villette (Paris), 154, *11.3*
Barrières, 154–5, *11.3*
Barry, Charles, 41, *3.1*
  National Gallery, 41, *3.1*
  Trafalgar Square, 7, 40–3
Barthes, Roland, 6
Bartlesville, 234–5
  Price Tower, 234–5
Bassae, 24
Bathroom Tower (London), 279–80, *20.6*
Bathrooms, 218, 272, 278–80
Battery Park (New York), 49, 378, *27.4*
Battleship Potemkin, 245
Baudelaire, Charles, 17, 308–9
Baudrillard, Jean, 6, 355, 389
  America, 355
Bauer, Catherine, 324
Bauhaus, 216, 271–2
Bear Run, 231, 233
  Fallingwater, 231, 233, *17.5*
Beaudouin, Eugène, 272
  Maison du Peuple, 272
Beauty, 59, 78, 90, 177–9, 308
Beauvais, 70, 75
  Beauvais Cathedral, 70, 75, *5.4*
Bedrooms, 218, 223
Beethoven, Ludwig van, 142
  Diabelli Variations, 142
Belgium, 122–3, 296, 297
Bell, Daniel, 354
Benedetto da Maiano, 115, *9.1*
  Palazzo Strozzi, 9, 115, 122, 125, *9.1*

Benedictines, 75, 81
Benjamin, Walter, 6, 17, 311
  Arcades Project, 311
Berlin, 189, 197, 292, 297, 301, 310–3, 340, 350, 368
  Altes Museum, 197, *14.2*
  Internationale Bauausstellung, 368, *26.8*
  New National Gallery, 301, *21.11*
  South Friedrichstrasse, Masterplan, 340
Berman, Marshall, 6
Bernini, Gianlorenzo, 61, 138–41, 144, *10.5, 10.6*
  Louvre, 61
  S. Andrea Quirinale, 9, 138, 139, 140, 141, *10.5, 10.6*
  St. Peter's, colonnade, 144
Bespoke buildings, 382, 383
Beth-Shalom Synagogue (Elkins Park), 234, 236
Bevan, Aneurin, 265
Bible, 79, 86, 88, 90, 107
Biology, 216, 294, 297, 317, 345
Birmingham, 377
  International Convention Centre, 377
Blondel, Jacques-François, 150–1, 172
Blore, Edward, 112–3
  Buckingham Palace, 112–3, *8.3*
Bodies, 219, 278, 279, 298, 300, 390, 395–6
Bofill, Ricardo, 49, *3.8*
  Antigone housing, 49, *3.8*
  Palais d'Abraxas, 49
Bohemia, 327
Boissonas, Frédéric, 24, 32, 34–5, *2.1, 2.7, 2.9, 2.10*
Bologna, 95, 122, 334
Bolsheviks, 244–5, 248–9
Bombing, 260, 262, 267, 332, 340
Boosterism, 45, 377–9
Borgia, 133
Borromeo, St. Carlo, 139–40
Borromini, Franceso, 138–42, *10.7, 10.8*
  S. Carlo alle Quattro Fontane, 9, 138, 139, 140, 141, 142, *10.7, 10.8*
Boston, 113, 320, 376
  Boston City Hall, 113, *8.4*
  John Hancock Tower, 376, *27.1*
Boston City Hall (Boston), 113, *8.4*
Boulevard St. Germain (Paris), 349, *25.3*
Boulevards, 291, 349
Boullée, Étienne-Louis, 11, 150–4, 163, *11.1, 11.2*
  Royal Library, 153–4, *11.2*
  Cenotaph for Newton, 152, *11.1*
Bourgeoisie, 122, 246, 253, 291–3, 296, 302, 318–20, 323–4, 327, 337, 349, 353
Bovingdon, John, 222
Braghieri, Gianni, 334–5, *24.2, 24.3*

S. Cataldo Cemetery, 334–5, *24.2, 24.3*
Bramante, Donato, 134–5, *10.1*
  Tempietto, 134–5, *10.1*
Brass, 299
Braudel, Fernand, 6
Brazil, 350
Brecht, Berthold, 310
Breuer, Marcel, 259
Brick, 41, 121, 179, 272, 299
Bridges, 12
Briefs, 373, 382–4
Briseux, Charles Etienne, 170
  Architecture moderne, 170
Britain, 1, 3, 7, 9, 12, 14, 38–43, 68–70, 74–6, 78, 83–5, 88–9, 106, 123, 127–8, 176–83, 193, 200–13, 258–69, 272, 274–82, 284–5, 297, 304, 306–8, 311, 321, 324–5, 331, 339, 347–52, 372–84
British Library (London), 180
British Museum (London), 40
British Property Federation, 374
Brixton (London), 267
Broadacre City, 229, 304, *17.1*
Broadgate (London), 49, 383, *27.9*
Brockhampton Church (Herefordshire), 211, *15.10*
Bronze, 301
Brooklyn Bridge (New York), 12, *1.6*
Brown, Denise Scott, 324–5, 388
  Learning from Las Vegas, 388
  Philadelphia Crosstown Community, 325
  see also Venturi, Scott Brown and Associates
Bruges, 123
Brunelleschi, Filippo, 9, 19, 93, 97–102, 120
  S. Lorenzo, 101
Brussels, 296–7
  Palais Stoclet, 296–7, *21.5*
Buckingham Palace (London), 113
Budapest, 292, 349
Building cycle, 374
Building economists, 375, 383
Building of Renaissance Florence, The, 9, 119
Building industry, see Construction industry
Building regulations, see Legislation
Building users, 4, 7, 8, 13, 78, 88–90, 111, 121–2, 154, 163, 214–24, 268, 275–6, 283, 318–24, 373, 377–84, 391–2, 395
Burckhardt, Jacob, 132
Bureaucracy, 240, 250, 252, 254, 259, 351, 354
Burgee, John, 381, *27.6*
  AT&T Building, 381, *27.6*
Burke, Edmund, 177–8, 181
  A Philosophical Enquiry into the Origins of Our Ideas of the Sublime and Beautiful, 177–8

Burnham, Daniel, 40, 43–5, *3.3*, *3.4*
  First National Bank, 44–5, *3.4*
  Park Commission plan, 43–4, *3.3*
Business parks, 377
Butterfield, William, 209–10, *15.7*
  Balbersby, 210, *15.7*
Byzantine art, 98

Cafés, 298, 300, 327
Cage, John, 222
Calatrava, Santiago, 367, *26.7*
  Stadelhofen Train Station, 367, *26.7*
Calendar, Christian, 5
Callicrates, 24
Cambridge, 181
  Kings College Chapel, 181
Camus system, 347, *25.2*
Canals, 201, 294
Canary Wharf (London), 379, *27.5*
Canterbury, 75, 83, 85, 88–9
  Canterbury Cathedral, 75, 83, 85, 88–9
Cantilever, 232–3, 252
Capitalism, 7, 14–5, 17, 19, 44–5, 119–128,
    163–75, 200–2, 207, 209, 243–6, 252, 322–3,
    344–55, 372–84, 389–90
  intensification of, 17, 322–3, 352–5, 390
  late capitalism, 7, 15, 17, 19, 352–5, 372–84,
    389–90,
  monopoly capitalism, 44
  renaissance, 119–27
  eighteenth century, 163–75
  nineteenth century, 200–2, 207, 209, 372, 380
Capitoline hill (Rome), 135
Capsules, 278–9
Capsule Homes Tower, 278
Capsule Village Project, 279, *20.5*
Car, *see* Automobiles
Carignan, Prince de, 164
Carlyle, Thomas, 202
Carlzon, Jan, 382
Carpentry, 26–8, 126–7, 227–8, 347
Carter, E.J., 262, 263
  The Future of London, 263
Carthage, 136
Cartography, 334
Castelfranco di Sopra, 96–7
Castells, Manuel, 389
Castles, 331
Castrae, 332
Catholicism, 78, 131, 138, 202, 207
Cellini, Benevenuto, 120
Cemeteries 334–5
Cenotaph for Newton, 152, *11.1*
Cenotaphs, 152

Censorship, 326–7
Centralized plan 133, 135
Centre Point (London), 376, *27.2*
Ceramics 227, 245, 294, 296
Chace, Clyde, 221–2
Chace, Marian, 221–2, 224
Chalk, Warren, 277–8
  Capsule Homes Tower 278
Chambre des Bâtiments, 169
Chaos, 369
Charing Cross, 40
Charity. 325
Charity Organization Society, 325
Charles I, 60
Charles V, 134
Charles, Prince, 176, 181, 183
  A Vision of Britain, 176
Chartism, 41, 202
Chartres, 73, 387
  Chartres Cathedral, 73, 387
Checkpoint Charlie, 368
Chiat Day Offices (Los Angeles), 18, *1.12*
Chicago, 7, 18, 40, 43–5, 50, 291, 312–3, 320,
    325, 362, 376
  Chicago Plan, 45
  Chicago Tribune Tower, 312–3, *22.6*
  Commonwealth Edison Substation, 50, *3.9*
  City Beautiful, 7, 44, 45
  60 East Lake Parking Facility, 362, *26.1*
  First National Bank, 44–5, *3.4*
  John Hancock Center, 18
  900 North Michigan Avenue, 18, *1.13*
  World's Fair, 44
Chicago Plan, 45
Chicago Tribune Tower (Chicago), 312–3, *22.6*
Child care, 250–1, 326
Children, 317–22
Chimneys, 334
Choisy, Auguste, 6, 26–7, 29, 33–6, *2.2*, *2.3*,
    2.4, *2.8*
  Histoire de l'architecture, 33–6, *2.2*, *2.3*, *2.4*,
    2.8
Christianity, 5, 67, 79, 88, 131, 135, 190–1, 196,
    202–4, 207, 295
CIAM (*Congrès International d'Architecture
    Moderne*), 215–9, 272
Circulation, 160, 163, 214, 224
Cistercians, 81, 82, 89
Cité Industrielle, 304
Cities, 5, 7, 13, 15–7, 25, 38–50, 75–6, 85,
    93–102, 107, 109–10, 123–5, 127–8, 131–44,
    200–2, 220, 228–9, 236–8, 247–50, 253–4,
    263, 265, 267–72, 274, 276–9, 291–302,
    304–14, 317–28, 331–42, 344–55, 377–9,
    389–98

Città Nuova, 304–5, *22.1*
City Beautiful movement, 7, 43–5
City of Quartz, 397
City of Tomorrow and its Planning, 271, 305
City walls, 93, 164, 334
Civil war, 60, 245
Cladding, 273, 299
Clapham Common (London), 318, *23.1*
Clark, T.J., 6, 309
Clarke, Linda, 128
Class, 2, 4, 7, 9, 12, 38–9, 41–6, 49–50, 78, 90,
    111, 119–24, 128, 163, 182, 185, 220, 243–4,
    250, 252, 256, 262, 291, 317–20, 323, 325,
    327, 344, 349, 351, 380, 392, 397
Class struggle, 4, 243–4, 248, 291, 344–5
Classical art (Hegel), 191, 196
Classicism 6–7, 10–11, 23–36, 38–50, 53–63, 79,
    93–5, 99–100, 106–17, 119–28, 131–44,
    149–61, 163–75, 192–3, 196, 202–4, 206,
    209, 247–8, 253–5, 293–4, 298, 333–4, 388
    residential 11, 26, 53–63, 106–17, 119–127,
        136–8, 160–1, 163–75, 254
    see also Orders
Cleveland, 291
Clichy, 272
    Maison du Peuple, 272
Climate, 224, 361, 366
Clothes, 120, 123, 245, 278–9, 298, 317, 322
Cluny 80–1
Cluster block, 269
CNN International 353, *25.8*
Coates, Wells, 258–9, 268, *19.1*
    Isokon Flats, 259, *19.1*
Cobbett, William, 201–2
    Rural Rides, 201
Coch, Georg, 295
Coffee houses, 319
Coffee pots, 341
Cognitive mapping, 395–7
Colbert, Jean Baptiste, 54–5, 58–9, 61
Collage, 245, 333–4
Collective living, 250–1, 253–4, 259, 323–4, 326
Collective memory, 333–5, 341, 369
Collectivity, 189–90, 215–6, 240, 249, 250–4, 259,
    312–4, 323–4, 326
Cologne, 75, 336, 339
    Cologne Cathedral, 75
Colomina, Beatriz, 327–8
    Sexuality and Space, 327–8
Colonization, 390
Colonna, 132
Colour, 283, 294
Columbia University, 50
Columbus, 369
    Wexner Center for Visual Arts, 369, *26.9*

Commodification, 17, 321–3, 352–5, 372–84,
    391–2
Common sense, 12, 176–85
Commonwealth Edison Substation (Chicago), 50,
    3.9
Communes, 250, 253–4, 323
Communication, 246, 249, 252, 349, 352–3,
    361–4, 366–9, 395
Communism, 243–56, 351
Communist Party, 250, 252, 351
Community, 158, 233, 276, 306, 314
Compact discs, 353
Competence, 363
Competitions, 170, 254–5, 283, 384
Competitive advantage, 374
Concrete, 67, 229, 232, 252, 272, 294, 347–8,
    351–2, 392
Condé, Prince de, 164
Condition of the Working Class in England, The,
    307
Conference centres, 364, 377, 392
Conferences, 325
Congestion, 313
Connoisseurship, 268
Conservation, 14, 268–9, 332–42
Conservative Party, 261, 265
Conspicuous consumption, 9, 107, 117, 119–23
Constant (Nieuewenhuys), 274
Constantin, A., 168
Constantine, 131
Constantinople, 131
Construction and structure, 2, 4, 8, 67–76, 86–7,
    116–7, 127, 169, 171, 184, 190, 192–5, 198,
    204, 206, 211, 214–6, 219, 221, 224, 227,
    231–3, 236, 238, 248, 252, 272–3, 275–6,
    279–80, 282–4, 294, 296, 347, 351–2, 366,
    373, 381, 387
Construction industry, 4, 17, 19, 119–28, 132,
    163–75, 215, 219, 244–5, 247, 252, 261, 273,
    345–52, 366, 372–84
Constructivism, 14, 247, 250
Consumerism, 17, 321–3, 341, 352–5, 392
Consumption, 17, 321–3, 352–5, 392
Contractors and contracting, 126, 167–8, 233,
    245, 372–84
Contracts, 372–4
Contradictions, 4–5, 180, 224, 243, 246–8, 252,
    256, 295, 344–5, 348, 350, 355, 367, 372
Contrasts, 202–4
Conversation, 298, 319, 324
Cook, Eric, 261–3
Cook, Peter, 277–8, *20.3*
    Plug-In City, 278, *20.3*
Corn exchanges, 164–6, 169, 172–3
Corner triglyph problem, 28–30

Correspondences, 308
Corsignano, 135
Cortona, Pietro da, 139
Cosham, 281–2
   IBM Office, 281–2, *20.8*
Cosmetics, 308
Cosmic cities, 249
Cottage estates, 261
Cottages, 344
Council of Trent, 139
Counter Reformation, 135–44
Country and western music, 328
Countryside, 5, 39, 46, 109–11, 113, 200–1, 248,
   307, 319–20, 331, 344
County of London Plan, 260, 263
Courtyards, 113, 169, 299
Covent Garden (London), 180
Crafts, 4, 38, 61, 86, 112–3, 123, 125–8, 167,
   198, 200, 207–9, 211, 272, 296–7, 302,
   345–7
Cremona, 114
Cricket, 285
Crompton, Dennis, 277
Cultural theory, 4, 6, 19, 311, 327–8, 354,
   389–98
Culture, 5–7, 15, 38, 49, 119, 123, 176, 229,
   245–6, 253, 273–5, 292–3, 298, 310–4,
   352–3, 366, 389–98
   hegemony, 7, 38, 352–3
Cumberland Terrace (London), 261, *19.3*
Cumbernauld Town Centre (Cumbernauld), 274
Cushicle 278–9, *20.4*
Czech republic, 292, 300

Dadaism, 300
Dance, 227, 229, 275, 319
Danger and safety, 169, 326, 327
Dante Alighieri, 131
   Paradiso, 131
Danube canal (Vienna), 294
Das Neue Frankfurt, 217, *16.2*
Davis, Mike, 397
   City of Quartz, 397
De Architectura, 24–8, 366
De Re Aedificatoria, 100–1, 115, 117, 137, *7.5*
Death and Life of Great American Cities, The,
   304
Death, 194, 202, 236, 259, 334–5
Debord, Guy, 274
Deconstruction, 362, 389
Decor, 28
Decoration, *see* Ornament
Deertrack (Michigan), 239
Dégagement, 150–1
Deleuze, Gilles, 6

Della Pittura, 101
Democracy, 39, 44, 46, 50, 149, 202, 246–50,
   252, 254, 256, 292–3, 353
Democritus, 97
Demolition, 14, 259, 268
Denington, Evelyn, 262–3, 266
Density, 95, 163–4, 169, 261, 265–6, 307–8
Depthlessness, 391
Der Scutt and Swanke, Hayden, Connell, 355
   Trump Tower, 355, *25.10*
Derrida, Jacques, 6, 362, 389
Description sommaire du chateau du Versaillies,
   58
Design management, 375
Design-and-build, 373–4
Deskilling, 352
Despenser, 84
Detective stories, 309
Detroit, 346
   Highland Park Plant (Detroit), 346, *25.1*
   Deutscher Werkbund, 263
Developing world, 390
Development corporations, 266
Dewey, John, 239
Dialectic, 191, 222, 224, 345, 367–8
Dialectical heightening, 392–5
Diana, 27, 151
Dickens, Charles, 202
Dictionnaire raisonné de l'architecture française,
   184, *13.5*
Didyma, 101
   Temple of Apollo, 101
Diller, Elizabeth and Scofidio, Ricardo, 362, *26.2*
   Slow House, 362, *26.2*
Dining rooms, 218, 297, 323
Disurbanism, 249, 253
Division of labour, 347–9, 366
Dixon, Jeremy, 180
   Royal Opera House, 180
Do-it-yourself, 353
Docklands (London), 379, *27.5*
Doctors' surgeries, 233
Dombar, Benjamin 230, *17.2*
Domes, 273
Domesticity, 17, 111, 121–2, 163, 192, 215–24,
   227–9, 248, 250, 259, 275, 317–24, 348, 353
Donatello, 120
Donestk Basin, 244
Doors, 79, 134, 169–70, 214, 222, 347
Doré, Gustav, 307–8, *22.4*
   London: a Pilgrimage, 307, *22.4*
Goetheanum (Dornach), 13, *1.7*
Drawing, 25, 86, 88, 93, 95, 121, 154, 170,
   214–5, 224, 228, 233, 235, 313, 334, 373
Dreiser, Theodore, 222

Dresden, 331
Drew, Jane, 324
Duccio, 96
   Christ Opens the Eyes of a Man Born Blind,
      96, *7.2*
Duma, 244
Dunn, Peter, 379
'Digital Highways', 379
Dunster village, 304, 306, *22.3*
Duomo, *see* Sta. Maria del Fiore and Piazza del
   Duomo
Duralumin, 272
Durandus, Bishop, 79
Dürer, Albrecht, 99, *7.4*
   Artist Drawing a Reclining Woman, 99, *7.4*
Durham, 9, 68–71, 74, 82–3
   Durham Cathedral, 9, 68–71, 74, 82–3, *6.3*
Dymaxion Bathroom, 272
Dymaxion Car, 272
Dymaxion House, 272–3

Eagleton, Terry, 6
Early English, 83
Earth, 236
Earth houses, 236
60 East Lake Parking Facility (Chicago), 362,
   26.1
Eco, Umberto, 6
École Centrale des Travaux Publics, 170
École des Beaux-Arts, 170
École Polytechnique, 170
Economic geography, 122–4, 201
Economic recession, 167, 173, 202, 211, 374
Economics, 3, 5–6, 9, 15, 19, 39, 46, 59–61, 75,
      78, 85, 106, 109, 111, 119–28, 138, 149,
      154, 163–75, 200, 202, 215, 219, 221, 223,
      227, 236, 244–6, 254, 258, 261, 273–4, 292,
      297–8, 302, 317–8, 320, 323, 332, 345, 349,
      351, 353, 361, 367, 372–84, 387–8, 397
Edinburgh, 201
Education and training, 4, 12–3, 25, 61, 87, 150,
      167–8, 182–3, 185, 214, 227–40, 247, 250,
      252, 272, 276, 292–4, 319–20, 324
Egypt, 136, 194, 196, 387
   sphinxes, 193, 194, 195, *14.1*
   temples, 195
Eisenman, Peter, 368–9, 381, *26.8*, *26.9*
   Internationale Bauausstellung housing, 368,
      26.8
   Wexner Center for Visual Arts, 369, *26.9*
Eisenstein, Sergei, 245–6, *18.1*
   Battleship Potemkin, 245
   Strike, 245–6, *18.1*
Ekberg, Anita, 144
Elections, 260, 263, 265, 321, 369

Electricity, 229, 245, 247, 283
Eleusis, 24
Elevators, 392, 394–5
Eliot, T.S., 189
Elkins Park, 234, 236
   Beth-Shalom Synagogue, 234, 236
Ely, 75, 106
   Ely Cathedral, 75, 106
Emerson, Ralph Waldo, 176
Emotional intensities, 391–2
Empiricism 1–2
Enabler, architect as, 274–9
Endell, August, 304
   Die Schonheit der Grossen Stadt, 304
Engels, Friedrich, 17, 243, 307
   *The Condition of the Working Class in
      England*, 307
Engineering, 12, 210, 221, 272, 367
English Heritage, 268–9
Enlightenment, 38, 150, 155, 353, 363
Enschede, 336
   Student Residence Hall, 336, *24.4*
Entasis, 100–1
Entresol, 169–70
Environment, 236–8, 361
Ephemerality, 273, 275–8, 280, 283, 286
Ergonomics, 219
Escalators, 395
Essai sur l'architecture, 10, 150, *1.4*
*Essay on National and Sepulchral Monuments,
   An*, 40
Étages nobles, 169
Ethnicity, *see* Race
Euromus, 7, *1.1*
Evangelicalism, 319–20
Everyday life, 4–5, 17, 152, 216, 248, 250, 317,
      322–3, 344–55, 397
Existenzminimum, 13, 215–21, 224, 259, 321
Experience, 12, 177–8, 180–3, 214, 304–14, 317,
      325–8, 387, 390–8
Expertise, 363
Experts, 183, 185, 220, 268, 375, 384
Exploitation, 243–4, 250
Expositions, 282, 309
Expressionism, 272, 298

Fabius Maximus Cunctator, 136
Façade, 93, 95, 98, 102, 108–9, 111, 115–7, 121,
      167, 169–72, 214, 229–30, 283, 294, 299,
      339–40, 368, 391
Fackel, Die, 293, 298
Factories, 155–9, 200–2, 207, 209, 219, 244–5,
      247, 250, 252, 279–80, 282, 331, 334, 344,
      346–8, 351–2, 354
Facts, 1, 6, 20

Failure, 232–3, 266–9, 331, 381
Fallingwater (Bear Run), 231, 233, *17.5*
Family, the, 9, 84, 215, 217, 220–1, 262, 317–25
Fanelli, Giovanni, 112
Farnese, 132, 136–7
    Palazzo Farnese, 9, 136–7, *10.2*
Farrell, Terry, 279–80, *20.6*
    Bathroom Tower, 279–80, *20.6*
Fascism, 7, 40, 46–9, 262, 305
Fashion effects, 379–82
Fast food, 352
Favelas, 349–50, *25.4*
Fear 16, 307–9
Félibien, André, 58
    *Description sommaire du chateau du
        Versaillies*, 58
Feminism, 326, *see also* Gender
Fermiers Généraux (Paris), 164
Ferrara, 95
Fêtes, 56–7, *4.2*
Feudalism, 60, 125, 331, 344–5
Filarete, Antonio Averlino, 135
    Sforzinda, 135
Filling stations, 233
Film, 245, 275, 344
Fire, 67–8, 223, 239, 281
Fire stations, 364
First National Bank of Chicago, (Chicago), 44–5,
    3.4
Flagship projects, 375–9
Flâneur, 308–9
Flats, *see* Apartments
Fletcher, Banister, 1
    A History of Architecture, 1
Flexibility, 163, 217, 272, 274–7, 278, 280–6, 355
Florence, 3, 9, 19, 93–103, 106–17, 119–28, 137,
    332
    Baptistery, 93, 98–9, 107
    city walls, 93, 109
    Loggia dei Lanzi, 94
    medieval towers, 108–11, 113
    New Towns, 96–7
    Palazzo Davanzati, 110, *8.2*
    Palazzo del Priori, 94
    Palazzo Medici, 9, 114–5, *8.5*
    Palazzo Rucellai, 9, 115–7, 137, *8.4*
    Palazzo Strozzi, 9, 115, 122, 125, *9.1*
    Palazzo Vecchio, 94–5, 98, 100, 102
    Piazza del Duomo, 93–4, 98–99
    Piazza della Signoria, 94, 95, 98–100, *7.1*
    S. Lorenzo, 101
    Sta. Croce, 93
    Sta. Maria del Fiore, 8, 93–4, 98, 107, *1.3*
    Sta. Maria Novella, 93
    Sta. Reparta, 93

Via del Calzaioli, 95
Florida Southern College (Lakeland), 233–4
Flying buttress, 72–3, 204–6
Fomin, Ivan, 247
Fontaine, Pierre-François-Léonard, 167–8, 172,
    12.6
    rue de Rivoli, 167, 172, *12.6*
Ford, Henry, 346
Fordism, 215, 218, 346–8, 351
Formalism, 106, 111–2, 114, 149, 247, 268, 294,
    299, 334, 340, 363–4, 366
Fortifications, 25, 48, 93, 108–10, 291–3, 332
Forum (Rome), 135
Foster Associates, 281–5, *20.8, 20.11, 20.12,
    20.13*
    Hongkong and Shanghai Bank, 283, 285,
        20.12, 20.13
    IBM Office, 281–2, *20.8*
    Sainsbury Centre, 283–4, *20.11*
Foster, Norman, 15, 280–5, *20.7*
    Reliance Controls Factory, 280, 282, *20.7*
Foster, Wendy, 280, 282, 324, *20.7*
    Reliance Controls Factory, 280, 282, *20.7*
Foucault, Michel, 6, 389
Fountains Abbey (Yorkshire), 81, *6.2*
Fourier, Charles, 243
Fragmentation, 349
France, 1, 7, 9, 11, 14, 53–63, 69–76, 81–2,
    84–5, 122, 132–3, 149–61, 163–75, 183,
    203–4, 209, 266, 272, 274, 281–5, 291, 293,
    297, 300, 304, 308–9, 333–4, 340, 347,
    349–50, 387
Francesco di Giorgio Martini, 111
Franciscans, 120
François Xavier, St., 140
Frankfurt, 215–21, 291, 337–8
    Das Neue Frankfurt, 217, *16.2*
    Frankfurt kitchen, 219–21, *16.4*
    Gleisdreieck Tower, 337–8, *24.5, 24.6*
    housing, 215–21, *16.1*
Frankfurt kitchen, 219–21, *16.4*
Frederick, Christine, 218–9, *16.3*
    Scientific Management in the Home, 218, *16.3*
Freedom, 243, 246–7, 252, 293, 310–1, 327, 354
Freemasons, 160
French revolution (1789), 62, 164
Freud, Sigmund, 6, 293–4, 302
Friedman, David, 97
Frondes, 60
Fuller, (Richard) Buckminster, 15, 272–3
    Dymaxion Bathroom, 272
    Dymaxion Car, 272
    Dymaxion House, 272–3
    geodesic domes, 273
Fun Palace (London), 275, *20.1*

Function, 4, 15, 107, 109, 111, 119, 127, 150–2, 155, 158, 160–1, 163, 190–3, 196, 206, 214–5, 218, 224, 235, 239, 248, 300, 334, 340–1
Functionalism, 215–21, 247, 271–2, 274, 286
Furness, Frank, 210, *15.9*
  Academy of Fine Arts, 210, *15.9*
Furniture, 61, 67, 112, 120, 218–20, 228, 245, 298, 322, 331
Future of London, The, 263
Futurism, 272–3, 304–5

Gables, 169
Gammage Auditorium (Arizona), 236
Garden Cities of Tomorrow, 304
Garden City, 249, 261, 304, 311, 323–4, 331
Gardens, 113, 137, 164, 221–3, 228, 319, 323–4, 378
Garnier, Tony, 304
  Cité Industrielle, 304
Gates, 143–4, 152, 334–5, 337–8
Gays, 327
Gehry, Frank O., and Associates, 18, 363, *1.12,* *26.3*
  Chiat Day Offices, 18, *1.12*
  Vitra Design Museum, 363, *26.3*
Gender, 4–5, 17, 26–8, 38, 50, 89–90, 111, 151, 220–1, 223–4, 250, 317–28, 349
  representation, 325, 327–8
  see also Feminism
General public, 183, 185, 214, 268–9, 281, 285, 334, 340–1, 366, 392
Geodesic domes, 273
Geometry 25, 86–7, 99, 141–3, 152–5, 194, 247, 252, 305, 313, 333, 335–9
Georgian London, 127
Germany, 13, 15, 75, 85, 134, 176, 183, 189, 197–8, 207, 215–21, 224, 262–4, 272, 291–2, 297, 301, 304, 307, 310, 312–4, 321, 331–2, 335–8, 339, 341, 350, 361, 363–4, 368
  Weimar Republic 215–21
Gesù (Rome), 138–40, *10.4*
Ghent, 123
Ghibellines, 109–10
Ghirardo, Diane, 46
Gibberd, Frederick, 265
  Regent's Park Estate, 265
Gibbs, James, 181
Gibling, Pauline, 221–4
Giddens, Anthony, 6
Giedion, Siegfried, 189
  Space, Time and Architecture, 189
Ginzburg, Moisei, 247, 250–1, 259
  Narkomfin, 250–1, 259, 323, *18.4*
  Style and Epoch, 250

Giotto, 96, 98
Glasgow, 259, 299, 349
  Glasgow School of Art, 299
  Hutchestown-Gorbals Area C Development, 259, *19.2*
Glasgow School of Art (Glasgow), 299
Glass, 69–71, 74–5, 78, 82, 84, 89, 231, 248, 252, 296, 298–9, 304, 392, 394
GLC (Greater London Council), 266
Gleisdreieck Tower (Frankfurt), 337–8, *24.5,* *24.6*
Globalization, 200, 248, 349–5, 377, 388–98
Gobelins, 61
GOELRO, 247
Goethe, Johann, 198
Goldman and Salatsch Store (Vienna), 298–9, *21.8*
Goldthwaite, Richard, 9, 119–28
  The Building of Renaissance Florence, 9, 119
Gordon Strong Planetarium, 234
Gothic architecture, 8–9, 67–76, 78–90, 106–7, 181, 200, 202–4, 206–7, 209, 387, 388
  All Saints, 89, *6.7*
  Amiens Cathedral, 74–5
  Beauvais Cathedral, 70, 75, *5.4*
  Canterbury Cathedral, 75, 83, 85, 88–9
  Chartres Cathedral, 73, 387
  clergy, 8, 78–83, 90
  Cologne Cathedral, 75
  construction and structure, 8, 67–76, 86–7, *5.1, 5.4, 15.4*
  Durham Cathedral, 9, 68–71, 74, 82–3, *6.3*
  Early English, 83
  Ely Cathedral, 75, 106
  Fountains Abbey, 81, *6.2*
  Kings College Chapel, 181
  laity, 9, 78, 84–5, 88–90
  Le Mans Cathedral, 74
  Lincoln Cathedral, 74, 106
  Mainz Cathedral, 67
  Masons, 85–8
  Meaux Abbey, 89
  Milan Cathedral, 86
  Norwich Cathedral, 76
  Notre-Dame Cathedral, 9, 71–3, *5.3*
  patronage, 8, 78, 84–6, 88, 90
  Rouen Cathedral, 209, *15.6*
  St.-Denis Abbey, 9, 71–2, 75, 81–2, 85, *5.2*
  St. Paul's Cathedral, 76
  St. Remi, Reims, 67
  Salisbury Cathedral, 9, 74–5, 83, *5.1, 5.5*
  Speyer Cathedral, 67
  Tewkesbury Abbey, 9, 83–4, *6.4*
  Vézelay, La Madeleine, 71, 81, *6.1*
  Wells Cathedral, 74, 79, 106, *5.1*

Gothic architecture (*cont.*)
  Westminster Abbey, 9, 75, 84–5, *6.5*
  Winchester Cathedral, 75
  Worcester Cathedral, 74, 76
  York Minster, 76
Gothic House, 160–1, *11.11*
Gothic revival, 13, 202–11, 293
Graffiti, 298
Grain elevators, 15, 391, *1.10*
Graphic design, 245, 277
Graves, Michael, 381, 387, *27.7*
  Public Services Building, 381, *27.7*
Gray, Eileen, 324
Greece, ancient, 6, 19, 23–36, 38, 97, 101, 141,
  151, 190, 196, 293, 306, 388, *2.4*
Greek revival, 31, 293
Green issues, *see* Environment
Greene, David, 271–2, 277–8
  Living Pod, 278
Gregory I, 79, 88
Grids, 332, 335–8, 349, 368
Griffin, Walter Burley, 236
  Knit-Lock, 236
Grimshaw, Nicholas, 279–80, 285–6, *20.6, 20.15*
  Bathroom Tower, 279–80, *20.6*
  Ladkarn Haulage Building, 285–6, *20.15*
Gropius, Walter, 216–7, 229, 262–3, 272, 302
  Weissenhof housing, 263
Grosstadtarchitektur, 313–4, *22.7*
Grosstadtbauten, 312, *22.6*
Grotto of Thetis (Versailles), 57–8, *4.3*
Guattari, Félix, 6
Guelphs, 109–10
Guggenheim Museum (New York), 234, 236, *17.6*
Guilds, 9, 86–8, 125–7, 167, 245, 345
Guimard, Hector, 297
Gulf War, 353
Gürtel Line (Vienna), 294
Gwathmey, Charles, 381

Hadid, Zaha, 364, *26.4*
  Vitra Fire Station, 364, *26.4*
Halbwachs, Maurice, 334
Halle au Blé (Paris), 11, 164, 166, 169, 171–3,
  12.1, 12.2
Hamilton, Thomas, 31
Hammond, Beeby and Babka, 180, *13.3*
  Paternoster Square, 180, *13.3*
Hampstead (London), 262
Hampton Court (London), 44
Hannibal, 136
Hansen, Theophil, 292, *21.1*
  Reichsrat, 292–3, *21.1*
Harmony, 44, 171, 181
Harvey, David, 6, 389

Haussmann, Georges-Eugène, 291, 349, *25.3*
  Boulevard St. Germain, 349, *25.3*
Hayden, Dolores, 326–7
Health, 163, 271, 293, 325, 331, 369
Hearth, 239, 320
Heathrow (London), 377
Heating, 216, 217, 229, 296
Hegel, G.W.F., 6, 12–3, 189–98, 243
  Aesthetics, 12, 189–98
Heidegger, Martin, 6, 362
Heisenberg, Werner, 361
Hellerau, 331
Henry III, 84, 85
Henry VIII, 202
Hepburn, Audrey, 144
Hermogenes, 27–8
Herron, Ron, 277
Heyduk, John, 381
Hieroglyphics, 153
High-tech, 15, 19, 181, 271–86, 376–7
Highland Park Plant (Detroit), 346, *25.1*
Hilberseimer, Ludwig, 17, 312–4, *22.6, 22.7*
  Chicago Tribune Tower, 312–3, *22.6*
  Grosstadtarchitektur, 313–4, *22.7*
  Grosstadtbauten, 312, *22.6*
Hill, Octavia, 325
Hillside (Taliesin), 227–8
Histoire de l'architecture, 27, 33–6, *2.2, 2.3, 2.4,*
  2.8
Histoire de ma vie, 309
Historical determinism, 189–90, 198, 243
Historical materialism, 200
Historical surveys, 1–3, 387–8
Historicism, 302, 391
History, 1–6, 19–20, 25, 106, 115, 150, 189–90,
  243, 331, 345, 363, 387–9, 396–8
  theorized history 6, 387–9, 396–8
History of Architecture, A, (Fletcher), 1
History of Architecture, A, (Kostof), 3
History of Building Types, A, 107
Hobsbawm, Eric, 6
Hoffmann, Josef, 296–7, *21.5*
  Palais Stoclet, 296–7, *21.5*
Holl, Stephen, 365, *26.6*
  Porta Vittoria, 365, *26.6*
Holland, 123
Hollyhock House, *see* Barnsdall House
Holmes, Sherlock, 309
Holy Roman Empire, 134
Homesgarth (Letchworth), 323–4, *23.6*
Homo ludens, 274
Homosexuality, 327
Hong Kong, 283, 285
  Hongkong and Shanghai Bank, 285, *20.12,*
  20.13

Hopkins, Michael, and Partners, 285, *20.14*
    Mound Stand, 285, *20.14*
Hoppen, Donald, 235
Horta, Victor, 297
Hospitals, 119, 292
Hôtel de Soissons (Paris),164
Hotels 304, 323, 327, 392–8
    foyers 327
Hôtels 163–5, 170
Housekeeping, 218–21, 223–4, 228–9, 250,
    317–24
Housing, 11, 14, 16, 45–6, 49, 156, 158, 163–75,
    214–24, 228–9, 231, 233, 235–6, 247,
    249–51, 253–4, 258–69, 271–3, 276–9, 292,
    294, 300, 304, 311, 313, 318–24, 334–7, 344,
    348–53, 368
Howard, Ebenezer, 249, 304, 323–4, 331
    *To-Morrow: a Peaceful Path to Real Reform/
        Garden Cities of Tomorrow*, 304, 331
    Homesgarth, 323–4, *23.6*
Howe, John, 230, 231, 233, *17.2*
Humanism, 9, 98–9, 101, 112–7, 293
Hungary, 349
Hunger, 244
Hutchestown-Gorbals Area C Development
    (Glasgow), 259, *19.2*
Hygiene, 221, 271, 298, 325, 331

IBM Office (Cosham), 281–2, *20.8*
ICA (Institute of Contemporary Arts), (London),
    272
Iconography, *see* Symbolism
Ideal towns, 135, 156, 304, *3.5, 3.6, 3.7*
Ideology, 7, 38–50, 185, 219–21, 224, 235, 243,
    254, 259, 267, 322, 324
Iktinos, 23–4
Imagination, 177, 239, 308, 370
Imitation, 380
Immeubles (Paris),163–75
Imperialism, 44, 245
Independent Group, 272
Indies, 123
Individuality, 189–90, 215–6, 240, 308, 310,
    312–3, 387, 397
Industrial revolution, 13, 123, 200–13, 344, 363
Industrialization, 14–7, 200–13, 215, 244, 245,
    252, 297, 344–55
Information explosion, 274
Information technology, 273, 283, 349, 352–3,
    362, 366–7, 391, 395, 397
Infrastructure, 378
Inner city, 261, 318, 327
Innocent III, 83
Innocent X, 132
Innovation, 381

Intensification, 17, 322–3, 352–5, 390
Internationale Bauausstellung (IBA) housing
    (Berlin), 368, *26.8*
Internationalism, 248–9, 252
Interpretation, 1–8, 14, 20, 63, 106, 111, 368–70,
    397–8
Investment appraisal, 381–4
Iofan, Boris, 254–5, *18.10*
    Palace of the Soviets, 254–5, *18.10*
Iron, 297
Iron Age, 363
Isokon Flats (London), 259, *19.1*
Italian Pavilion (Osaka), 282
Italy, 3, 7, 9, 38–9, 40, 46–9, 86, 93–103,
    106–17, 119–28, 131–44, 291, 304–5, 311,
    332–5, 365
    New towns, 7, 40, 46–9, *3.5, 3.6, 3.7*
Izenour, Stephen, 388
    Learning from Las Vegas, 388

Jacobs, Jane, 304
    The Death and Life of Great American Cities,
        304
Jameson, Fredric, 6, 19, 389–98
    *Postmodernism, Or, the Cultural Logic of Late
        Capitalism*, 19, 389–98
Japan, 279, 282, 349
Jarzombeck, Mark, 115, 117
Jeanneret, Charles Edouard, *see* Le Corbusier
Jefferson, Thomas, 43, 228
Jesuits, 139
Jesus Christ, 82, 142
John Hancock Center (Chicago), 18
John Hancock Tower (Boston), 376, *27.1*
Johnson Wax Administration Building and
    Laboratory Tower (Racine), 231, 234, *17.3,
        17.4*
Johnson, Philip, 301, 381, *21.10, 27.6*
    AT&T Building, 381, *27.6*
    Seagram Building, 301, *21.10*
Jombert, Charles Antoine, 170
    Architecture moderne, 170
Journey Through Ruins, A, 259
Journey to the East, 23
Judaism, 295
Julius II, 132–4, 136

Kallmann, G., 113, *8.4*
    Boston City Hall, 113, *8.4*
Kärntner Bar (Vienna), 298–9, *21.7*
Kaufmann Sr., Edgar, 231, 233
Kaufmann, Emil, 149
Keeling House (London), 269, *19.9*
Kepler, Johannes, 103
Kings College Chapel (Cambridge), 181

Kings Road Studios (Los Angeles), 13, 215,
  221–4, 238, 323, *16.5, 16.6*
Kingship, 6–63, 84–5, 133
Kitchens, 217–23, 251, 278, 322–3
Klein, Alexander, 219
Klimt, Gustav, 297
Knight, Richard Payne, 179, 181–2
  *An Analytical Enquiry into the Principles of
    Taste,* 179, 181–2
Knit-Lock, 236
Knowledge structures, 365–6
Knowles, E., 113, *8.4*
  Boston City Hall, 113, *8.4*
Kohn, Pederson and Fox, 18, *1.13*
  900 North Michigan Avenue, 18, *1.13*
Kokoschka, Oscar, 298
Korea, 3
Kornmann, 168
Kostof, Spiro, 3
  A History of Architecture, 3
Krauss, Karl, 293–4, 298–9
Krier, Leon, 49
Krier, Rob, 17, 332–3, 339–42, *24.7*
  South Friedrichsstrasse, Masterplan, 340
  Urban Space, 340
Kristeva, Julia, 6
Kurokawa, Kisho, 279, *20.5*
  Capsule Village Project, 279, *20.5*

L'Enfant, Pierre, 43
Labour, 9, 13, 17, 41, 86, 119, 123,-8, 158, 200,
  202, 207–9, 211, 215, 219, 227–9, 243–5,
  250, 252–3, 317–24, 344–55, 374
Labour Party, 260–1, 263–5
Ladkarn Haulage Building (London), 285–6,
  20.15
Ladovski, Nikolai, 247, 249
Laing, 351
Lakeland, 233–4
  Florida Southern College, 233–4
Land 164–7, 169, 202, 228, 245, 292, 331, 351,
  387
  nationalization, 245
Land Army, *23.2*
Land ownership, 135, 164, 244, 292
Lander, Harold Clapham, 323–4, *23.6*
  Homesgarth, 323–4, *23.6*
Landscape, 5, 45, 54, 57, 59, 62, 113, 179,
  182–3, 203, 221–3, 227, 229, 239
Lang, Fritz, 344
  Metropolis, 344
Lang, k.d., 328
Language, 17, 53, 149, 151–2, 154, 161, 182,
  230, 246, 299, 332, 361–4, 368–70
Las Vegas, 388

Lasdun, Denys, 269, *19.9*
  Keeling House, 269, *19.9*
Late capitalism, 7, 15, 17, 19, 352–5, 372–84,
  389–90, *see also* Capitalism
Lateran (Rome), 135
Lateran Council, 83
Latin America, 349–50
Laubin, Carl, 180, *13.3*
  Paternoster Square, 180, *13.3*
Laugier, Marc-Antoine, 150
  Essai sur l'architecture, 110, 150, *1.4*
Laundries, 250
Lautner House (Los Angeles), 238, *17.9*
Lautner, John, 228–31, 235–6, 238–9, *17.9*
  Lautner House, 238, *17.9*
LCC (London County Council) 263, 265–7,
  19.7, 19.8
  Alton East Estate, 266–7
  Alton West Estate, 265–7, *19.7*
  Loughborough Road Estate, 267, *19.8*
Le Camus de Mézières, Nicolas, 166, *12.1, 12.2*
  Halle au Blé, 11, 164, 166, 169, 171–3, *12.1,
    12.2*
Le Corbusier, 6, 9, 14, 23–4, 31–6, 229, 263,
  266, 271–3, 302, 304–5, 327–8, 388, *1.8,
    2.1, 2.7, 2.9, 2.10, 22.2, 23.8*
  City of Tomorrow and its Planning, 271, 305
  Journey to the East, 23
  and photography, 327–8
  Towards a New Architecture, 32–6, 271, 388,
    2.1, 2.7, 2.9, 2.10
  Unité d'Habitation, 266
  Villa Savoye, 14, 328, *1.8, 23.8*
  Ville Contemporaine, 304–5, *22.2*
  Weissenhof housing, 263
Le Mans, 74
  Le Mans Cathedral, 74
Le Nôtre, André, 59
Learning from Las Vegas, 388
Leases, 164
Leather, 299
Ledoux, Claude-Nicolas, 11, 50–1, 154–9, 163,
  *11.3, 11.4, 11.5, 11.6, 11.7, 11.8, 11.9,
    11.10*
  Barrière de la Villette, 154, *11.3*
  Royal Saltworks, 155–9, *11.4, 11.5, 11.6,
    11.7, 11.8, 11.9, 11.10*
Leeson, Loraine, 379
  'Digital Highways', 379
Lefebvre, Henri, 6, 103, 354, 389
Legislation, 167–9, 171, 201, 351, 366
Leicester, 201
Leisure, 56–8, 122, 144, 182, 219, 229, 250–1,
  274–5, 319–20, 327, 341, 353–4, 392
Lenin Institute of Librarianship 252, 254, *18.6*

Lenin, Vladimir Ilich, 243–6
Leningrad, 347
  Precasting Combine No. 2, Obuhov, 347, *25.2*
Lenoir de Romain, Samson-Nicolas, 168, *12.5*
  rue de Saintonge,168, *12.5*
Leonidov, Ivan, 249, 252, 254, 304, *18.3*, *18.6*
  Lenin Institute of Librarianship, 252, 254, *18.6*
  Magnitogorsk, 249–50, 304, *18.3*
Lequeu, Jean-Jacques, 11, 150, 160–1, *11.11*
  Gothic House, 160–1, *11.11*
Lesbians 327
Letchworth 323, 324, 331
  Homesgarth 323, 324, *23.6*
Lethaby, W.R. 211, *15.10*
  Brockhampton Church, 211, *15.10*
Lévi-Strauss, Claude 334
Levittown (New York), 352
Liberal arts, 24–5, 87, 168
Libertarianism, 327
Libraries, 152–3, 180, 252, 254, 283, 319
Life-cycle, 278, 282
Light, 35, 67, 69–71, 74–6, 141, 153, 216, 220,
  231, 238, 275, 296, 334
Lincoln, 74, 106
  Lincoln Cathedral, 74, 106
Lincoln Income Life Insurance Company
  Building (Louisville), 236–7, *17.7*
Linear cities, 249–50
Linguistics, 151, 332, 361–2
Listing, 14, 268–9
Literary criticism, 6, 362, 389, 398
Literature, 6, 25, 308–10, 311, 331, 362
Littlewood, Joan, 275
Liturgy, 67, 78, 88, 135, 139–40
Living Pod, 278
Lloyds Building (London), 282, 284–5, *20.10*
Local politics, 14, 109–10, 120, 258–69
Locality 377–8
Location 1, 375–9
Lods, Marcel, 272
  Maison du Peuple, 272
Loggia dei Lanzi (Florence), 94
Lollards, 90
London, 3, 7, 11, 14, 40–3, 49, 76, 79, 84–5,
  112–3, 123, 127–8, 180, 201, 204–6, 209–11,
  259–69, 272, 275, 279–80, 284–6, 297,
  307–8, 318, 339, 348–51, 354, 376–7, 379,
  383
  Alton East Estate, 266–7
  Alton West Estate, 265–7, *19.7*
  Bathroom Tower, 279–80, *20.6*
  British Library, 180
  British Museum, 40
  Brixton, 267
  Broadgate, 49, 383, *27.9*

  Buckingham Palace, 112–3, *8.3*
  Canary Wharf, 379, *27.5*
  Centre Point, 376, *27.2*
  Charing Cross, 40
  Clapham Common, 318, *23.1*
  Covent Garden, 180
  Cumberland Terrace, 261, *19.3*
  Docklands, 286, 379
  Fun Palace, 275, *20.1*
  Hampstead, 262
  Heathrow, 377
  Isokon Flats, 259, *19.1*
  Keeling House, 269, *19.9*
  Ladkarn Haulage Building, 285–6, *20.15*
  Lloyds Building, 282, 284–5, *20.10*
  Loughborough Road Estate, 267, *19.8*
  Midland Hotel, 210, *15.8*
  Moriarty Place, 351, *25.6*
  Mound Stand, 285, *20.14*
  National Gallery 7, 41, *1.2*, *3.1*
  Nelson's Column, 41–2, *3.2*
  Pall Mall, 40
  Paternoster Square, 180, *13.3*
  Regent Street, 339
  Regent's Park, 260–2, 339
  Regent's Park Estate, 14, 260–8, *19.5*, *19.6*
  Roehampton, 267
  Royal Academy, 41
  Royal Opera House, 180
  Sainsbury Wing, National Gallery, 7, *1.2*
  St. Martin's, 40
  St. Pancras Station, 180, 210
  St. Paul's Cathedral, 76, 180, 204–6, *15.3*
  Stockley Park, 377, *27.3*
  Surrey Square, 11, *1.5*
  Temple Church, 79
  Trafalgar Square, 7, 40–3
  Westminster Abbey, 84–5, *6.5*
  Whitehall, 40
  Yaohan shopping mall, 354, *25.9*
London: a Pilgrimage, 307, *22.4*
Loos House (Vienna), 298–9
Loos, Adolph, 16, 19, 193, 298–300, 341, *21.7*,
  21.8, *21.9*
  Goldman and Salatsch Store, 298–99, *21.8*
  Kärntner Bar, 298–9, *21.7*
  Loos House, 298–9
  Muller House, 300, *21.9*
  Ornament and Crime, 298, 300
  raumplan, 300
  Tzara House, 300
Lorenzetti, Ambrogio, 96, 98
Los Angeles, 13, 18, 215, 221–4, 238–9, 320,
  323, 390, 392–8, *1.11*
  Barnsdall House, 238

Los Angeles (*cont.*)
  Chiat Day Offices, 18, *1.12*
  Downtown/Bunker Hill, 392
  Kings Road Studios, 13, 215, 221–4, 238, 323, *16.5*, *16.6*
  Lautner House, 238, *17.9*
  Sturges House, 238–9, *17.10*
  Westin Bonaventure Hotel, 390, 392–8, *28.1*, *28.2*, *28.3*, *28.4*, *28.5*, *28.6*
Lotissement, 167
Loughborough Road Estate (London), 267, *19.8*
Louis XIII, 55, 59
Louis XIV, 54–63
Louisville, 236–7
  Lincoln Income Life Insurance Company Building 236–7, *17.7*
Louvre (Paris), 54, 61, 163, 167
Lower East Side (New York), 19, *1.14*
Luther, Martin, 134
Lutyens, Edwin, 43, 297
Luxembourg, 332
Lyotard, Jean-François, 354

McDonald's, 352, *25.7*
McKim, Charles, 43
McKinnell, M., 113, *8.4*
  Boston City Hall, 113, *8.4*
McMillan, James, 43
Mace, Rodney, 40
Machiavelli, Nicolo, 133
  The Prince, 133
Machines, 25, 200, 207, 216, 227, 244, 247, 273, 278, 344–52
Machino-facture, 345–6
Mackintosh, Charles Rennie, 299
  Glasgow School of Art, 299
MacManus, Frederick, 265, *19.6*
  Regent's Park Estate, 265, *19.6*
Maderno, Carlo, 144
  St. Peter's, west front, 144
Maestri, 126
Magnesia, 27
  Temple of Artemis, 27
Magnesis, 27
Magnitogorsk, 249–50, 304, *18.3*
Maintenance, 282, 382
Mainz, 67
  Mainz Cathedral, 67
Maison du Peuple (Clichy), 272
Maison partagés (Paris),163
Majolica House (Vienna), 294, *21.2*
Malevich, Kasimir, 245, 253–4, *18.7*, *18.8*
  Red Square, 253, *18.7*
  Female Worker, 254, *18.8*
Man Without Qualities, 310

Management contracting, 374
Manchester, 123, 350
Mandel, Ernst 6, 19, 389
Manet, Edouard, 309, *22.5*
  Exposition Universelle, 309, *22.5*
Mansard roof, 169
Mantua, 95, 132
Manufacture, 345
Maps, 336, 368, 395
Marathon, battle of, 40
Marble, 298–9
Marcuse, Herbert, 354
Marin County, 236
  Marin County Civic Center, 236
Market segmentation, 376–7
Marketing, 19, 375, 383–4
Markets, 179, 306, 311, 344
Marne-la-Vallé, 49
  Palais d'Abraxas, 49
Mars, 27
Marseilles, 266
  Unité d'Habitation, 266
Martin, (John) Leslie, 214, 265–7, *19.7*
  Alton West Estate, 266–7, *19.7*
  Loughborough Road Estate, 267
Martines, Lauro, 111, 114–5
Marx, Karl, 6, 124, 189, 243
Marxism, 244, 274, 389, 398
Masculinity, 327–8
Masons, 85–8, 125–7, 141, 209
Mass production, 273, 297, 345–4
Masselink, Eugene, 230–1, 233, *17.2*
Massimi, 132, 136–8
  Palazzo Massimi, 136–7, *10.3*
Mastroianni, Marcello, 144
Materials, 4, 24, 61, 67–76, 82, 85, 115, 121, 127, 150, 153, 170, 181, 209, 214–5, 219–20, 227–8, 233, 235–8, 248, 252, 271–3, 275, 279, 282, 294, 296, 298–9, 301, 348, 351–2, 392
Mathematics, 25, 86–7, 361
May, Ernst, 217, *16.1*
  Frankfurt housing, 216–21, *16.1*
Mayakovski, Vladimir, 245–6
Meaning, 53, 62–3, 78–90, 149, 150–1, 176, 178, 191–2, 327–8, 364, 367
Meaux, 89
  Meaux Abbey, 89
Medici, 9, 114–5, 120–1
  Cosimo de Medici, 114
  Lorenzo de Medici, 121
  Palazzo Medici, 9, 114–5, *8.5*
Medicine, 25, 214–5, 293, 366
Medieval towers, 9, 108–11, 113
Medieval towns, 9, 47, 76, 78, 85, 93–7, 108–11, 163, 168, 202–3, 291–3, 311

Megastructures, 277–8
Meier, Richard, 381
Melnikov, Konstantin, 250–3, 255, *18.5*, *18.9*
   People's Commissariat of Heavy Industry, 253, 255, *18.9*
   Russakova workers' club, 250–3, *18.5*
Mercantilism, 61
Mercator, Gerhardus, 368
Merrie England, 201–3
Metabolism, 279
Metal, 273, 296
Metalwork, 82, 227, 272
Metaphor, 34, 151, 154, 238, 249, 397
Metonym, 11, 151, 153–8
Metropolis, 344
Metropolis and Mental Life, The, 310
Meyer, Hannes, 214
Michelangelo (Buonarroti) 120, 133, 144
   St. Peter's, dome, 144
Michelozzo di Bartolommeo, 115, *8.5*
   Palazzo Medici, 9, 114–5, *8.5*
Michigan, 39
   Deertrack, 239
Micro-region housing (Moscow), 350, *25.5*
Midland Hotel (London), 210, *15.8*
Mies van der Rohe, Ludwig, 229, 263, 301–2, *19.4*, *21.10*, *21.11*
   New National Gallery, 301, *21.11*
   Seagram Building, 301, *21.10*
   Weissenhof housing, 263, *19.4*
Milan, 86, 291, 334, 365
   Milan Cathedral, 86
   Porta Vittoria, 365, *26.6*
Milinis, I., 250–1, 259, *18.4*
   Narkomfin 250–1, 259, 323, *18.4*
Minimalism, 301–2
Minneapolis, 320
Mittel Europa, 292–3
Mobility, 249, 259, 273–4, 276, 279, 352, 392, 395
Models, 384
Modena, 334–5
   S. Cataldo Cemetery, 334–5, *24.2*, *24.3*
Modénature, 33, 35
Modern Architecture, 294
Modern Houses, Beautiful Homes, 320, *23.3*
Modern Painters, 207
Modernism, 1, 3, 13–4, 16, 36, 149, 177–8, 181, 183, 185, 189–90, 193, 214–24, 227–40, 243–56, 258–69, 271–86, 291–302, 304–14, 321–5, 327–8, 331–42, 344–55, 388, 391–2, 395
Modernity, 2, 16–7, 304–14, 317–28, 344–55, 389–98
Money, 310, 322

Montpellier, 49, *3.8*
   Antigone housing, 49, *3.8*
Monument to the Third International, 248–9, *18.2*
Monuments and monumentality, 5, 40–4, 46, 48, 90, 95, 100, 107, 112–3, 117, 121, 127, 131, 135–6, 141, 151, 163, 170–3, 234, 248, 253, 292, 302, 304, 312–3, 333–4
Morality, 182–3, 202–4, 207, 300, 320, 325, 350
Moriarty Place (London), 351, *25.6*
Morin, Edgar, 377
   Sociologie, 377
Moscow, 39, 244, 247, 250–5, 323, 350, 352
   micro-region housing, 350, *25.5*
   Narkomfin, 250, 259, 323, *18.4*
   Russakova workers' club, 250–3, *18.5*
Mosher, Robert, 233
Motherhood, 322–3
Mound Stand (London), 285, *20.14*
Muller House (Prague), 300, *21.9*
Museums and art galleries, 7, 15, 40, 114, 152, 176, 195, 210, 234, 236, 281–5, 363, 369
Music, 25, 86, 142, 191, 227, 229, 275, 296, 298, 328, 392
Musil, Robert, 310
   Man Without Qualities, 310
Mussolini, Benito, 40, 46
Mysticism, 11, 297, 363

Nancy, 340
Naples, 122
Napoleon I, 167, 169, 172
Napoleon III, 291
Narkomfin (Moscow), 250, 259, 323, *18.4*
Narrative, 89, 151, 161, 387, 395
Nash, John, 40, 112–3, 209, 261, 262, *8.3*, *19.3*
   Buckingham Palace, 112–3, *8.3*
   Cumberland Terrace, 261, *19.3*
   Regent Street, 339
   Regent's Park, 60, 261–2, 339
National Gallery (London), 7, 41, *1.2*, *3.1*
Nationalism, 38, 40–3, 46, 61, 322
Nationalization, 245, 351
Nature, 55, 58–9, 62, 113, 124, 150, 179, 182–3, 194, 222–3, 230, 294, 297, 308, 319–20, 322, 344, 354, 363, 389–90
Nazi party, 262
Neighbourhood, 263, 265, 304, 311
Nelson's Column (London), 41–2, *3.2*
Nelson, Horatio, 40–1
Neo-classicism, 11, 40–1, 44, 149–61, 163, 171, 192–3, 209, 248, 253–5, 293
Neo-renaissance, 247
Neue Sachlichkeit, 216–21
Neue Staatsgalerie (Stuttgart), 15, *1.9*

Neutra, Dione, 222
Neutra, Richard, 222
Neveu, Charles, 172–3, *12.7*
   12 rue de Tournon, 172–3, *12.7*
New Deal, 46
New Economic Policy (NEP), 245, 246, 247
New Left, 245
New Left Review, 389
New National Gallery (Berlin), 301, *21.11*
New Objectivity, 216–21
New Right, 259
New Science, 151
New towns 7, 40, 46–9, 96–7, 247–50, 265–6,
   304, 311, *3.5, 3.6, 3.7, see also* Ideal
   Towns
New York, 12, 19, 49, 234–6, 273, 301, 304,
   311, 349, 352, 355, 376, 378, 381, *1.14*
   AT&T Building, 381, *27.6*
   Battery Park, 49, 378, *27.4*
   Brooklyn Bridge, 12, *1.6*
   Geodesic Dome, 273
   Guggenheim Museum, 234, 236, *17.6*
   Levittown, 352
   Lower East Side, 19, *1.14*
   Radburn, 304, 311
   St. Mark's-in-the-Bouwerie, 235
   Seagram Building, 301, *21.10*
   Trump Tower 355, *25.10*
New York Five, 381
New York University, 231
Newspapers, 283, 312, 353
Newton, Isaac, 152
Nicholas V, 131
Nietzsche, Friedrich, 362
Non-architecture, 274–9
Norman Conquest, 78, 85
North Haven Point, 362
   Slow House, 362, *26.2*
900 North Michigan Avenue (Chicago), 18, *1.13*
Norwich, 76, 283–4
   Norwich Cathedral, 76
   Sainsbury Centre, 283–4, *20.11*
Notre-Dame Cathedral (Paris), 9, 71–3, *5.3*
Nuclear power, 389, 391
Nylon, 275

Obelisks, 136, 194
Objectivity, 101–2, 160, 216, 361
Oblin, Bernard and Charles, 166
Oculus, 170
Offices, 18, 49, 114, 180, 234–5, 266, 281–2,
   284–5, 294, 313, 334, 337–8, 349, 352, 355,
   372–84, 387, 391
Oil crisis, 268

Okhitovich, Mikhail, 249
Olbrich, Joseph, 297, 298, *21.6*
   Secession Pavilion, 297, *21.6*
Oldenburg, Claes, 18, *1.12*
   Chiat Day Offices, 18, *1.12*
Olmstead Junior, Frederick Law, 43
Olympia and York, 378–9
Onyx, 299
Opera House (Vienna), 292
Opera houses, 180, 292, 327
Operative Stonemasons Union, 42
Orders, 26–31, 33, 35–6, 41, 101, 141, 153, 170,
   298, *2.2, 2.3, 2.4, 2.5, 2.6, 2.8*
Organicism, 150, 193–, 196, 235–8, 294, 297
Orientation, 57, 214–7, 339
Ornament, 19, 78, 81, 88, 115–, 127, 151, 173,
   190, 193–5, 198, 206, 294, 296, 298–300,
   302, 311
Ornament and Crime, 298, 300
Osaka, 282
   Italian Pavilion, 282
Ottoman empire, 124
Oud, J.J.P., 263
   Weissenhof housing, 263
Outline of European Architecture, An, 23
Owen, Robert, 243

Padua, 334
Paestum, 31, 34
Pagan architecture, 88
Pagans, 88, 90, 202–3, 207
Painting, 25, 53, 61, 78, 95–102, 120, 127, 132,
   141, 177, 179–81, 191, 203, 209, 245, 253,
   297–8, 309, 331, 391
Palace of the Soviets, 254–5, *18.10*
Palais d'Abraxas (Marne-la-Vallée), 49
Palais de Bourbon (Paris), 164
Palais Stoclet (Brussels), 296–7, *21.5*
Palatine hill (Rome), 135
Palazzi, 9, 106–17, 119–28, 136–7, 144, 171
Palazzo Davanzati (Florence),110, *8.2*
Palazzo del Priori (Florence), 94, *see also*
   Palazzo Vecchio
Palazzo Farnese (Rome), 9, 136–7, *10.2*
Palazzo Massimi (Rome), 136–7, *10.3*
Palazzo Medici (Florence), 9, 114–5, *8.5*
Palazzo Riccardi (Florence), *see* Palazzo Medici
Palazzo Rucellai (Florence), 9, 115–7, 137, *8.6*
Palazzo Strozzi (Florence), 9, 115, 122, 125, *9.1*
Palazzo Vecchio (Florence), 94, 95, 98, 100, 102
Pall Mall (London), 40
Panofsky, Erwin 85
Pantheon (Rome), 79
Papacy, 4, 9, 122, 131–44
Paradiso, 131

Paris, 9, 11, 44, 49, 54, 61, 70–3, 75–6, 81–2,
    85, 122, 154–5, 163–75, 281–5, 291, 297,
    300, 308–9, 311, 327, 340, 349–50
  Académie Royale d'Architecture, 170–1
  Barrière de la Villette, 154, *11.3*
  Boulevard St. Germain, 349, *25.3*
  Chambre des Bâtiments, 169
  École de Travaux Publics, 170
  École des Beaux Arts, 170
  École Polytechnique, 170
  Fermiers Généraux, 164
  Généralité de Paris, 169
  Halle au Blé, 11, 164, 166, 169, 171–3, *12.1,
    12.2*
  Haussmannization, 291
  Hôtel de Soissons, 164
  Louvre, 54, 61, 163, 167
  Notre-Dame, 9, 71–3, *5.3*
  Nouveau quartier Poissonière, 164
  Palais de Bourbon, 164
  Passy, 327
  Place de l'Odeon, 166, *12.3*
  Pompidou Centre, 281–5, *20.9*
  rue de Rivoli, 11, 167, 172, 340, *12.6*
  rue de Saintonge, 168, *12.5*
  12 rue de Tournon, 172–3, *12.7*
  Saint-Antoine, 163
  St.-Denis Abbey, 9, 71–2, 75, 81–2, 85, *5.2*
  Théâtre de l'Odeon, 11, 164, 166–7, 172, *12.4*
  Tuileries, 167
  Tzara House, 300
Park Commission plan, 43–4, *3.3*
Parking structures, 362
Parks, 45, 54, 57–9, 62, 76, 260–2, 292, 304,
    331, 339
Parliament, 60–2, 244, 292–3
Parma, 95, 109
Parry, Eric, 377, *27.3*
  W3 Building, Stockley Park, 377, *27.3*
Parthenon (Athens), 23–4, 29–30, 32–4, 101, *2.1,
    2.5, 2.7, 2.9, 2.10*
Passy, 327
Paternoster Square (London), 180, *13.3*
Patriarchy, 317–8, 326
Patronage, 2, 4, 8–9, 44, 78, 84–6, 88, 90,
    109–10, 114–17, 119–25, 128, 131–44, 380,
    387
Paul III, 132, 136
Pavilions, 282
Pazzi, 120
Peasantry, 244–6
Peck, Gregory, 144
Pedestrians, 313, 395
Pei, I.M., 376, *27.1*
  John Hancock Tower, 376, *27.1*

Pelli, Cesar, 378–9, *27.4, 27.5*
  Battery Park, 49, 378, *27.4*
  Canary Wharf, 379, *27.5*
  Winter Garden, World Financial Center, 378,
    27.4
People's Commissariat of Heavy Industry, 253,
    255, *18.9*
Percier, Charles, 167–8, 172, *12.6*
  rue de Rivoli, 167, 172, *12.6*
Periodization, 2, 4, 345, 363
Perrault, Claude, 61
Perspective, 9, 25, 93–103, 144, 263, 365
Peruzzi, Baldassare, 136–7, *10.3*
  Palazzo Massimi, 136–7, *10.3*
Peto, 42
Pevsner, Nikolaus, 23, 107, 189
  A History of Building Types, 107
  Outline of European Architecture, 23
  Pioneers of Modern Design, 189
Peyre, Marie-Joseph, 166–8, *12.3, 12.4*
  Place de l'Odeon, 166, *12.3*
  Théâtre de l'Odeon, 11, 164, 166–7, 172, *12.4*
Pheidias, 23
Philadelphia, 210
  Academy of Fine Arts, 210, *15.9*
Philadelphia Crosstown Community, 325
Philanthropy, 325
*Philosophical Enquiry into the Origins of Our
    Ideas of the Sublime and Beautiful, A*,
    177–8
Philosophy, 2, 4, 6, 12–3, 17, 25, 79, 86, 176,
    189–98, 207, 239, 274, 293, 306, 362, 365,
    367, 389
Photography, 53, 327–8, 354
Photomontage, 245
Physics, 361
Piano, Renzo, 281–5, *20.9*
  Italian Pavilion, 282
  Pompidou Centre 281–5, *20.9*
Piazza del Duomo (Florence), 93–4, 98–9
Piazza del Popolo (Rome), 9, 142–4, *10.9*
Piazza della Signoria (Florence), 94–5, 98–100,
    7.1
Picturesque, 3, 12, 176–85, 193, 203, 206, 209,
    311
Pienza, 95, 135
Piero di Cosimo, 125, *9.2*
  Building a Palace, 125, *9.2*
Pilgrimage, 82–3, 144
Pilotis, 250
Pioneers of Modern Design, 189
Piranesi, Giovanni Battista, 31
Pisa, 107
Pius II, 114, 135
Place de l'Odeon (Paris), 166, *12.3*

Place royale, 171, 173

Plan, 13, 26, 39, 113–4, 121, 133, 135, 137, 138, 140–2, 153, 156, 163, 170–1, 196, 204, 206, 214–24, 228–9, 233, 238, 250, 263, 272, 300, 313, 321, 365
  centralized 133, 135

Plan of Work, 373

Planners, 260–1, 268, 274, 294, 299, 304, 311–4, 324–6, 331–42

Planning, 7, 17, 43–9, 93–7, 132, 134–6, 138, 142–4, 155–6, 239, 245–50, 253–4, 258, 260–3, 265–8, 271, 274–5, 291, 294, 297, 299, 304–6, 311–4, 324–6, 331–42, 351, 376–9

Plastic, 279, 282

Plato, 46, 79, 306

Plug-In City, 278, *20.3*

Plumbing, 229, 283, 298

Plutarch, 23

Poetics and poetry, 57, 191, 207, 235–6, 239–40, 245, 310

Poissy, 14, 328
  Villa Savoye, 14, 328, *1.8, 23.8*

Poland, 292

Police, 307

Politicians, 14, 201, 239, 254, 260–1, 267

Politics, 5–7, 9, 14, 26, 39, 45–6, 53–63, 78, 84–5, 131–3, 138, 149, 243–56, 258–69, 292, 305, 345, 349–50, 353, 388, 397

Pollock, Griselda, 6, 327

Polykleitos, 25

Pompidou Centre (Paris), 281–5, *20.9*

Poore, Richard, 83

Popova, Lyubov, 245

Popper, Karl, 189

Population, 109, 163, 181, 200–1, 215, 244, 307, 308, 331, 350

Pornography, 326

Porphyrios, Demetri, 49, 180, *13.3*
  Paternoster Square, 180, *13.3*

Porta, Giacomo della, 139, *10.4*
  Gesù, 138–40, *10.4*

Porta Vittoria (Milan), 365, *26.6*

Porte-cochère 169–70

Portland, 381, *27.7*
  Public Services Building, 381, *27.7*

Portman, John, 392, *28.1, 28.2, 28.3, 28.4, 28.5, 28.6*
  Westin Bonaventure Hotel, 390, 392–8, *28.1, 28.2, 28.3, 28.4, 28.5, 28.6*

Post-industrial, 354

Post-rationalization, 238

Postal Savings Bank (Vienna), 294–6, *21.3, 21.4*

Postmodernism, 19, 49, 302, 362, 389–98

Postmodernism, Or, the Cultural Logic of Late Capitalism, 19, 389–98

Potteries Thinkbelt, 276, *20.2*

Poverty, 46, 120, 202, 325, 331, 346, 354

Prague, 292, 300
  Muller House, 300, *21.9*

Precasting Combine No. 2, Obuhov (Leningrad), 347, *25.2*

Prefabrication, 347, 351–2

Price Tower (Bartlesville), 234–5

Price, Cedric, 15, 275–7, 285, *20.1, 20.2*
  Fun Palace 275, *20.1*
  Planning for Pleasure, 275
  Potteries Thinkbelt, 276, *20.2*

Priene, 29, 31
  Temple of Athena Polias, 29, 31, *2.6*

Primitive hut, 10, *1.4*

Primitivism, 298

Prince, The, 133

Princeton University, 227

Prisons, 201–2

Privacy, 224, 354

Private sector, 374–84

Production, 155–6, 163, 200, 207–9, 211, 215, 248–9, 252, 273, 297, 313, 317, 344–54, 367, 387, 392

Production line, 218–9, 346–8, *25.1*

Professionalism, 221, 273, 317, 321, 324–5, 367–8, 372–84, 389

Progress, 4, 155, 243, 345, 353–4

Project management, 372–84

Projection screens, 275, 283

Proletarian classicism, 247

Proletariat, 244–8, 254, 353

Proletkult, 246

Property development, 4, 19, 49, 163–75, 292, 294, 355, 372–84, 392, *see also* Speculative development

Proportion, 170–1, 190–3

Propriety, 28, 206, 294, 297

Prostitutes and prostitution, 327, 381

Protestantism, 202, 207

Proust, Marcel, 310
  Remembrance of Things Past, 310

Prouvé, Jean, 15, 272–3
  Maison du Peuple, 272

Psychoanalysis, 6, 293, 366, 390

Psychology, 119, 149

Public sector, 374

Public Services Building (Portland), 381, *27.7*

Public/private, 25, 111, 121–2, 265, 317–28, 333, 378, 397

Publishing, 2–4, 170, 219, 243, 245, 277, 293, 298, 367

Pugin, A.W.N., 13, 200, 202–7, 209, 211, *15.1*, *15.2*, *15.4*
  Contrasts, 202–4, *15.1*, *15.2*
  St. Augustine's, 206, *15.5*
  True Principles of Pointed or Christian Architecture, 204–5, *15.4*
Purposeful writing, 387, 388
Pyramids, 387

Quantity surveying, 383
Quatremère de Quincy, Antoine, 333–4

Race, 38, 50, 349, 392, 397
Racine, 231, 234
  Johnson Wax Administration Building and Laboratory Tower, 231, 234, *17.3*, *17.4*
Radburn (New York), 304, 311
Radial cities, 249
Radio, 249, 252, 278, 353
Railton, William, 41, *3.2*
  Nelson's Column, 41–2, *3.2*
Railway stations, 180, 210, 367
Railways, 201, 247, 276–7, 294, 320, 391
Rainaldi, Carlo, 144, *10.9*
  Sta. Maria in Monte Santo, 144, *10.9*
  Sta. Maria dei Miracoli, 143–4, *10.9*
Ramsgate, 206
  St. Augustine's, 206, *15.5*
Raphael (Sanzio), 133
Rathaus (Vienna), 292–3
Ratiocinatio, 366
Rationalism, 14, 204, 247, 332
Rattenbury, John, 228, *17.1*
  Broadacre City, 228, *17.1*
Raumplan, 300
Realism, 151
Reason, 177–83, 185, 353, 363
Reconstruction, 14, 247, 258–69, 271, 331–42
Reformation, 78, 134, 202
Regent Street (London), 339
Regent's Park (London), 260–2, 339
Regent's Park Estate (London), 14, 260–8, *19.5*, *19.6*
Regionalism, 236
Rehousing, 261
Reichsrat (Vienna), 292–3, *21.1*
Reilly, Charles, 260
Reims, 67
  St. Remi, 67
Reliance Controls Factory (Swindon), 279–80, 282, *20.7*
Religion, 8–9, 13, 38, 53, 63, 67, 75–6, 78–90, 107, 117, 120, 131–44, 164, 190–2, 196, 202–4, 207, 245, 318–20, 366
Remembrance of Things Past, 310

Renaissance, 3, 9, 19, 38, 93–103, 106–17, 119–28, 131–44, 192, 202, 247, 293, 327
Rentiers, 123, 164
Repton, Humphrey, 178–9, 182–3, *13.1*, *13.2*, *13.4*
  Sketches and Hints on Landscape Gardening, 183, *13.4*
  Theory and Practice of Landscape Gardening, 182
Restaurants, 233, 327, 392, 394–5
Retail, 163, 165, 169–70, 228, 233, 277, 283, 294, 298, 300, 304, 320, 327, 331, 334, 352, 372–84, 392
Revolution, 14, 62, 164, 243–56, 291–2, 323
  1789 French revolution, 62, 164
  1830, 291
  1848, 291–2
  1870, 291
  1905 Russian revolution, 244
  1917 Russian revolution, 14, 243–56, 323
RFG (*Reichsforschungsgesellschaft für Wirtschaftlichkeit im Bau- und Wohnungswesen*), 216, 219
Rhetoric, 25, 366
RIBA (Royal Institute of British Architects), 260, 262, 266–7
Riboutté, 168
Ricoeur, Paul, 6
Ringstrasse (Vienna),16, 291–4, 387
Rio de Janeiro, 350
Ritual, 88, 135, 160, 192, 366
Roads, 16, 40–1, 45, 47, 94–5, 97, 108, 133, 136, 144, 163, 166–7, 172, 201, 228–9, 249–50, 265–6, 271, 276–7, 291–4, 304, 307–8, 311, 326, 331, 333–5, 339–40, 349, 387–8
Rodchenko, Alexander, 245
Roebling, John A., 12, *1.6*
  Brooklyn Bridge, 12, *1.6*
Roehampton (London), 267
Rogers, Richard, 15, 181, 280–5, *20.7*, *20.9*
  Pompidou Centre 281–5, *20.9*
  Reliance Controls Factory 280, 282, *20.7*
Rogers, Richard, Partnership, 282, 284–5, *20.10*
  Lloyds Building 282, 284–5, *20.10*
Rogers, Su, 280, 282, *20.7*
  Reliance Controls Factory, 280, 282, *20.7*
Roman architecture, 6–7, 44, 48, 67, 79, 99, 135, 141, 332, 336,
Roman republic and empire, 38–40, 46, 48, 136, 254, 336
Romanesque architecture, 9, 68–71, 74, 81–3, 85–6
  Durham Cathedral, 9, 68–71, 74, 82–3, *6.3*
  Vézelay, La Madeleine, 71, 81, *6.1*
Romanesque art, 98

Romantic art (Hegel), 191, 196
Romanticism, 201, 207
Rome, 9, 39, 44, 46, 61, 79, 99, 122, 131–44
  Capitoline hill, 135
  Forum, 135
  Gesù, 138–40, *10.4*
  Lateran, 135
  obelisks, 136
  Palatine hill, 135
  Palazzo Farnese, 9, 136–7, *10.2*
  Palazzo Massimi 136–7, *10.3*
  Pantheon, 79
  Piazza del Popolo, 9, 142–4, *10.9*
  S. Andrea Quirinale, 9, 138–41, *10.5, 10.6*
  S. Carlo alle Quattro Fontane, 9, 138–42,
    10.7, 10.8
  St. Peter's, 9, 79, 133–5, 144
  Sta. Maria in Monte Santo, 144
  Sta. Maria dei Miracoli, 143–4, *10.9*
  Sta. Maria del Popolo, 143–4, *10.9*
  Tempietto, 134–5, *10.1*
  Vatican, 135
  Via Babuini, 144
  Via del Corso, 144
  Via Ripiena, 144
Roosevelt, Franklin, 46
Roosevelt, Theodore, 45, 239
Roriczer, Matthias, 88, *6.6*
Rosehaugh Stanhope, 383 *see also* Stanhope
Rossi, Aldo, 17, 302, 332–5, 339–42, *24.1, 24.2,*
  24.3
  Analogous City, 333–4, *24.1*
  Architecture and the City, 333
  S. Cataldo Cemetery, 334–5, *24.2, 24.3*
Rouen, 209
  Rouen Cathedral, 209, *15.6*
Rovere, Cesare, 133
Royal Academy (London), 41
Royal Institute of British Architects (RIBA),
  373
  Plan of Work, 373
Royal Library, 153–4, *11.2*
Royal Opera House (London), 180
Royal Saltworks (Arc-et-Senans),155–9, *11.4,*
  11.5, 11.6, 11.7, 11.8, 11.9, 11.10
Rucellai, 9, 115–7, 120–1, 137
  Giovanni Rucellai, 121
  Palazzo Rucellai, 9, 115–7, 137, *8.6*
Rue de Rivoli (Paris), 11, 167, 172, 340, *12.6*
Rue de Saintonge (Paris),168, *12.5*
12 rue de Tournon (Paris), 172–3, *12.7*
Rueger, Werner, 367, *26.7*
  Stadelhofen Train Station, 367, *26.7*
Rural, *see* Countryside
Rural Rides, 201

Ruskin, John, 13, 183, 193, 197, 200, 207–9,
  211, 294, 296, 336, *15.6*
  Modern Painters, 207
  The Seven Lamps of Architecture, 207
  The Stones of Venice, 207, 209
Russakova workers' club (Moscow), 250–3, *18.5*
Russia, *see* USSR
Russian revolution (1905), 244
Russian revolution (1917), 14, 243–56, 323
Russki Moderne, 248
Rustication, 158

Sabaudia, *3.5, 3.6, 3.7*
Sabsovich, Leonid, 249
Sainsbury Centre (Norwich), 283–4, *20.11*
Sainsbury Wing, National Gallery (London), 7,
  1.2
S. Andrea Quirinale (Rome), 9, 138, 139, 140,
  141, *10.5, 10.6*
St. Andrew, 141
Saint-Antoine (Paris), 163
St. Augustine, 88
St. Augustine's (Ramsgate), 206, *15.5*
St. Bernard, 81
S. Carlo alle Quattro Fontane (Rome), 9, 138,
  139, 140–2, *10.7, 10.8*
S. Cataldo Cemetery (Modena), 334–5, *24.2,*
  24.3
Sta. Croce (Florence), 93
St. Cuthbert, 83
St.-Denis Abbey (Paris), 9, 71–2, 75, 81–2, 85,
  5.2
St. Ignatius, 139–40
Saint-Lazare, house of, 164
S. Lorenzo (Florence), 101
Sta. Maria dei Miracoli (Rome), 143–4, *10.9*
Sta. Maria del Fiore (Florence), 8, 93, 94, 98,
  107, *1.3*
Sta. Maria del Popolo (Rome), 143–4, *10.9*
Sta. Maria in Monte Santo (Rome), 144, *10.9*
Sta. Maria Novella (Florence), 93
Sta. Reparta (Florence), 93
St. Mark's-in-the-Bouwerie (New York), 235
St. Martin's (London), 40
St. Pancras Metropolitan Borough Council,
  260–8
St. Pancras Station (London), 180, 210
St. Paul's Cathedral (London), 76, 180, 204–6,
  15.3
St. Peter, 131, 135, 142
St. Peter's (Rome), 9, 79, 133–5, 144
St. Petersburg, 244
St. Remi (Reims), 67
Saint Simon, Duc de, 62, 243
St. Thomas Becket, 83, 85

Salisbury, 9, 74–5, 83
  Salisbury Cathedral, 9, 74–5, 83, *5.1*, *5.5*
San Francisco, 348
San Gimignano, 108–9, *8.1*
San Giovanni, 97
Sand, George, 309
  Histoire de ma vie, 309
Sangallo, Antonio da, 136–7, *10.2*
  Palazzo Farnese, 9, 136–7, *10.2*
Sanitation, 325
Sant'Elia, Antonio, 304–5, *22.1*
  Città Nuova, 304–5, *22.1*
Santayana, George, 239
SAS Building (Stockholm), 382, *27.8*
SAS (Scandinavian Airline Systems), 382
  SAS Building, 382, *27.8*
Satellite television, 352–3, 391
Saturday Evening Post, 320, *23.5*
Scale, 44, 70, 75, 115, 142, 151–2, 154–5, 181,
  338–41
Scarperia, 96
Scenographia, 98
Scharoun, Hans, 263
  Weissenhof housing, 263
Scheyer, Galka, 222
Schiller, Friedrich, 198
Schimkowitz, Othmar, 296
Schindler, Rudolph, 13, 221–4, 238, 323, *16.5,*
  16.6
  Kings Road Studios, 13, 215, 221–4, 238, 323,
    16.5, *16.6*
Schinkel, Karl Friedrich, 197, 341, *14.2*
  Altes Museum, 197, *14.2*
Schlegel, Karl, 198
Schlegel, Wilhelm, 198
Schönberg, Arnold, 298–9, 302
Schonheit der Grossen Stadt, Die, 304
Schools, 228, 233, 248
Schütte-Lihotsky, Grette, 219–20, *16.4*
  Frankfurt kitchen, 219–21, *16.4*
Schwagenscheidt, Walter, 216
Science, 2, 17, 93, 103, 151, 182, 198, 216,
  274–6, 292, 345, 349, 353, 361–4, 367–8
Science parks, 377
Scientific management, 218–9, 252–3
Scientific Management in the Home, 218,
  16.3
Scott, George Gilbert, 209–10, *15.8*
  Midland Hotel, 210, *15.8*
Sculpture, 18, 23, 25, 40–1, 43, 55, 58, 61, 78–9,
  90, 107, 120, 127, 133, 141, 151, 191,
  193–7, 209, 228, 245, 255, 295–6
Seagram Building (New York), 301, *21.10*
Secession, 297–8, 300
Secession Building (Vienna), 297, *29.6*

Section, 68–76, 85–6, 109–10, 113, 121, 137,
  151, 153, 155, 158–60, 161, 163, 169–71,
  184, 204–6, 214, 238, 250, 300, 365
Segal, Walter, 178
Seifert, Richard, and Partners, 375–6
  Centre Point, 376, *27.2*
Selling, 375, 382–4
Semiotics, 6
Semper, Gottfried, 13, 183, 197–8
Seoul, 3
Servants, 221, 323
Serviced shed, 279–84
Services, 163, 169, 216, 223, 229, 250, 273,
  279–84, 373
Seven Lamps of Architecture, The, 207
Sexism, 326, 328
Sexuality, 325, 328
Sexuality and Space, 327–8
Sforzinda, 135
Shaftesbury, Lord, 202
Shaw, Richard Norman, 297
Shekhtel, Fedor, 248
Shell and core, 373
Shepherd, Peter, 263–6, *19.5*
  Regent's Park Estate, 263–6, *19.5*
Shoppell, Robert, *Modern Houses, Beautiful
  Homes*, 320, *23.3*
Shopping malls, 304, 344, 349, 354–5, *see also*
  Retail
*Sieben Variationem des Raumes über die Sieben
  Leuchter der Baukunst von John Ruskin*,
  336, *24.4*
Siena, 96, 109
Simmel, Georg, 6, 16–7, 310
  The Metropolis and Mental Life, 310
Simone del Cronaca, 115, *9.1*
  Palazzo Strozzi, 9, 115, 122, 125, *9.1*
Simpson, John, 49, 180, *13.3*
  Paternoster Square, 180, *13.3*
Site and topography, 4, 25, 121, 135–7, 163–4,
  167, 169–71, 235–9, 263, 276, 283, 376, 384
Site planning, 264–5, 365
Sitte, Camillo, 304, 341
  Der Städtebau, 304
Situationist International, 274, 279
Sixtus V, 136
Sketches and Hints on Landscape Gardening,
  181, *13.4*
Skidmore, Owings and Merrill, 383
  Broadgate, 49, 383, *27.9*
Skyline, 271
Slovak republic, 292
Slow House (North Haven Point), 362, *26.2*
Smirke, Robert, 209
Soane, John, 209

Social condenser, 250–2
Social engineering, 268
Social justice, 243
Social reproduction, 4, 219–21, 317–24, 346–55
Social theory, 6, 354
Socialism, 243–56, 259, 264, 323
Socialist Realism, 14, 252–6
Société de nouveau quartier Poisonnière, 167–8
Société des terrains de Ruggieri et Saint-Georges, 167–8
Sociologie, 377
Sociology, 6, 9, 106–7, 114, 310, 327, 389
Soja, Edward, 6, 389
Soldiers, 244, 248, 291
Soleri, Paolo, 236–8, *17.8*
   Arcosanti, 236–8, *17.8*
Solomon's Temple, 79
South Friedrichstrasse, Masterplan (Berlin), 340
Southey, Robert, 201
Soviet Councils, 244–5, 252, 254
Space and spatiality, 4–6, 9, 13, 17, 48, 53, 93–103, 106, 119–20, 153, 156, 160, 176–85, 214–24, 238, 247–8, 274–5, 298, 300, 309, 317–28, 331–42, 344, 346–55, 367–8, 372, 375–6, 392–8
   representation, 9, 13, 93–103, 214–24, 336–8
Space technology 273, 278, 352–3
Space, Time and Architecture, 189
Spain, 85, 132, 133, 332
Spectacle, 18–9
Speculative development, 11, 127–8, 163–75, 294, 321, 350–2, 372–84, *see also* Property development
Spence, Basil, 259, *19.2*
   Hutchestown-Gorbals Area C Development, 259, *19.2*
Spengler, Oswald, 189
Speyer, 67
   Speyer Cathedral, 67
Sphinx in the City, The, 327
Sphinxes, 193–5
Spirals 234–5, 280
Spirit 190–2, 194–7, 207, 363
Sports stadia, 285
Stadelhofen Train Station (Zurich), 367, *26.7*
Städtebau, Der, 304
Staffordshire, 276
   Potteries Thinkbelt, 276, *20.2*
Stained glass, 75, 78, 82, 84, 89
Stalin, Joseph, 248, 253, 256
Stalinism, 39
Stam, Mart, 263
   Weissenhof housing exhibition, 263
Standardization, 95, 163, 215, 217, 219, 235, 311, 349, 352, 380

Stanga, 114
Stanhope, 374, 377, 383 *see also* Rosehaugh Stanhope
Star system, 324–5
State, the, 14, 16, 46, 49, 56–9, 117, 131–44, 149, 167, 192, 243–56, 258–69, 292, 298, 351, 354, 374, 379
Steam-power, 200–1
Steel, 248, 252, 272, 282, 284, 294, 299
Steinberg, Leo, 142
Steiner, Rudolf, 13, *1.7*
   Goetheanum, 13, *1.7*
Stern, Robert, 49
Stevenage New Town, 266
Stirling, James, *see* Stirling, Wilford and Associates
Stirling, Wilford and Associates, 15, *1.9*
   Neue Staatsgalerie, 15, *1.9*
Stockholm, 382
   SAS Building 382, *27.8*
Stockley Park (Heathrow), 377
   W3 Building, 377, *27.3*
Stone, 23, 28, 29, 41, 67, 68, 69, 72, 73, 74, 75, 79, 95, 108, 109, 115, 126, 153, 209, 228, 272, 294, 296, 297, 299
Stone Age, 3
Stones of Venice, The, 207, 209
Stravinsky, Igor 222
Street, *see* Roads
Street, G.E., 209
Streetscape, 311
Strike, 245–6, *18.1*
Strozzi, 9, 115, 120, 125
   Palazzo Strozzi, 9, 115, 122, 125, *9.1*
Structural engineering, 373, *see also* engineering
Structural rationalism, 183, 203–4, 206–7, 211
Structuralism, 334
Structure, *see* Construction and structure
Student Residence Hall (Enschede), 336, *24.4*
Studios, 221–4
Sturges House (Los Angeles), 238–9, *17.10*
Stuttgart, 15, 263
   Neue Staatsgalerie, 15, *1.9*
   Weissenhof housing exhibition, 263, *19.4*
Style, 2, 4, 13, 114, 119, 171, 173, 194, 206, 209, 211, 258, 284–5, 293–4, 377, 379–80, 391
Style and Epoch, 250
Sub-contracting, 374
Sublime, 178, 391
Suburbs, 17, 261, 292, 311, 317–23, 325, 327, 331–2, 337, 349, 351–2
Suger, Abbot, 75, 81–2
Suitaloon, 279
Sullivan, Louis, 216

Summerson, John, 127
  Georgian London, 127
Suprematism, 253
Surrealism, 338, 341
Surrey Square (London), 11, *1.5*
Surveillance, 354, 397
Surveying, 375, 383–4
Sweden, 382
Swindon, 280, 282
  Reliance Controls Factory, 280, 282, *20.7*
Switzerland, 13, 178, 304, 367
Symbolic art (Hegel), 191, 196
Symbolism, 9, 11, 42, 54, 57–8, 79, 82, 84, 86,
    88–9, 107, 121, 141–3, 151, 326, 328
Symmetry, 34, 97, 137, 172, 192–5, 294
Synagogues, 234, 236
System building, 340, 347, 351–2

Tafel, Edgar, 230–1, 233, 236, *17.2*
Taliesin, 13, 221, 227–40
  Hillside, 227–8
Taliesin Associated Architects (TAA), 234–7,
    17.6, 17.7
  Beth-Shalom Synagogue, 234, 236
  Gammage Auditorium, 236
  Guggenheim Museum, 234, 236, *17.6*
  Lincoln Income Life Insurance Company
    Building, 236–7, *17.7*
  Marin County Civic Center, 236
Taller de Arquitectura, 49, *3.8*
  Antigone housing, 49, *3.8*
Taste, 12, 62, 119–21, 127, 176–85
Tatlin, Vladimir, 248–9, *18.2*
  Monument to the Third International, 248–9,
    18.2
Tattoos, 298, 300
Tax, 166–7
Taylor Woodrow, 351
Taylor, Frederick Winslow, 253, 346
Taylorism, 252–3, 346–8
Team Four, 280, 282, *20.7*
  Reliance Controls Factory, 280, 282, *20.7*
Teamwork, 240, 373
Technology, 4, 12, 14–6, 38, 126–7, 200, 207,
    227–9, 233, 246, 248, 252, 255, 271–86, 305,
    345–54, 367–8, 380–1, 389, 391
Telephones, 249
Television, 176, 243, 278, 352–3, 391
Tempietto (Rome), 134–5, *10.1*
Temple Church (London), 79
Temple of Apollo (Didyma), 101
Temple of Artemis (Magnesia), 27
Temple of Athena Polias (Priene), 29, 31, *2.6*
Temple of Dionysus (Teos), 27
Temple of Zeus (Euromus), 7, *1.1*

Tendering, 374
Teos, 27
  Temple of Dionysus, 27
Terranuova, 96–7, *7.3*
Terrorism of everyday life, 354
Terry, Quinlan, 49
Tewkesbury Abbey, 9, 83–4, *6.4*
Text, 368–70
Textile block, 236
Textiles, 109, 227, 245
Thatcher, Margaret, 379
Théâtre de l'Odeon (Paris), 11, 164, 166–7, 172,
    12.4
Theatres, 164, 166–7, 229, 275, 319, 327
Theatricality, 56–9, 62–3, 144
Theme parks, 62
Theorized history 6, 387–9, 396–8
Theory and Design in the First Machine Age,
    272–3
Theory and Practice of Landscape Gardening,
    182
Thermopylae, battle of, 40
Thetis, 57–8, *4.3*
Third Machine Age, 391
Tiercelet, 170
Tigerman Fugman McCurry, 362, *26.1*
  60 East Lake Parking Facility, 362, *26.1*
Tigerman McCurry, 50, *3.9*
  Commonwealth Edison Substation, 50, *3.9*
Timber frame, 352
Time, 1, 5, 6, 23, 102, 189, 221, 243, 247, 323,
    334, 340, 346–8, 355
Time-space compression, 349
Tokyo, 349
Tombs, 302, 334–5, 387
To-Morrow: a Peaceful Path to Real Reform, 331
Torp, Nils, 382, *27.8*
  SAS Building, 382, *27.8*
Totality, 1, 3, 387–9, 397
Tourism, 144, 283, 341, 392
Towards a New Architecture, 32–6, 271, 388,
    2.1, 2.7, 2.9, 2.10
Towers and tower blocks, 152, 231, 234–5, 248,
    259, 263, 266, 271, 278–80, 312–3, 337, 350,
    376, 379, 392, *see also* Medieval towers
Town halls, 152, 292, *293*
Town planning, *see* Planning
Town Planning in Practice, 304, 306, *22.3*
Trade unions, 41–2, 244
Trafalgar Square (London), 7, 40–3
Trams, 252, 320
Treatises, 24–5, 28, 88, 98, 100–1, 111, 115, 117,
    121, 137, 150, 170, 179, 181–2, 202, 204,
    207, 209, 304, 313–4, 340, 388
Trier, 336

Trinitarians, 139
Triumphal arches, 152
Trope, 366
Trotsky, Leon, 246, 253
Trott, Richard, 369, *26.9*
   Wexner Center for Visual Arts 369, *26.9*
*True Principles of Pointed or Christian
   Architecture*, 204–5
Trump Tower (New York), 355, *25.10*
Truth, 182–4, 190
Tuileries (Paris), 167
Turbines, 391
Turkey, 139
Turner, J.M.W., 209
Tuscany, 96–7, 110–1, 123
Twelve tone theory, 298
Two-stage tendering. 374
Type and typology, 9, 17, 26, 39, 106–17, 119,
   121, 136, 144, 164, 219, 333–42, 352
Typography, 245, 277
Tzara House (Paris), 300
Tzara, Tristan, 300
   Tzara House, 300

Uncertainty principle, 361
Ungers, O.M., 17, 332–3, 335–42, *24.4, 24.5,
   24.6*
   Gleisdreieck Tower, 337–8, *24.5, 24.6*
   *Sieben Variationem des Raumes über die
      Sieben Leuchter der Baukunst von John
      Ruskin*, 336, *24.4*
   Student Residence Hall, 336, *24.4*
Unité d'Habitation (Marseilles), 266
United States, 7, 13, 38–9, 40, 43–6, 49, 123,
   133, 209–10, 215–6, 219, 221–4, 227–40,
   272–3, 291, 298, 302, 304, 312–3, 320–1,
   323–6, 332, 348–9, 352, 355, 362, 369,
   372–84, 388, 392–8
Universality, 184, 313, 363–4
Universities, 50, 114, 276, 292–3, 336
University of East Anglia, 284
   Sainsbury Centre, 283–4, *20.11*
Unwin, Raymond, 304, 306, 311, *22.3*
   Dunster village, 304, 306, *22.3*
   Town Planning in Practice, 304, 306, *22.3*
Urban design, *see* Planning
Urban geography, 6, 332–4, 389
Urban III, 132
Urban regeneration, 377–9
Urban space, 1, 7, 9, 15–7, 39, 42, 44, 47–8,
   93–103, 107, 109, 119–20, 133–7, 14–4, 249,
   283, 291, 304, 308–9, 317, 377–9
Urban Space, 340
Urbanism, *see* Cities

Urbanization, 13, 17, 123–5, 200–2, 248–9,
   304–14, 317–23, 325–8, 331–42, 344–55,
   392–8
Urbino, 132
Usonian housing, 229
USSR, 14, 39, 243–56, 304, 323, 348, 350–1
Utopia, 228–9, 236–8, 243, 250, 253, 256, 267,
   269, 304–5

Van Gogh, Vincent, 391
   A Pair of Boots, 391
Vatican (Rome), 135
Vaulting, 67–75, 85, 87
Veblen, Thorstein, 6, 120
Venice, 123, 132
Ventilation, 216, 275, 283
Venturi, Robert, 324, 325, 388
   Learning from Las Vegas, 388
Venturi, Scott Brown and Associates, 7, *1.2*
   Sainsbury Wing, National Gallery, 7, *1.2*
Ver Sacrum, 297
Vernacular, 5, 333, 344, 388
Versailles, 7, 44, 53–63, *4.1, 4.2, 4.3, 4.4, 4.5*
   Grotto of Thetis, 57–8, *4.3*
Vertical cities, 249
Vesnin, Aleksandr, 247
Vesnin, Leonid, 247
Vesnin, Viktor, 247
Vézelay, 71, 80, 81
   Vézelay, La Madeleine, 71, 80, 81, *6.1*
Via Babuini (Rome), 144
Via del Calzaioli (Florence), 95
Via del Corso (Rome), 144
Via Ripiena, 144
Vico, Giambattista, 151
   New Science, 151
Vidal de la Blache, Paul, 334
Video, 353
Vienna, 16, 193, 291–302, 311, 341, 387
   glacis, 292
   Goldman and Salatsch Store, 298–9, *21.8*
   Kärntner Bar, 298–9, *21.7*
   Loos House, 298–9
   Majolica House, 294, *21.2*
   Opera House, 292
   Postal Savings Bank, 294–6, *21.3, 21.4*
   Rathaus, 292–3
   Reichsrat, 292–3, *21.1*
   Ringstrasse, 16, 291–4, 387
   Secession, 297–8, 300
   Secession Pavilion, 297, *21.6*
   University, 292–3
Vignola, Giacomo Barozzi da, 138–9, *10.4*
   Gesù, 138–40, *10.4*
Villages, 304, 331

Villa Savoye (Poissy), 14, 328, *1.8*, *23.8*
Ville Contemporaine, 304–5, *22.2*
Viollet-le-Duc, Eugéne-Emanuel, 13, 183–4, 197, 198, *13.5*
   Dictionnaire raisonné de l'architecture française, 184, *13.5*
Virtual reality, 362
Vision, 1, 3, 9, 12, 35, 93–103, 144, 176–85, 202–4, 206, 233
Vision of Britain, A, 176
Vitruvius, 6, 24–9, 35–6, 98, 366
   De Architectura, 24–8, 366
VKhUTEMAS, 247
Voysey, C.F.A., 211
Vitra Conference Centre (Weil am Rhein), 364, *26.5*
Vitra Design Museum (Weil am Rhein), 363, *26.3*
Vitra Fire Station (Weil am Rhein), 364, *26.4*

Wade, C., 306, *22.3*
Wagner, Otto, 16, 294–7, 311, 341, *21.2*, *21.3*, *21.4*
   Danube canal, 294
   Gürtel Line, 294
   Majolica House, 294, *21.2*
   Modern Architecture, 294
   Postal Savings Bank, 294–6, *21.3*, *21.4*
Wailly, Charles de, 166–8, *12.3*, *12.4*
   Place de l'Odeon, 166, *12.3*
   Théâtre de l'Odeon, 11, 164, 166, 167, 172, *12.4*
War communism, 245
Warfare, 25, 39, 40–2, 46, 48, 55, 59–61, 124, 136, 244–5, 260, 262, 268, 291, 319, 332, 340, 350, 353, 369
Warhol, Andy, 391
   Diamond Dust Shoes, 391
Washington, 7, 19, 40, 43–4, 291
   City Beautiful, 7, 43–4
   Park Commission plan, 43–4, *3.3*
   White House, 113
Water, 24–5, 54, 59, 62, 233, 278, 292, 331, 392
Water-power, 200
Webb, Aston, 112–3, *8.3*
   Buckingham Palace, 112–3, *8.3*
Webb, Michael, 277–9, *20.4*
   Cushicle, 278–9, *20.4*
   Suitaloon, 279
Weil am Rhein, 363, 364
   Vitra Conference Centre, 364, *26.5*
   Vitra Design Museum, 363, *26.3*
   Vitra Fire Station 364, *26.4*
Weimar Republic, 215–21, 272
Weissenhof housing exhibition, 263, *19.4*

Welfare State, 258–69
Wells, 74, 79, 106
   Wells Cathedral, 74, 79, 106, *5.1*
Welwyn, 331
Wesley Peters, William, 231, 233, 237
Westin Bonaventure Hotel (Los Angeles), 390, 392–8, *28.1*, *28.2*, *28.3*, *28.4*, *28.5*, *28.6*
Westminster Abbey (London), 9, 75, 84–5, *6.5*
White House (Washington), 113
White, Hayden, 6
White, John, 102
Whitehall (London), 40, 261, 266
Wiener Werkstätte, 296, 300
Wilberforce, William, 319
Wilkins, William, 41, *3.1*
   National Gallery, 41, *3.1*
   Trafalgar Square, 7, 40, 41, 42, 43
Williams, Raymond, 6
Wilson, Colin St John, 180
   British Library, 180
Wilson, Elizabeth, 6, 327
   The Sphinx in the City, 327
Wilson, Harold, 260, 261, 267
Wilson, Hugh, 274
   Cumbernauld Town Centre, 274
Wimpey, 351–2
Winchester, 75
   Winchester Cathedral, 75
Winckelmann, Johann, 198
Windows, 68, 70–1, 75, 84, 111, 192, 214, 239, 250, 252, 299, 334, 347
Wisconsin, 221, 227
Wittenberg, 134
Wittgenstein, Ludwig, 53, 293, 294, 302
   Wittgenstein House 293
Wohnküche, 217, 219
Wolff, Janet, 6, 327
Wölfflin, Heinrich, 6
Woman Question, 323–4
Wood, 26–8, 67, 72–3, 95, 126, 227–8, 299, 352
Wood, Edith Elmer, 324
Wood, William, 40
   An Essay on National and Sepulchral Monuments, 40
Worcester, 74, 76
   Worcester Cathedral, 74, 76
Work, 182–3, 200, 207–9, 211, 245, 248, 252–3, 274, 313, 317–24, 326–7, 344–55, 374
Workers' clubs, 247, 250–3
Workhouses, 202
World War I, 46, 215, 227, 244
World War II, 239, 261–3, 268, 272, 274, 302, 331–2, 340
Wren, Christopher, 204–6, *15.3*
   St. Paul's Cathedral, 76, 180, 204–6, *15.3*

Wright, Frank Lloyd, 13, 221–2, 227–40, 304,
    17.1, 17.2, 17.3, 17.4, 17.5, 17.6, 17.10
  Barnsdall House, 238
  Beth-Shalom Synagogue, 234, 236
  Broadacre City, 229, 304, *17.1*
  Deertrack, 239
  Fallingwater, 231, 233, *17.5*
  Florida Southern College, 233–4
  Gammage Auditorium, 236
  Guggenheim Museum, 234, 236, *17.6*
  Hillside, 227–8
  Johnson Wax Administration Building and
    Laboratory Tower, 231, 234, *17.3, 17.4*
  Marin County Civic Center, 236
  Price Tower, 234–5
  St. Mark's-in-the-Bouwerie, 235
  Sturges House, 238–9, *17.10*
  Taliesin, 227–40
  Usonian housing, 229
Wright, Patrick, 259
  A Journey Through Ruins, 259

Yale University, 50
Yaohan shopping mall (London), 354, *25.9*
York, 76, 89
  All Saints, 89, *6.7*
  York Minster, 76
Yosemite, 222
Zeilenbau, 263–4
Zholtovski, Ivan, 247
Zocchi, 93, 114, 122, *7.1, 8.5, 9.1*
Zoning, 332, 349
Zurich, 367
  Stadelhofen Train Station, 367, *26.7*